The Amphibians
of Tennessee

The Amphibians of Tennessee

Edited by Matthew L. Niemiller
and R. Graham Reynolds

THE UNIVERSITY OF TENNESSEE PRESS / KNOXVILLE

Support for this book was provided in part by the Tennessee Wildlife Resources Agency, Division of Environmental Services, and by Furthermore: a program of the J. M. Kaplan Fund.

Copyright © 2011 by The University of Tennessee Press / Knoxville.
All Rights Reserved. Manufactured in China.
First Edition.

For *The Amphibians of Tennessee* website, visit: http://www.AmphibiansofTN.com.

Library of Congress Cataloging-in-Publication Data

The amphibians of Tennessee / edited by Matthew L. Niemiller and R. Graham Reynolds. — 1st ed.
      p. cm.
Includes bibliographical references and index.
ISBN-13: 978-1-57233-762-6 (hardcover)
ISBN-10: 1-57233-762-1 (hardcover)
 1. Amphibians—Tennessee.
 2. Amphibians—Tennessee—Classification.
 I. Niemiller, Matthew L.
 II. Reynolds, R. Graham.

QL653.T3A47 2011
597.809768—dc22
2011012376

Contributors

Brian T. Miller
Department of Biology
Middle Tennessee State University

Stesha A. Pasachnik
Department of Ecology and Evolutionary Biology
University of Tennessee

Brad M. Glorioso
IAP World Services, Inc.
USGS National Wetlands Research Center, Lafayette, Louisiana

George R. Wyckoff
ATA Conservation
Arnold Air Force Base, Tennessee

Jason R. Jones
Department of Ecology and Evolutionary Biology
University of Tennessee

Elizabeth K. Timpe
Department of Ecology and Evolutionary Biology
University of Connecticut

Sean P. Graham
Department of Biological Sciences
Auburn University

To our teachers: past, present, and future

To the future scientists of Tennessee

and

To our families for their unyielding support

All the phenomena of nature need to be seen
from the point of view of wonder and awe.

                Henry David Thoreau

Contents

Foreword   xiii
    Brian T. Miller
Acknowledgments   xv

Part 1: Amphibians, Habitats, and Conservation

1. What is an Amphibian? Amphibian Anatomy and Life History   1
2. Physiography, Climate, and Habitats of Tennessee   11
3. Amphibian Conservation   29
4. Finding Amphibians in Tennessee   37
5. How to Use the Species Accounts   47
6. How to Use the Taxonomic Keys   51

Part 2: Salamanders

7. Key to the Salamanders of Tennessee   57
8. Key to the Larval and Adult Larviform Salamanders of Tennessee   69
9. Family Ambystomatidae (Mole Salamanders)   73
       Streamside Salamander (*Ambystoma barbouri*)   73
       Spotted Salamander (*Ambystoma maculatum*)   77
       Marbled Salamander (*Ambystoma opacum*)   80
       Mole Salamander (*Ambystoma talpoideum*)   83
       Small-Mouthed Salamander (*Ambystoma texanum*)   86
       Eastern Tiger Salamander (*Ambystoma tigrinum*)   88
10. Family Amphiumidae (Amphiumas)   91
        Three-Toed Amphiuma (*Amphiuma tridactylum*)   91
11. Family Cryptobranchidae (Giant Salamanders)   95
        Eastern Hellbender (*Cryptobranchus alleganiensis*)   95
12. Family Plethodontidae (Lungless Salamanders)   99
        Green Salamander (*Aneides aeneus*)   102
        Cumberland Dusky Salamander (*Desmognathus abditus*)   105
        Seepage Salamander (*Desmognathus aeneus*)   108
        Carolina Mountain Dusky Salamander (*Desmognathus carolinensis*)   110
        Spotted Dusky Salamander (*Desmognathus conanti*)   113
        Northern Dusky Salamander (*Desmognathus fuscus*)   116

Imitator Salamander (*Desmognathus imitator*) 119
Shovel-Nosed Salamander (*Desmognathus marmoratus*) 122
Seal Salamander (*Desmognathus monticola*) 125
Allegheny Mountain Dusky Salamander (*Desmognathus ochrophaeus*) 128
Ocoee Salamander (*Desmognathus ocoee*) 131
Blue Ridge Dusky Salamander (*Desmognathus orestes*) 134
Northern Pygmy Salamander (*Desmognathus organi*) 136
Black-Bellied Salamander (*Desmognathus quadramaculatus*) 139
Santeetlah Dusky Salamander (*Desmognathus santeetlah*) 142
Black Mountain Dusky Salamander (*Desmognathus welteri*) 145
Pygmy Salamander (*Desmognathus wrighti*) 147
Brownback Salamander (*Eurycea aquatica*) 150
Southern Two-Lined Salamander (*Eurycea cirrigera*) 154
Three-Lined Salamander (*Eurycea guttolineata*) 157
Junaluska Salamander (*Eurycea junaluska*) 160
Long-Tailed Salamander (*Eurycea longicauda*) 163
Cave Salamander (*Eurycea lucifuga*) 166
Blue Ridge Two-Lined Salamander (*Eurycea wilderae*) 169
Berry Cave Salamander (*Gyrinophilus gulolineatus*) 172
Tennessee Cave Salamander (*Gyrinophilus palleucus*) 175
Spring Salamander (*Gyrinophilus porphyriticus*) 178
Four-Toed Salamander (*Hemidactylium scutatum*) 181
Tellico Salamander (*Plethodon aureolus*) 184
Eastern Red-Backed Salamander (*Plethodon cinereus*) 186
Zigzag Salamander Complex (*Plethodon dorsalis/ventralis*) 189
Slimy Salamander Complex (*Plethodon cylindraceus/glutinosus/mississippi*) 192
Jordan's Red-Cheeked Salamander (*Plethodon jordani*) 197
Cumberland Plateau Salamander (*Plethodon kentucki*) 199
Northern Gray-Cheeked Salamander (*Plethodon montanus*) 202
Southern Ravine Salamander (*Plethodon richmondi*) 204
Southern Red-Backed Salamander (*Plethodon serratus*) 207
Red-Legged Salamander (*Plethodon shermani*) 210
Southern Appalachian Salamander (*Plethodon teyahalee*) 213
Wehrle's Salamander (*Plethodon wehrlei*) 215
Weller's Salamander (*Plethodon welleri*) 218
Yonahlossee Salamander (*Plethodon yonahlossee*) 221
Mud Salamander (*Pseudotriton montanus*) 223
Red Salamander (*Pseudotriton ruber*) 226

13. Family Proteidae (Waterdogs and Mudpuppies)   231
      Common Mudpuppy (*Necturus maculosus*)   231
14. Family Salamandridae (Newts)   235
      Eastern Newt (*Notophthalmus viridescens*)   235
15. Family Sirenidae (Sirens)   239
      Lesser Siren (*Siren intermedia*)   239

Part 3: Frogs

16. Key to the Adult Frogs of Tennessee   245
17. Key to the Tadpoles of Tennessee   249
18. Family Bufonidae (True Toads)   253
      American Toad (*Anaxyrus americanus*)   253
      Fowler's Toad (*Anaxyrus fowleri*)   257
19. Family Hylidae (Treefrogs)   265
      Northern Cricket Frog (*Acris crepitans*)   265
      Southern Cricket Frog (*Acris gryllus*)   266
      Bird-Voiced Treefrog (*Hyla avivoca*)   268
      Cope's Gray/Gray Treefrog (*Hyla chrysoscelis/versicolor*)   271
      Green Treefrog (*Hyla cinerea*)   274
      Barking Treefrog (*Hyla gratiosa*)   277
      Mountain Chorus Frog (*Pseudacris brachyphona*)   280
      Spring Peeper (*Pseudacris crucifer*)   283
      Upland Chorus Frog (*Pseudacris feriarum*)   286
      Western Chorus Frog (*Pseudacris triseriata*)   289
20. Family Microhylidae (Narrow-Mouthed Toads)   293
      Eastern Narrow-Mouthed Toad (*Gastrophryne carolinensis*)   293
21. Family Ranidae (True Frogs)   297
      Crawfish Frog (*Lithobates areolatus*)   297
      Gopher Frog (*Lithobates capito*)   300
      American Bullfrog (*Lithobates catesbeianus*)   304
      Green Frog (*Lithobates clamitans*)   307
      Pickerel Frog (*Lithobates palustris*)   310
      Southern Leopard Frog (*Lithobates sphenocephalus*)   313
      Wood Frog (*Lithobates sylvaticus*)   316
22. Family Scaphiopodidae (American Spadefoot Toads)   319
      Eastern Spadefoot (*Scaphiopus holbrookii*)   319

23. Erroneous Species and Species of Possible Occurrence   323
    Family Ambystomatidae: Jefferson's Salamander (*Ambystoma jeffersonianum*)   323
    Family Proteidae: Gulf Coast Waterdog (*Necturus beyeri*)   324
    Family Bufonidae: Southern Toad (*Anaxyrus terrestris*)   324
    Family Hylidae: Squirrel Treefrog (*Hyla squirella*)   325
    Family Hylidae: Illinois Chorus Frog (*Pseudacris streckeri illinoensis*)   326
    Family Ranidae: Plains Leopard Frog (*Lithobates blairi*)   326
    Family Ranidae: Northern Leopard Frog (*Lithobates pipiens*)   326
    Other Erroneous Amphibians   327

Checklist of the Amphibians of Tennessee   329
Glossary   333
Recommended Readings, Organizations, and Websites   343
Selected References   349
Index of Common and Scientific Names   363

Field Notes

A Heavy Rain, an Elevational Gradient, and a Road Full of Amphibians   46
A Plethora of Plethodontids   100
Jordani by the Hundreds   196
Swamps and Frogs   260

Foreword

Ten years ago, a colleague of mine wrote a book on wildflowers of the central and southern United States. While attending a fund raiser for a local discovery center, I overheard a community leader make the following comment on the book's then-recent publication: "That's just what we need, another book on flowers. How many books on the natural history of this region do we need?" I was a bit dismayed by the comment, in part because I had hoped that community leaders were better informed, but also because I had hopes of writing a similar book on the amphibians of Tennessee. This had been a dream of mine since Bill Redmond and Floyd Scott published their *Annotated Bibliography of Amphibians and Reptiles of Tennessee* in 1990. Life took me in different directions and I never got around to writing that book, but the dream persisted, and the need for such a book increased.

Contrary to the views of some politicians, regional and state guides on flora and fauna are especially timely because affronts on biodiversity abound. Some argue that the public is barraged with stories about the loss of biodiversity, but generally these stories concern a loss of habitat and diversity in the tropical rainforests. Too infrequently we are informed about the extent of, and jeopardy to, biodiversity of the temperate regions, including Tennessee. Indeed, most people are unaware of the tremendous diversity of life in the southeastern United States in general and in Tennessee in particular. For example, at least 102 species of salamanders occur in the southeastern United States, which accounts for nearly one-fifth of all salamander species known worldwide. Furthermore, 58 of these species are found in Tennessee (roughly 10% of the world's salamander species). Currently, only North Carolina can boast of having a greater diversity of salamanders. However, the total number of species recognized changes as we explore our countryside and as our understanding of species changes. For example, during the past 20 years we have added to our faunal lists a couple species of amphibians that were known to occur in neighboring states but were not known to occur in Tennessee (e.g., the Gopher Frog and Streamside Salamander). Furthermore, by use of molecular techniques to examine relatedness among amphibian populations, we have uncovered a hidden diversity of species, particularly within salamanders. We now know that what we previously recognized as single species are indeed complexes of similarly appearing species (e.g., members of the Slimy Salamander complex, Two-Lined Salamander complex, Tennessee Cave Salamander complex, Dusky Salamanders, Pygmy Salamanders, etc.). With more study, we likely will uncover more hidden diversity. Tennessee's diversity is in large part associated with variations in altitude, topography, and climate, as may be noted when traveling from Memphis to Johnson City. The amphibian community of West Tennessee is similar to that of the Coastal Plain states and includes species adapted to sluggish waters in this region of low relief (e.g., the eel-like Three-Toed Amphiuma, gilled Lesser Siren, and burrowing Crayfish Frog). The amphibian communities of East Tennessee include species adapted to mountains with fast-flowing water and cooler temperatures; some of these species have large distributions (e.g., Hellbenders) that extend throughout the Appalachian range, whereas other species have extremely small distributions and are found only on the sides of one or two mountains (e.g., several species of lungless salamanders in the genus *Plethodon*). The amphibian community of Middle Tennessee overlaps with both West and East Tennessee, as well as with western Kentucky and northern Alabama and Mississippi. With books such as this one, the citizens, and especially the children, of Tennessee will garner an appreciation and understanding of the amphibian species and their diversity in the state. Hopefully, these leaders of tomorrow will then be more willing to preserve the state's natural biodiversity.

I feel compelled to comment on the editors of this book. Both are graduate students at the University of Tennessee, working on their doctoral degrees in Ben Fitzpatrick's laboratory (Graham is working with lizards, boas, and frogs in the Caribbean, Matt with cavefish throughout the eastern half of the United States.) I have known Matt Niemiller for 10 years, Graham Reynolds for five years. Each of them has seemingly tireless energy, which allows them to spend inordinate time in the field in search of amphibians and reptiles. They are true students of nature, and their understanding of the biology of so much of Tennessee's wildlife allows them to recognize which of their observations are important or novel discoveries. Consequently, although they are early in their careers, each has made many significant contributions to our understanding of the distribution, ecology, and evolutionary biology of the amphibians and reptiles in this region. Furthermore, both Matt and Graham are accomplished photographers. Nearly all of the photographs in the book were taken by one of them. In addition, they are not only the editors of this book but also the major contributors. Collectively, they authored or co-authored the sections on amphibians, habitats, and conservation, the various keys to salamanders and frogs, and the vast majority of species accounts. Fortunately for us, they saw a great need to provide the citizens of Tennessee and surrounding states with a book that showcased the state's dazzling array of amphibians and used their energy to accomplish what I could not—a wonderful compilation of information on the state's amphibians.

Brian T. Miller, Ph.D.
Department of Biology
Middle Tennessee State University

Acknowledgments

We would like to extend a special thanks to Dr. Brian Miller, who has been a mentor in amphibian biology to both of us and has encouraged this project for quite some time. His willingness to share his expertise on Tennessee amphibians over many years has benefited us as scientists and has contributed greatly to our ability to complete this book. Thanks as well to Dr. Ben Fitzpatrick, our graduate advisor and renowned amphibian biologist, who encouraged this project despite the potential for detriment to our respective dissertations.

This book was greatly improved by the expertise of the contributors and we wish to acknowledge them for their outstanding contributions. The manuscript was greatly improved by two reviewers: an anonymous reader and C. Kenneth Dodd Jr. A special thank you to Brook Corwin for directing, filming, and editing the video introduction to this book, and for designing and building the book's website: http://www.AmphibiansofTN.com.

We also would like to thank the many volunteers, friends, and family members who have joined us in our field adventures documenting and photographing amphibians in Tennessee or assisted with various aspects of this endeavor (in alphabetical order): Bob Biddix, John Bills, Crystal Bishop, Vince Cobb, Phil Colclough, Noa Davidai, Chris Davis, Terry Deal, Dylan Dittrich-Reed, Joe Douglas, Sarah Duncan, Sandy Echternacht, Bob English, Pandy English, Dante Fenolio, Ben Fitzpatrick, Heather Garland, Brad and Melita Glorioso, Troy Glorioso, Erin Gray, Matt Gray, Jeff Green, Nathan Haislip, Kevin Hamed, Kerry Hansknecht, Heather Hensley, Cory Holliday, Jason Hoverman, Darrin Hulsey, J. R. Jones, Denise Kendall, Chris Kerr, Richard Kirk, Katie Koss, Michael Lawton, Thany Mann, Laura Marsh, Roger McCoy, Brian Miller, Jacob Miller, Joshua Miller, Avis Moni, Gerald Moni, Brad Moxley, Stephen Nelson, Trent Niemiller, Michael Ogle, Michael Osbourn, Stesha Pasachnik, Lisa Powers, Rebecca Quasney, Elizabeth Reed, Jennifer Reynolds, Bob and Kim Reynolds, Floyd Scott, Premal Shah, Jeremy Spiess, Kyle Sykes, Mark Thurman, Steve Tilley, Jason Todd, Megan Todd-Thompson, Nathan and Jess Turnbough, Bill Walter, Jessica Welch, David Withers, Richie Wyckoff, Elizabeth Young, Dr. Brian Miller's herpetology students from Middle Tennessee State University, and any others we have forgotten to mention.

We are also grateful to the staff and personnel we have interacted with during the course of this project in the Tennessee Wildlife Resources Agency, Tennessee Department of Environment and Conservation–Division of Natural Heritage, Tennessee Department of Environment and Conservation–State Parks, Tennessee Department of Agriculture–State Forests, Tennessee Valley Authority, Tennessee Cave Survey, Tennessee Herpetological Society, National Park Service, U.S. Forest Service, and U.S. Fish and Wildlife Service. We also thank all those in the Department of Biology at Middle Tennessee State University and the Department of Ecology and Evolutionary Biology at the University of Tennessee, Knoxville. Data gathered for this book by the editors has been associated with various projects funded by the Tennessee Wildlife Resources Agency, National Speleological

Society, American Society of Ichthyologists and Herpetologists, the Department of Biology at Middle Tennessee State University, and the Department of Ecology and Evolutionary Biology at the University of Tennessee, Knoxville.

We would like to thank Carl Brune, Andrew Durso, Bob English, Dante Fenolio, Brad Glorioso, Nathan Haislip, Pierson Hill, John Jensen, Brian Miller, Bill Peterman, and Todd Pierson for providing photographs used in this book.

Matt wishes to thank his family, who has tolerated his obsessive passion for biology and, in particular, herpetology. He also thanks all his past teachers for ultimately guiding him into a career in biology and academia. At the very top of this list is Brian Miller, whose tutelage instilled a deep appreciate for natural history and ultimately inspired a career in academia. Lastly, Matt thanks all his friends who have supported him over the years, but especially Brad Glorioso, Richie Wyckoff, and Graham Reynolds. Hopefully, we will all have many more years of friendships and stories to share of our herping excursions.

Graham wishes to thank Jennifer Reynolds, his incredibly supportive and loving wife, who has tolerated his frequent herping excursions as well as his late-night returns home from road cruising with Matt, which elicit a cacophony from alarmed pets when she has to get up for work in the morning. He also is grateful to his family for encouraging the pursuit of his passion for science and the natural world, as well as to his many teachers, particularly his advisors Joanne Bartsch (Carolina Day School), Erika Deinert (Organization for Tropical Studies), Susan Alberts (Duke University), and Ben Fitzpatrick (University of Tennessee) for their knowledge and encouragement.

Lastly, a big thank you to the staff of the University of Tennessee Press—especially Kerry Webb, Scot Danforth, Thomas Wells, Gene Adair, Chad Pelton, Barbara Karwhite, Cheryl Carson, Tom Post, and freelance copyeditor Karin Kaufman—for taking on this project and understanding the vision of two young editors.

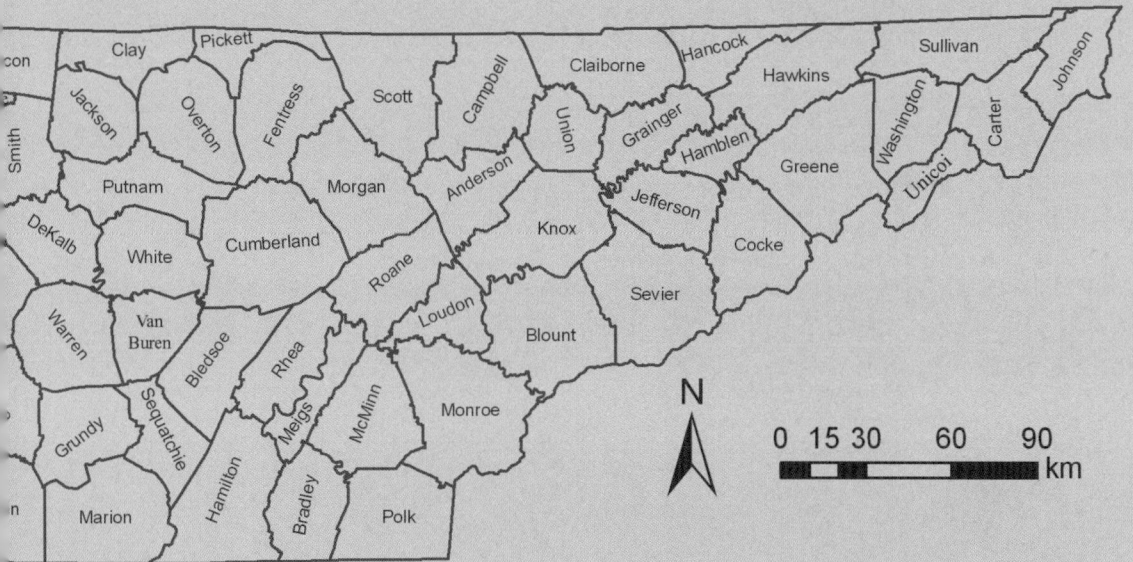

Part 1

Amphibians, Habitats, and Conservation

1

What is an Amphibian? Amphibian Anatomy and Life History

Amphibians constitute all members of the class Amphibia, both extinct and extant. From their first appearance in the mid-Devonian some 350 million years ago, they have diversified considerably to occupy a wide range of habitats both on the land and in the water. These are the original vertebrate pioneers of land—the ancestors of which began to move from the water to colonize the terrestrial habitats of the mid-Paleozoic. As we will see, this adaptation to dry land necessitated some morphological and physiological changes to allow these amphibian ancestors to deal with water loss, fluctuating daily temperatures, terrestrial respiration, and the acquisition of food, among other things. Evolutionary processes have since led to a spectacular diversification of amphibians constituting three main groups: the frogs, the salamanders, and the caecilians. Today about 6,350 species of amphibians are recognized, with many new species being discovered each year, especially in places such as Southeast Asia, South America, southern Asia, and Madagascar. In addition, many populations of amphibians are considered to be incipient species—in other words, in the process of diverging to become separate species, giving us a view of speciation in action.

The word "amphibian" is from the Greek *amphi* "double" or "both" and *bios* "life," hence giving the meaning "double life." This refers to the two life stages of these animals—a larval stage and an adult stage. There is quite a bit of variation among groups in these life stages, with some amphibians never metamorphosing and instead maturing as larvae and others that nearly skip the larval stage while in the egg to hatch as miniature adults. The generalized transition, however, is characterized by tremendous changes as aquatic larvae metamorphose into adults, involving reorganization of much of the body morphology and physiology. All amphibians are ectothermic, that is, they regulate their body temperature via their surrounding environment. Below we explore the two groups of amphibians found here in Tennessee: salamanders and frogs.

Salamanders

Salamanders are a less diverse group globally than the frogs, with only about 600 species belonging to the order Caudata, from the Latin *cauda* "tail." However, and of particular importance to this volume, the Southern Appalachian Mountains are considered the world center of biodiversity of salamanders. The age of the mountains, combined with the varying habitats from low to high elevation and periodic separation during climate shifts over millions of years, has led to a spectacular diversification of salamanders in our own backyard. Salamanders, unlike frogs, appear to be much less diverse in the tropics than in temperate North America, with the exception of the

Generalized salamander external anatomy. Key characteristics for identifying salamanders include the total length (TL) and snout-vent length (SVL). 1 = vent; 2 = toe tips; 3 = costal grooves; 4 = nasolabial groove; 5 = cirri (males only); 6 = mental gland underneath the chin (males only), 7 = gular fold underneath head, 8 = tail keel, and 9 = nares.

radiation of bolitoglossine slamanders in Central America. In Tennessee, we have at least 58 species of salamanders, with 31 of those occurring just within the Great Smoky Mountains National Park alone. Indeed, the Southern Appalachians are an extremely important area for amphibians, with over 101 species, 37% of which are endemic or found nowhere else in the world. We have some of the most beautiful and unusual salamanders here in Tennessee, including Jordan's Red-Cheeked Salamander and the giant Hellbender. There are few outdoor pleasures greater than exploring the mountains and valleys of Tennessee in search of these fascinating and handsome salamanders.

Salamanders exhibit a biphasic lifestyle, though it is often much less apparent than that of frogs. Ambystomatid salamanders, such as the Tiger Salamander, lay eggs in the water, producing gilled aquatic larvae, while some plethodontids, like the Pygmy Salamander, lay their eggs on land, which hatch into fully developed miniature adults. This variation in reproductive modes is an adaptation to different habitats and allows some salamanders to be completely divorced from the necessity of large quantities of water, instead relying on moist microhabitats to maintain appropriate osmotic balance.

Salamanders for the most part breed in the spring and summer, though some, such as Marbled Salamanders, start much later in the calendar year during autumn. Unlike the frogs, salamanders do not use sound to locate conspecifics or potential mates. Instead, some species (the plethodontids) rely on highly developed chemosensory organs consisting of nostrils, nasolabial grooves, vomeronasal or-

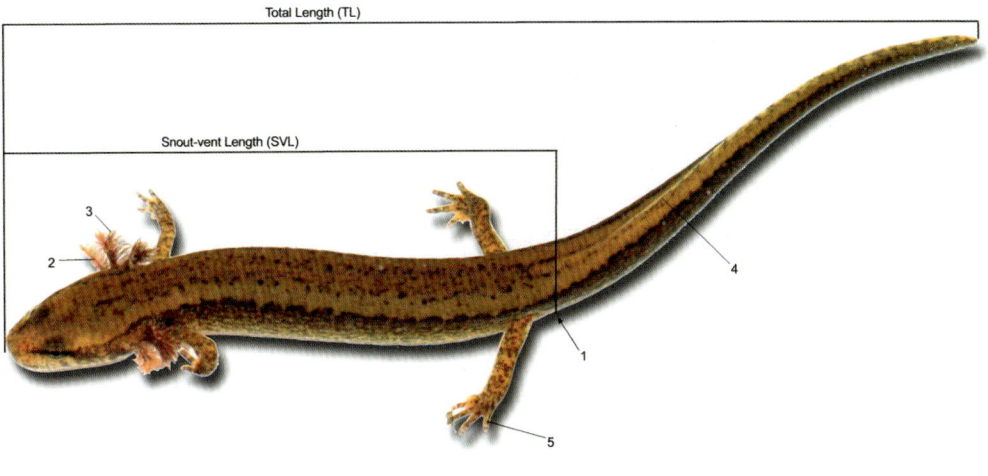

Larval salamander anatomy. Key characteristics of larval salamanders include the total length (TL) and snout-vent length (SVL). 1 = vent; 2 = external gill branch (ramus); 3 = gill fimbriae; 4 = tail fins; and 5 = number of toes.

gans, and cirri. They are capable of detecting faint odor trails left by prey or by other salamanders and hence are fully capable of living in complete darkness—and most salamanders are indeed nocturnal. Much information can be gathered from scent trails, including species recognition, sex, and even nutrient content of feces left by males in their territories, which might signal whether the male is healthy and well fed. In terrestrial salamanders, males track sexually receptive females through olfaction, though courtship doesn't occur in all species. Some males simply deposit spermatophores, which are packets of sperm placed atop a gelatinous base that females find and pick up with their cloaca. In other species, courtship can be elaborate, with the male prodding the female with his snout, dousing or even injecting her with mental gland secretions, or guiding the female to a spermatophore. Physical restraint of the female is also sometimes used, including what is known as cephalic amplexus, or amplexus of the head, in Eastern Newts.

Fertilization is accomplished internally in most salamanders when the female picks the sperm off of the spermatophore with her cloaca, oftentimes storing it for up to several years. Others, like the Hellbenders, use external fertilization, with the males depositing sperm on the eggs laid in a depression under a rock. Females lay eggs either attached to rocks in streams (aquatic and semi-aquatic salamanders), in clumps or strands along the shoreline of ephemeral pools (Mole Salamanders), under moist leaf litter or in rotten logs (terrestrial salamanders), or scattered about in the water (Sirens). Many species of salamanders exhibit parental care and guard eggs after laying

A Northern Red Salamander female laying an egg in a cave rimstone pool, Cannon County. (Photo by R. Graham Reynolds)

until they hatch. Aquatic and semi-aquatic salamanders hatch into larvae, which resemble miniature salamanders but with tail fins and large external gills. These gills look like feathery protrusions just behind the eyes and consist of thin tissue with many capillaries that allow efficient gas exchange. Larval salamanders are predatory, and some are even cannibalistic, especially the Mole Salamanders. Larval periods might last a few weeks or many years, often depending on the conditions of the aquatic habitat and the density of larvae. Metamorphosis includes the loss of external gills and the flattening of the tail, with some species replacing their gills with lungs and others (plethodontids) relying on their moist skin to allow cutaneous respiration, or gas exchange through the skin. Some salamanders are paedomorphic, in that they mature into reproductive adults without undergoing metamorphosis. Facultative paedomorphs include the Tiger Salamanders, which can either metamorphose or become sexually mature in the larval stage. Obligate paedomorphs include the Tennessee Cave Salamander Complex (*Gyrinophilus*), which nearly always mature without undergoing metamorphosis. This is thought to be an adaptation to caves, where more food exists in the water and prey detection is facilitated by the lateral line system. Some metamorphosed cave salamanders have been found, but these frequently appear emaciated and the transformation might be due to extreme environmental stressors.

In terrestrial salamanders, the larval stage is completed while in the egg, and the parents often guard the nest from predators and parasites. The eggs hatch after a few weeks into fully formed miniature adults, which then disperse and mature over a period of one to several years.

Frogs

More than 5,600 species belong to the order Anura, what we refer to as the frogs, which is from the Greek *an* "without" and *oura* "tail." Of these, most are found in moist tropical areas, with some small countries such as Ecuador being home to hundreds of species. In the southeastern United States, diversity is much lower, and only 22 species reside in Tennessee.

Most people probably have some idea of the life cycle of a frog, whether from elementary school pet tadpoles or high school science dissection labs, whose favorite subject is often the Leopard Frog. The generalized life cycle of a frog consists of eggs laid in masses in shallow water, which hatch after a few days into tadpoles and then metamorphose into adults after several weeks. This is the process employed by frogs here in Tennessee but is by no means idiosyncratic of the whole group. Many variations exist in other parts of the world, where eggs might be laid on vegetation above water (*Agalychnis*), in leaf litter (*Eleutherodactylus*),

Generalized anuran life cycle. Shown are the major life stages of the Wood Frog (*Lithobates sylvaticus*), illustrating the biphasic life cycle consisting of the aquatic stages (eggs, tadpole, late-stage tadpole) and terrestrial stages (metamorph and adult).

or even on pouches on the female's back (*Pipa*). Some species have direct development, where the larval stage occurs while still in the egg and a fully formed miniature froglet emerges straight from the egg (*Eleutherodactylus*). Others spend larval stages isolated in bromeliad tanks (*Oophaga*) or even in the vocal sac of the male (*Rhinoderma*). These variations likely represent adaptations to habitats where freshwater might be minimal, ephemeral, or full of predators.

In Tennessee, male frogs begin calling near breeding areas in the spring, with some species, like the Wood Frog, starting as early as January or February. Males produce sound by moving air over their vocal cords and then into their vocal sacs. The sacs are variable among species and serve to fine tune and amplify the sound. The sac can conduct sound through the air, water, and perhaps the ground—indeed, some species of frogs call underwater. Males call in specific ways and transfer a good bit of information in their calls. In some species, smaller or inferior males might call less rapidly, less loudly, or less frequently than large, virile males—and females understand this, often choosing mates based on call characteristics. Calling is energetically expensive, in that it requires a great deal

An Eastern American Toad male calling, Knox County. (Photo by Nathan Haislip)

of energy to call for long periods of time; hence healthy males produce the best and most prolonged song. However, males must often strike a balance between attracting females and not drawing attention to themselves from predators. Therefore, some songs contain frequencies that are difficult to locate, such as Spring Peepers. We have even had a hard time locating a male Peeper when it is calling just a few feet away. Others use complex notes in their songs, which include difficult to locate frequencies punctuated by easily locatable song elements. Some species, such as Bullfrogs and Green Frogs, use sound to startle predators, emitting a loud squawk (Green Frogs) or even a loud nasal squeal lasting several seconds that sounds most unfroglike (Bullfrogs).

Frogs have finely tuned hearing, optimized to the range of frequencies at which members of their species call. The ears are located beneath the tympanum, which is a patch of translucent skin behind the eyes that acts as an eardrum. Sound is transmitted through the tympanum to the middle ear and then to the papilla in the inner ear. Males can recognize the song of other males, and they stake out and maintain territories using sound to maintain proper distances from one another. Sexually reproductive females respond to male song, often arriving at a breeding pond from long distances, drawn by loud calls or calls that transmit over great distances. Other females live near breeding areas, and males' calls have no need to travel very far. Females actively listen to calling males, making initial selections of potential mates by orienting toward males with the best songs. Some further courtship is often required after a female approaches a male, but the song is certainly one

Anuran external anatomy. Key characteristics of anurans include body length. 1 = toe webbing; 2 = toe tips; 3 = tympanum; 4 = dorsolateral fold; and 5 = nares.

of the most important elements in successful reproduction. Some closely related species, such as American and Fowler's Toads, have similar songs, and indeed females are known to respond to either species' calls. This problem is often avoided by what is known as temporal sexual isolation. In other words, American Toads begin to call early in the spring and complete much of the breeding by the time Fowler's Toads begin the process. This is not a perfect situation, however, and these two species are thought to interbreed in some locations, a scenario that could be exacerbated by patterns of global climate change.

Once male and female meet, the male, which is usually smaller, climbs on the back of the female and hooks his front feet under her shoulders, a grip known as amplexus. This position might be maintained for days, and other males often try to dislodge the amplexed couple to

Larval anuran anatomy. Key characteristics of larval anurans include body length and tail length. 1 = relative location of the mouth, either subterminal, terminal, or upturned; 2 = tail musculature; 3 = dorsal tail fin; 4 = ventral tail fin; 5 = developing legs, 6 = vent, and 7 = spiracle, which is the exit tube for water passing over the gills.

take the lucky male's place, which of course necessitates a firm grip. When the female is ready to lay, the eggs begin to stream out of her cloaca, and the male positions himself to spread sperm over the emerging eggs. Oviposition frequently occurs in bouts, with females laying clutches over a period of days, with some species producing a tremendous number of eggs: on the order of several thousand. No parental care exists in frogs in Tennessee, and hence after being laid along the shoreline, the eggs are on their own.

Frog eggs can take several days to several weeks to hatch, at which point a tadpole, or pollywog, emerges. This larval stage of the frogs is fully aquatic, possessing gills to breathe underwater and a tail to swim. Tadpoles have specialized mouthparts, very different from those of adults and often a useful characteristic to distinguish species. They feed on aquatic plankton and organic detritus, and the mouthparts are often a giveaway of the diet. Benthic feeders have subterminal mouths with scraping parts, while those that feed on plankton have terminal mouths. Some even have mouths that point upward, allowing them to feed on organic surface film. Larvae develop over a period of weeks to months in the spring and summer, avoiding the many aquatic predators, such as beetles, dragonfly larvae, fish, and birds. As they approach metamorphosis, several changes become apparent. The tails shrink, legs sprout, and lungs develop, and soon they begin to resemble miniature frogs. When metamorphosis is complete, they leave the water and begin their terrestrial lives, taking from one to several years to mature into reproductive adults.

Though they are terrestrial, frogs must still maintain proper hydration—a difficult task in xeric environments. Frog skin is variable, with the more terrestrial toads having thick, dry skin to prevent water loss and the more aquatic ranids having moist soft skin, which can still act as a surface for gas exchange. Some frogs, such as the Spadefoots, deal with seasonal water availability by burrowing underground and becoming inactive until sufficient rains come. Winter, with its freezing temperatures, can also present

Top left: Eastern American Toads in amplexus, Coffee County. (Photo by Brad M. Glorioso) *Top right:* A Northern Spring Salamander eating a Cumberland Dusky Salamander, Morgan County. (Photo by Matthew L. Niemiller) *Bottom:* Diversity of amphibian species in Tennessee based on county records. Note that low diversity in some counties (e.g., Loudon) is likely due to limited sampling.

a hazard, which frogs deal with by burrowing into mud banks, under leaf litter, or in rotten logs, or by moving into subterranean haunts such as mammal burrows and even caves. Others produce their own antifreeze by converting glycogen to glucose, which reduces damage to tissues caused by the expansion of ice crystals. The Wood Frog can tolerate being completely frozen, going into a state of suspended animation and often appearing dead—a handy trick as their early breeding often gets interrupted by winter storms.

Frogs and salamanders are wonderful examples of adaptation to a "double life" and provide interesting examples of solutions to living both in and out of the water. Frog calls fill spring and summer evenings and together with their intricate and handsome forms give a great deal of pleasure to those who choose to observe them. Salamanders are amazingly diverse and occupy some of the most beautiful habitats in Tennessee, from the peak of Clingman's Dome in the Smokies to the cypress swamps around Reelfoot Lake. Searching for frogs and salamanders will lead you toward a greater appreciation for the beauty of our state and the fascinating complexity of the world beneath the rocks and leaves.

2

Physiography, Climate, and Habitats of Tennessee

Our state is home to a wonderful diversity of amphibians. The rich amphibian fauna in Tennessee is due in large part to the state's size and geographic position, and because it contains much physiographic, climatic, and habitat heterogeneity. This heterogeneity can be plainly observed as one drives Interstate 40 from Memphis on the Mississippi River east across the state toward the Blue Ridge Mountains in East Tennessee. Although several species of frogs and salamanders are distributed statewide, many species (particularly salamanders) are restricted to distinct areas within specific habitats. These areas, known as ecoregions, vary with respect to geology, topography, soils, vegetation, hydrology, and climate. Maps of the state's topography, precipitation, average temperatures, and hydrology clearly illustrate the abiotic heterogeneity found within Tennessee. Accordingly, these ecoregions provide a wealth

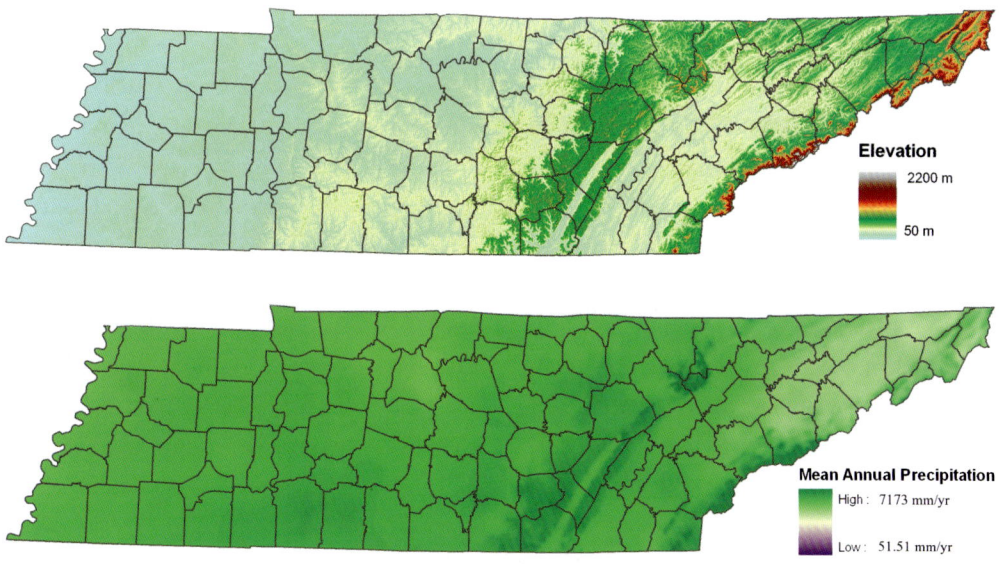

Top: Digital elevation model for Tennessee. The lowest point in Tennessee is the Mississippi River at 52 m, and the highest point is Clingman's Dome in the Great Smoky Mountains National Park at 2,025 m. *Bottom:* Mean annual precipitation in Tennessee, 1971–2000. Note that the range reflects high and low values for the continental United States, and that mean annual rainfall varies between 1,000 and 2,000 mm a year in Tennessee. The region with the least precipitation is the Ridge and Valley in northeast Tennessee, while the areas receiving the most precipitation are the high Blue Ridge Mountains and portions of the Cumberland Plateau. (From: PRISM Group, Oregon State University, Corvallis, http://www.prismclimate.org)

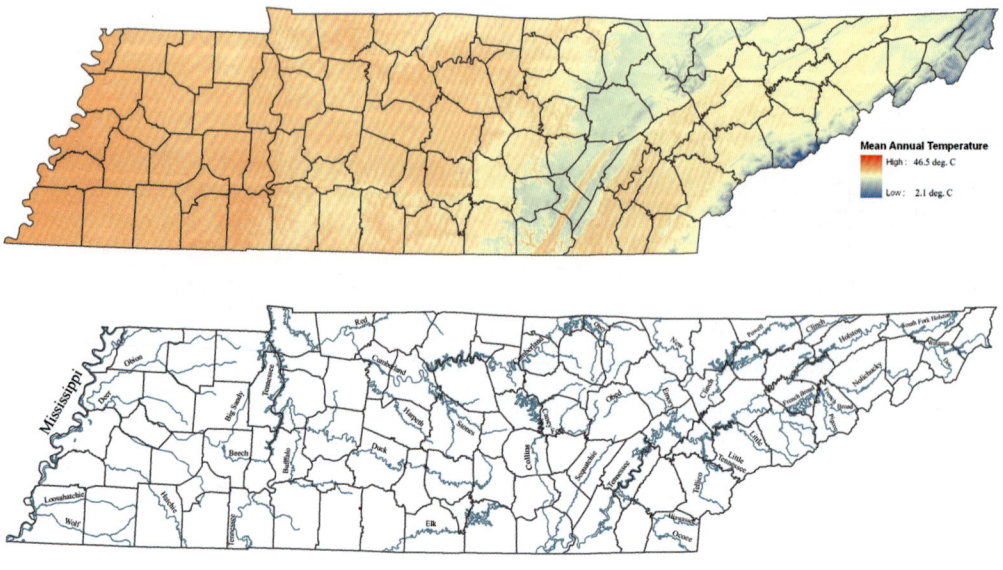

Top: Mean annual temperature in Tennessee, July 1971–2000. Note that the range reflects high and low temperatures for the continental United States, and that mean annual temperature in Tennessee varies between 6°C on top of Clingman's Dome and 17°C in southwest Tennessee. From: PRISM Group, Oregon State University, Corvallis (http://www.prismclimate.org). *Bottom:* Major rivers and tributaries in Tennessee.

of habitats for amphibians and greatly influence the distribution and abundance of the state's diverse amphibian fauna.

In general, Tennessee has a temperate climate, with warm summers and mild winters, but a variety of climatic conditions occur because of the range of topography across the state. Indeed, the warmest areas are in the Mississippi Alluvial Plain along the Mississippi River in West Tennessee and have growing seasons up to 235 days. The Nashville Basin is also quite warm, with a growing season of about 225 days. In contrast, the mountainous regions in East Tennessee (Southwestern Appalachians and Blue Ridge Mountains) have considerably cooler temperatures and shorter growing seasons (as low as 130 days). Although cooler, these regions also receive the most precipitation in the state, particularly the Blue Ridge Mountains, where precipitation occurs in excess of 78 inches (2 m) per year on average. The driest areas occur within the Ridge and Valley of northeast Tennessee, which receive less than 46 inches (1.16 m) of precipitation a year on average. The warmest temperature recorded in the state was 113°F (45°C) in August at Perryville along the Tennessee River in West Tennessee, whereas the coldest temperature on record was -32°F (-36°C) in December at Mountain City in extreme northeast Tennessee.

Eight main ecoregions are recognized in Tennessee. Amphibian diversity and community composition vary substantially from one ecoregion to another (Table 1). Indeed, ecoregions with greater topography, such as the Blue Ridge Mountains and Southwestern Appalachians,

Table 1

Numbers of Species of Amphibians Associated with Ecoregions in Tennessee

Ecoregion	All Species	Anurans	Salamanders
Mississippi Alluvial Plain	**30**	**18**	**12**
Northern Mississippi Alluvial Plain	30	18	12
Mississippi Valley Loess Plains	**33**	**18**	**15**
Bluff Hills	33	18	15
Loess Plains	31	18	13
Southeastern Plains	**39**	**18**	**21**
Blackland Prairie	30	15	15
Flatwoods/Alluvial Prairie Margins	32	17	15
Southeastern Plains and Hills	32	17	15
Fall Line Hills	29	15	14
Transition Hills	31	14	17
Interior Plateau	**42**	**19**	**23**
Western Pennyroyal Karst	33	15	18
Western Highland Rim	37	18	19
Outer Nashville Basin	32	13	19
Inner Nashville Basin	29	11	18
Eastern Highland Rim	37	15	22
Southwestern Appalachians	**40**	**15**	**25**
Plateau Escarpment	40	15	25
Cumberland Plateau	38	14	24
Sequatchie Valley	31	13	18
Central Appalachians	**36**	**14**	**22**
Cumberland Mountains	36	14	22
Ridge and Valley	**41**	**16**	**25**
Southern Limestone/Dolomite Valleys and Low Rolling Hills	38	15	23
Southern Shale Valleys	35	14	21
Southern Sandstone Ridges	33	14	19
Southern Dissected Ridges and Knobs	34	14	20
Blue Ridge Mountains	**56**	**14**	**42**
Southern Igneous Ridges and Mountains	22	4	18
Southern Sedimentary Ridges	43	13	30
Limestone Valleys and Coves	41	13	28
Southern Metasedimentary Mountains	51	14	37

are cooler on average and receive more precipitation than those with less topography. These regions have greater salamander diversity than other ecoregions in the state. Conversely, ecoregions that are warmer with less topography, such as the Mississippi Alluvial Plain and Mississippi Valley Loess Plains, support greater frog diversity.

In this section, we briefly describe each of the major ecoregions and associated subregions found in Tennessee. In particular, we discuss the topography, geology, prominent natural vegetation, hydrology, and unique amphibian fauna for each ecoregion and subregion.

Mississippi Alluvial Plain

The Mississippi Alluvial Plain is a flat and broad floodplain 60–90 m in elevation that lies between the Mississippi River to west and the Bluff Hills to the east in western Tennessee. This ecoregion is composed of Quaternary alluvial deposits of silt, clay, sand, and gravel. Although most of this ecoregion has been converted to cropland, some southern floodplain forest remains, consisting of oak, tupelo, and bald cypress stands. Streams in this ecoregion are sluggish and meandering with many oxbow lakes and cypress swamps. Reelfoot Lake, formed by subsidence and backflow of the Mississippi River during the New Madrid earthquake of 1811–12, occurs within this ecoregion in northwest Tennessee. Bird-Voiced Treefrogs, Green Treefrogs, Mole Salamanders, Small-Mouthed Salamanders, Lesser Sirens, and Three-Toed Amphiumas are characteristic amphibians of the Mississippi Alluvial Plain.

Mississippi Valley Loess Plains

The Mississippi Valley Loess Plains extend from near the Ohio River in western Kentucky south into Louisiana, and thick loess deposits define this ecoregion. Natural vegetation is primarily irregular plains with oak-hickory to oak-hickory-pine forest, but most of this land has been converted for agricultural use in Tennessee. Two subregions of the Mississippi Valley Loess Plains occur in Tennessee, the Bluff Hills and the Loess Plains.

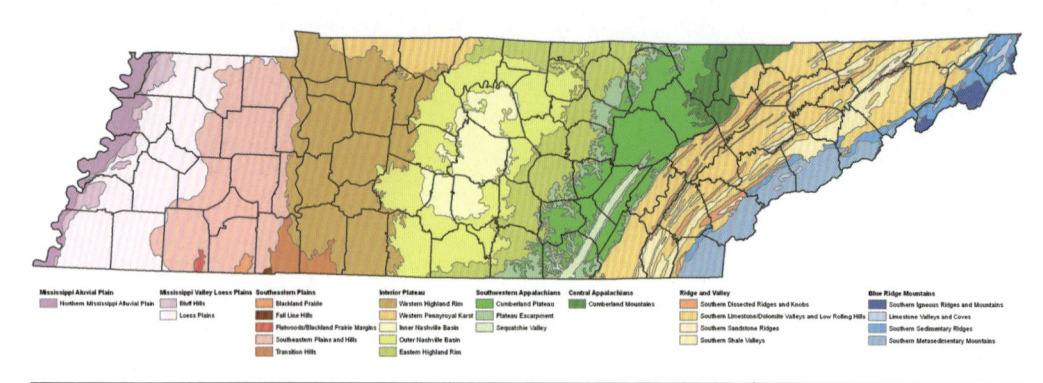

Major ecoregions of Tennessee; see text for details. From Griffith et al. 1998.

Left: Reelfoot Lake in the Mississippi Alluvial Plain at dusk, Obion County. (Photo by Brad M. Glorioso)
Right: Roadside slough in the Mississippi Alluvial Plain, Obion County. (Photo by Brad M. Glorioso)

Bluff Hills

The Bluff Hills consist of disjunct areas of generally dissected and forested terrain over deposits of sand, silt, clay, and lignite that are capped by substantial loess greater than 18 m thick. The Bluff Hills form a narrow border along the Mississippi Alluvial Plain that lies to the west. A variety of habitats exist in this subregion, including xeric slopes and ridges, more mesic slopes and ravines, bottomland forest, and small cypress swamps. Upland areas are primarily oak-hickory to mixed oak forest, whereas more mesic ravines and bottomland forest are dominated by maple, hickory, yellow poplar, and beech. Many streams in this subregion are intermittent or ephemeral with sandy to silty substrates; however, higher gradient streams also occur and have gravel substrates. Mississippi Slimy Salamanders occur in this subregion.

Loess Plains

Gently undulating, irregular plains with broad bottomlands and terraces characterize the Loess Plains, with loess deposits up to 15 m thick at elevations of 75–150 m. This subregion is a very productive agricultural area and much of the natural mosaic of oak-hickory forest, southern floodplain forest, and bluestem prairie has been replaced by cropland. However, some bottomland forest and cypress-gum swamp forest still remain. Most streams in the subregion have been channelized and are low gradient and murky with sand to silt substrates. Agricultural runoff has degraded water quality in many river systems. Crawfish Frogs, Bird-Voiced Treefrogs, Green Treefrogs, Lesser Sirens, Mississippi Slimy Salamanders, Mole Salamanders, and Small-Mouthed Salamanders are known from this subregion. Southern Cricket Frogs occur in the southern part of the Loess Plains in southwest Tennessee.

Southeastern Plains

The Southeastern Plains consist of irregular plains, broad areas between streams that contain a mosaic of oak-hickory-pine forest, woodlands, pasture, and croplands. This ecoregion is underlain with Cretaceous- to Tertiary-aged silts, sands, and clays. Elevation and relief are generally greater than the Mississippi Valley

A swamp in the Southeastern Plains and Hills is home to Three-Toed Amphiumas and Western Lesser Sirens and is breeding habitat for Bird-Voiced Treefrogs, Hardeman County. (Photo by Matthew L. Niemiller)

Loess Plains to the west but less than the Interior Plateau to the east. Streams in this ecoregion are generally low gradient with sand substrates. Five subregions occur in Tennessee: the Blackland Prairie, Flatwoods/Alluvial Prairie Margins, Southeastern Plains and Hills, Fall Line Hills, and Transition Hills.

Southeastern Plains and Hills

The Southeastern Plains and Hills is the largest subregion of the Southeastern Plains in Tennessee. This subregion is characterized by several bands of sand and clay formations oriented north to south. These formations are Tertiary-aged and have greater relief, with undulating topography to the west and some elevations reaching over 190 m. Natural vegetation is oak-hickory forest that transitions into oak-hickory-pine forest to the south. Streams are located in wide-bottomed areas with broad, rolling terraces and are moderate to low gradient with sandy substrates. Crawfish Frogs, Bird-Voiced Treefrogs, Lesser Sirens, Mississippi Slimy Salamanders, Red Salamanders, Spotted Dusky Salamanders, Mole Salamanders, and Small-Mouthed Salamanders are known from this subregion. Southern Cricket Frogs occur in the southern part of the Southeastern Plains and Hills in southwest Tennessee.

Transition Hills

The Transition Hills are characterized by dissected open hills 120–305 m in elevation with steep slopes caused by the downcutting of streams into the Mississippian-, Devonian-, and Silurian-aged strata. However, Cretaceous-aged clay, silt, sand, and gravel have been deposited above these older limestones, shales, and chert. This subregion is adjacent to the Western Highland Rim of the Interior Plateau in Hardin and Wayne counties. The natural vegetation of most of this subregion is oak-hickory-pine forest. Streams are moderate to low gradient with sand and gravel substrates. Mississippi Slimy Salamanders occur in this subregion.

Blackland Prairie, Flatwoods/Alluvial Prairie Margins, and Falls Line Hills

These three subregions have small areas at elevations of 120–210 m in southwest Tennessee, which extend from the south in Mississippi. The Blackland Prairie extends into a small portion of southeast McNairy County and is characterized as irregular plains and undulating lowlands. Natural vegetation is oak-hickory forest and blackbelt forest of sweetgum, oak, and cedar with patches of bluestem prairie. Streams in this subregion are low gradient with clay, sand, and silt substrates. The Flatwoods/Alluvial Prairie Margins is characterized by undulating plains and lowlands with sluggish, low-gradient streams with sand substrates. This subregion encompasses a small area in southeast Hardeman County. Natural vegetation is oak-hickory to oak-hickory-pine forest with bottomland hardwood forest. The Fall Line Hills are dissected open hills composed primarily of Cretaceous-aged sand deposits at elevations of 140–210 m in southwest Hardin County. Natural vegetation is oak-hickory-pine forest and streams are moderate to low gradient with sand substrates. Southern Cricket Frogs are known from the Flatwoods/Alluvial Prairie Margins.

Interior Plateau

The Interior Plateau ecoregion consists of a diverse landscape of generally hilly topography extending from north Alabama to southern Illinois, Indiana, and Ohio. Within Tennessee, the Interior Plateau is bordered by the Southwestern Appalachians ecoregion to the east and the Southeastern Plains to the west. There are five subregions within the Interior Plateau of Tennessee: the Western Pennyroyal Karst, Western Highland Rim, Eastern Highland Rim, Outer Nashville Basin, and Inner Nashville Basin. The Highland Rim encircles the oval-shaped Nashville Basin (also called the Central Basin) and is 150–180 m higher in elevation. The Nashville Basin can be divided into two concentric zones: the relatively flat Inner Nashville Basin and the hillier Outer Nashville Basin.

Western Pennyroyal Karst

This subregion is characterized by relatively flat, weakly dissected terrain with irregular open plains and few perennial streams; however, sinking streams, sinkholes, and depressions are common and subterranean drainages are well developed. The Western Pennyroyal Karst is composed primarily of Middle Mississippian–aged limestones. The natural vegetation of this subregion is oak-hickory forest interspersed with patches of bluestem prairie, but much of this subregion has been cultivated for agriculture or is pastureland. Barking Treefrogs, Western Chorus Frogs, Zigzag Salamanders, Spotted Dusky Salamanders, Long-Tailed Salamanders,

A borrow pit used as a breeding site by American Toads, Cope's Gray Treefrogs, and Barking Treefrogs in the Eastern Highland Rim, Coffee County. (Photo by Matthew L. Niemiller)

Northern Slimy Salamanders, Mole Salamanders, Small-Mouthed Salamanders, and Tiger Salamanders occur in this subregion.

Western Highland Rim

This subregion is characterized by dissected, hilly terrain with open hills but heavily forested valleys at 120–300 m in elevation. Both the Tennessee and Cumberland rivers bisect this subregion. The Western Highland Rim is composed of Mississippian limestone, chert, and shale covered by cherty, acidic soils. Upland areas have cherty soils and mixed oak forests predominate, whereas oak-hickory forests are the natural vegetation throughout other areas. However, most of the subregion was deforested in the mid- to late 1800s. Streams are of moderate gradient with sand-gravel substrates. Long-Tailed Salamanders, Cave Salamanders, Spotted Dusky Salamanders, Northern Slimy Salamanders, and Red Salamanders are characteristic amphibian fauna of this subregion. Green Treefrogs have been reported from the major river bottomlands. Bird-Voiced Treefrogs have been documented along the Cumberland River. Hellbenders are known from several rivers.

Eastern Highland Rim

The Eastern Highland Rim averages 305 m in elevation (up to 430 m) and is only 24 to 32 km wide. This subregion is characterized by gently rolling to nearly flat terrain with numerous springs, sinkholes, and other karst features. The highest point on the Eastern Highland Rim,

Vernal pond on the Eastern Highland Rim, Coffee County. (Photo by Matthew L. Niemiller)

Short Mountain in Cannon County (632 m), is a remnant of a formerly much broader Cumberland Plateau. Like the Western Highland Rim, the periphery of the Eastern Highland Rim is characterized by steep-sloping valleys that mark the transition into the Outer Nashville Basin. A mosaic of open canopy woodlands and an understory consisting of grasslands called the Barrens is found within the headwaters of the Caney Fork, Duck, and Elk river watersheds. The hardpan soils of this region and low topographic relief keep soils saturated in the winter yet very dry during the summer inhibiting forest development but fostering a prairie community. This subregion is composed of Mississippian-aged limestones, chert, shale, and dolomite. The natural vegetation is a transition from the oak-hickory forest to mixed mesophytic forest. Streams in this subregion are moderate gradient and nutrient rich with bedrock, cobble, and gravel substrates. Barking Treefrogs, Gopher Frogs, Mole Salamanders, Small-Mouthed Salamanders, Southern Two-Lined Salamanders, Mud Salamanders, Northern Slimy Salamanders, and Red Salamanders are known from the Barrens region. Hellbenders are known from several rivers. Tennessee Cave Salamanders are known from several caves.

Outer Nashville Basin

The Outer Nashville Basin is characterized by rolling hills with numerous knobs slightly higher in elevation than the Inner Nashville Basin. Predominant groundcover includes oak-hickory forest with pasture and cropland. This

Top left: American Bullfrog in an ephemeral wetland in the Inner Nashville Basin, Wilson County. (Photo by Brad M. Glorioso) *Top right:* Subterranean stream in the Inner Nashville Basin, Wilson County. (Photo by Matthew L. Niemiller) *Bottom:* A rocky, ephemeral stream in the Inner Central Basin is a breeding site for Streamside Salamanders, Rutherford County. (Photo by Brad M. Glorioso)

subregion is underlain primarily by noncherty Ordovician-aged limestones, although the higher knobs and hills contain more cherty Mississippian-aged limestones and Devonian-aged Chattanooga shale, which are remnants of a once broader Highland Rim. Streams in this subregion are low to moderate in gradient and nutrient rich. Cope's Gray Treefrogs, Southern Two-Lined Salamanders and Zigzag Salamanders occur in this subregion.

Inner Nashville Basin

The Inner Nashville Basin is considerably flatter and lower in elevation than the Outer Nashville Basin. Additionally, this subregion has thinner soils and greater karst development. This subregion is underlain by Ordovician-aged limestones. Most of this subregion is cropland and pasture with scattered maple-oak-hickory forests. Cedar glades also are found within the Inner Nashville basin and contain a unique assemblage of plants and animals adapted to a harsh, xeric environment. The shallow and rocky soils of cedar glades limit forest development and typically are open areas surrounded by eastern red cedar where soils are thicker. Streams are low gradient and nutrient rich with bedrock the predominant substrate. Tiger Salamanders, Streamside Salamanders, Cave Salamanders, and Zigzag Salamanders occur in this subregion. Hellbenders are historically known from several rivers. Tennessee Cave Salamanders are known from several caves.

Stream on Cumberland Plateau Escarpment, Warren County. (Photo by Matthew L. Niemiller)

Southwestern Appalachians

The Southwestern Appalachians ecoregion consists of forest and woodland habitats interspersed with some cropland and pasture on low mountainous terrain. This region extends from Kentucky southwest through Tennessee and into Alabama and northwest Georgia. The eastern edge of this ecoregion, where it meets the Ridge and Valley, is only slightly dissected by eastward flowing streams. In contrast, the western edge, where it meets the Eastern Highland Rim of the Interior Plateau, is much more rugged and deeply incised. Upland areas are primarily mixed oak–shortleaf pine forest, whereas deeper ravines and escarpment slopes are characterized by mixed mesophytic forest. Three subregions occur within the Southwestern Appalachians: the Cumberland Plateau, Plateau Escarpment, and Sequatchie Valley.

Cumberland Plateau

The Cumberland Plateau is characterized by low hills, undulating uplands, valleys, and ridges about 300 m higher in elevation than the Eastern Highland Rim to west. Elevations range from 360 to 610 m, although the Crab Orchard Mountains reach over 900 m in elevation. Accordingly, this subregion is slightly cooler and receives more precipitation than surrounding ecoregions. This subregion is underlain by Pennsylvanian-aged conglomerate, sandstone, siltstone, coal, and shale and is covered by acidic, well-drained soils. Although forested, forest composition is highly variable and logging is common. Streams within this subregion are of low to moderate gradient with broader floodplains and more riparian wetlands than in the Plateau Escarpment. Mountain Chorus Frogs, Mud Salamanders, Northern Slimy Salamanders, and Zigzag Salamanders occur in this subregion. Green Salamanders are known from rock outcrops.

Plateau Escarpment
Narrow ridges, cliffs, gorges, and steep, forested slopes characterize the Plateau Escarpment, where local relief can be in excess of 340 m. This subregion is underlain by Mississippian-aged limestones, sandstone, shale, and siltstone in the lower slopes and western valleys, whereas the upland areas are underlain by Pennsylvanian-aged conglomerate, sandstone, shale, and siltstone. Ravines and gorges are characterized by mixed oak forest on the upper slopes to more mesic forests of beech, tulip-poplar, ash, buckeye, and maple on the middle and lower slopes. Hemlock is common along riparian areas and river birch along floodplain terraces. Streams are of high quality and gradient with numerous riffles and pools and boulder to bedrock substrates. Several streams have cut down into the Mississippian-aged limestones and have lower gradients, wider valleys, and higher productivity. Green Frogs, Pickerel Frogs, Cumberland Dusky Salamanders, Southern Two-Lined Salamanders, Long-Tailed Salamanders, Cave Salamanders, and Zigzag Salamanders are characteristic amphibians of this subregion. Green Salamanders are known from rock outcrops at higher elevations. Tennessee Cave Salamanders are known from several caves.

Sequatchie Valley
The Sequatchie Valley is an open, rolling valley averaging 6.4 km wide running from just south of the Crab Orchard Mountains south-southwest for 240 km into northwest Alabama. This subregion is associated with an anticline where erosion has formed a deep valley 180–300 m in elevation and bounded on either side by the Cumberland Plateau. The eastern section boundary is much narrower and is known as Walden Ridge. The valley floor is nearly 300 m lower in elevation than the surrounding highlands. This subregion is underlain with Mississippian-aged and Ordovician-aged limestones and shale. The Sequatchie Valley is characterized by mixed oak-hickory-maple forest, but there are several areas of cropland and pasture. Streams in this subregion are moderate to low gradient and several springs are present. Cope's Gray Treefrogs, Eastern Spadefoots, American Bullfrogs, Common Mudpuppies, and Spring Salamanders are known from this subregion.

Central Appalachians
The Central Appalachians span from northern Tennessee northeast to central Pennsylvania. This ecoregion is characterized as a high plateau of rugged terrain that is highly dissected. Most of this ecoregion is blanketed with Appalachian oak and northern hardwoods forest because of the rugged terrain, cool, moist climate, and infertile soils; however, coal mining is prominent in this ecoregion. The Cumberland Mountains is the only subregion of the Central Appalachians in Tennessee.

Cumberland Mountains

The Cumberland Mountains are characterized as low mountains with long, steep slopes and narrow, winding valleys. This subregion is higher in elevation (360–1060 m) and much more highly dissected than the adjacent Cumberland Plateau, with local relief up to 610 m. This subregion is underlain with Pennsylvanian-aged sandstones, shales, siltstones, and coal. This natural vegetation is mixed mesophytic forest consisting of oak, maple, buckeye, beech, and tulip poplar, although the forest composition varies greatly depending on local topography. Streams are high to moderate gradient that are clear with principally bedrock substrates, waterfalls, and many riffles. However, many streams have been negatively impacted by coal mining and logging operations. Wood Frogs, Seal Salamanders, Spring Salamanders, Cumberland Plateau Salamanders, Wehrle's Salamanders, Black Mountain Salamanders, and Allegheny Mountain Dusky Salamanders are known from this subregion.

Ridge and Valley

The Ridge and Valley consists of lower elevation, roughly parallel ridges and valleys generally running from southwest to northeast between the Cumberland Plateau to the west and the Blue Ridge Mountains to the east. This topography is varied in height, width, and geology because of past tectonic events. This ecoregion is underlain with Paleozoic sandstones, siltstone, shale, chert, limestones, and dolomites that have been folded and faulted. Ridges tend to be composed of more resistant strata, whereas valleys are

John Bills looking for salamanders in the splash zone of a waterfall in the Cumberland Mountains, Cumberland County. (Photo by Matthew L. Niemiller)

composed by weaker strata, such as limestones and shales. Dominant natural vegetation is Appalachian oak forest, although only about 50% of this ecoregion is now forested. Streams vary in gradient and substrate composition and are very productive. Springs and caves are also numerous in this ecoregion. Four subregions occur in Tennessee: the Southern Limestone/Dolomite Valleys and Low Rolling Hills, Southern Shale Valleys, Southern Sandstone Ridges, and Southern Dissected Ridges and Knobs.

Southern Limestone/Dolomite Valleys and Low Rolling Hills

This subregion encompasses the largest area of the Ridge and Valley in Tennessee and is characterized by Ordovician-aged limestones and cherty dolomite forming broad, rolling, fertile valleys and numerous springs and caves. Elevation ranges from 210 to 610 m with local relief up to 210 m. Natural vegetation is Appalachian oak forest, although bottomland oak and sycamore-ash-elm riparian forests also occur in this subregion. Grassland barren and cedar-pine glades also occur. However, much of this subregion has been converted to cropland and pasture. Streams are moderate to low gradient with sand, gravel, cobble, and bedrock substrates. Green Frogs, Zigzag Salamanders, Northern Slimy Salamanders, and Southern Two-Lined Salamanders occur in this subregion. Hellbenders are known from the larger streams and rivers. Cave Salamanders, Spring Salamanders, and Berry Cave Salamanders are known from several caves.

Southern Shale Valleys

The Southern Shale Valleys region is characterized by lowlands, rolling valleys, and low hills with Ordovician- and Cambrian-aged shale deposits at elevations of 240–460 m. Natural vegetation is Appalachian oak forest, but much of the land has been converted to pasture and small farms. Streams are moderate to low gradient with sand, gravel, cobble, and bedrock substrates. Southern Two-Lined Salamanders, Spotted Dusky Salamanders, Northern Slimy Salamanders, and Green Frogs are known from this subregion.

Southern Sandstone Ridges

The Southern Sandstone Ridges are high, steep-sided, forested ridges with narrow crests ranging from 270 to 910 m in elevation with up to 365 m of local relief. These ridges are comprised of Ordovician-, Silurian-, Devonian-, and Mississippian-aged sandstones, shales, siltstones, and conglomerates. Natural vegetation is Appalachian oak forest with some mixed mesophytic forest. Streams are high to moderate gradient with cobble and bedrock substrates. Northern Slimy Salamanders are known from this subregion.

Southern Dissected Ridges and Knobs

The Southern Dissected Ridges and Knobs are characterized by hills, ridges, and knobs that are lower in elevation (240–610 m) and more dissected than the Southern Sandstone Ridges. The ridges on the east side of the Ridge and Valley ecoregion typically are associated with Ordovician-aged shales, sandstones, and limestones, whereas those in the central and western Ridge and Valley tend to be associated with Cambrian-aged formations. Natural vegetation of higher elevations is chestnut oak-pine forest with Appalachian oak and mixed mesophytic forest at lower elevations. Streams are small in this subregion, with high to moderate gradient and gravel, cobble, bedrock substrates. Spotted Dusky Salamanders and Southern Two-Lined Salamanders occur in this subregion.

Blue Ridge Mountains

The Blue Ridge Mountains are characterized by narrow mountain ridges that are forested and highly dissected at elevations of 305–2,025 m. These mountains are rugged with high-gradient streams that are cool and clear. This is the wettest ecoregion in Tennessee, with some peaks in the Great Smoky Mountains receiving over 80 inches (2 m) of precipitation. Four subregions occur in Tennessee: the Southern Igneous Ridges and Mountains, Southern Sedimentary Ridges, Limestone Valleys and Coves, and Southern Metasedimentary Mountains.

Southern Igneous Ridges and Mountains

The Southern Igneous Ridges and Mountains are characterized by prominent, highly dissected

Stream in Blue Ridge Mountains, Cocke County. (Photo by Brad M. Glorioso)

A view of the Great Smoky Mountains from within Cades Cove in the Blue Ridge Mountains, Blount County. (Photo by Matthew L. Niemiller)

ridges and mountains separated by high gaps and coves with steep slopes. This subregion occurs in northeast Tennessee near the North Carolina border in Unicoi, Carter, and Johnson counties. These ridges and mountains are composed primarily of Precambrian-aged igneous and metamorphic strata. Elevations range from 610 to 1,915 m. This area is primarily covered in Appalachian oak, mixed mesophytic, and northern hardwoods forest. Streams are high gradient, cool, and clear with boulder and bedrock substrates. Northern Pygmy Salamanders, Blue Ridge Dusky Salamanders, White-Spotted Slimy Salamanders, Northern Gray-Cheeked Salamanders, Weller's Salamanders, Yonahlossee Salamanders, and Eastern Red-Backed Salamanders occur in this subregion.

Southern Sedimentary Ridges

The Southern Sedimentary Ridges are high-elevation (305–1,370 m), steep-sloped ridges with deep, narrow valleys—primarily composed of Cambrian-aged shale, sandstones, siltstones, quartzite, and conglomerates—and include some of the westernmost foothills areas, such as the Bean, Starr, Chilhowee, English, Stone, Bald, and Iron mountains. Natural vegetation is Appalachian oak forest with some mixed mesophytic and northern hardwoods forest. Streams are high gradient with cool, clear water and with boulder and bedrock substrates. Black-Bellied Salamanders, Blue Ridge Two-Lined Salamanders, Southern Ravine Salamanders, Weller's Salamanders, Yonahlossee Salamanders, White-Spotted Slimy Salamanders, and Eastern Red-Backed Salamanders occur in this subregion.

Prime habitat for Hellbenders and Common Mudpuppies in a river in the Blue Ridge Mountains, Polk County. (Photo by Matthew L. Niemiller)

Limestone Valleys and Coves

The Limestone Valleys and Coves is the smallest subregion of the Blue Ridge Mountains in Tennessee. This subregion is characterized by small but distinct lowland areas between 450 and 760 m that have flat to rolling valleys and coves surrounded by high mountains. Cades Cove, Wear Cove, and Tuckaleehee Cove are part of this subregion. Limestone sinks are common. Appalachian oak forest is the dominant natural vegetation although much of this land has been converted into pasture and cropland. Streams are moderate gradient with boulder and cobble substrates. Shovel-Nosed Salamanders, Red Salamanders, Southern Red-Backed Salamanders, and Long-Tailed Salamanders occur in this subregion.

Southern Metasedimentary Mountains

The Southern Metasedimentary Mountains are highly dissected, steep-sloped mountains composed primarily of Precambrian-aged metamorphic and sedimentary strata. Elevations range from 305 to 2,010 m. Lower and middle elevations have Appalachian oak and northern hardwood forests while the higher elevations (above 1,675 m) have southeastern spruce-fir forest as the dominant natural vegetation. Cool, clear streams are high gradient with boulder and bedrock substrates. Wood Frogs, Hellbenders, Blue Ridge Two-Lined Salamanders, Junaluska Salamanders, Southern Red-Backed Salamanders, Southern Appalachian Slimy Salamanders, Blue Ridge Spring Salamanders, Seal Salamanders, Ocoee Salamanders, Santeetlah Dusky Salamanders, Shovel-Nosed Salamanders, and Black-Bellied Salamanders are characteristic amphibians of this subregion. Imitator Salamanders, Pygmy Salamanders, and Jordan's Red-Cheeked Salamanders occur at higher elevations in the Great Smoky Mountains. Mountain Chorus Frogs, Seepage Salamanders, and Tellico Salamanders occur in Monroe and Polk counties.

3
Amphibian Conservation

Amphibians have recently risen to the forefront of conservation biology due to massive global population declines and species extinctions. Certain regions of the world, including Central and South America, Australia, Sri Lanka, and the western United States, have experienced tremendous amphibian losses, with many species lost forever to extinction. The rapid loss of amphibian diversity is both heartbreaking and extremely alarming, as amphibians are sometimes considered bioindicators, a sort of canary-in-the-coal-mine whose demise might indicate serious environmental problems to come. The year 2008 was officially declared the Year of the Frog, a campaign which aimed to raise awareness for the global amphibian crisis.

In Tennessee, amphibians are not immune to the problems faced by other populations around the globe, and declining populations are being noted with increasing frequency in our state. We are justly proud of the fact that the Southern Appalachians harbor the greatest salamander diversity in the world and that Tennessee is home to many of these unique and beautiful species. Yet the ominous fact that an amphibian extinction crises could wipe out the world's center of salamander diversity should not go unnoticed. Many of these species occur in small ranges and are adapted to a particular range of environmental variables, such that they would not be able to tolerate any great environmental perturbation.

This is why we have included a conservation section for each species account in this book, so that readers might be aware of the diverse threats faced by our state's amphibians. We further hope that perhaps by learning about particular threats faced by individual populations and species, Tennesseans will participate in mitigation and conservation projects to protect their beautiful but vulnerable amphibian neighbors.

Below are some examples of threats faced by amphibians, both around the world and in the state of Tennessee. We hope that our readers will consider these threats and take personal action to assist in the conservation of amphibian biodiversity.

Threats to Amphibians

Global Threats

These threats are taking a large toll on amphibian diversity and abundance worldwide, including here in Tennessee.

GLOBAL CLIMATE CHANGE

The unfortunate arrival of anthropogenic global climate change due to increased input of greenhouse gases in the atmosphere has greatly alarmed the conservation community. What this will eventually mean for future biodiversity is yet to be understood, though many scientists and policy makers are modeling the potential consequences so that mitigation action plans can be put into place. Though much of the potential environmental damage has yet to come, amphibians are already being drastically affected.

Global climate change involves the rapid shifting of climate patterns, such as temperature and precipitation. The frequency and severity of periodic global climactic oscillations, such as El Niño/Southern Oscillation, might be increased as a result of warmer ocean temperatures. Such an event has been implicated in the extinction of the Golden Toad (*Bufo periglenes*) from the cloud forests of Costa Rica, which was lost during the late 1980s during a shift in the altitude of moisture-laden clouds brought on by the loss of lowland rainforest, which traps moisture, and exacerbated by an El Niño event. The temporary and seasonal high-altitude streams that the toads relied on to breed never formed due to a reduction in low cloud cover, and hence there was a period of no juvenile recruitment. As amphibians are so reliant on moisture, any rapid change in seasonal precipitation could have a drastic impact on amphibian populations.

Warming temperatures in temperate latitudes have also brought about earlier breeding in some amphibians. As many closely related communal breeders, such as Fowler's Toad and American Toad found in Tennessee, are temporally separated breeders, a change in breeding time could cause these temporal barriers to relax and overlap. This might result in increased hybridization between the species, as has already been observed with these toads.

Many amphibians are adapted to specialized habitats, such as *Atelopus* frogs, which are mostly found in cool, high-elevation streams in the Neotropics. Changes in climate patterns, such as a reduction in precipitation and an increase in temperature, would drive these frogs higher and higher into the mountains, where they would eventually run out of real estate. Additionally, amphibians with specialized habitat preferences might be unable to move or adapt quickly enough to cope with changing environmental conditions. These factors have been implicated in the reduction or loss of several amphibian populations worldwide.

Disease

Disease-causing pathogens have played a major role in the recent decline and loss of amphibians, perhaps constituting one of the greatest threats they face in the short term. The fungal pathogen *Batrachochytrium dendrobatidis,* known in brevis as chytrid, is a particularly insidious threat and has directly caused massive population declines. First discovered only recently during tremendous frog die-offs, the fungus grows inside adult and recently metamorphosed frogs, and interferes with osmoregulation and respiration which in most cases leads to death. This fungus grows in water 4–25°C but seems to be unable to grow and survive in warmer water. This means that some amphibian populations might be less susceptible to the fungus. Low-elevation populations of *Atelopus* in Panama, which as of March 2009 appear stable, might be less affected by the pathogen than their high-elevation congeners, which are in drastic decline and are rapidly disappearing. Chytrid, which is hypothesized to have been spread by the use of African Clawed Frogs (*Xenopus*) in laboratory research and early pregnancy tests, is now found nearly worldwide and is taking a massive toll in the Neotropics, Australia, and the western United States, among other locations.

In the Great Smoky Mountains National Park, researchers from the University of Tennessee and elsewhere have been documenting spring die-offs of larval amphibians in breeding pools, which is thought to be due to the presence of ranavirus, a group of iridoviruses (Iridoviridae) which causes tissue necrosis resulting in visible lesions and can result in up to 90% mortality of an exposed amphibian population. Using molecular techniques, these researchers have identified ranavirus in several populations of amphibians, which breed in standing water such as ponds. This represents yet another insidious disease pathogen, which might occur simultaneously with chytrid and other pathogens within a population, a perfect storm of disease that is a great threat to global amphibian biodiversity.

Dead ambystomatid salamander larvae in Gourley Pond, Cades Cove, Great Smoky Mountains National Park, Blount County. Found after confirmation of a ranavirus outbreak in the park, spring 2009. (Photo by Matthew L. Niemiller)

INVASIVE ANIMAL SPECIES

Invasive animal species are one of the top three major causes for global biodiversity decline, and they are taking a toll on amphibians as well. In the western United States, the introduction of fish species such as Rainbow Trout (*Oncorhynchus mykiss*) and Largemouth Bass (*Micropterus salmoides*) are implicated in the decline of Yellow-Legged Frogs (*Rana muscosa* and *Rana boylii*) and Red-Legged Frogs (*Rana aurora*). Fish likely consume tadpoles and metamorphs, while larger fish, such as bass, might take adult frogs.

Introduced amphibians might also play a role in the loss of native species. Bullfrogs (*Lithobates catesbeianus*) and Cane Toads (*Rhinella marina*), which are native to eastern North America and Central America respectively, have been introduced worldwide for food (*Lithobates*) and pest control (*Rhinella*). Neither species is very good for either of these purposes, but the introductions have led to greatly increasing populations outside of their native ranges. In the western United States, Bullfrogs are thought to be contributing to local declines of native amphibians due to competition for food between their tadpoles and those of the natives. In Australia, where the Cane Toad has exploded in numbers and range, declines have been noted in native amphibians due to competition as well as direct predation, as Cane Toads will consume nearly anything that will fit into their mouth.

In California, a particularly troublesome situation is leading to the extinction of the endangered California Tiger Salamander (*Ambystoma californiense*). Non-native larvae of the Barred Tiger Salamander (*Ambystoma tigrinum mavortium*) from Texas were introduced into the Central Valley as a source of bass bait for fishermen. These invaders are now interbreeding with the native California Tiger Salamanders, producing hybrids that are capable of outcompeting the native parents. Hence, the unique genome of the California Tiger Salamander is being swamped by introgression of alleles from the invasive Barred Tiger Salamander, and California Tiger Salamanders are unable to compete with their own hybrid offspring. This is leading to what will surely be the imminent demise of this unique ambystomatid salamander.

Habitat Loss and Pollution

Perhaps the greatest threat to amphibian biodiversity, habitat modification due to human destruction of natural environments, has led to the loss of many local populations of amphibians and, if extensive enough, will certainly lead to the ultimate extinction of amphibian species. Amphibians, like most organisms, are adapted to particular habitats and require certain conditions to be present in order to survive. If forests are cut down, wetlands drained, habitats bulldozed, and rivers dammed, then amphibians are left with much less or in some cases no suitable habitat in which to live or breed. These environmental changes might also increase stress levels of local amphibian populations, which could lead to increased susceptibility to viral or fungal infection or reduced breeding success. Countries such as Haiti, with a formerly high diversity of frog species and recently near-complete deforestation, are sure to lose many species to extinction.

Pollution can greatly harm amphibian populations, as it directly damages or alters the environment in which they live. Acid rain reduces the pH of breeding habitat; nitrogenous fertilizer or waste causes algal blooms, which reduce the available oxygen in the water; runoff leads to siltation; and chemicals leached into the water might be directly absorbed through the skin—all potentially devastating to amphibian populations. In the Sierra Nevada Mountains of California, the use of agricultural chemicals has been directly linked to declines of amphibian populations. Heavy use of pesticides in the Central Valley might be transported by coastal winds up the mountains, depositing these toxins in what should be pristine Sierra habitat. Hence, pollution has a nasty ability to affect remote populations of amphibians that might otherwise be protected within reserves.

Xenobiotics

Xenobiotics are chemicals found in organisms that are not produced by that organism. Human input of chemicals into the environment through industrial, residential, or agricultural processes results in the accumulation of xenobiotics in native wildlife. For example, the herbicide atrazine causes malformation of reproductive organs or leads to reproductive failure in frogs. Polychlorinated biphenyls (PCBs), a component of the manufacture of items such as telephone wire insulation and which might travel long distances from their site of release, have been shown to accumulate in the tissues of aquatic amphibians, such as Mudpuppies (*Necturus*). One mechanism for this is known as bioaccumulation, where the prey consumed by mudpuppies contain the chemical, and over time it becomes more and more concentrated in the tissues of the predator. The toxin might then lead to death at sufficient levels or might be present in eggs, which could reduce breeding success.

Cuban Treefrog (*Osteopilus septentrionalis*) captured in Davidson County after having hitched a ride on a rental car driven from Miami, Florida. (Photo by Nathan Haislip)

Local Threats

Amphibians in Tennessee are experiencing the effects of the global threats listed above, but the threats below are occurring on a local scale here in Tennessee.

Habitat Alteration

In East Tennessee, mountaintop removal for coal mining and acid rain are two factors responsible for changing habitats in the mountains. The practice of mountaintop removal to gain access to coal deposits is a controversial though continuing practice. This type of mining can lead to the input of large amounts of silt into streams, which impacts amphibian populations far downstream from the site. Acid rain has already caused the degradation of high-altitude forest and has implications for the health of montane amphibian populations through both a reduction in stream and soil pH and the loss of unique forest cover.

Invasive Animal Species

It is worth mentioning the imminent impact of the Hemlock Wooly Adelgid (*Adelges tsugae*) on amphibians in East Tennessee. Originally from Japan, this invasive pest is causing massive mortality among the native hemlock trees (*Tsuga caroliniana*), which frequently grow in riparian areas. Hemlocks serve to stabilize the banks of streams, which reduce erosion and silt runoff, and to shade the water, which helps keep it cool. If the mature hemlocks die back, the loss of these trees along streams could cause a cascade of effects, which ultimately would harm local amphibians through both increasing siltation and water temperature.

Interestingly, one Cuban Treefrog (*Osteopilus septentrionalis*) was found in Davidson County. This animal hitched a ride on a rental car from Miami and was captured by wildlife authorities. Cuban Treefrogs are introduced to many areas of the southeastern United States and are having a major detrimental impact on local ecosystems in areas such as South Florida. While it is unlikely that Cuban Treefrogs could survive long term in Tennessee, it is important to note and report all appearances of non-native species to wildlife authorities.

Collection for the Pet Trade

Amphibians are frequently regarded as pleasant or interesting pets. Though this frequently isn't the case, amphibians might be taken out of the wild by collectors or hobbyists. It should be noted that some amphibian species in Tennessee do make good pets, if responsibly obtained, though most do not. Of particular concern is the collection of Eastern Hellbenders for the pet trade. Hellbenders, while handsome and fascinating creatures, make very poor pets. They are extremely difficult to maintain in captivity due to their narrow range of tolerance of water temperature, turbidity, and dissolved oxygen content. However, collection from the wild has undoubtedly taken a toll on local populations.

In other parts of the southeastern United States, escaped non-native pets are causing problems for local amphibian communities. In Florida, the Cuban Treefrog (*O. septentrionalis*) was (and, alas, still is) a popular pet. They have subsequently been released into the wild and have become well established, even abundant in many areas. These frogs are competing with the native treefrogs, and are voracious predators that might be consuming native frogs.

Roads

Roads are a threat to amphibian populations because they (inexplicably!) are frequently designed without a thought to the potential impacts on local fauna, including amphibians. Roads might bisect territory or isolate a seasonal habitat from a breeding habitat. This inevitably leads to the necessity of amphibians to cross the roads, which can result in extremely high mortality. Amphibians, especially salamanders and small frogs, are often difficult to see on blacktop roadways and might be easily run over while they attempt to cross. It is common knowledge that "cruising" roadways on warm rainy nights is an excellent way to find amphibians, but it also highlights the peril that these constructions pose. We have frequently been out on such nights, when the roads are literally covered with amphibians, and motorists continue on their way without slowing, leaving a mass of squished amphibians in their wake. It is likely that the drivers never even noticed the amount of death that was perpetrated under their tires. Roads, such as those in the Great Smoky Mountains National Park, receive heavy traffic, especially during the summer and fall months. Many amphibians meet their demise here—we have seen road-killed representatives of nearly every species of amphibian found in the park on a short stretch of road from Tremont to Cades Cove.

As one of the hottest current topics in conservation, the global loss of amphibian diversity demands attention and rectification. This chapter highlights some of the threats and a few examples of obstacles faced by amphibian populations both worldwide and here in Tennessee. We encourage readers interested in learning more to consult the many excellent references on amphibian conservation and declines, some of which are listed in the "Recommended Readings, Organizations, and Websites" section toward the end of this book.

Road-killed Green Frog (*Lithobates clamitans*) in Cherokee National Forest, Monroe County. This scene is all too common on many roads in Tennessee, even in protected areas. This is a good example of why amphibians are not completely safe from human activities, even in national parks and other "safe" havens. (Photo by Matthew L. Niemiller)

4
Finding Amphibians in Tennessee

Although observing amphibians at a zoo, aquarium, or pet store can be interesting and satisfying, searching for and discovering the diversity of amphibians that reside in Tennessee in their natural environment can be a truly rewarding experience. This is how we became "hooked" on studying amphibians and reptiles and decided to make a career of it. Even when we were children, catching salamanders in neighborhood creeks proved a meaningful pastime that brought us a deeper understanding of and appreciation for the natural world. Since then, searching for unique and unusual amphibians has taken us to some of the most beautiful natural areas in Tennessee, North America, and the rest of the world. We firmly believe that an appreciation for wildlife and, indeed, all of Mother Nature must be instilled in children and adults alike, so that they will understand the value of preserving these threatened treasures. We also believe that amphibian appreciation is a grand entry to this end, and below we give advice on observing amphibians in Tennessee to novices and professionals alike.

Marbled Salamanders and Spotted Salamanders caught while migrating in mass to a breeding pond at night, Coffee County. (Photo by Brad M. Glorioso)

Preparation

It is important to remember that any foray into the field calls for an understanding of the potential hazards associated with such endeavors. Whether you are a professional herpetologist or just someone with a basic interest in amphibians, preparation is very important. You should pay attention to the weather, preparing and dressing accordingly. Be aware of the potential for severe weather, particularly thunderstorms and heavy rainfall. We have been caught out in the field on several occasions during heavy thunderstorms and had to seek shelter beneath a rock ledge or huddle underneath a tree (but *not* a very tall tree). Likewise, many streams in Tennessee can rise rapidly after heavy rainfall. Avoid parking or hiking in areas prone to flooding or hiking across such streams when there is a threat of heavy rainfall. You could easily become stranded on the wrong side of a stream and have to look for alternative routes to cross it again. Several natural areas (e.g., state parks, state natural areas, wildlife management areas) are dissected with trails making traversing the terrain much easier. We advise searching for amphibians on and around trail systems to avoid becoming lost or disorientated, especially in dense vegetation. Off-trail searches should only be conducted with those individuals familiar with and experienced in such activities. Be mindful of the presence of venomous snakes in the areas you are walking through. You should always scan the ground around any log or rock you intend to flip to avoid an unpleasant and potentially life-threatening encounter with our scaly friends.

Legal and Ethical Issues

Almost all species of amphibians *cannot* be collected in Tennessee without a valid scientific collection permit issued by the Tennessee Wildlife Resources Agency (TWRA). American Bullfrogs are the only amphibians considered game animals and can be legally hunted in Tennessee. All aquatic habitats are open to bullfrog hunting with a valid hunting license, with the exception of those located on state and federal wildlife refuges. Bullfrog hunting is open year-round (except on TWRA-managed lakes) and the daily bag limit is 20 per person. Firearms, gigs, and angling gear are all legal for taking bullfrogs; however, firearms are prohibited on wildlife management areas and TWRA-managed lakes. Salamanders, often called "spring lizards" by locals and fishermen, are used as fish bait in many states. In Tennessee, only Dusky Salamanders (*Desmognathus fuscus* and *D. conanti*) can be collected or used for bait with a valid fishing license. All other amphibians can be collected legally for scientific purposes only via a scientific collection permit issued by TWRA. Moreover, collection of amphibians on state parks and state natural areas requires an additional scientific collection permit from the Tennessee Department of Environment and Conservation (TDEC), Division of Natural Heritage. Likewise, collection of amphibians on federal lands requires a proper permit. Several species of amphibians are considered threatened or endangered and are therefore protected in Tennessee. These species are listed in Table 2 and should not be taken from the wild unless there is authorization to do so. If you have any questions regarding any restrictions or legality of collecting or observing amphibians in Tennessee, contact your regional TWRA office.

Table 2

Protected and Rare Amphibians in Tennessee (after Withers 2009)

State status is a formal listing by TWRA. State ranks derive from a ranking system by the Nature Conservancy for estimating the abundance of animals tracked by Natural Heritage programs. Some species do not have a formal state status but are tracked by Tennessee's state agencies.

State Status	Definition
E	***Endangered:*** any species or subspecies of wildlife whose prospects of survival or recruitment within the state are in jeopardy or are likely to become so within the foreseeable future
T	***Threatened:*** any species or subspecies of wildlife that is likely to become an endangered species within the foreseeable future
D	***Deemed in Need of Management:*** any species or subspecies of nongame wildlife which the executive director of the TWRA believes should be investigated in order to develop information relating to populations, distribution, habitat needs, limiting factors, and other biological and ecological data to determine management measures necessary for their continued ability to sustain themselves successfully

State Rank	Definition
S1	Extremely rare and *critically imperiled* in the state (often with five or fewer occurrences), or very few remaining individuals, or because of some special condition where the species is particularly vulnerable to extirpation
S2	Very rare and *imperiled* within the state, six to twenty occurrences, or few remaining individuals, or because of some factor(s) making it vulnerable to extirpation
S3	*Vulnerable,* rare, and uncommon in the state due to a restricted range, relatively few populations (often 80 or fewer), recent and widespread declines, or other factors making it vulnerable to extirpation
S4	Uncommon but not rare, and *apparently secure* within the state, but with cause for long-term concern due to declines or other factors

Table 2 (cont.)

Common Name	Scientific Name	State Status	State Rank
Salamanders			
Streamside Salamander	*Ambystoma barbouri*	D	S2
Green Salamander	*Aneides aeneus*		S3, S4
Eastern Hellbender	*Cryptobranchus alleganiensis*	D	S3
Cumberland Dusky Salamander	*Desmognathus abditus*		S2, S3
Seepage Salamander	*Desmognathus aeneus*	D	S1
Carolina Mountain Dusky Salamander	*Desmognathus carolinensis*		S2, S3
Northern Pygmy Salamander	*Desmognathus organi*	D	S2, S3
Santeetlah Dusky Salamander	*Desmognathus santeetlah*		S2, S3
Black Mountain Dusky Salamander	*Desmognathus welteri*	D	S3
Pygmy Salamander	*Desmognathus wrighti*	D	S2, S3
Junaluska Salamander	*Eurycea junaluska*	D	S2
Berry Cave Salamander	*Gyrinophilus gulolineatus*	T	S1
Tennessee Cave Salamander	*Gyrinophilus palleucus*	T	S2
Four-Toed Salamander	*Hemidactylium scutatum*	D	S3
Tellico Salamander	*Plethodon aureolus*		S2
Cumberland Plateau Salamander	*Plethodon kentucki*		S1, S2
Red-Legged Salamander	*Plethodon shermani*		S2
Wehrle's Salamander	*Plethodon wehrlei*	D	S1
Weller's Salamander	*Plethodon welleri*	D	S2
Yonahlossee Salamander	*Plethodon yonahlossee*		S2
Frogs			
Southern Cricket Frog	*Acris gryllus*		S2, S3
Barking Treefrog	*Hyla gratiosa*	D	S3
Dusky Gopher Frog	*Lithobates capito*		S1

Handling

We do not generally recommend capturing or otherwise harassing wild amphibians, preferring to admire them *in situ,* but we give advice to those who might wish to physically interact with amphibians and hope that it will be heeded to ensure the well-being of the capture.

After capturing an amphibian (see below), they can be temporarily placed in a sterile plastic bag or container with a handful of moist moss and leaves to prevent desiccation. Plastic bags and containers should be disinfected between uses or thrown away to prevent the spread of infectious diseases, such as ranavirus and chytrid fungus. On hot days, bags or containers should be placed in an ice chest or cooler to prevent overheating. Small holes can be punched in the containers and plastic bags can be periodically opened to allow the flow of fresh air.

Care should be taken when handling amphibians to prevent harming these delicate creatures and to prevent harm to yourself. Although most species are harmless to humans, all amphibians possess poison glands in their skin. You should always wash your hands after handling amphibians to avoid accidentally rubbing their irritating secretions in and around your mucous membranes (i.e., mouth, nose, and eyes). Secretions from several species, such as toads and newts, are highly irritating. If you are unfortunate enough to get these secretions in your eyes or mouth (as one of the editors [MLN] has experienced), rinse repeatedly with water for several seconds. If discomfort persists or if you begin to experience symptoms other than mild irritation (e.g., nausea or blurred vision), you should probably seek medical attention. Because most amphibians are slippery, they need to be held firmly but gently to prevent escape. Larger anurans can be held by encircling their waist with your fingers, while smaller individuals should be held by their hind limbs. Larger salamanders should be held with the entire hand such than their head protrudes slightly. Smaller salamanders can be restrained briefly with a clenched hand, but care should be taken so that their tails are not accidentally dropped (autotomized).

Location and Capture

Amphibians can be captured using a variety of techniques, and the effectiveness of these techniques varies from season to season. Below we describe several of the most common methods employed by herpetologists and wildlife biologists to capture and document amphibians in nature. Several other techniques exist and we encourage readers seeking additional information on such methods to several references listed under the "Recommended Readings, Organizations, and Websites" section of this book.

Visual Encounter Surveys

One of the best approaches to observing amphibians is simply walking along a stream, edge of a pond, or trail through a forest using your eyes and ears to detect frogs and salamanders at night with the aid of a headlamp or flashlight. Indeed, this can be very productive for several species, particularly when it is rainy and humid. Many amphibians spend daylight hours underneath cover objects, such as rocks and logs, or within crevices in rock outcrops to avoid direct sunlight and the heat of the day. Semi-aquatic and terrestrial salamanders and occasionally anurans can be found underneath rocks, logs, and other debris along streams, other aquatic habitats, and on the forest floor. Although some people use garden tools such as potato rakes to overturn rocks and logs, we recommend wearing a pair of gloves and using your hands to overturn cover objects, as salamanders often will escape into burrows quickly once they are exposed. Gloves will protect you from abrasions and from plants that might cause skin irritation, such as poison ivy. However—*and this is paramount*—all cover objects should be returned to their original positions in order to preserve the delicate microhabitats found underneath them. Using a potato rake, snake stick, or snake hook can be useful for those with back problems or in habitats frequented by venomous snakes.

Night Driving (Road Cruising)

Another highly productive technique for observing amphibians at night is driving along roads (also known as road cruising) to detect more mobile species as they are migrating to and from breeding locations or are out foraging. This technique is most productive on warmer, rainy nights in areas with low vehicle traffic and relatively undisturbed surrounding habitats. Although a single person can perform night driving, it is best if two or more individuals are involved so that one person can drive and the others can spot and capture amphibians. This technique can be highly productive. For instance, we have observed as many as 17 species of amphibians during a single night drive. However, stopping for amphibians at night on a road can be very dangerous and drivers should use common sense and the necessary precautions when night driving for amphibians (do not stop around a curve or at the base of a hill).

Calling Surveys and Frogloggers

Because male frogs use advertisement calls to attract females during their respective breeding seasons, frog species can be identified and relative abundance qualitatively determined by listening for their unique vocalizations. Two methods often are implemented to detect calling anurans: calling surveys and "frogloggers."

Calling surveys are typically performed by vehicle along a predetermined route, making a series of stops at wetlands and other potential breeding localities along rural roads. Most surveys begin within an hour of sunset and last no more than two to three hours. At a stop, observers usually wait at least one minute to reduce the effects of disturbance by an approaching vehicle and then listen for three to five minutes. Observers record both which species were heard calling and an index value corresponding to the number of individuals heard for a given species. Frogloggers consist of a microphone attached via cable to a recording device, solid-state timers, and a battery housed within a weather-resistant box. Frogloggers are positioned in secure areas or hidden to avoid human disturbance and theft in close proximity to a breeding wetland. These devices can be programmed to record in intervals (e.g., for a minute every hour) or at certain times when frogs are most likely to vocalize.

Graham Reynolds dipnetting for tadpoles in a wetland in the Southeastern Plains and Hills, Hardeman County. (Photo by Matthew L. Niemiller)

Calling surveys are inexpensive other than the cost of gas; however, frogloggers can be very expensive, ranging in price from $300 for a basic unit to as much as $2,000. Frogloggers have the added advantage of potentially documenting more rare species than traditional calling surveys. There are a few considerations that must be taken into account to successfully implement a frog call monitoring program. Some species, such as the Eastern Spadefoot, might only call vigorously for one or two days after heavy rainfall. Therefore, calling surveys and the use of frogloggers should be conducted at multiple times of the year, often in concert with rainfall events to optimize detection. Other species are more inclined to vocalize at certain times of the day. For instance, some ranid frogs call most often in the early morning before sunrise, and hence monitoring programs should account for this diel variation among species.

Dipnetting

Both long-handled and aquarium dipnets are useful for collecting frogs, tadpoles, and aquatic salamanders (larvae and adults). Long-handled dipnets are typically triangular or rectangular in shape and can be used to sample amphibians in a variety of habitats. In water bodies with little flow, such as ponds and ditches, dipnets are run through aquatic vegetation or mats of aquatic vegetative debris. Caution should be taken while dipnetting in the late winter and early spring when many amphibian species are breeding, as dipnetting could damage developing egg masses. In faster flowing water or aquatic habitats with rocks, dipnets can be positioned downstream or adjacent to rocks as they are lifted. This is a particularly useful technique to sample stream-dwelling salamanders, such as Shovel-Nosed Salamanders, and larvae of several other stream-associated salamanders. Likewise, we have used this technique to capture Tennessee Cave Salamanders and Northern Spring Salamanders in subterranean streams. All nets and gear should be disinfected between uses to prevent the spread of diseases.

Minnow and Crayfish Traps

Aquatic minnow and crayfish traps are effective at catching aquatic amphibians in a variety of habitats, including ephemeral ponds, ditches, swamps, stream pools, and even caves. We have used these traps to capture a variety of amphibians, including pond-breeding salamanders (family Ambystomatidae), sirens, amphiumas, larval stream-dwelling salamanders (family Plethodontidae), and larval and adult ranid frogs and hylid frogs. Minnow traps typically are either made of plastic or galvanized steel with 3–12 mm mesh and 0.3–1.0 m in total length with a funnel on each end. Traps are usually partially submerged so trapped animals can reach the surface to breathe. However, in well-oxygenated water (e.g., flowing streams) they can be submerged if they are to be checked within 12 hours and water temperatures are cold. Otherwise, traps are placed in shallow water and attached with twine to a tree or other object so that they cannot be displaced and should be checked regularly, usually within 24 hours. An additional consideration is that traps should not be placed in direct sunlight.

Crayfish traps are large, bell-shaped funnel traps that have three funnels located near their base and a vertical column on the top of the trap allowing captured animals to reach the surface to breathe. These traps are significantly larger (up to 0.75 m high) than traditional minnow traps and, therefore, can be placed in deeper water. Crayfish traps are highly effective at capturing larger aquatic salamanders, such as Lesser Sirens and Three-Toed Amphiumas, and cause little habitat disturbance. However, crayfish traps can be pricy (up to $25/trap) and are difficult to transport in large numbers because of their size. Minnow traps are less expensive and can be broken down and stacked to conserve space. Both minnow and crayfish traps must be checked often to prevent mortality.

Leaf Litter Bags

Leaf litter refugia bags are an effective method to survey for larval and juvenile stream salamanders (family Plethodontidae). This method is relatively inexpensive and causes minimal habitat disturbance. The basic technique consists of filling plastic mesh (1.5–4 cm mesh) bags constructed from plastic netting with small rocks, leaves, and moss and partially submerging the bags at the edge of a stream. It is important that the bags are well marked with brightly colored flagging tape and either surrounded or placed beneath larger rocks to prevent the bags from washing downstream after rain events. The bags are left in place for one to two weeks before first checking them. The leaf litter bags are checked by carefully moving the larger rocks away from the bag and quickly placing and shaking the bag in a large dipnet for 10–15 seconds to separate the salamanders from the bag. The leaf debris that falls into the dipnet should also be searched through to look for salamanders. Leaf litter decays over time, so it should be replaced regularly if bags are checked repeatedly.

Other Techniques for Aquatic Amphibians

Several other methods have proven successful at observing or capturing aquatic amphibians, including hook and line, seines, electroshocking, and snorkeling. Larger salamanders (e.g., Mudpuppies and Hellbenders) have been taken on hook and line on occasion. Small-meshed seines are effective at sampling for aquatic salamanders and tadpoles in habitats with few snags (e.g., large rocks, branches, or debris) on the bottom. Seines range in size from 1 to 3 m in depth and one to several meters in length with lead weights along the bottom edge to maintain contact with the substrate and floats along the top to keep the net extended. The seine is attached to poles on each side, and two people run the seine through an aquatic habitat ensuring the lead line maintains contact with the substrate as much as possible. The seine typically is pulled up onto land and the contents of the catch are assessed. Although electroshocking is used primarily to survey for fishes, this technique also can be effective for several salamander species. A backpack electroshocker consists of a generator or battery unit connect to electrodes that are placed in the water to produce an electric field that stuns aquatic organisms (e.g., fish and salamanders). Electroshocking has the advantage of permitting the collection of salamanders in areas where seines or dipetting are ineffective, but electroshocking units are bulky, expensive, and can cause some mortality and hence are not prefered. Snorkeling is an approach often used to search for Hellbenders and Mudpuppies beneath rocks in fast-flowing water, though we recommend wearing a wetsuit, as the cold water will rapidly deplete your energy. Care should be taken to not disturb Hellbenders in their burrows, as they are highly territorial and removing them from their burrow could cause them to have fatal encounters with other Hellbenders. Hellbenders can be enjoyed by watching them wait at the entrance of their burrow for passing food items.

It is our hope that this section will aid in the appreciation of amphibians, not the harm or illegal collection of them. Amphibians are an extremely important component of terrestrial and aquatic ecosystems and tend to fair poorly in captivity. Please be responsible when enjoying these animals and be sure that you leave as little a footprint as possible in their environment so that others might share equally in the experience.

Field Notes

A Heavy Rain, an Elevational Gradient, and a Road Full of Amphibians

LOTS OF RAIN IN THE FORECAST for a warm May evening had Matt, Jennifer, and I excited about the prospect of exploring the amphibian diversity of a new area in southeastern Tennessee. As we geared up at my house in west Knoxville, a Black Kingsnake (*Lampropeltis getula nigra*) appeared in the garden, a sure sign that tonight was going to be special. We were headed for Cherokee National Forest, in an area we had recently surveyed during the day and discovered a variety of interesting salamander species. As we began our cruise, Spring Peepers (*Pseudacris crucifer*), Upland Chorus Frogs (*P. feriarum*), American Toads (*Anaxyrus americanus*), and Cope's Gray Treefrogs (*Hyla chrysoscelis*) called from small ponds on the side of the road that were rapidly filling from the deluge. We paused to photograph some of these specimens, admiring the acoustic qualities of the calls, which made locating the callers quite difficult in the pouring rain. Back on the road, the salamanders appeared by the hundreds. In fact, we had to abandon the vehicle in several areas to clear the road of amphibians before proceeding. At lower elevations, the Dusky Salamanders (*Desmognathus*) were abundant. Eight Seal (*D. monticola*), two Spotted Dusky (*D. conanti*), and 12 Black-Bellied (*D. quadramaculatus*) Salamanders mingled on the roadways with more than 100 Ocoee Salamanders (*D. ocoee*). Wood Frogs (*Lithobates sylvatica*), Pickerel Frogs (*L. palustris*), and Green Frogs (*L. clamitans melanotus*) leaped across the road in their characteristic legs-splayed fashion. As we moved higher, neon Red Salamanders (*Pseudotriton ruber schencki*) and orange Blue Ridge Two-Lined Salamanders (*Eurycea wilderae*) appeared by the dozens, shining like colored lights all over the dark pavement. As we headed toward the highest elevation, Southern Appalachian Salamanders (*Plethodon teyahalee*) appeared by the hundreds, a perfect exhibition of their large numbers, which easily go overlooked during diurnal surveys, while dozens of Blue Ridge Spring Salamanders (*Gyrinophilus porphyriticus danielsi*) punctuated the spaces between gray Southern Appalachian Salamanders with their fluorescent orange coloration. As we descended back down along a river, we considered the number of species and the abundance of each that we had seen to that point, but there were two species that had thus far not shown themselves: the Tellico Salamander (*Plethodon aureolus*) and the Junaluska Salamander (*Eurycea junaluska*). We badly needed to get better pictures of these species, but as daylight approached we began to doubt our chances of finding these elusive caudates. As we neared the highway toward the bottom of the river, we decided to call it a night and head back to Knoxville. Within a minute of this declaration, a small, dark form appeared on the road, followed by a pale shape 10 meters beyond. We swung out of the car and joyously exclaimed that here, nearly on top of each other, were a Tellico and a Junaluska Salamander! A flurry of flashes later and we had secured our photos, retiring the salamanders to a safe distance from the road. As we headed home, we reflected on how special a place East Tennessee is—where in a single evening one might encounter over a thousand individuals representing seventeen species of amphibians in a few short hours.

R. Graham Reynolds

5
How to Use the Species Accounts

We provide an overview of each major group of amphibians (frogs and salamanders) and an overview of each family preceding species accounts. Species accounts are arranged alphabetically by scientific name within their respective families. Families are also arranged alphabetically.

Within family accounts, we provide general information on the family. Following the organization of Etnier and Starnes (1993), general family information includes information on classification, fossil record, diagnostic characters, overall family distribution, biology, and economic importance where available. Taxonomic keys include page number references to easily reference species accounts. Readers should refer to the "How to Use Taxonomic Keys" section for assistance in using the keys provided to properly identify Tennessee amphibians.

Species accounts are provided for all amphibians native to Tennessee. Readers should refer to the "Erroneous Species and Species of Possible Occurrence" section for species that have been reported but are believed to be misidentifications and other species that might be added to the Tennessee's herpetofaunal list. Classification of the species included in this book largely follows *Scientific and Standard English Names of Amphibians and Reptiles of North America, North of Mexico,* by Crother (2008) with exceptions noted under individual species accounts. In some cases, we combined two or more species accounts into one for so-called cryptic species—closely related species that exhibit little if any morphological differentiation. Variation in life history, ecology, and distribution among cryptic species are treated within the account. Subspecies are not treated separately, as there is often disagreement about the status of subspecific nomenclature. Where appropriate, we mention subspecific variation in individual species accounts, and subspecific variation is included in the taxonomic keys.

Information for each species account comes from a variety of sources including peer-reviewed journals, government reports, and other available scientific literature, museum records, and individual observations made by the authors of accounts and the editors. We also relied on previous information gathered and presented in the *Atlas of Tennessee Amphibians* by Redmond and Scott (1996), *The Amphibians of Great Smoky Mountains National Park* by Dodd (2004), *Frogs and Toads of the Southeast* by Dorcas and Gibbons (2008), AmphibiaWeb, and *Salamanders of the Southeast* by Mitchell and Gibbons (2010). Readers should refer to these works and the "Selected References" section for additional information on a particular species.

A typical species account has the following sections and information.

Scientific and Common Names

The scientific name is composed of the genus name and the unique specific epithet and is italicized (see chapter 6, "How to Use the Taxonomic Keys").

Scientific names for several amphibian species in Tennessee have changed in recent years as a result of numerous morphological and molecular phylogenetic studies. We include the most recent accepted names in this text in an effort to be consistent with current and future references to these species.

Similarly, common names for a given species can also vary. For this reason, herpetologists maintain standardized lists of common names. Here, we largely follow *Scientific and Standard English Names of Amphibians and Reptiles of North America, North of Mexico,* by Crother (2008) for common names. For many species there are a number of local and regional colloquial names, especially those frequently encountered by the general public. We have included the well-known colloquial names under the "Comments" section of a species account.

Etymology

We provide the derivation of the Latinized scientific name for each species. In many cases, scientific names are based on morphological characters or geography. Other scientific names are based on the last name of an individual, or individuals, often as a tribute to him, her, or them.

Description

This section provides information on size, physical appearance, and coloration of adults, juveniles, and larvae. Sizes of adults and juveniles are given in snout-vent length or total length. Snout-vent length (SVL) is measured from the tip of the snout to the posterior margin of the vent and is the preferred measurement, as many salamanders might lose a portion of their tail after an attack by a predator. Total length (TL) is measured from the tip of the snout to the tip of the tail in salamanders and both salamander and anuran larvae (tadpoles). In adult frogs, total length is measured to the posterior margin of the body. Measurements are presented in metric units. Refer to chapter 1, "What is an Amphibian? Amphibian Anatomy and Life History," as well as taxonomic keys for diagrams showing how measurements are obtained.

We provide diagnostic characters of each species and discuss potential morphological variation within species and between subspecies if warranted. We have provided many photographs to aid in the accurate identification of our state's amphibians. However, accurate identification requires knowledge of the terminology used to describe the many morphological characters that might be unfamiliar to those who are not herpetologists. Therefore, readers should refer to chapter 1 and the glossary to better familiarize themselves with these characters. Descriptions of coloration and pattern are for living specimens. In many cases, preservation or death results in the loss of brightly colored pigmentation, but pattern usually remains evident. Coloration and pattern often vary ontogenetically (with age) and between males and females. Therefore, we have attempted to discuss ontogenetic morphological variation and sexual dimorphism in sufficient detail for metamorphosed individuals. Salamander larvae and anuran tadpoles exhibit substantial phenotypic variation from hatching to metamorphosis. However, we provide only general description herein and briefly discuss variation among individuals.

We have included several photographs with each species account to illustrate variation in color, pattern, and other morphological characters. In addition, we have tried to include representative photographs of different life stages for as many species as possible. We strived to provide photographs of individuals actually collected from Tennessee, in spite of the investment of time and energy (and gas) required to locate species that might be rare in our state but abundant elsewhere. Hence, most photographs are of Tennessee populations with county of collection noted. Photographs of specimens collected outside of Tennessee are noted.

Similar Species

Many species, particularly salamanders, are very similar in appearance. Therefore, we have included this section to quickly alert readers to similar looking species that can be easily confused with that particular species. We provide diagnostic characters for distinguishing between these species when appropriate. However, some species can only be distinguished using molecular methods, as they cannot be accurately differentiated using morphology. In some cases, geography can be used to discern a species identity, so it is important to keep track of where a particular specimen was observed. However, some individuals can be nearly impossible to identify to species because of hybridization between two or more species. Therefore, we tried to provide detailed and accurate information on documented cases of hybridization involving a species and where it is known to occur.

Distribution

A range map is illustrated for each species with delineation of subspecific ranges when warranted. We have not provided a generalized overall range map depicting the range of the species in North America. However, readers can easily find this information online or in several other texts listed in the "Selected References" section. Range maps show the distribution of the species in light green with confirmed county records depicted in darker green. Individual subspecies are illustrated in additional light and dark colors, with dark colors always indicating confirmed county records. Readers should note that for counties within which the range of the species only partially occurs, the darker green shading for county records only appears for that the portion of the range within the county and not the entire county itself. This differs from many other state herpetological texts, which highlight the entire county instead of just a portion of the county. Ranges and county records were determined from a number of sources, including museum collections, the scientific literature, and personal observations, though not all county records have a museum voucher associated with them. The depicted range within the state represents an estimated distribution generated from known locality data and information on habitat preferences and availability, physiography, and hydrology. Questionable records are discussed in the written account. Likewise, information on physiography or river drainages that cannot be easily determined from the range maps is discussed when appropriate.

Habitat

We provide information for each species on the general habitat and, for some species, microhabitat preferences. Readers should refer to chapter 2, "Physiography, Climate, and Habitats of Tennessee," for a discussion of major habitats found in the state. We also provide discussion on the breeding habitat of each species if this information is available.

Natural History

In this section we provide a brief discussion on the life history and ecology of each species. We present information on reproduction and development, including courtship, breeding, hatching, larval period, and metamorphosis. We also present information on the ecology and behavior of each species, including daily and seasonal activity patterns, diet, predators, and defense. We relied mainly on information available from Tennessee but expanded our review to include information obtained in adjacent states when such data were not available for Tennessee populations.

Call

This section is only applicable to frogs. We describe the advertisement and occasionally alarm calls of every species of frog in the state. There are a number of quality CDs that have recently been produced on frog calls for most species that occur in Tennessee and we have provide a list of these in the "Recommended Readings, Organizations, and Websites" section.

Conservation Status

We comment on the status of each species referring to the relative abundance or rarity within its range and within Tennessee. We provide state and federal listings along with potential causes of decline or threats to particular species when applicable. Readers should refer to chapter 3, "Amphibian Conservation," for more information on major threats facing many amphibian species in Tennessee and worldwide.

Comments

This section contains other anecdotal information that is not included in other sections of a species account, such as common colloquial names.

Example Range Map (*Pseudotriton ruber*)

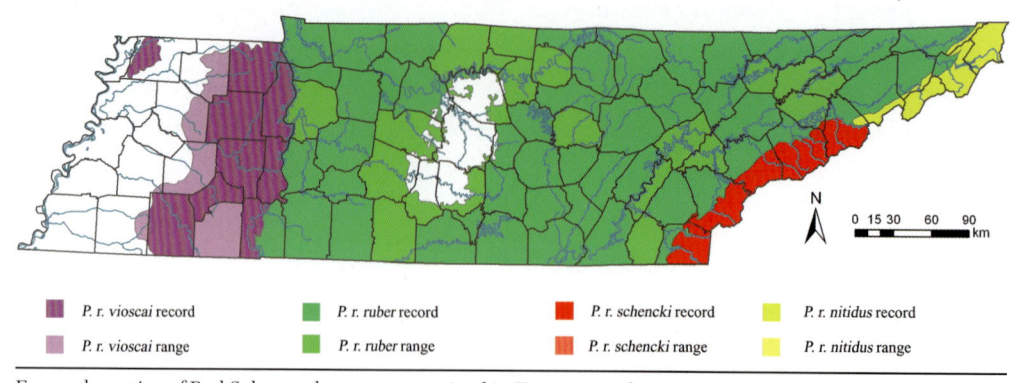

Four subspecies of Red Salamanders are recognized in Tennessee: the Northern Red Salamander (*P. r. ruber*), whose range appears in green; the Southern Red Salamander (*P. r. vioscai*), whose range appears in purple; the Black-Chinned Red Salamander (*P. r. schencki*), whose range appears in red; and the Blue Ridge Red Salamander (*P. r. nitidus*), whose range appears in yellow.

6
How to Use Taxonomic Keys

Standardized taxonomy, or the classification and naming of living organisms, is an important pursuit in modern science. Taxonomy allows us to give names to groups of organisms in a way that reduces confusion about what organism is being referred to, a situation that frequently arises when using common names. Common names are limited in their utility, as they tend to vary from place to place and often encompass many colloquial names. For instance, Hellbenders (*Cryptobranchus alleganiensis*) are referred to as Devil Dogs, Water Dogs, and Mudpuppies, depending on whom you ask and where you are asking. Hence, taxonomists give each species a scientific name, also known as a Latin binomial, which places the organism within a hierarchical framework of Linnaean taxonomy. These names include two or three parts—first the name of the genus to which the organism belongs, in this case *Cryptobranchus,* followed by the specific epithet *alleganiensis*. The species name is occasionally followed by an additional name, which is known as the subspecies name. Subspecies, though widely used, are frequently in debate, as they usually just describe regional variation within a species. The Latin binomial for the Hellbender tells us more than just the proper name of the species; it gives us an idea of its evolutionary relationship to other organisms on the planet in a hierarchical manner. The species is nested within the genus, which is in turn nested within the successively more inclusive groups of family, order, class, phylum, kingdom, and domain. So for the Eastern Hellbender, we have: **domain** Eukaryota, **kingdom** Animalia, **phylum** Chordata, **class** Amphibia, **order** Caudata, **family** Cryptobranchidae, **genus** Cryptobranchus, **species** *Cryptobranchus alleganiensis*. Hence from the name we can deduce that the Eastern Hellbender is a species of North American giant salamander (*Cryptobranchus*) sharing ancestry with the giant salamanders of Asia (Cryptobranchidae).

Taxonomic keys are scientific tools used to identify unknown organisms. Most keys are dichotomous, in that for each step there are two options to choose from. You may think of them as a sort of choose-your-own-adventure book, where at each step you are asked a question about the characteristics of the organism in question and then proceed according to the instructions given by the option you select. The goal is to eventually reach the correct name of the organism that you are "keying" based on a series of steps that list the characteristics of that organism. One uses a key by starting at number 1 and selecting one of the two options: **1a** or **1b**. Following the boldface arrow (**→**) is a number, instructing you to go to that number in the key to select from two additional options. For instance, a salamander with two pairs of limbs (**1b** . . . go to **2**), more than 3 toes on each foot (**2b** . . . go to **3**), and external gills present (**3a**) will key to a **Common Mudpuppy (*Necturus maculosus*)**. Populations of some species may be morphologically variable—that is, individuals within a population of a particular species exhibit morphological differences. Consequently, we have attempted to document and account for this variation in the keys where possible. For example, larvae of the Black-Bellied Salamander vary in coloration geographically in Tennessee. When using the key, the reader could end at one of two options for the Black-Bellied Salamander reflecting this variation. We added the phrase "in part" after the species name to reflect this situation, and to notify the reader that the characters used in the key to reach a particular identification do not represent all individuals of that species. If identifying an amphibian is difficult based on the description and photographs, use of the key should allow positive identification in most cases. For more information on amphibian taxonomy, we refer the reader to "Recommended Readings, Organizations, and Websites."

Hellbender (*Cryptobranchus a. alleganiensis*) adult, Polk County. (Photo by Dante Fenolio)

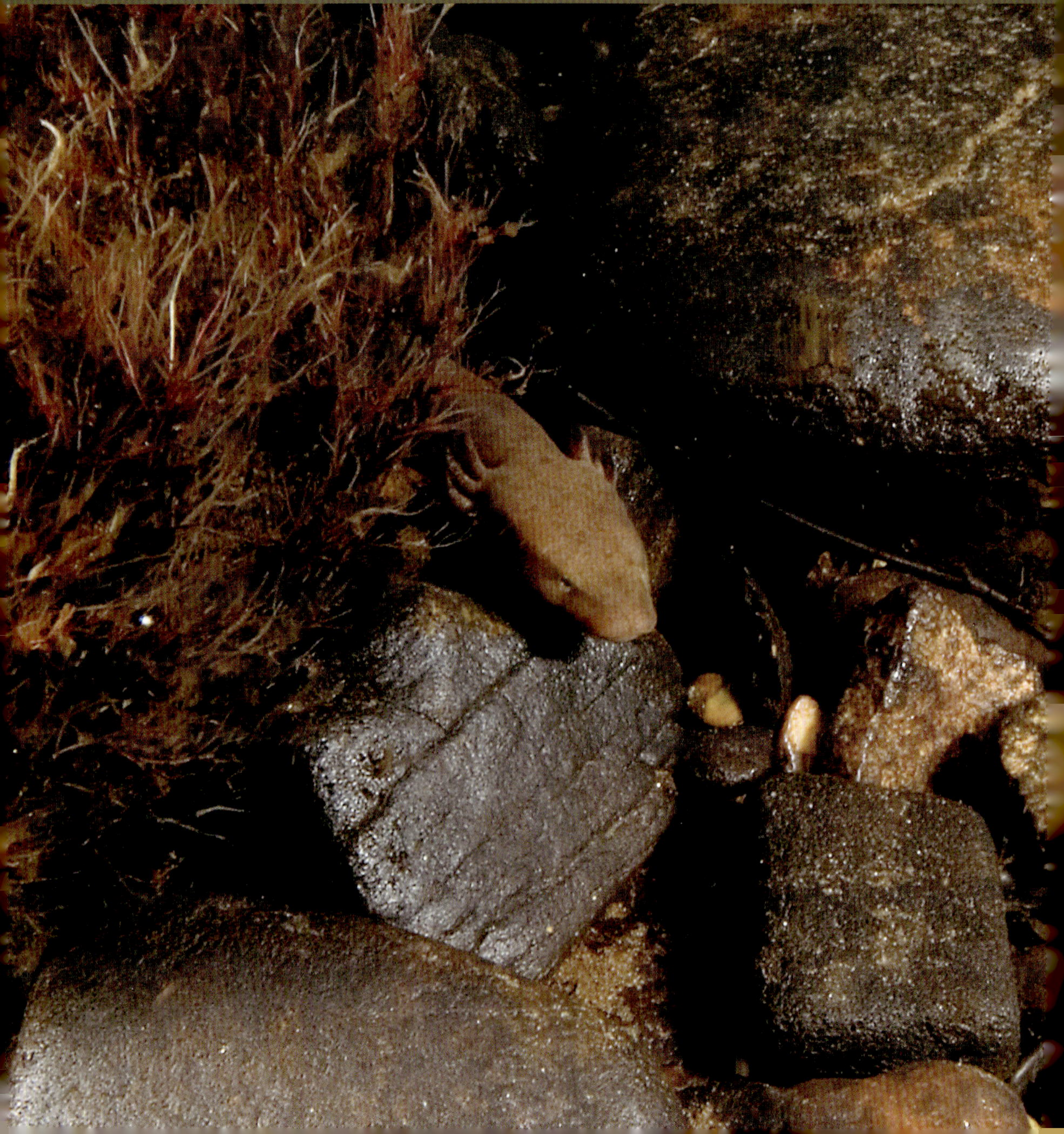

Part 2

Salamanders

Mudpuppy (*Necturus maculosus*) adult emerging from vegetation, Polk County. (Photo by Dante Fenolio)

7

Key to the Salamanders of Tennessee

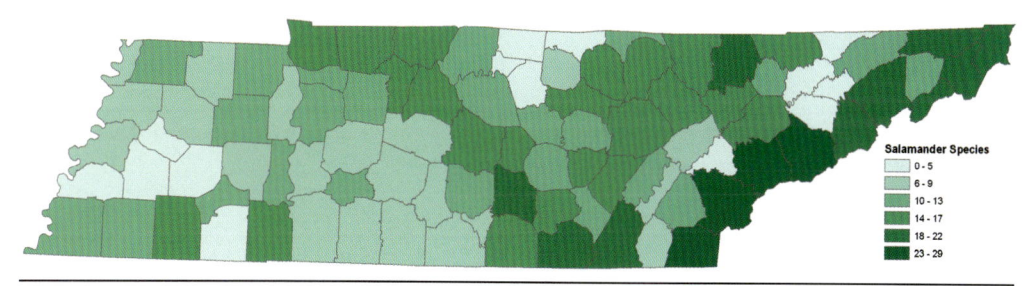

Diversity of salamander species in Tennessee based on county records. Note that low diversity in some counties (e.g., Loudon) is likely due to limited sampling.

1a. One pair of limbs; external gills present; hind limbs absent—**Western Lesser Siren (*Siren intermedia nettingi*), Family Sirenidae**

1b. Two pairs of limbs; external gills present or absent ➔ **2**

2a. External gills absent; limbs reduced with three or fewer toes on each foot; body eel-like—**Three-Toed Amphiuma (*Amphiuma tridactylum*), Family Amphiumidae**

2b. External gills present or absent; limbs not reduced with four or more toes on each foot ➔ **3**

3a. External gills present; four toes on each hind foot; laterally compressed tail; permanently aquatic—**Common Mudpuppy (*Necturus maculosus*), Family Proteidae**

3b. Five toes on each hind foot, or if four, tail round with basal constriction ➔ **4**

Anterior anatomical features of salamanders. Note the lack of nasolabial grooves on the Spotted Salamander (*Ambystoma maculatum*) and the canthus rostralis, which is unique to Spring Salamanders (*Gyrinophilus porphyriticus*).

Streamside Salamanders (*Ambystoma barbouri*) possess costal grooves along each flank, while Eastern Newts (*Notophthalmus viridescens*) have no costal grooves.

4a. Gill slits present; body dorsoventrally compressed; highly folded and wrinkled skin along sides—**Eastern Hellbender (*Cryptobranchus alleganiensis alleganiensis*), Family Cryptobranchidae**

4b. Gill slits absent; body not dorsoventrally compressed and lacking folded, wrinkled skin ➔ **5**

5a. Nasolabial grooves absent ➔ **6**

5b. Nasolabial grooves present ➔ **13 (Family Plethodontidae)**

6a. Costal grooves absent; gular fold absent ➔ **7 (Family Salamandridae)**

6b. Costal grooves present; gular fold present ➔ **8 (Family Ambystomatidae)**

7a. Red spots that are outlined with black present—**Eastern Newt (*Notophthalmus viridescens viridescens*)**

7b. Normally without red spots or, if present, spots small and only partially outlined in black—**Central Newt (*Notophthalmus viridescens louisianensis*)**

8a. Body pattern of white or silvery crossbands—**Marbled Salamander (*Ambystoma opacum*)**

8b. Body pattern without crossbands ➔ **9**

9a. Body patterned with yellow or orange spots or blotches ➔ **10**

9b. Body patterned without yellow or orange spots or blotches ➔ **11**

10a. Dorsolateral irregular spots, blotches, or bars present that are light yellow to olive in color; venter and lower lateral surface often with markings—**Eastern Tiger Salamander (*Ambystoma tigrinum*)**

Key to the Salamanders of Tennessee | 59

Seepage Salamander

Black Mountain Dusky Salamander

Tennessee salamander tail shapes range from round to triangular in cross section at the base of the tail and from unkeeled to strongly keeled and dorsolaterally compressed toward the posterior end of the tail. The terrestrial Seepage Salamander (*Desmognathus aeneus*) possesses a tail that is round in cross section and no keel, while the more aquatic Black Mountain Dusky Salamander (*D. welteri*) has a tail that is triangular in cross section at the base and becomes strongly keeled towards the tip. This individual also has a regenerating tail tip.

10b. Dorsolateral spots situated in irregular rows present that are rounded and yellow to orange in color; venter typically gray—**Spotted Salamander (*Ambystoma maculatum*)**

11a. Head small and generally narrower than neck; snout short and rounded ➜ **12**

11b. Conspicuously large head that is wider than neck and broader than trunk; 10–11 costal groves—**Mole Salamander (*Ambystoma talpoideum*)**

12a. Maxillary and premaxillary teeth with long, pointed cusps; from the Nashville Basin in Tennessee; 14–15 costal grooves—**Streamside Salamander (*Ambystoma barbouri*)**

12b. Maxillary and premaxillary teeth more rounded—**Small-Mouthed Salamander (*Ambystoma texanum*)**

13a. Tail with basal constriction; all limbs with four toes; venter white with black spots—**Four-Toed Salamander (*Hemidactylium scutatum*)**

13b. Tail without basal constriction; hind limbs with five toes ➜ **14**

14a. Hind limbs conspicuously larger than fore limbs; light diagonal line running from eye to angle of jaw ➜ **15**

14b. Hind and fore limbs about the same size; light diagonal line absent ➜ **32**

15a. Basal third of tail round or oval in cross section; posterior half of tail not laterally compressed and without a distinct keel ➜ **16**

15b. Basal third of tail triangular in cross section; posterior half of tail laterally compressed and often with a distinct keel ➔ **26**

16a. Dorsum variable but usually lacking chevron pattern or Y-shaped marking on the head behind the eyes; adults usually > 30 mm SVL ➔ **17**

16b. Dorsum usually with a chevron pattern or Y-shaped marking on the head behind the eyes; adults usually < 30 mm SVL ➔ **24**

17a. Occurring in the Cumberland Plateau or Cumberland Mountains ➔ **18**

17b. Occurring in the Blue Ridge Mountains ➔ **20**

18a. Larval spotting almost always evident on dorsum; dorsal patterning usually a strongly undulating stripe; tail round throughout length—**Cumberland Dusky Salamander (*Desmognathus abditus*)**

18b. Larval spotting may or may not be evident on dorsum; dorsal pattern usually with a straight-edged or wavy, blotched patterning; tail round through length or with slight keel along posterior third ➔ **19**

19a. Tail usually round in cross section throughout length; from northern Cumberland Plateau and Cumberland Mountains—**Allegheny Mountain Dusky Salamander (*Desmognathus ochrophaeus*)**

19b. Tail usually with slight keel along posterior third; from southern Cumberland Plateau on Walden's Ridge—**Ocoee Salamander (*Desmognathus ocoee*) (in part)**

20a. Red or yellowish cheek patch present; from Great Smoky and Balsam mountains— **Imitator Salamander (*Desmognathus imitator*)**

20b. Cheek patch absent ➔ **21**

21a. Dorsum usually without straight-edged or wavy, blotched patterning; from Great Smoky and Balsam mountains—**Imitator Salamander (*Desmognathus imitator*) dark phase**

21b. Dorsum usually without straight-edged or wavy, blotched patterning ➔ **22**

22a. From Roan Mountain in Carter County northeast to Virginia state line—**Blue Ridge Dusky Salamander (*Desmognathus orestes*)**

22b. From southwest of Roan Mountain in Carter County ➔ **23**

23a. From Round Mountain in Cocke County northeast to Birchlog Creek in Unicoi County—**Carolina Mountain Dusky Salamander (*Desmognathus carolinensis*)**

23b. From Georgia state line northeast to Indian Gap in Sevier County—**Ocoee Salamander (*Desmognathus ocoee*) (in part)**

Underside of hind limb of an adult Black Mountain Dusky Salamander, showing the dark cornified toe tips.

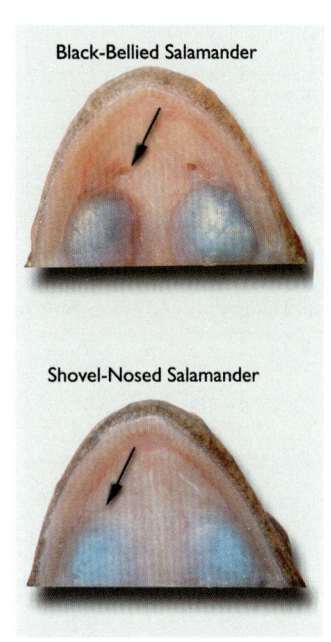

Internal nares of Black-Bellied (*Desmognathus quadramaculatus*) and Shovel-Nosed (*D. marmoratus*) Salamanders. View is of the roof of the mouth, showing the rounded internal nares of the Black-Bellied Salamander and the barely visible slit-shaped internal nares of the Shovel-Nosed Salamander.

24a. Dorsum without chevron pattern or faint if present; top of head smooth; Y-shaped marking usually present on head behind the eyes; mental gland of males kidney-shaped—**Seepage Salamander (*Desmognathus aeneus*)**

24b. Dorsum with chevron pattern; top of head rugose; eyelids and dorsum of legs bronze to copper in color; mental gland of males large and U-shaped ➜ **25**

25a. Found north of the French Broad River in the Blue Ridge Mountains at elevations above 1,100 m—**Northern Pygmy Salamander (*Desmognathus organi*)**

25b. Found south of the French Broad River in the Blue Ridge Mountains at elevations above 950 m—**Pygmy Salamander (*Desmognathus wrighti*)**

26a. Internal nares slit-like; head distinctly flattened sloping from behind small eyes to snout—**Shovel-Nosed Salamander (*Desmognathus marmoratus*)**

26b. Internal nares round; head not distinctly flattened; eyes large and froglike in appearance ➜ **27**

27a. Toe tips cornified and dark in appearance ➜ **28**

27b. Toe tips not cornified ➜ **30**

28a. Venter distinctly dark gray to black—**Black-Bellied Salamander (*Desmognathus quadramaculatus*)**

28b. Venter white, light gray, or mottled with brown ➜ **29**

29a. Venter uniformly colored white to light gray; sharp transition from dorsal to ventral ground coloration—**Seal Salamander (*Desmognathus monticola*)**

29b. Venter heavily mottled and brown; no sharp transition from dorsal to ventral ground coloration; base of tail laterally compressed—**Black Mountain Dusky Salamander (*Desmognathus welteri*)**

30a. Undersurfaces of limbs and tail usually with light yellow wash; from the Great Smoky, Balsam, and Unicoi mountains—**Santeetlah Dusky Salamander (*Desmognathus santeetlah*)**

30b. Undersurfaces of limbs and tail usually without light yellow wash → **31**

31a. Remnants of larval dorsal spotting (6–8 pairs of large spots) fused into a band in adults; from northeast section of Tennessee—**Northern Dusky Salamander (*Desmognathus fuscus*)**

31b. Remnants of larval dorsal spotting still evident and usually not fused in adults; not from northeast Tennessee—**Spotted Dusky Salamander (*Desmognathus conanti*)**

32a. Toe tips square-shaped; green blotches on dorsum—**Green Salamander (*Aneides aeneus*)**

32b. Toe tips rounded; green blotches lacking on dorsum → **33**

33a. External gills present in adults; greatly reduced eyes; from caves → **34**

33b. External gills absent; eyes not reduced → **36**

34a. Dorsum flesh colored and lacking spotting; from caves in southern Franklin and Marion counties—**Pale Salamander (*Gyrinophilus palleucus palleucus*)**

34b. Dorsum dark, usually yellowish brown, reddish brown, or purplish brown, with numerous flecks or spots → **35**

35a. From caves in the Nashville Basin, Eastern Highland Rim, and Western Escarpment of the Cumberland Plateau—**Big Mouth Cave Salamander (*Gyrinophilus palleucus necturoides*)**

35b. Some individuals with distinct throat stripe or blotch; from caves in the Valley and Ridge of East Tennessee—**Berry Cave Salamander (*Gyrinophilus gulolineatus*)**

36a. Canthus rostralis present → **37**

36b. Canthus rostralis absent → **38**

37a. Dorsum a dull red, salmon, to brownish pink, usually with darker markings forming a mottled or cloudy appearance; dark pigmentation bordering canthus rostralis not as distinct; from Valley and Ridge, Cumberland Mountains, Cumberland Plateau, and Eastern Highland Rim—**Northern Spring Salamander (*Gyrinophilus porphyriticus porphyriticus*)**

37b. Dorsum reddish, salmon, or orangish yellow with small brown to black flecks or spots; canthus rostralis bordered by a dark brown or black line; from Blue Ridge Mountains—**Blue Ridge Spring Salamander (*Gyrinophilus porphyriticus danielsi*)**

38a. Body robust; tail short in relation to body length; ground color bright orangish red, reddish, salmon, to purplish that fades with age and with conspicuous black spots or flecks → **39**

38b. Body more slender; tail longer in relation to body length → **43**

39a. Black spots on dorsum round and few in number; venter unmarked; iris of eye usually brown—**Midland Mud Salamander (*Pseudotriton montanus diastictus*)**

39b. Black spots on dorsum more numerous and irregular in shape; iris of eye usually yellow → **40**

40a. Ground coloration purplish brown with tiny white flecks on the snout and sides of the head; dark spots on dorsum often fusing to form chevron pattern; from West Tennessee—**Southern Red Salamander (*Pseudotriton ruber vioscai*)**

40b. Usually lacking white flecking on snout and sides of head; not from West Tennessee → **41**

41a. Little to no dark spotting on the posterior half of the tail; chin with little to no black flecking; from northern Blue Ridge Mountains in Tennessee—**Blue Ridge Red Salamander (*Pseudotriton ruber nitidus*)**

41b. Black flecking usually present on chin → **42**

42a. Ground coloration more variable ranging from red to reddish orange to purple; some black flecking along margin of the chin; from Valley and Ridge, Cumberland Plateau, and Highland Rim—**Northern Red Salamander (*Pseudotriton ruber ruber*)**

42b. Heavy black flecking on chin; from southern Blue Ridge Mountains in Tennessee— **Black-Chinned Red Salamander (*Pseudotriton ruber schencki*)**

43a. Tongue attached on a central pedicel and free all around; ground color usually yellowish, orangish, or reddish → **44**

43b. Tongue attached in front and free on sides and behind; ground color of dorsum not brightly colored → **50**

44a. Tail about half of body length; 2–5 costal grooves between adpressed limbs → **45**

44b. Tail more than half of body length; 0–2 costal grooves between adpressed limbs → **48**

45a. Dorsolateral stripes or streaks usually not continuous and not extending onto tail; from Blue Ridge Mountains of east-central Tennessee—**Junaluska Salamander (*Eurycea junaluska*)**

45b. Dorsolateral stripes present and extending onto tail → **46**

46a. Body robust, head relatively wide, trunk thick, limbs and tail relatively short; dorsum brownish with dark brown to dusky black sides; from Ridge and Valley—**Brownback Salamander (*Eurycea aquatica*)**

46b. Body less robust and slender, head more narrow, trunk less thick, and tail long; dorsum lighter in coloration and usually yellow to orange or tan ➔ **47**

47a. Dorsolateral stripes unbroken and extending past midpoint of the tail—**Southern Two-Lined Salamander (*Eurycea cirrigera*)**

47b. Dorsolateral stripes rarely extending unbroken past midpoint of the tail—**Blue Ridge Two-Lined Salamander (*Eurycea wilderae*)**

48a. Vertical bars or chevrons lacking on sides of tail; small black flecks or spots on dorsum—**Cave Salamander (*Eurycea lucifuga*)**

48b. Vertical bars or chevrons usually present on sides of tail ➔ **49**

49a. Dorsolateral and middorsal stripes forming a distinct three-lined appearance—**Three-Lined Salamander (*Eurycea guttolineata*)**

49b. Middorsal line or line of spots usually not present—**Long-Tailed Salamander (*Eurycea longicauda longicauda*)**

50a. Dorsum and lateral surfaces without conspicuous spotting or blotches ➔ **51**

50b. Dorsum and lateral surfaces with conspicuous white to brassy spotting and/or blotches ➔ **63**

51a. Bright red to orange or yellow pigment on cheeks or legs present ➔ **52**

51b. Bright red to orange or yellow pigment on cheeks or legs absent ➔ **53**

52a. Bright red to orange or yellow pigment on cheeks only—**Red-Cheeked Salamander (*Plethodon jordani*)**

52b. Bright red to orange pigmentation on upper surfaces of limbs—**Red-Legged Salamander (*Plethodon shermani*)**

53a. Dorsum with straight, wavy, or serrate-edged stripe that is tan, red, orange, or yellow in color ➔ **54**

53b. Dorsum without evidence of a stripe ➔ **56**

54a. Dorsal stripe wavy or zigzag-shaped—**Northern Zigzag Salamander (*Plethodon dorsalis*) and Southern Zigzag Salamander (*Plethodon ventralis*)**

54b. Dorsal stripe serrated or straight-edged ➔ **55**

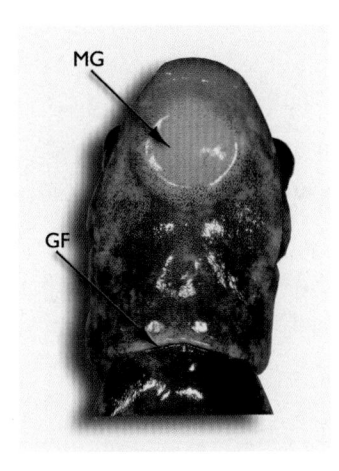

Underside of the head of a male Tellico Salamander (*Plethodon aureolus*) showing the mental gland (MG) and the gular fold (GF).

55a.   From northern Blue Ridge Mountains north of the French Broad River—**Northern Red-Backed Salamander (*Plethodon cinereus*)**

55b.   From southern Blue Ridge Mountains south of the French Broad River—**Southern Red-Backed Salamander (*Plethodon serratus*)**

56a.   Ground coloration of dorsum and venter typically slate gray to purplish black with little to no flecking, spotting, or blotches ➔ **57**

56b.   Ground coloration of dorsum and especially venter often with flecks, spotting, or blotches ➔ **58**

57a.   From Unicoi Mountains in Monroe County—**Red-Legged Salamander (*Plethodon shermani*) dark phase**

57b.   From Blue Ridge Mountains northeast of Great Smoky Mountain National Park—**Northern Gray-Cheeked Salamander (*Plethodon montanus*)**

58a.   Body long and slender with disproportionally short limbs; venter dark and plain; lightly mottled chin; from northeast Tennessee—**Southern Ravine Salamander (*Plethodon richmondi*)**

58b.   Body and limbs not disproportionate ➔ **59**

59a.   Dorsum dark with large brassy to coppery blotches or striations that are metallic in appearance; venter dark with light mottling; from mountains of extreme northeast Tennessee—**Weller's Salamander (*Plethodon welleri*)**

59b.   Dorsum without large metallic-colored blotches or striations ➔ **60**

60a.   Venter uniformly gray; throat white or with white blotches; dorsum purplish brown with numerous small light flecks and bronze mottling; some individuals with two rows of large yellow spots on dorsum—**Wehrle's Salamander (*Plethodon wehrlei*)**

60b.   Venter with distinct mottling ➔ **61**

61a.   Venter with salt-and-pepper mottling without red or orange pigment ➔ **62**

61b.   Venter with salt-and-pepper mottling with red or orange pigment—**Northern Zigzag Salamander (*Plethodon dorsalis*)** and **Southern Zigzag Salamander (*Plethodon ventralis*) unstriped phase**

62a.   From northern Blue Ridge Mountains north of the French Broad River—**Northern Red-Backed Salamander (*Plethodon cinereus*) leadback phase**

62b.   From southern Blue Ridge Mountains south of the French Broad River—**Southern Red-Backed Salamander (*Plethodon serratus*) leadback phase**

63a.   Dorsum with large chestnut blotches that often fuse into large streak; sides with large white blotches that often fuse—**Yonahlossee Salamander (*Plethodon yonahlossee*)**

63b.   Dorsum without chestnut blotches ➔ **64**

64a.   Chin lighter than overall ground coloration ➔ **65**

64b.   Chin nearly as or as dark as overall ground coloration ➔ **67**

65a.   Dorsum with numerous brassy spots and flecks; sides with greater concentration of yellowish to white spotting or blotches; from Monroe and Polk counties—**Tellico Salamander (*Plethodon aureolus*)**

65b.   Spotting, flecks, and blotches not brassy in coloration; from northern Cumberland Plateau or southern Blue Ridge Mountains ➔ **66**

66a.   Dorsum and sides with scattered, tiny white flecks or spots; from Blue Ridge Mountains—**Southern Appalachian Salamander (*Plethodon teyahalee*)**

66b.   Dorsum and sides with scattered, white spots that become larger on the sides; from the Cumberland Mountains—**Cumberland Plateau Salamander (*Plethodon kentucki*)**

67a.   Dorsum with variable white spots that become larger and often fuse to form blotches along sides; from west of Tennessee River in West Tennessee—**Mississippi Slimy Salamander (*Plethodon mississippi*)**

67b.   Dorsum as in 67a but from east of Tennessee River ➔ **68**

68a.   Dorsum with large white spots and abundant white or yellow spotting or blotches on sides; from northeast Tennessee—**White-Spotted Slimy Salamander (*Plethodon cylindraceus*)**

68b.   Dorsum with small to medium spots; spots and blotches numerous but not abundant; not from northeast Tennessee—**Northern Slimy Salamander (*Plethodon glutinosus*)**

8
Key to the Larval and Adult Larviform Salamanders of Tennessee

1a. Hind limbs absent in all larval stages; toes with keratinized toe pads; body eel-like—**Western Lesser Siren (*Siren intermedia nettingi*) (Family Sirenidae)**

1b. Hind limbs present except in young larval stages → **2**

2a. Body elongate, eel-like and cylindrical; limbs reduced with three or fewer toes; a single open gill slit; gills thin and transparent if present; up to 106 cm TL—**Three-Toed Amphiuma (*Amphiuma tridactylum*) (Family Amphiumidae)**

2b. Body not elongate, eel-like and cylindrical; limbs normal with four or five toes; one to four open gill slits; gills usually thicker and pigmented if present → **3**

3a. Body dorsoventrally compressed; skin loose with conspicuous lateral skin folds present; toes flattened and fleshy; limbs with folds posteriorly; one open gill slit; gills unpigmented—**Eastern Hellbender (*Cryptobranchus alleganiensis alleganiensis*) (Family Cryptobranchidae)**

3b. Body not dorsoventrally compressed; skin not loose with conspicuous lateral skin folds → **4**

4a. Hind limbs with four toes → **5**

4b. Hind limbs with five toes → **6**

5a. Dorsal fin extending onto body; snout round; to 35 mm TL—**Four-Toed Salamander (*Hemidactylium scutatum*) (Family Plethodontidae)**

5b. Dorsal fin limited to tail; snout angular; to 330 mm TL—**Common Mudpuppy (*Necturus maculosus*) (Family Proteidae)**

6a. Gills white to silvery in life; four gill slits; gill rami shorter than gill filaments; toes often keratinized → **7 *Desmognathus* (Family Plethodontidae)**

6b. Gills pigmented; three to four gill slits; gill rami longer than gill filaments → **17**

7a. Partially metamorphosed with small eyelids; dark occipital spot present; labial folds absent; gills short; partial dorsal fin; to 15 mm TL—**Seepage Salamander (*Desmognathus aeneus*)**

7b. Not as in 7a ➔ **8**

8a. Toe pads cornified and black ➔ **9**

8b. Toe pads not cornified and black ➔ **13**

9a. Dorsum with series of paired light spots; body more slender ➔ **10**

9b. Dorsum lacking series of paired light spots; body more robust ➔ **12**

10a. Dorsum with 4–5 pairs of light spots between limbs that might fuse in larger larvae; rarely > 18 mm SVL; gill fimbriae number 11–18 per side—**Seal Salamander (*Desmognathus monticola*) (in part)**

10b. Dorsum with 5–8 pairs of light spots between limbs that might fuse in larger larvae; often > 18 mm SVL ➔ **11**

11a. Dorsum with 5–7 pairs of light spots between limbs that might fuse in larger larvae; ground coloration usually lighter brown; rarely > 36 mm SVL; gill fimbriae number 17–27 per side; restricted to Cumberland Mountains and northern Cumberland Plateau—**Black Mountain Dusky Salamander (*Desmognathus welteri*)**

11b. Dorsum with 6–8 pairs of diffuse light spots between limbs that might fuse in larger larvae; ground coloration darker brown; often > 36 mm SVL; restricted to Blue Ridge Mountains—**Black-Bellied Salamander (*Desmognathus quadramaculatus*) (in part)**

12a. Dorsum typically lighter in color; lateral surfaces lacking conspicuous light flecks; often > 36 mm SVL—**Black-Bellied Salamander (*Desmognathus quadramaculatus*) (in part)**

12b. Dorsum darker in color; lateral surfaces with conspicuous light flecks; rarely > 36 mm SVL—**Shovel-Nosed Salamander (*Desmognathus marmoratus*)**

13a. Dorsum usually uniformly pigmented or with 6–8 pairs of diffuse light spots between limbs; often > 36 mm SVL; restricted to Blue Ridge Mountains—**Black-Bellied Salamander (*Desmognathus quadramaculatus*) (in part)**

13b. Dorsum with a series of spots, middorsal stripe, or dorsolateral stripes or spots; rarely > 36 mm SVL ➔ **14**

14a. Undersurface of tail diffusely blotched; angle of mouth falls within vertical lines from anterior to posterior margin of eyes; ventrolateral lateral line pores partially or entirely outside pigment margin dorsal spots without dark margins—**Seal Salamander (*Desmognathus monticola*) (in part)**

14b.   Undersurface of tail not diffusely blotched; dorsal spots with or without dark margins ➔ **15**

15a.   From Blue Ridge Mountains—**Blue Ridge Dusky Salamander (*Desmognathus orestes*), Carolina Mountain Dusky Salamander (*D. carolinensis*), Imitator Salamander (*D. imitator*), Ocoee Salamander (*D. ocoee*), Santeetlah Dusky Salamander (*D. santeetlah*), Spotted Dusky Salamander (*D. conanti*), and Northern Dusky Salamander (*D. fuscus*)**

15b.   Not from Blue Ridge Mountains ➔ **16**

16a.   From Cumberland Plateau or Cumberland Mountains—**Cumberland Dusky Salamander (*Desmognathus abditus*), Ocoee Salamander (*D. ocoee*), Allegheny Mountain Dusky Salamander (*D. ochrophaeus*), and Spotted Dusky Salamander (*D. conanti*)**

16b.   Not from Cumberland Plateau or Cumberland Mountains—**Northern Dusky Salamander (*Desmognathus fuscus*), Spotted Dusky Salamander (*D. conanti*), and Allegheny Mountain Dusky Salamander (*D. ochrophaeus*)**

17a.   Dorsal fin extends onto body unless partially metamorphosed; rarely collected in lotic water ➔ **18**

17b.   Dorsal fin usually terminates on tail or near junction of tail with the body; usually collected in lotic water ➔ **26**

18a.   Four open gill slits unless partially metamorphosed or absent in neotenic adults; keratinized jaw sheath absent; costal grooves absent; body usually slender; older larvae and neotenic adults usually with granular skin and distinct red spots on dorsum; dark stripe on side of head continuing through eye onto snout; head appearing pointed in dorsal view and not enlarged—**Eastern Newt (*Notophthalmus viridescens viridescens*) and Central Newt (*N. v. louisianensis*) (Family Salamandridae)**

18b.   Three open gill slits unless partially metamorphosed; keratinized jaw sheath present; costal grooves usually distinct in older larvae; body robust; head broadly rounded in dorsal view and large; dark stripe on side of head or snout usually not continuing through eye if present; skin smooth ➔ **19 (Family Ambystomatidae)**

19a.   Chin or throat heavily or lightly pigmented ➔ **20**

19b.   Chin and throat without pigment ➔ **23**

20a.   Costal grooves 10–11; dark band on each side of snout to the eye and often continuing through eye onto the side of the head; older larvae with one to two dark longitudinal stripes on venter and two cream or dull yellow stripes on each side (striped patterning absent in neotenic adults)—**Mole Salamander (*Ambystoma talpoideum*)**

20b.   Costal grooves 11–16; dark band limited to snout if present; older larvae without dark longitudinal stripes on venter ➔ **21**

21a. Costal grooves 11–13; conspicuous ventrolateral white spots present; dorsum without squarish blotches separated by vertical light bars—**Marbled Salamander (*Ambystoma opacum*)**

21b. Costal grooves 14–16; ventrolateral white spots not conspicuous; dorsum with squarish blotches separated by vertical light bars ➔ **22**

22a. Typically from lotic habitats within Nashville Basin—**Streamside Salamander (*Ambystoma barbouri*) (in part)**

22b. Typically from lentic habitats outside of range of 22a—**Small-Mouthed Salamander (*Ambystoma texanum*) (in part)**

23a. Toes flattened in cross section, broad at base and pointed at tip with a slight flange along each side; up to 20 cm TL in neotenic adults—**Eastern Tiger Salamander (*Ambystoma tigrinum*)**

23b. Toes rounded in cross section, not broad at base or pointed at tip; usually < 80 mm TL ➔ **24**

24a. Costal grooves 11–13; ventrolateral white spots present but not as conspicuous as in 21a; dorsum without squarish blotches separated by vertical light bars—**Spotted Salamander (*Ambystoma maculatum*)**

24b. Costal grooves 14–16; ventrolateral white spots often indistinct; dorsum with squarish blotches separated by vertical light bars ➔ **25**

25a. Typically from lotic habitats within Nashville Basin—**Streamside Salamander (*Ambystoma barbouri*) (in part)**

25b. Typically from lentic habitats outside of range of 22a—**Small-Mouthed Salamander (*Ambystoma texanum*) (in part)**

26a. Costal grooves 13–16 ➔ **27**

26b. Costal grooves 17–19 ➔ **31**

27a. Heavy pigmentation on anterior half of gular region; ventral surface of hind feet pigmented (absent in small larvae); lateral pigmentation extending onto belly beyond bases of limbs—**Cave Salamander (*Eurycea lucifuga*)**

27b. Pigmentation sparse or lacking on anterior half of gular region; ventral surface of hind feet not pigmented or very sparsely pigmented in larger larvae; lateral pigmentation not extending onto belly beyond bases of limbs ➔ **28**

28a. Dorsum lacking pairs of light spots; light middorsal stripe present; gular pigmentation usually sparse and confined to anterior third of gular region—**Long-Tailed Salamander (*Eurycea longicauda longicauda*)** and **Three-Lined Salamander (*Eurycea guttolineata*)**

28b. Dorsum with 6–9 pairs of light spots that often fuse in older larvae into a middorsal stripe; pigmentation absent on gular region ➔ **29**

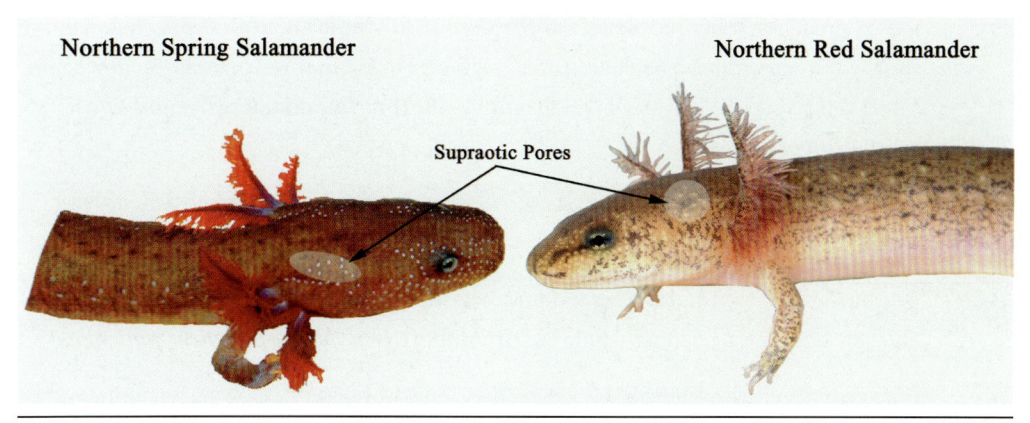

Oval orientation of supraotic pores of Northern Spring Salamanders (*Gyrinophilus p. porphyriticus*) and rounded supraotic pores of Northern Salamanders (*Pseudotriton r. ruber*).

29a. Margin pigmentation on venter straight; iridophores absent on venter; body more robust; distinct dark cheek patches anterior to gill slits present—**Junaluska Salamander (*Eurycea junaluska*)**

29b. Margin of pigmentation on venter wavy; iridophores usually present on venter; body slender; cheek patches anterior to gill slits usually indistinct ➔ **30**

30a. Lateral surface of body uniformly dark; typically found in springs in Valley and Ridge of Tennessee—**Brownback Salamander (*Eurycea aquatica*)**

30b. Lateral surface of body usually not uniformly dark; not confined to springs in Valley and Ridge of Tennessee—**Southern Two-Lined Salamander (*Eurycea cirrigera*) and Blue Ridge Two-Lined Salamander (*Eurycea wilderae*)**

31a. Costal grooves 16–17; snout short; eyes larger with eye diameter usually 0.5 or greater the length of the snout; supraotic lateral line pores typically arranged in a circle ➔ **32**

31b. Costal grooves 17–19; snout longer; eyes smaller with eye diameter usually less than 0.5 the length of the snout; supraotic lateral line pores typically arrange in an ellipse ➔ **33**

32a. Dorsum and sides uniformly brown to reddish brown with widely scattered dark spots, flecks, or reticulations; body more slender; typically from more sluggish bodies of water including muddy ponds, swamps, and sluggish bottomland streams—**Midland Mud Salamander (*Pseudotriton montanus diastictus*)**

32b. Dorsum and sides usually mottled or streaked with darker pigment and without distinct spots or flecks (except in larger larvae); body more robust; typically from higher gradient streams—**Red Salamander (*Pseudotriton ruber*) (differentiate between subspecies by geography)**

33a. Eyes not reduced; snout moderate; eye diameter 0.3–0.5 the length of the snout; found in surface and subterranean habitats; surface larvae up to 110 mm TL while larvae from some subterranean populations reaching 180 mm TL—**Spring Salamander (*Gyrinophilus porphyriticus*)**

33b. Eyes reduced; snout long; eye diameter 0.2–0.3 the length of the snout; almost exclusively found in subterranean habitats ➔ **34**

34a. Dorsum flesh colored and lacking spotting in larvae > 50 mm SVL; from caves in southern Franklin and Marion counties—**Pale Salamander (*Gyrinophilus palleucus palleucus*)**

34b. Dorsum dark, usually yellowish brown, reddish brown, or purplish brown with numerous flecks or spots in larvae > 50 mm SVL (smaller larvae nearly identical to 34a) ➔ **35**

35a. From caves in the Nashville Basin, Eastern Highland Rim, and Western Escarpment of the Cumberland Plateau—**Big Mouth Cave Salamander (*Gyrinophilus palleucus necturoides*)**

35b. Some individuals with distinct throat stripe or blotch; from caves in the Ridge and Valley of East Tennessee—**Berry Cave Salamander (*Gyrinophilus gulolineatus*)**

9

Family Ambystomatidae (Mole Salamanders)

Mole Salamanders are large, robust salamanders typically with large, rounded heads. Metamorphosed adults have conspicuous costal grooves, lack nasolabial grooves, and possess lungs. Larvae are also robust with broad heads and well-developed caudal fins that extend well anterior on the dorsum. Larvae have three pairs of large, bushy gills with well-developed rachises. Several species are neotenic (attaining sexual maturity during the larval stage) and do not readily undergo metamorphosis. About 30 species are recognized in the family and all are endemic to North America. Six species occur in Tennessee and are found statewide. Fossils of Mole Salamanders date back to the lower Oligocene 30 million years ago, and many of the species living today have fossils dating to the Pleistocene and Pliocene. Mole Salamanders inhabit a variety of habitats in Tennessee but are most common in forests in close proximity to breeding sites, such as ephemeral ponds and flooded meadows. Throughout the majority of the year, adults reside underground in burrows but come to the surface during the breeding season.

Streamside Salamander

Ambystoma barbouri

Description: The Streamside Salamander is a medium-sized and slender member of the genus; adults reach a TL of 168 mm and an SVL of 96 mm. The head is relatively small and narrow, and the snout is short and blunt. The body is roughly cylindrical, although the belly is flattened. There are usually 14–15 distinct costal grooves from the armpit to the groin. The tail is cylindrical, thick, and short. The front limbs are slender with four toes, whereas the hind limbs are stout with five toes. The ground color of the back and sides varies from dark brown to jet-black and is covered with light-colored flecks (white, gray, silver, or olive) that often coalesce into a lichen-like stippling. The ground color of the belly is lighter, and the flecks are smaller and less numerous, than those of the back and sides. The teeth of the upper and lower jaws occur in multiple rows. The inner (lingual) cusp of the teeth of the upper jaw in juveniles and adults is short and spade-like, whereas the lingual cusp of teeth of the lower jaw can be either short and blade-like or, in older individuals, elongate and pointed. The larvae are of the pond type: the gills are bushy and the tail fin is broad and extends to the base of the head. The coloration of the larvae is brown, gray or black. No subspecies are recognized.

Etymology: The specific epithet, *barbouri*, honors Roger Barbour, a herpetologist at the University of Kentucky.

Similar Species: Morphologically, Streamside Salamanders are nearly indistinguishable from Small-Mouthed Salamanders (*Ambystoma texanum*) and experts have difficulty in distinguishing between individuals of these two

Streamside Salamander adult, Rutherford County. (Photo by Matthew L. Niemiller)

species. Coloration is variable in both species and cannot be used to aid in identification and dentition is the only reliable morphological feature used in species differentiation. Furthermore, the mode of egg deposition and related life history parameters differ between the two species. Streamside Salamanders typically use low-order streams and lay their eggs on the undersurface of rocks in flowing water, whereas Small-Mouthed Salamanders typically breed in ephemeral ponds and attach a small cluster of eggs to vegetation.

Distribution: Streamside Salamanders breed in low-order streams in the Inner Nashville Basin, with historic records from Jackson and Davidson counties and extant populations in southern Rutherford, northern Bedford, northern Marshall, southern Trousdale, and south-central Wilson counties.

Habitat: The Streamside Salamander breeds in first- to second-order streams, where the larvae remain until metamorphosis. Many of the streams used as breeding sites are ephemeral and, therefore, dry during the summer months.

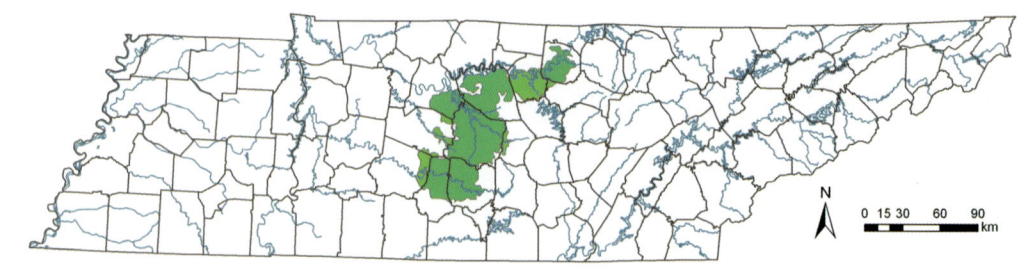

Top left: Streamside Salamander adult, Rutherford County. (Photo by Matthew L. Niemiller) *Top right:* Streamside Salamander larva, Wilson County. (Photo by Matthew L. Niemiller) *Bottom:* Streamside Salamander eggs attached to undersurface of a rock, Rutherford County. (Photo by Brad M. Glorioso)

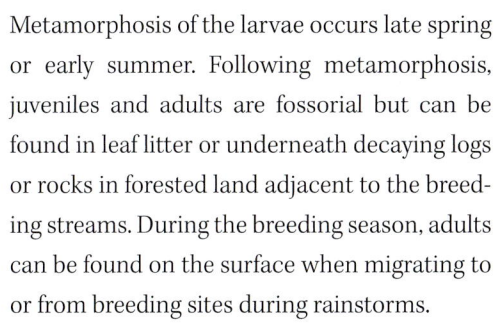

Metamorphosis of the larvae occurs late spring or early summer. Following metamorphosis, juveniles and adults are fossorial but can be found in leaf litter or underneath decaying logs or rocks in forested land adjacent to the breeding streams. During the breeding season, adults can be found on the surface when migrating to or from breeding sites during rainstorms.

Natural History: Streamside Salamanders breed during the winter months after low-order streams begin to flow continually. Depending on the weather and stream conditions, breeding is initiated in early to late December to early January. Adults begin moving toward breeding streams during autumn rainstorms and are found underneath rocks in the streams as early as November. Courtship is thought to occur beneath rocks in the streams. Following mating, eggs are attached one at a time to the undersurface of rocks, logs, or other submerged or partially submerged cover objects. To oviposit, a female will flip onto her back and brace herself with her legs, back, and tail while pressing her cloaca upward against the undersurface of the cover object. She then extrudes an egg, repositions herself, and continues to oviposit. She deposits eggs rapidly, one every 15–45 seconds. The number of eggs a female can oviposit is positively correlated with her body size and is, therefore, highly variable. Maximum reported number of mature ova counted by dissection of preserved specimens is 397. Therefore, a large female can deposit nearly 400 eggs, which she can spread onto several rocks. However, the number of eggs found on the undersurface of the same rock is highly variable and often represents eggs deposited by more than one female. Indeed, clusters of eggs at different developmental stages are found often on the undersurface of rocks. Larval Streamside Salamanders are opportunistic in feeding and eat a variety of aquatic prey including zooplankton, benthic invertebrates, amphipods, isopods, worms, and other invertebrates. Adults are also opportunistic in feeding and eat most invertebrates that they encounter on and underneath the forest floor. Predators likely include frogs, fishes, crayfish, snakes, birds, and mammals. Transformed Streamside Salamanders will release a white exudate from their poison glands when threatened. Because Streamside Salamanders inhabit the Nashville Basin, which is becoming largely urban and suburban, metamorphosed Streamside Salamanders wandering above ground during and following rainstorms frequently are killed by automobile traffic.

Conservation Status: The Streamside Salamander is listed as "Deemed in Need of Management" by the Tennessee Wildlife Resources Agency, state listed as "Imperiled" and "Near Threatened" by the International Union for Conservation of Nature (IUCN), but currently is not afforded protection by the U.S. Fish and Wildlife Service. Conversion of forests and fields to subdivisions and retail space threaten extant populations. Disturbance of forest surrounding streams used for breeding seems to greatly affect this species as well.

Brian T. Miller

Family Ambystomatidae (Mole Salamanders) | 77

Spotted Salamander adult, Blount County. (Photo by Matthew L. Niemiller)

Spotted Salamander

Ambystoma maculatum

Description: The Spotted Salamander is one of the larger ambystomatid salamanders. Adults are 112–197 mm TL but can reach lengths up to 248 mm TL with 12 costal grooves on average. The dorsal ground color ranges from black to gray and the venter is slate gray. Adults have two irregular rows of yellow to orange spots that extend from the eye to the tip of the tail. Albinism and individuals lacking spots have been reported. The tail is moderately compressed laterally. The head is distinctly round. The front limbs have four toes, whereas the hind limbs have five toes. During the breeding season, males have conspicuously swollen vents. Juveniles resemble adults in appearance but might have less significant spotting and be lighter in ground coloration. Hatchlings are dull green and measure 12–17 mm TL. A dull greenish dorsum, a light venter, and a lack of markings characterize larger larvae. The tail fin is extensive and extends anterior to the insertion

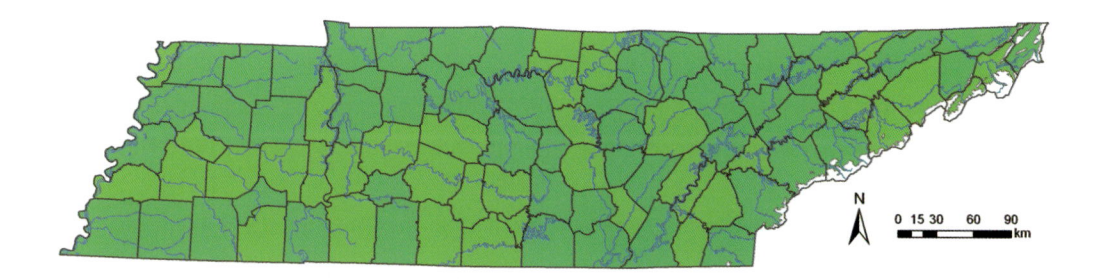

Top left: An unspotted Spotted Salamander female, Rutherford County. (Photo by Matthew L. Niemiller) *Top right:* Spotted Salamander egg mass, Coffee County. (Photo by Brad M. Glorioso) *Bottom:* Spotted Salamander larva, Coffee County. (Photo by Matthew L. Niemiller)

of the front limbs and is mottled. No subspecies are recognized.

Etymology: The specific epithet, *maculatum*, is Latin for "spotted," referring to the large spots found on most individuals.

Similar Species: Adult Spotted Salamanders resemble Tiger Salamanders (*A. tigrinum*). When Tiger Salamanders are found with spots instead of blotches, they are usually more elongated, irregular, and brownish yellow in color. Additionally, the venter of Tiger Salamanders is marked with yellow blotches, whereas that of Spotted Salamanders is slate gray. Recently transformed Spotted Salamanders, whose spots have not fully developed, can be confused with Mole and Marbled Salamanders (*A. talpoideum* and *A. opacum,* respectively). However, Marbled Salamanders metamorphose earlier in the season than Spotted Salamanders. Mole Salamanders have much broader heads than Spotted Salamanders.

Distribution: Spotted Salamanders occur across a wide range, from southeastern Canada to the southeastern Gulf Coast. In Tennessee, this species has been reported nearly statewide, though the records are scattered and frequently clustered. This might indicate that the density of Spotted Salamanders is greatly reduced in some areas, such as in western, southern, and central Tennessee, or that suitable habitat does not exist in these areas. Due to the secretive nature of this species during most of the year, it could be that populations have simply been overlooked.

Habitat: Spotted Salamanders are most common in bottomland deciduous forest habitats, usually below 600 m in elevation. Areas with multiple vernal pools or swamps are ideal for this species, thus forests occurring near floodplains are optimal. Rarely, this species has been reported from mountainous regions consisting of coniferous forests, and populations do exist in lower elevation hardwood cove forest in the Great Smoky Mountains National Park.

Natural History: Adult Spotted Salamanders migrate to ephemeral, fish-free areas to breed in late winter to early spring. Mass migrations are known to occur following warm rains; however, multiple migrations throughout the breeding season are common. Breeding site fidelity has been observed within this species, though individuals tend not to breed every year. Breeding might occur over as few as several days or might last for months depending on the weather conditions. Egg masses, consisting of up to 370 eggs, vary in color from clear to white. Other egg masses are greenish because of the presence of symbiotic, photosynthetic algae (*Oophila ambystomatis*). It is thought that the developing salamander embryos produce nitrogen-rich waste that is useful to the algae, while the algae increase the oxygen content of the water surrounding the eggs. Egg deposition occurs from January to April. Hatchlings are usually found as early as March and are known to consume a variety of foods, such as zooplankton, cladocerans, copepods, and larval Red-Spotted Newts. Two to four months after hatching, larvae undergo metamorphosis and emerge from breeding ponds (rarely has overwintering been reported). Metamorphs aggregate under rocks and logs, but the most successful individuals burrow beneath the surface. Adults forage on a variety of larval and adult insects, earthworms, spiders, millipedes, and centipedes. Spotted Salamander egg predators include a variety of aquatic insects, such as caddisfly and midge larvae, adult Eastern Newts, and Wood Frog tadpoles. Aquatic insect larvae, birds, and raccoons often consume larval Spotted Salamanders. Adult Spotted Salamanders secret noxious chemicals from their tails, have a butting defensive behavior and will bite, all of which reduces their predation risk by birds, mammals, and reptiles.

Conservation Status: The Spotted Salamander is not currently listed with any agency and populations in Tennessee are secure. However, habitat destruction, fragmentation, and acidic pollution are all factors that affect this species' survival. Continued monitoring of this species is recommended as the habitat continues to be altered.

Stesha A. Pasachnik

Marbled Salamander adult, Coffee County. (Photo by Matthew L. Niemiller)

Marbled Salamander

Ambystoma opacum

Description: The Marbled Salamander is one of the smaller ambystomatid species. Adults are 80–107 mm TL but can reach 127 mm TL. Costal grooves number 11–13. Adults have black ground coloration with prominent white dorsal crossbands and exhibit sexual dimorphism in coloration. In females the bands are grayish white, whereas in males they are a much brighter white. These crossbands often coalesce and become broader laterally. On rare occasion individuals lack crossbands altogether or have a dorsolateral stripe. The venter is solid black. The front limbs have four toes, whereas the hind limbs have five toes. Within a few weeks following metamorphosis, individuals begin to develop light white patches, which have been described as lichen-like in appearance. Within 1–2 months the adult pattern is present. Hatchlings are 10–19 mm TL and are drab black. Larvae have large gills, a dorsal tail fin that extends to the front limbs. Larvae are dark brown to black, often with yellow to green coloration dorsally. A series of light

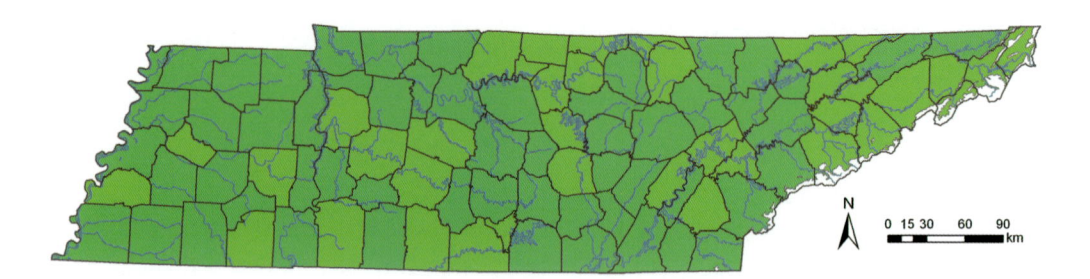

Top left: Female (top) and male (bottom) Marbled Salamanders, Coffee County. (Photo by Brad M. Glorioso) *Top right:* Marbled Salamander female with eggs, Blount County. (Photo by Matthew L. Niemiller) *Bottom:* Marbled Salamander larva, Blount County. (Photo by Matthew L. Niemiller)

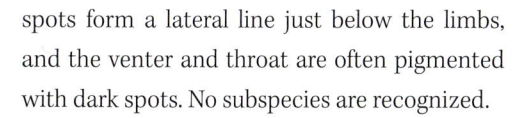

spots form a lateral line just below the limbs, and the venter and throat are often pigmented with dark spots. No subspecies are recognized.

Etymology: The specific epithet, *opacum,* is Latin for "shaded," "dark," or "obscure," referring to the adult dorsal color pattern.

Similar Species: Adult Marbled Salamanders are easily distinguishable from all other species within Tennessee. Larval and recently transformed *Ambystoma* can be difficult to tell apart. Recent Marbled Salamander metamorphs are usually darker in color with narrower heads than the Mole Salamanders (*A. talpoideum*) and metamorphose earlier in the year than other species of *Ambystoma.*

Distribution: The Marbled Salamander ranges from Massachusetts and southern Vermont to northern Florida and the Gulf Coast. In Tennessee, this species can most likely be found in lower elevations statewide; however, some published distribution maps show that this species does not occur in the northeastern part of the state.

Habitat: Marbled Salamanders are most common under debris in woodland areas associated with floodplains, swamps, oxbows, and terminal stream channels when at the surface during the breeding season. In some instances outside of the breeding season, individuals have been recorded from drier sandy areas, ridges, and rocky hillsides. Adults can most often be encountered during and around the breeding season. Recently transformed individuals are often encountered under debris on the edge of the breeding ponds.

Natural History: Adult Marbled Salamanders migrate to breeding sites in late summer and fall. This species is unique in that it mates and oviposits on land instead of in water like most other *Ambystoma*. Breeding most likely occurs in October and November. Females lay clusters of 50–200 eggs, under debris or in burrows within vernal pools, floodplains, and swamps that will flood in the coming months. Females remain with the eggs in order to help prevent desiccation and for protection from predators. In rare cases communal nests have been observed. The incubation period is 90–120 days. However, embryos are developed to the point at which they could hatch only 9–15 days after oviposition. Thus, in most instances hatching occurs within a 1–2 days after the brooding sites become submerged. After approximately three months, larvae undergo metamorphosis, usually in March and April at 30–40 mm TL. However, size at metamorphosis varies greatly. Metamorphs remain around breeding ponds for a short time. Longer distance dispersal occurs subsequently during periods of heavy rain. Little is know about the biology of juveniles and adults as they spend the vast majority of their time underground, surfacing only rarely following rains. No data is available on the prey of adult Marbled Salamanders though it can be assumed that their diet is similar to other ambystomatids, thus including a variety of larval and adult insects, earthworms, spiders, millipedes, and centipedes. Larvae immediately begin to feed after hatching. Food items include zooplankton, aquatic insects, mites, snails, and copepods. Once larvae are larger, they feed on a variety of other amphibians, such as the eggs and larvae of Upland Chorus Frogs (*Pseudacris feriarum*), Wood Frogs (*Lithobates sylvaticus*), and other salamander species, including their own. Adult Marbled Salamanders secret noxious chemicals from their tails and perform defensive posturing, which reduces their predation risk by birds, mammals and reptiles. However, there have been reports of predation by snakes, and it can be assumed that a variety of forest predators forage on this species at all life stages.

Conservation Status: The Marbled Salamander is not currently listed with any agency and populations in Tennessee are secure. The destruction and fragmentation of bottomland hardwood forests as well as acid deposition are factors that can affect this species' survival. Continued monitoring of this species is recommended as the habitat continues to be altered.

Stesha A. Pasachnik and
Matthew L. Niemiller

Mole Salamander adult, Obion County. (Photo by Brad M. Glorioso)

Mole Salamander

Ambystoma talpoideum

Description: Mole Salamanders are small, robust ambystomatid salamanders characterized by their stout bodies and large heads. Adults are 80–120 mm TL with relatively large limbs. Costal grooves usually number 11. Metamorphosed adults and juveniles are brown, bluish, gray, or black, often with light-colored flecks on the dorsum and sides. The venter is bluish gray, also with light-colored flecks. The tail is short, laterally compressed, and glandular. Parotid glands are present on the head. The front limbs have four toes, whereas the hind limbs are stout with five toes. During the breeding season, the vent swells in males, allowing for easy visual differentiation between the sexes during this period. Aquatic, neotenic adults also occur and have a compressed oarlike tail with a distinct

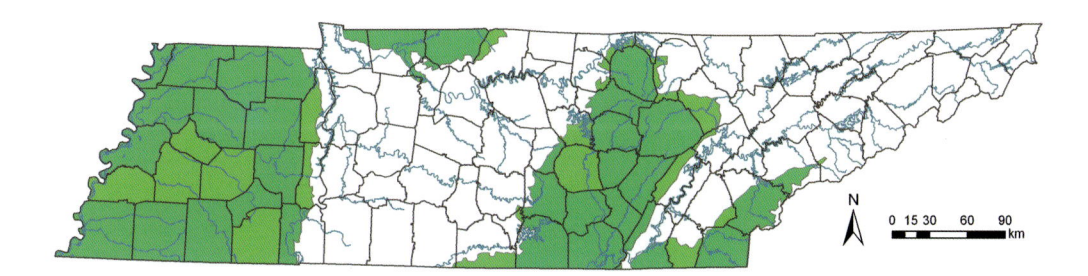

Left: Mole Salamander adult exhibiting defensive posture, Obion County. (Photo by Brad M. Glorioso) *Right:* Mole Salamander larva, Coffee County. (Photo by Matthew L. Niemiller)

caudal fin that extends onto the back. Neotenic adults resemble larvae but are darker in color and are considerably smaller in body size compared to metamorphosed adults. Hatchlings are 10–18 mm TL and have distinct black and yellow blotching on the dorsum. Larvae also have conspicuous cream-colored stripes along each side and large feathery gills. Recent metamorphs are 70–82 mm TL, drab olive green in color and begin to develop adult coloration a few weeks after metamorphosis. No subspecies are recognized.

Etymology: The specific epithet, *talpoideum,* is from the Latin for *talpa* "mole" and *-oides* (similar to *-eum*), roughly meaning "having the quality of."

Similar Species: Adult Mole Salamanders can be easily distinguished from all other ambystomatids by their drab coloration, gray flecking, and stout appearance. Small-Mouthed Salamanders (*A. texanum*) have a similar coloration but are generally longer, more slender, and have small heads relative to their stout bodies. Streamside Salamanders (*A. barbouri*) also have small heads relative to their body size, closely resemble Small-Mouthed Salamanders, and are very narrowly distributed in Tennessee. Mole Salamander larvae can be easily confused with other species of *Ambystoma*. However, the dark abdominal vein usually is clearly visible running the length of the body along the midline in Mole Salamander larvae.

Distribution: Mole Salamanders are patchily distributed throughout the southeastern United States, with continuous populations occurring along the Mississippi and Gulf Coastal Plains. In Tennessee, this species ranges across the state in disjunct units. Mole Salamanders are found in the Southeastern Plains and Mississippi Valley Loess Plains, the Western Pennyroyal Karst and Eastern Highland Rim of the Interior Low Plateau, the Cumberland Plateau of the Southwestern Appalachians, and southern sections of the Blue Ridge Mountains. The Southeastern Plains, Mississippi Valley Loess Plains, and Western Pennyroyal Karst populations appear contiguous with the main distribution of the species, which ranges throughout the Coastal Plain. The Eastern Highland Rim and Cumberland Plateau populations are contiguous, as are the southern Blue Ridge populations with North Carolina's highland populations. Both of these units are disjunct from the main distribution. Additionally, a small population occurs in the Great Smoky Mountains National Park near Cades Cove, though it is unknown whether other populations exist nearby.

Habitat: Mole Salamanders inhabit upland hardwood and floodplain forests surrounding breeding ponds. Breeding ponds are often temporary wetlands, such as open grassy ponds, woodland ponds, roadside ditches, and borrow pits; however, permanent fish-free ponds are also used. Neotenic adults typically inhabit permanent to semipermanent ponds, and both neotenic and terrestrial adults can be found in the same pond. Adults can be found under rotten logs and other surface debris within 500 m of breeding ponds and are often encountered as they await spring rains in the basin of ephemeral wetlands.

Natural History: Migrations of adult Mole Salamanders occur from upland habitats to breeding ponds in late fall or winter. Breeding occurs from December to late February. Females lay an average of 200–600 eggs into masses of 4–50 eggs, though this is highly variable geographically. Eggs are dark above and white below, and masses are 30–57 mm long, 24–34 mm wide, and usually attached to submerged vegetation and twigs. Eggs hatch within a few weeks and the larval period lasts 3–6 months. However, some larvae might metamorphose the following spring or even bypass metamorphosis, maturing into neotenic adults. Sexually maturity occurs in two years and adults can live up to eight years or longer. Metamorphosed Mole Salamanders are fossorial but will feed on the surface during rainy nights. Main prey items are invertebrates, either terrestrial or aquatic depending upon the adult habitat. Larvae also consume aquatic invertebrates. Aquatic predators of larvae and neotenic adults include aquatic insects, fish, and amphibians. Terrestrial predators include snakes, skunks, and raccoons. Both adults and juveniles produce noxious secretions from glands on the head and tail to deter predators.

Conservation Status: The Mole Salamander was previously listed as "Deemed in Need of Management" by the Tennessee Wildlife Resources Agency but was subsequently removed. Populations appear stable, but loss of forested wetland habitat continues to threaten local populations. Special attention should be paid to presumably isolated populations, such as the one occurring in the Great Smoky Mountains.

George R. Wyckoff and Matthew L. Niemiller

Small-Mouthed Salamander adult, Coffee County. (Photo by Brian T. Miller)

Small-Mouthed Salamander

Ambystoma texanum

Description: As its name suggests, the Small-Mouthed Salamander has a small mouth and narrow head relative to the rest of its body. Adults are 100–140 mm TL with a maximum length around 178 mm TL. Costal grooves number 13–15. The dorsum is gray to black with light lichen-like flecking that extend onto the sides, but this flecking can be absent in some individuals. The venter typically is dark gray to black and usually lacks the prominent flecking of the dorsum. The front limbs have four toes, whereas the hind limbs have five toes. Males may be differentiated from females in the breeding season by a swollen vent. Young larvae are yellowish brown to olive green and have light yellow to olive green saddles or paired spots along the back. As larvae develop, these spots fade, becoming inconspicuous, and a weak broken light stripe forms along each side of the body. Metamorphs are brownish to brownish gray in color and begin to exhibit the light gray flecking and lichen-like patterning of adults within a few weeks. No subspecies are recognized.

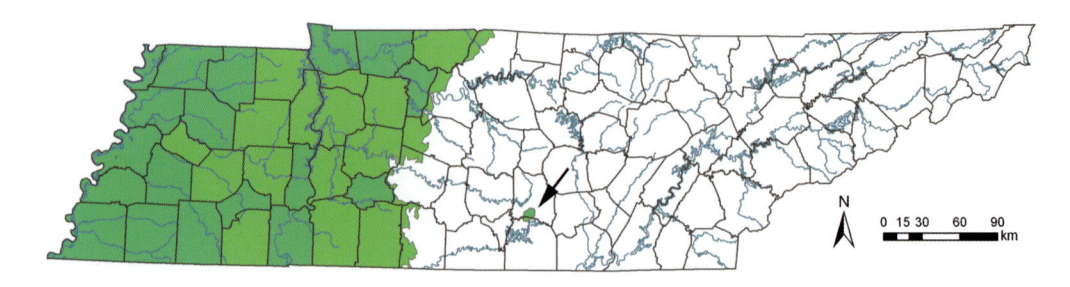

Etymology: The specific epithet, *texanum,* means "belonging to the state of Texas," which is where the type locality of this species is located.

Similar Species: Small-Mouthed Salamanders are identical externally to Streamside Salamanders (*A. barbouri*). Location is the most reliable method for differentiating between these two species. Breeding location also can be useful in species identification; Small-Mouthed Salamanders typically breed in lentic habitats, such as woodland ponds, roadside ditches, and borrow pits, whereas Streamside Salamanders breed in lotic habitats, such as small streams. Laboratory examination of the teeth can also be used to differentiate species. Streamside Salamanders have rounded cusps on the maxillary and premaxillary teeth, whereas Small-Mouthed Salamanders have elongate pointed cusps. Small-Mouthed Salamanders resemble Mole Salamanders (*A. talpoideum*) in coloration but are less robust and have conspicuously narrower heads than Mole Salamanders.

Distribution: Small-Mouthed Salamanders occur throughout much of the Mississippi River drainage, from the Great Lakes to the Gulf of Mexico. They are found in the western part of our state and along the Cumberland River basin in north-central Tennessee. Populations have also been reported in Coffee and Lewis counties in the south-central part of the state.

Habitat: Small-Mouthed Salamanders typically inhabit bottomland and floodplain forests surrounding breeding ponds but also can be found in more open habitats. Breeding occurs in shallow temporary habitats, including wetlands, woodland ponds, ditches, flooded fields, sluggish streams, and borrow pits. Breeding sites are typically shallower than other ambystomatid species. Adults and juveniles can be found underneath logs and other cover at the surface from February to June but can be found at the surface while feeding during rainy nights at other times of the year.

Small-Mouthed Salamander larva, Gibson County. (Photo by Matthew L. Niemiller)

Natural History: Adults migrate from their fossorial haunts to breed during rainy nights in late winter to early spring (late January to late February). Females deposit 400–700 eggs in small, sausage-shaped masses of 6–25 eggs on submerged vegetation and twigs. Eggs are bicolored, 1.6–2.5 mm in diameter, and hatch in 2–8 weeks depending on water temperature. Larvae develop for 8 to 12 weeks and metamorphose at 50–65 mm TL in May to June. Larvae feed on a plethora of prey, including water fleas, ostracods, isopods, chrionomids, amphipods, copepods, gastropods, odonates, and coleopterans. Adults and juveniles feed on earthworms, centipedes, caterpillars, isopods, and other invertebrates. Documented predators of larvae include Tiger Salamander larvae (*A. tigrinum*) and aquatic insects, whereas adults are prey for gartersnakes, watersnakes, and small mammals. Adults produce noxious secretions from their tails and exhibit defensive posturing to deter predation.

Conservation Status: The species is not listed in Tennessee. Populations appear stable but are threatened by habitat loss.

George R. Wyckoff and
Matthew L. Niemiller

Eastern Tiger Salamander adult, Rutherford County. (Photo by Matthew L. Niemiller)

Eastern Tiger Salamander

Ambystoma tigrinum

Description: The Tiger Salamander is the largest of the ambystomatid salamanders and is one of the largest salamanders in North America. Adults are 180–210 mm TL but have been recorded to reach 350 mm TL. This species is characterized as having small eyes, a large blunt head, and a stout body. The dorsal ground coloration of the adults is grayish black to dark brown. A pattern of dorsal markings is almost always present on the head, body, and tail but varies in color from brownish yellow to greenish yellow. These dorsal markings also vary in pattern from spots to blotches to crossbands. The venter is yellowish with irregular spots and some mottling. Costal grooves number 12–13. The front limbs have four toes; the hind limbs have five toes. Four adult morphs are documented for this species. The most common adult is described above. Adults can

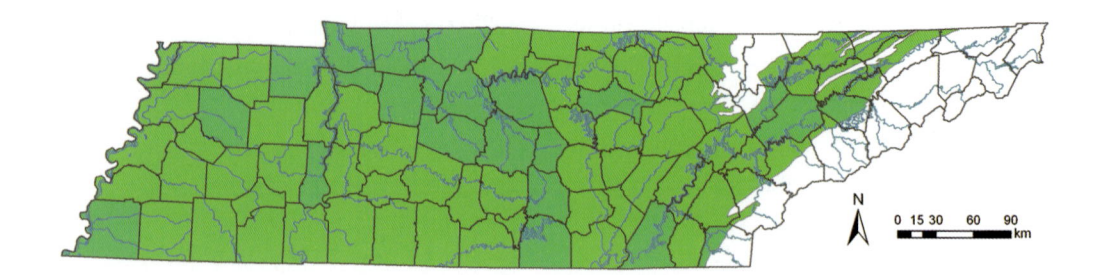

Left: Eastern Tiger Salamander larva, Loudon County. (Photo by Nathan Haislip) *Right:* Eastern Tiger Salamander metamorph, Wilson County. (Photo by Matthew L. Niemiller)

also be metamorphosed and cannibalistic, in which case they have an enlarged head. Neotenic adults, of both the cannibalistic and common form also can be found, but only rarely within this species. Males have a conspicuously swollen vent during the breeding season. Both hatchlings and more developed larvae have stout heads, large gills, broad dorsal fins, and typically have paired irregular spots along the dorsum. Hatchlings are 13–17 mm TL. Larval dorsal coloration is greenish gray, while the venter is white and sometimes has dark spots. Larger larvae possess a light-colored lateral stripe that is bordered by darker, mottled bands both above and below. As has been documented in adults, larvae can be found in both cannibalistic and noncannibalistic forms. Metamorphs are dark gray to black with lighter mottling of gray, yellow, and olive yellow. Several subspecies of Tiger Salamanders have been described, only one of which, the Eastern Tiger Salamander (*A. t. tigrinum*), occurs in Tennessee.

Etymology: The specific and subspecific epithets, *tigrinum,* are Latin for "tiger," referring to the striped coloration in some individuals, and perhaps the voracious appetite.

Similar Species: Adult Eastern Tiger Salamanders most closely resemble Spotted Salamanders. Unlike Eastern Tiger Salamanders, Spotted Salamanders have yellow to orange spots aligned in two rows on the dorsum and have slate gray venters. Eastern Tiger Salamanders also can be found in much deeper pools than Spotted Salamanders and are often found in farm ponds. Larval Eastern Tiger Salamanders also resemble Spotted Salamander larvae but possess a lateral stripe (in larger individuals), have flattened digits, and grow to a much greater size (often > 80 mm TL).

Distribution: The Eastern Tiger Salamander is broadly distributed throughout much of the eastern United States. Most records from Tennessee are from the Interior Plateau of central Tennessee and the southern Ridge and Valley; however, this species probably has a much larger distribution in the Tennessee, including all but the Blue Ridge Mountains and northeast Ridge and Valley.

Habitat: Eastern Tiger Salamanders can be found in a variety of habitats within Tennessee, including conifer and deciduous woodlands, open fields, and grasslands. Preferable breeding habitats include cattle ponds, vernal pools, limestone ponds, borrow pits, and flooded woodlands. Adults are known to spend the majority of their time outside of the breeding season in burrows that they construct themselves and those that are already present.

Natural History: Adult Tiger Salamanders migrate to a variety of fish-free ephemeral and permanent water bodies to breed from November to late May, though peak migration occurs in January and February. Migration generally occurs at night during or following rain, with males arriving at ponds a few weeks earlier than females. Breeding does not necessarily occur every year. When there is very little rain, females are known not to migrate to ponds. Eggs are typically deposited in masses of 15–100 eggs on twigs and other structures usually in water > 20 cm in depth. Females can deposit anywhere from 400 to as many as 7,000 eggs, depending on body size. The incubation period typically lasts one month. Growth rates, length of the larval period, and size at metamorphosis are highly variable, but generally the larval period is 2–6 months with larvae metamorphosing at 60–110 mm TL. However, some individuals in permanent water bodies might overwinter and metamorphose the following year at a much larger size at 170–210 mm TL. As a means of thermoregulation, larvae travel to and from the edge of the pond to the deeper water in the center of ponds. Sexual maturity is reached in two years. Prey of larvae is greatly dependent on body size. The diet of larvae includes nematodes, insects, snails, clams, shrimp, crayfish, and a variety of amphibian eggs and larvae including conspecifics. Little is known about the diet of adults, but insects, worms, snails, lizards, and tadpoles have been found in gut content analyses. Egg predators include Eastern Newts, caddisflies and conspecifics. Though larvae are highly camouflaged, a variety of predators do exist, including gartersnakes, other ambystomatid larvae, many aquatic insect larvae, birds, and mammals. Birds, snakes, and mammals prey upon adults, but adults have a defensive posturing that greatly reduces the risk of predation.

Conservation Status: The Eastern Tiger Salamander is not currently listed in Tennessee, though declines in some populations have been recorded throughout its range. Habitat destruction of terrestrial and breeding habitats, acid rain and fish introductions are all factors that might affect the survival of this species. Continued research into these causes and monitoring of this species is recommended as the habitat continues to be altered.

Stesha A. Pasachnik and
Matthew L. Niemiller

10
Family Amphiumidae (Amphiumas)

Amphiumas are associated with the Coastal Plain of the southeastern United States and are the longest salamanders in North America, reaching total lengths of 1.25 m. Amphiumas have an extremely elongate body with greatly reduced (vestigial) limbs. Rather than the normal four toes on the front limbs, amphiumas have one, two, or three toes. Adults are permanently aquatic but lack external gills. Instead they have a single pair of gill slits and possess lungs, which gives rise to the family name Amphiumidae, which is from the Greek *amphi* "both" and *pneuma* "breathe." Three species occur in the southeastern United States and a single species is found in Tennessee. Amphiuma fossils date to the Late Cretaceous, when the family was widely distributed throughout North America. Amphiumas are voracious predators that live in swamps, ponds, ditches, sloughs, and sluggish streams with abundant vegetation and organic matter. Although aquatic, females often lay their eggs on land adjacent to water.

Three-Toed Amphiuma

Amphiuma tridactylum

Description: The Three-Toed Amphiuma is one of the longest salamanders in North America, ranging 50–75 cm TL and reaching a maximum length of 106 cm TL. It is an eel-like salamander that is completely aquatic but lacks external gills. Instead, adults have lungs but retain gill slits on the head. The body has smooth skin and is distinctly bicolored with a brown to black dorsum and a light brown to gray venter. A dark throat patch also is present. The head is pointed and narrow with small eyes that lack eyelids. Four diminutive legs are present, each typically with three toes; however, toe counts can vary if a limb has been lost and has regenerated. The tail is laterally compressed. Hatchlings are 43–64 mm TL, and both hatchlings and juveniles have short, whitish external gills that are lost at around 75 mm TL. No subspecies are recognized.

Etymology: The specific epithet, *tridactylum*, is from the Greek *tri-* for "three" and *daktylos* "finger or digit" and refers to the number of digits on each appendage.

Similar Species: Within its range, the Three-Toed Amphiuma can be confused with the Western Lesser Siren (*Siren intermedia nettingi*) and the American Eel (*Anguilla rostrata*). Unlike Three-Toed Amphiumas, Western Lesser Sirens have external gills and have just two front limbs each with four toes. American Eels lack limbs and have a pair of pectoral fins just behind the head.

Distribution: Three-Toed Amphiumas are found throughout the Coastal Plain of the lower Mississippi River Valley from southeastern

Three-Toed Amphiuma adult, Natchitoches Parish, Louisiana. (Photo by Matthew L. Niemiller)

Missouri and western Kentucky south to western Texas, Louisiana, Mississippi, and southwestern Alabama. In Tennessee, Three-Toed Amphiumas occur throughout the Coastal Plain of West Tennessee in river drainages that flow directly into the Mississippi River.

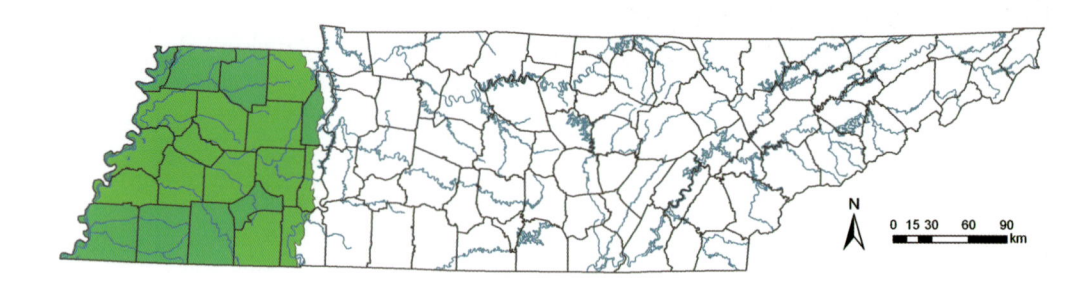

Habitat: Three-Toed Amphiumas occur in a variety of aquatic habitats, including cypress swamps, oxbow lakes, bayous, sloughs, roadside ditches, sluggish streams, and ponds with abundant vegetation and decaying organic matter. During the day, salamanders can be found in submerged crevices and beneath vegetation and debris. Amphiumas leave their daytime retreats at night to forage. During drought, Three-Toed Amphiumas are known to burrow into the substrate or occupy crayfish burrows to avoid desiccation and can remain there for several months without feeding.

Natural History: Three-Toed Amphiumas have internal fertilization. Courtship and mating occur underwater in late winter and spring. Females lay 40–200 eggs in a cavity underneath logs and other cover objects on land adjacent to water from late summer into early autumn. Females brood eggs that hatch in 4–5 months, when eggs are inundated by water and embryos are about 64 mm TL. Hatchlings lose their gills in 3–4 weeks. Females can reach sexual maturity at 33–46 cm TL. Adults can live more than 12 years. Three-Toed Amphiumas feed on earthworms, crayfish, aquatic insects, mollusks, and fishes. Both adults and juveniles scavenge and have been caught in turtle traps. Amphiumas are eaten by Mudsnakes (*Farancia abacura*) and Western Cottonmouths (*Agkistrodon piscivorus*). Birds of prey and herons also prey on Three-Toed Amphiumas. Three-Toed Amphiumas are very slimy and difficult to handle, and they are capable of inflicting a very painful bite.

Three-Toed Amphiuma adult, Lake County. (Photo by Matthew L. Niemiller)

Conservation Status: Three-Toed Amphiumas are not currently listed in Tennessee and are in no immediate danger of decline. Three-Toed Amphiumas are common where they occur.

Matthew L. Niemiller

11
Family Cryptobranchidae (Giant Salamanders)

Giant Salamanders are extremely large, stream-dwelling salamanders reaching lengths up to 1.8 m TL that are distributed in eastern North America and eastern Asia (China and Japan). A single species found in North America, the Hellbender, is considerably smaller (reaching up to 74 cm TL) than its Asian cousins. Giant Salamander fossils date back to the Upper Paleocene 56–59 million years ago in North America. Giant Salamanders lack visible external gills; instead, the gills are covered by skin. The family and genus names, Cryptobranchidae and *Cryptobranchus,* are from the Greek *kryptos* "hidden" and *branchion* "gill." Giant Salamanders have flattened heads with small eyes and conspicuously wrinkled skin along the sides of the body—a trait that increases the surface area of the skin to aid in cutaneous respiration. Additionally, Giant Salamanders have long oarlike tails and short, robust legs to facilitate in movement in their preferred habitat—depressions underneath rocks and logs in swift-flowing, oxygen-rich streams and rivers. Unlike most other salamanders, Giant Salamanders have external fertilization.

Eastern Hellbender

Cryptobranchus alleganiensis

Description: Adult Hellbenders are nearly unmistakable, as they are the largest salamanders by weight in North America. Adults reach a TL of 300–740 mm and an age exceeding 25 years. A key identifying rubric is the combination of a large flattened head, thick fleshy folds in the skin, and a lack of large external gills. The wrinkled skin is particularly apparent and is thought to increase the surface area of the skin to allow for more cutaneous absorption of dissolved oxygen. The body is wide and becomes more dorsolaterally flattened toward the head. The small eyes are located on top of the wide snout, the tail is thick and lobed, and there are four short, stout limbs, which the Hellbender uses to walk along the river bottom in search of prey. Hellbenders are usually varying shades of olive or brown, from khaki to dark chocolate or reddish brown, and often have dark black or brown spots sprinkled over the body. The coloration appears to closely match the shade of the large flat rocks that they hide under during the day. Hellbender larvae are dark brown to black dorsally with a white or cream-colored venter. Larvae also have prominent external gills and the stout, flattened body shape of adults. Hellbenders undergo partial metamorphosis, and as the larvae age, the body coloration becomes uniformly brown, dark spots appear, and the external gills become recessed and water flows to them through a single gill opening. By about 1–2 years of age, young Hellbenders resemble small adults. Two subspecies are recognized, and one occurs in Tennessee, the Eastern Hellbender

Eastern Hellbender adult, Polk County. (Photo by Matthew L. Niemiller)

(*C. a. alleganiensis*). The Ozark Hellbender (*C. a. bishopi*) occurs in a disjunct range in southeastern Missouri and northern Arkansas.

Etymology: The specific epithet, *alleganiensis,* is the Latinized name which refers to the Allegheny Mountains in the Appalachians, where this species was first discovered.

Similar Species: No other salamanders are similar in appearance to the Hellbender within its range. Nevertheless, many people confuse Hellbenders with the Mudpuppy (*Necturus maculosus*), which can be distinguished by the more slender body, lack of prominent folds and wrinkles in the skin, and large external gills. Larvae of other salamander species might be mistaken for larval Hellbenders due to the presence of external gills; however, the flattened head and stout body should easily distinguish the Hellbender.

Distribution: Historically, Hellbenders were distributed throughout the Appalachian Mountains, from New York south to north

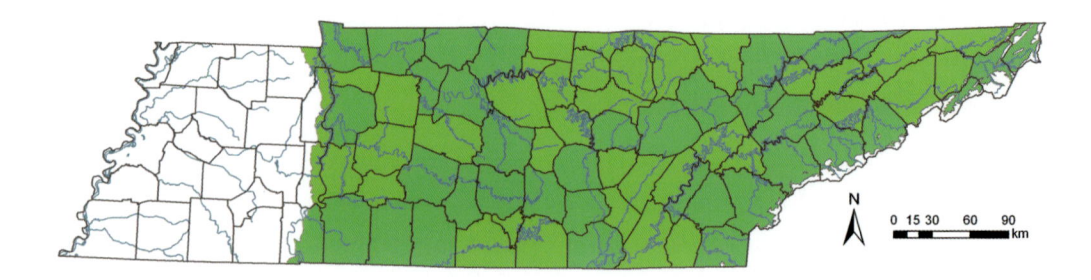

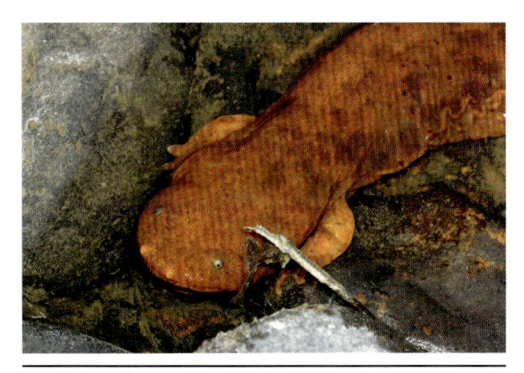

Top left: Eastern Hellbender adult, Polk County. (Photo by Matthew L. Niemiller) *Top right:* Eastern Hellbender adult, Polk County. (Photo by Matthew L. Niemiller) *Bottom:* Eastern Hellbender larva, Polk County. (Photo by Matthew L. Niemiller)

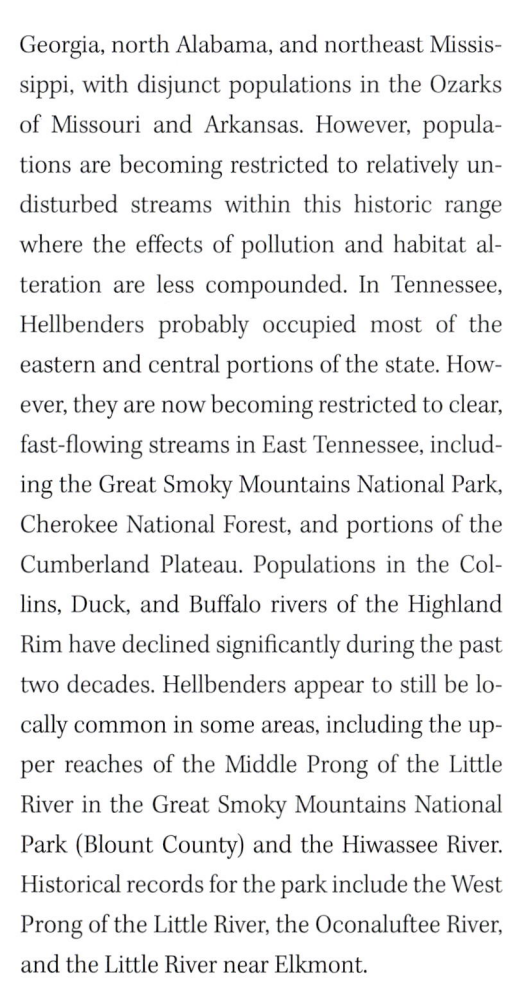

Georgia, north Alabama, and northeast Mississippi, with disjunct populations in the Ozarks of Missouri and Arkansas. However, populations are becoming restricted to relatively undisturbed streams within this historic range where the effects of pollution and habitat alteration are less compounded. In Tennessee, Hellbenders probably occupied most of the eastern and central portions of the state. However, they are now becoming restricted to clear, fast-flowing streams in East Tennessee, including the Great Smoky Mountains National Park, Cherokee National Forest, and portions of the Cumberland Plateau. Populations in the Collins, Duck, and Buffalo rivers of the Highland Rim have declined significantly during the past two decades. Hellbenders appear to still be locally common in some areas, including the upper reaches of the Middle Prong of the Little River in the Great Smoky Mountains National Park (Blount County) and the Hiwassee River. Historical records for the park include the West Prong of the Little River, the Oconaluftee River, and the Little River near Elkmont.

Habitat: Hellbenders are completely aquatic during all stages of their life cycle. They are habitat specialists and are confined to cool swift-flowing streams and rivers with clear, unpolluted water and a high dissolved oxygen content. They are mostly found in pools between rapids, where they hide during the day under large, flat rocks often with their head protruding from under the rock. They are generally infrequently encountered, although they can be locally abundant. Hellbenders are nocturnally active, though they can be occasionally found active during the day, particularly during the breeding season between August and October. The best way to locate this species is to look under rocks using snorkel gear and slowly lifting large flat rocks and waiting for the river current to clear the silt.

Natural History: Breeding and egg deposition take place in late summer or autumn (sometimes as late as December), when females lay strings of eggs in nests created and defended by the males. Male Hellbenders are territorial and defend suitable nesting sites, often violently, beneath large flat rocks. Male-male combat might include the shearing off and consumption of a rival's limbs or tail. Fecundity is variable and appears to depend on female size at the time of reproduction. Female Hellbenders in two river systems in Missouri were found to lay an average of about 440 eggs per female. Egg masses resemble long strings of beads, and nests are large depressions carved out underneath large rocks with openings that face downstream. Eggs begin to hatch after about two months, and newly hatched larvae are about 25 mm TL. Hellbenders are important large predators in stream ecosystems. Their primary prey is crayfish, though they will eat most anything that they can catch, including fish, frogs, and invertebrates, as well as other Hellbender eggs and larvae. Fishermen sometimes catch Hellbenders when using live bait, such as worms.

Conservation Status: In Tennessee, Hellbenders are state listed as "Vulnerable" and "Deemed in Need of Management." Possession of this species is illegal. Stream impoundment, channelization, siltation, acid mine drainage, and thermal pollution are typically implicated factors in the decline of Hellbender populations. Hellbenders appear to be extremely sensitive to changes in water quality, including pollution and eutrophication, and thus suitable habitat has been greatly reduced in recent times. Collection for the pet trade is another major factor contributing to declines, with some populations being heavily exploited after location by collectors. Hellbenders do not survive well in captivity, as they need cold, fast-flowing water with a high dissolved oxygen content; they should never be collected as pets. Conversion of riparian areas into pasture and the presence of cattle and livestock in suitable streams might impact populations as well. Because of their cutaneous respiration, any change in dissolved oxygen content, such as an increase in algae due to nitrogen runoff from animal waste and fertilizer, could render streams uninhabitable. Certain pesticides have also been implicated in reproductive failure by acting as endocrine disruptors, and the presence of organic chemicals in streams could impact juvenile survival.

Comments: Common names for this species vary by region but include mudpuppy, waterdog, or devil dog.

R. Graham Reynolds and
Brian T. Miller

12

Family Plethodontidae (Lungless Salamanders)

Lungless Salamanders represent the largest family of salamanders, containing about 275 described species from mainly North, Central, and South America; though a few species are known from Europe and Asia. Lungless Salamander fossils date as far back as the Late Oligocene to Early Miocene in North America. A major center of plethodontid salamander diversity is the Southern Appalachians, and Tennessee is well represented, with 47 species occurring in the state. The family name is from the Greek *plethore* "full of" and *odon* "teeth," an apt description of this group's various tooth types present in large quantities along the jaw and on the palate. Seven genera are represented in Tennessee: *Aneides, Desmognathus, Eurycea, Gyrinophilus, Hemidactylum, Plethodon,* and *Pseudotriton*. The etymology of these genera is as follows. The genus name, *Aneides,* is from the Greek *an-,* "lacking" and *eidos,* "shape." The genus name, *Desmognathus,* is from the Greek *desmos* "ligament" and *gnathos* "jaw," referring to the ligaments attached to the jaw. The genus name, *Eurycea,* is from Eurydice, the name of the wife of Orpheus from Greek mythology. The genus name, *Gyrinophilus,* is from the Greek *gyrinos* "tadpole" and *philos* "loving," which references the extended larval stage of this genus. The genus name, *Hemidactylium,* is from the Greek *hemi-* for "half" and *daktlion* "fusion of digits," referring to the lack of a fifth toe on the hind limbs. The genus name, *Plethodon,* is from the Greek *plethore* "full of" and *odon* "teeth." The genus name, *Pseudotriton,* is from the Greek *pseudos* "false" and *Triton,* a genus of European salamanders that this genus resembles.

All plethodontid salamanders lack lungs and possess nasolabial grooves that transport chemicals from the ground or substrate to the vomeronasal organ. Throughout Tennessee and rest of the Southeast, plethodontid salamanders are used as fish bait and called "spring lizards" by some because of their resemblance to true lizards and their abundance around springs and spring-fed streams. Lungless Salamanders occupy a plethora of other habitats, including swamps, larger rivers, seeps, caves, rock outcrops, and forests. Some species are neotenic, while others bypass the larval stage altogether in the egg (i.e., direct development). Several species exhibit parental care where females brood their eggs until hatching. In some cases, females will also remain with their hatchlings for a short time. In those species that do not have direct development, the larval period last from a couple of weeks to as long as eight years in some cave-dwelling populations.

Field Notes

A Plethora of Plethodontids

IN PREPARATION FOR WRITING THIS BOOK, Matt and I wanted to obtain our own photographs of as many species of amphibians in Tennessee as possible. Hence we found ourselves setting out one early May morning toward the extreme northeastern part of the state in search of plethodontid, or woodland, salamanders and anything else we could turn up. Our goal was to search Carter, Sullivan, and Unicoi counties for several species of salamanders for which we needed additional pictures. Our goal for the day was ambitious: find four elusive species of woodland salamanders, a task that would require flitting between various mountaintops up to 40 miles distant from one another before sundown (a self-imposed time limit). The conditions were excellent, one of the keys to finding plethodontids on the surface. May is one of the months when they are most active, and a series of warm rainy nights the week before gave us hope that we could find all four species. At our first stop, Roan Mountain State Park in Carter County, we geared up and headed out on a promising trail. Here we hoped to find Yonahlossee and Northern Gray-Cheeked Salamanders. Yonahlossee Salamanders are arguably one of the most attractive species in the state. They are a large, robust salamander with a handsome face and a beautiful brick red swath of color down their backs, almost as though they had been painted with a quick stroke from a thick brush. Northern Gray-Cheeked Salamanders are members of the *Plethodon jordani* complex, and though they lack red cheeks, their sleek gunmetal gray color is especially striking against a mossy background.

We should have guessed this day was going to be special when the third log I rolled over had a handsome gray salamander underneath: *"Montanus."* I called to Matt, who came jogging over, grinning widely. Our first target species, not five minutes in to the search! A short photo session ensued, and we continued up the trail. We found many salamanders as we made our way up a creek bed, including the Dusky Salamanders, *Desmognathus fuscus, D. orestes* and *D. quadramaculatus;* and the woodland salamanders, *Plethodon cylindraceus* and *P. cinereus*. These last two were welcome additions to our *Plethodon* count, though we had sufficient pictures of these species from other areas in Tennessee. We searched log after log and rock after rock beneath the beautiful spring canopy of Roan Mountain, an area that provides ideal habitat for salamanders. The trees are large, the ground is moist, and the setting is a spectacular backdrop for salamander hunting. With our tally now in the hundreds of individual salamanders, we began to work our way back, reluctant to leave until we came up with a Yonahlossee. Near a fork in the streambed, Matt moved up into the forest and began rolling over a series of large rocks. "Bingo! Got a Yonah!" he called. I sprinted up the hill and the strikingly colored amphibian greeted me from its resting place under the boulder. What an amazing specimen. Matt set up his camera equipment and an exciting photo session ensued.

Two species down and two to go, we headed back to the car. Next stop was the border of Carter and Sullivan counties, where the Southern Ravine Salamander was known to occur. We headed up a forested ridge in an unfamiliar area, contemplating what habitat and side of the mountain might yield our quarry. We decided to head to the top of the ridge and then work our way down, after some challenging though uneventful searches of very steep talus and boulder strewn ravines on the way up. The habitat consisted of a closed canopy and open understory forest on a moist slope covered in moss and spring wildflowers. We began to turn rocks and logs, and within minutes Matt had found another Yonahlossee. A good sign, but not a Ravine Salamander. Twenty minutes in, our lucky streak continued, as I rolled a small log and a slender, gold-flecked salamander came tumbling out. The Southern Ravine! An additional hour yielded a total of 12 Southern Ravine Salamanders. We excitedly photographed these individuals and released them, then checked our watches. We had a couple of hours of daylight left, and one more species to go. We headed down to Unicoi County in search of the high-elevation Weller's Salamander, which occurs on the highest mountaintops in East Tennessee. The habitat of this species is characterized by spruce-fir forest, in an area that has an isolated, wilderness feel to it. We parked on the state line and headed up a trail. We found several *P. montanus*, a welcome find, as well as a *P. cylindraceus*. If we could just find *welleri* we could cap a perfect day of East Tennessee salamander hunting. Well, we weren't disappointed, as Matt discovered a young *P. welleri* as the sun was setting and the cold was descending on the mountaintops. With the photograph session completed, we headed down the mountain and back to Knoxville, excited and exhausted by the marathon day of salamander hunting. It is days like this that remind us of what a special place Tennessee is and the beauty of the different habitats and the salamanders that occupy them.

R. Graham Reynolds

Green Salamander adult, Campbell County. (Photo by Matthew L. Niemiller)

Green Salamander

Aneides aeneus

Description: The Green Salamander is an incredibly colorful amphibian. Adults are small and slender (80–140 mm TL) and are slightly flattened (dorsoventrally compressed). The head is flat and broad with large, bulging eyes. The ground color of the back and sides is black and is overlain with green, lichen-like blotches. The ground color of the venter is paler than the back and sides and lacks the blotches. There are usually either 14 or 15 costal grooves. The tail is laterally compressed and very long, typically accounting for > 50% of TL in adults; however, the tail accounts for < 50% of body length in immature individuals. The front limbs are long and slender with four toes, whereas the hind limbs are stouter than the front limbs and have five toes. Nasolabial grooves are present. The tip of each toe is expanded into a square disc, and the hands and feet are slightly webbed. Sex of Green

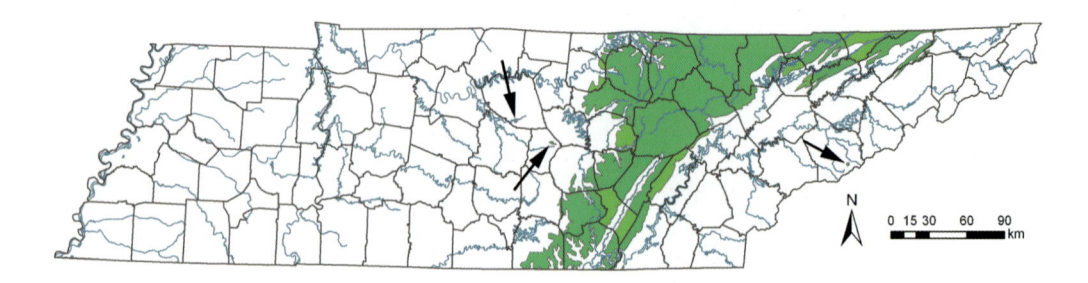

Left: Green Salamander adult, Campbell County. (Photo by Matthew L. Niemiller) *Right:* Green Salamander young juvenile, Campbell County. (Photo by Matthew L. Niemiller)

Salamanders is difficult to discern, although the anterior surface of the vent in mature males is covered in papillae, which are lacking in females. Furthermore, yolk-laden eggs can be visible through the body wall of the belly in gravid females. The tongue is boletoid, and the teeth of the upper and lower jaws occur in single rows. The premaxillary teeth protrude beyond the chin in males and, exceptionally, females during the breeding season. This species is direct developing. No subspecies are recognized.

Etymology: The specific epithet, *aeneus*, is Latin for "copper" or "bronze." This name is given because of the coloration of the patches on the dorsum.

Similar Species: Green Salamanders are most similar in morphology (flattened head and body, long, slender tail, protruding eyes) to species of the genus *Eurycea* (e.g., *E. lucifuga* and *E. longicauda*). However, green body coloration and square toe tips are unique to the Green Salamander and allow for immediate identification of members of this species.

Distribution: Green Salamanders range across much of the Cumberland Plateau and the foothills of the Southern Appalachians, from Alabama north to southern Pennsylvania. In Tennessee, this species is found roughly within the eastern half of the state and primarily in the Eastern Highland Rim, Cumberland Plateau, Cumberland Plateau Escarpment, and Cumberland Mountains. However, a population reportedly occurs in Cedars of Lebanon State Park in the Nashville Basin, though only two individuals have been recorded. A specimen was also collected in the Cherokee Orchard area of Great Smoky Mountains National Park in Sevier County in 1929, but this species has not been observed since in the park.

Habitat: Green Salamanders are associated with shaded rock outcroppings with abundant cracks and crevices and the trunks of trees in the vicinity of rock outcroppings, typically at elevations of 500–1,300 m. Rock outcroppings typically are sandstone, granite, and occasionally limestone. Generally they are located by searching cracks and crevices in rock faces, though the editors found one individual crossing a road on a rainy night at the base of a rocky road cut.

Natural History: Breeding activities of Green Salamanders are poorly documented in Tennessee. Courtship occurs on land and presumably occurs from spring through early autumn. Females deposit 10–30 white to pale yellow eggs attached to the ceiling of damp rock crevices or, presumably more rarely, underneath bark of rotting logs. Eggs are laid in June and July. The larval stage is bypassed in the egg, and hatchlings resemble adults but often have smaller concentrations of greenish blotches. Females remain with their eggs throughout the 2–3 month incubation period. Furthermore, the hatchlings often remain in the nest site for 2–3 weeks, and the female continues to brood her young during this time. Brooding females regularly consume dead eggs. Green Salamanders are likely opportunistic in feeding, although their diet has not been well studied. Males are highly territorial and will aggressively defend territories in rock crevices. A variety of small invertebrates have been reported in the diet, including small snails, spiders, and insects. Mites are also an important component of the diet, particularly in young individuals. Predation has seldom been observed, but likely predators include birds and mammals. When disturbed, Green Salamanders often respond by retreating deeper into cracks and crevices.

Conservation Status: The Green Salamander is patchily distributed and infrequently encountered outside of known aggregations. Accordingly, the species is state listed as "Imperiled/Vulnerable." Timbering in the vicinity of rock outcrops might lead to the extirpation of local populations. However, this species is locally abundant in appropriate habitat.

Brian T. Miller and
R. Graham Reynolds

Cumberland Dusky Salamander adult, Rhea County. (Photo by Matthew L. Niemiller)

Cumberland Dusky Salamander

Desmognathus abditus

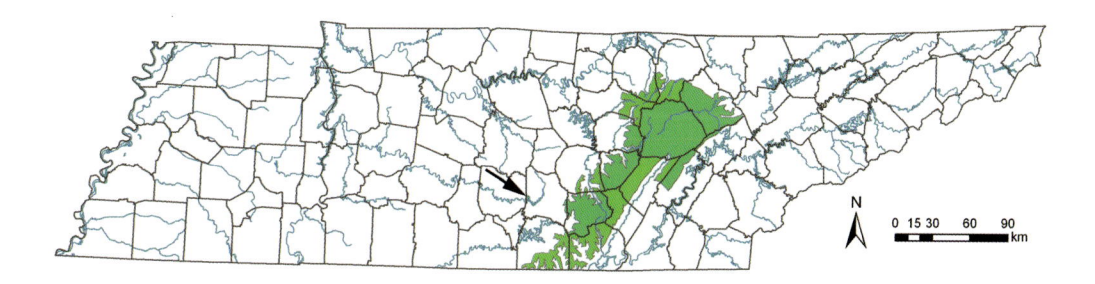

Description: The Cumberland Dusky Salamander is a small member of the Allegheny Mountain Dusky Salamander (*D. ochrophaeus*) complex reaching sexual maturity at 30–40 mm SVL. The tail is completely round in cross section and lacks even a trace of a keel. The dorsum of adults is brown in coloration and typically shows evidence of eight pairs of larval spots that are either reddish or yellowish in pigmentation or because their positions are bordered by darker pigmentation forming strongly undulating dorsolateral stripes, especially in older individuals. The venter is usually unmarked and gray to grayish black. A pale stripe runs from the eye to the rear angle of jaw. Fifteen costal grooves are present and the toe tips are not cornified. Four toes are found on the fore limbs and five toes on the hind limbs. Nasolabial grooves are present. Larvae have not been described. No subspecies are recognized.

Etymology: The specific epithet, *abditus,* is Latin for "concealed" or "secret," referring to its restricted range on the Cumberland Plateau and the difficulty in finding this species compared to other members of the genus.

Similar Species: As a member of the Allegheny Mountain Dusky Salamander (*D. ochrophaeus*) complex, this species closely resembles others in this group. Identification of species within this complex is generally based on distribution, although individuals from adjacent or overlapping ranges might be extremely difficult to identify without using molecular data. The Cumberland Dusky Salamander differs from the Allegheny Mountain Dusky Salamander by having a dorsal pattern in which the positions of larval spots are nearly always evident. In addition, the dorsal pattern of the Allegheny Mountain Dusky Salamander consists of nearly straight-edged dorsolateral stripes and indistinct larval spots with reddish or yellowish pigmentation not necessarily confined to distinct larval spots. Cumberland Dusky Salamanders also closely resemble Ocoee Salamanders. Ontogenetic darkening typically obscures the larval spotting in larger Ocoee Salamanders. In addition, the tails of Ocoee Salamanders from the southern Cumberland Plateau have a low but distinct keel, especially toward the tip of the tail, whereas Cumberland Dusky Salamanders lack a keel.

Distribution: The Cumberland Dusky Salamander has a scattered distribution along the margins of the Cumberland Plateau north and west of the Sequatchie Valley. This species has been documented from Cumberland, Grundy, Morgan, Rhea, Roane, Van Buren, and White counties. The northernmost distribution lies just south of the Cumberland Mountains section of the Cumberland Plateau in Morgan County, while the southern extent of its distribution occurs near Fiery Gizzard in Grundy County. Cumberland Dusky Salamanders also have been observed along the Western Escarpment of the Cumberland Plateau in Payne Cove, Grundy County. This species is replaced by the Allegheny Mountain Dusky Salamander to the north and the Ocoee Salamander to the south on Walden's Ridge. However, this species is difficult to locate and its distribution is likely more widespread than currently known. An isolated population along the Eastern Highland Rim in Coffee County is currently assigned to this species but likely represents a distinct taxon from both *D. ochrophaeus* and *D. abditus*.

Habitat: Cumberland Dusky Salamanders occur in or near cool streams and springs along the slopes of the Cumberland Plateau. As its name implies (*abditus* means "hidden" or "secret"), this species can be very difficult to locate. Most observations have occurred in the summer months where salamanders are found

Cumberland Dusky Salamander adult, Cumberland County. (Photo by Matthew L. Niemiller)

underneath rocks and logs along small streams and under moss and rocks on moist, vertical rock faces.

Natural History: Little is known about the ecology and life history of this recently described species. Larvae and brooding females have not been observed. This species is difficult to locate in the field, as repeated surveys at sites where salamanders have been observed in summer often are unsuccessful at other times of the year.

Conservation Status: The biggest threats facing populations of the Cumberland Dusky Salamander include habitat loss and degradation associated with housing development and mining. However, studies are needed to thoroughly document the status and distribution of this species and learn more about its natural history. Several localities of this species occur on state-owned property and are afforded some protection. This species is state listed as "Imperlied/Vulnerable."

Matthew L. Niemiller

Seepage Salamander adult, Monroe County. (Photo by Matthew L. Niemiller)

Seepage Salamander

Desmognathus aeneus

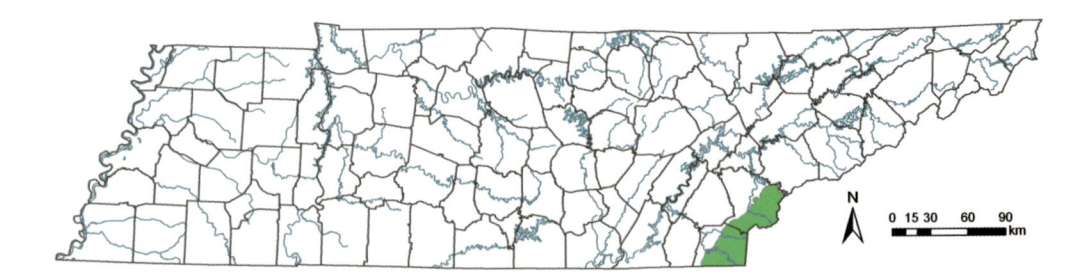

Description: A tiny, slender salamander, the Seepage Salamander can be distinguished from other desmognathine salamanders by its minute size as adults are only 38–64 mm TL. A dark Y-shaped mark is often found between the eyes with a faint mid-dorsal stripe that is usually straight-edged or a series of blotches extending the length of the dorsum onto the tail. This stripe varies in color from yellow to red to brown, and often darker chevrons are present that form a faint herringbone pattern. The dorsal surfaces of the hind limbs often have a light spot present. The venter is light colored and mottled. The tail is round in cross section, not keeled, and slightly shorter than the body. A light stripe runs from the eye to the rear angle of jaw. Costal grooves number 13–14. Nasolabial grooves are present. Four toes are found on the fore limbs and five toes on the hind limbs. The toe pads lack cornifications. Males can be differentiated from females during the breeding season by the small kidney-shaped mental gland under the chin. Larvae are direct developing and hatchlings measure 10–12 mm TL. Juveniles resemble adults. No subspecies are recognized.

Etymology: The specific epithet *aeneus* is Latin for "copper" or "bronze," referring to the color of the dorsum.

Similar Species: Seepage Salamanders can often be differentiated from Pygmy Salamanders (*D. aeneus*) by location; in Tennessee the two species distributions overlap only slightly in northern Monroe County and extreme southern Blount County. In areas where both species are found, the dark sides, smooth top of the head, inconspicuous dorsal herringbone pattern, and a small kidney-shaped mental gland in breeding males can identify Seepage Salamanders. Even experts might have a hard time distinguishing these species, as a museum record from Monroe County remains ambiguous due to an apparent combination of the above traits. Seepage Salamanders also resemble Southern Red-Backed Salamanders (*P. serratus*); however, Southern Red-Backed Salamanders do not have a light stripe running from the eye to the rear angle of the jaw and do not have disproportionately larger hind limbs.

Distribution: Seepage Salamanders occur in the Blue Ridge Mountains of southeastern Tennessee, southwestern North Carolina, and northern Georgia, and highland areas in central Alabama. In Tennessee this species can be readily found in Polk and Monroe counties, with some populations perhaps occurring in Blount County. This species appears to reach its northern limit at the Little Tennessee River.

Habitat: Seepage Salamanders are found in leaf litter in moist forested areas of the southern Blue Ridge Mountains, associated with seepages and small steams. They are more common at low to middle elevations (50–1,350 m), where salamanders are frequently found when surface active by flipping rotten logs, rocks, and other surface debris.

Seepage Salamander adult, Polk County. (Photo by Matthew L. Niemiller)

Natural History: Seepage Salamanders often forage under the leaf litter for invertebrates and rarely emerge onto the surface. Little is known about the timing of the breeding season. Mating apparently occurs in autumn, and nests are often found in and around seepages under mosses or other cover between April and May. Females lay grapelike masses of 6–17 eggs and attend the eggs until they hatch. Females will sometimes aggregate in seepages to nest. Eggs hatch in 6 to 9 weeks, usually from June to early August. Seepage Salamanders lack a true larval feeding stage and develop into juveniles inside the egg. Some individuals might hatch with gills but these are lost within a few days. Sexual maturity is reach in two years. Adults feed on a variety of invertebrates, including earthworms, mites, snails, spiders, and small insects. Predators are unknown but likely include woodland snakes and larger salamanders.

Conservation Status: Seepage Salamanders occur in isolated populations and are restricted by habitat, making them vulnerable to incompatible land management. Current logging practices and habitat loss are the prominent threats to this species in Tennessee. The species is state listed as "Critically Imperiled" and is "Deemed in Need of Management." The Seepage Salamander was once considered as a candidate for listing under the Endangered Species Act but is no longer considered.

George R. Wyckoff and Matthew L. Niemiller

Carolina Mountain Dusky Salamander adult, Cocke County. (Photo by Matthew L. Niemiller)

Carolina Mountain Dusky Salamander

Desmognathus carolinensis

Description: The Carolina Mountain Dusky Salamander is a medium-sized member of the Allegheny Mountain Dusky Salamander (*D. ochrophaeus*) complex, with adults measuring 70–110 mm TL. The tail is round in cross section, longer than the body, and lacks a keel. A light stripe runs from the eye to the rear angle of the jaw. Dorsal coloration is variable but ranges from blotched to striped in varying shades of greenish gray, brown to yellowish brown, or bright to brownish red. As individuals age, they often accrue melanistic deposits making them appear darker in color. Juveniles typically have yellowish to reddish dorsal stripes or blotches.

The venter is usually unmarked and gray to grayish black. Fourteen costal grooves are present and the toe tips are not cornified. Nasolabial grooves are present. Males possess small mental glands. Hatchlings and larvae have five to six pairs of alternating dorsal spots, but these can be faint in some individuals. The snout also is rounded in hatchlings and larvae. Hatchlings measure 13–18 mm TL and have small, whitish gills. No subspecies are recognized.

Etymology: The specific epithet, *carolinensis,* means "belonging to Carolina" and refers to this species' distribution, which is mostly in North Carolina.

Similar Species: A member of the Allegheny Mountain Dusky Salamander (*D. ochrophaeus*) complex, this species closely resembles others in the complex. Identification of species within this complex is generally based on distribution, although individuals from adjacent or overlapping ranges might be extremely difficult to identify without using molecular data. Carolina Mountain Dusky Salamanders can be confused with some species in the genus *Plethodon,* such as Northern Red-Backed Salamanders (*P. cinereus*). However, Carolina Mountain Dusky Salamanders, like all desmognathine salamanders, have larger hind limbs relative to the fore limbs and a light stripe running from the eye to the rear angle of the jaw.

Carolina Mountain Dusky Salamander adult, Cocke County. (Photo by Matthew L. Niemiller)

Distribution: The Carolina Mountain Dusky Salamander is found in west-central North Carolina and adjacent northeast Tennessee. In our state, populations can be found in the Blue Ridge Mountains along the North Carolina border in Cocke, Greene, Unicoi, and Washington counties. The Pigeon River separates Carolina Mountain Dusky Salamanders to the north and Ocoee Salamanders to the south.

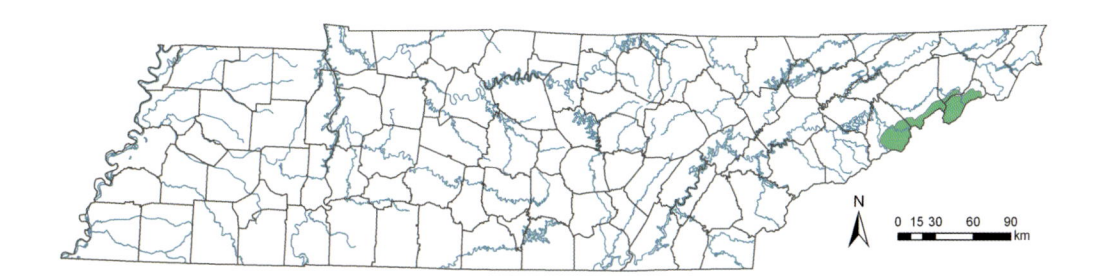

Habitat: Carolina Mountain Dusky Salamanders occur in or near cool streams, springs, seeps, and wet rock faces, and hence are usually found in mountainous areas with plenty of forest cover up to 1,900 m in elevation. They can be common in secondary growth, provided a closed canopy keeps the forest floor moist and some surface water exists. This species is frequently found by turning rocks, logs, leaf mats, and moss near streams, seeps, springs, and other moist areas, though they are occasionally found in the forest litter well away from water. Carolina Mountain Dusky Salamanders are nocturnal and remain hidden during the day. On rainy nights, they can be seen in large numbers moving about the forest floor and around streams.

Natural History: Carolina Mountain Dusky Salamanders are active year round but will retreat underground during especially cold weather. This species presumably mates in summer and females typically deposit 16–26 eggs in small, grapelike clusters in hollowed cavities at or slightly above the water surface beneath rocks, decaying logs, and within or under moss near springs, seeps, and streams in late May to early July. Females guard their nests and eggs hatch within 8–10 weeks. Larvae metamorphose in 2–8 months at 10–12 mm SVL. Adults reach sexual maturity in 3–4 years and live up to 10 years. Carolina Mountain Dusky Salamanders are generalists and feed on a variety of small invertebrates, including beetles, fly larvae, and caterpillars. One adult ate a Weller's Salamander (*Plethodon welleri*). Major predators include woodland birds, snakes, and large salamanders, including Spring Salamanders (*Gyrinophilus porphyriticus*).

Conservation Status: Carolina Mountain Dusky Salamanders are perhaps the most abundant salamanders in appropriate stream and seep habitats. Dozens of individuals can be found in a few minutes of rock turning in and around a small mountain stream. Like most salamanders, clear-cutting, stream siltation and eutrophication, and loss of forest cover will greatly impact populations of this species, which might take decades to recover. Because of their limited distribution in the state, Carolina Mountain Dusky Salamanders are state listed as "Imperiled/Vulnerable."

R. Graham Reynolds and
Matthew L. Niemiller

Spotted Dusky Salamander, Rhea County. (Photo by Matthew L. Niemiller)

Spotted Dusky Salamander

Desmognathus conanti

Description: The Spotted Dusky Salamander is a medium-sized, robust salamander, with adults measuring 60–130 mm TL. The head is relatively flat and broad with large bulging eyes. A distinct light line extends on each side of the head, from the eye to the angle of the jaw. The dorsal ground color is light brown to gray to even black often with the appearance of a relatively uniform, lighter and wavy mid-dorsal stripe extending onto the tail that is red to yellow to brown. However, dorsal patterning is quite variable, depending on the degree of retention of larval spotting. Older individuals often are melanistic. The venter is light to dark gray with apparent mottling. The tail is triangular in cross section anteriorly, while the posterior third is laterally compressed and

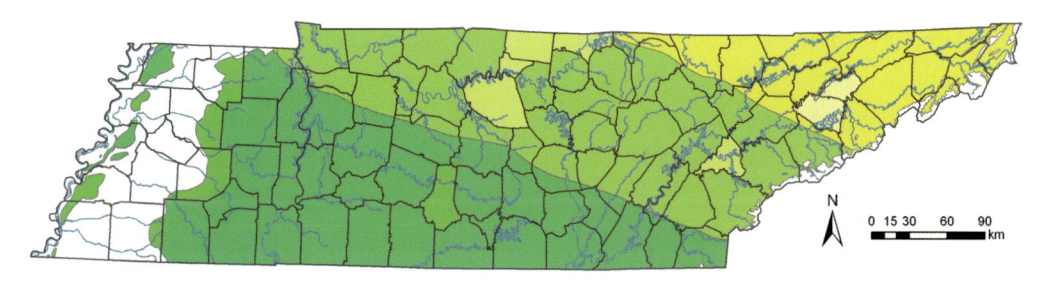

The Spotted Dusky Salamander range is in green, while the Northern Dusky Salamander *(D. fuscus)* range is in yellow. A large contact zone between these two species occurs and is represented by light green and light yellow. See the text for details.

Left: Spotted Dusky Salamander venter, Cumberland County. (Photo by Matthew L. Niemiller) *Right:* Spotted Dusky Salamander female with hatchlings, Franklin County. (Photo by Matthew L. Niemiller)

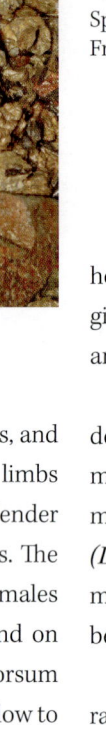

keeled. There are usually 14 costal grooves, and nasolabial grooves are present. The front limbs have four toes and are noticeably more slender than the hind limbs, which have five toes. The toe tips are not cornified. Sexually active males have a small, inconspicuous mental gland on the chin and papillose cloacal lips. The dorsum of hatchlings and small larvae is beige-yellow to light brown with five to eight pairs of even or alternative light spots on the dorsum between the limbs that continue onto the tail. As larvae grow, these spots can fade and coalesce to form a wavy, darker dorsolateral stripe. The gills are white. Hatchlings are 12–20 mm TL. This species was formerly considered a subspecies of the Northern Dusky Salamander (*D. fuscus*). No subspecies are recognized.

Etymology: The specific epithet *conanti* honors Roger Conant, a prominent herpetologist and expert on North American reptiles and amphibians.

Similar Species: Spotted Dusky Salamanders are very similar to Northern Dusky Salamanders (*D. fuscus*), Santeetlah Dusky Salamanders (*D. santeetlah*), and Seal Salamanders (*D. monticola*). See the Northern Dusky Salamander account for characters to distinguish between these species.

Distribution: Spotted Dusky Salamanders range from the Gulf Coast in eastern Louisiana, Mississippi, Alabama, and the panhandle of Florida northward into Georgia, northern Alabama, central and western Tennessee, and western Kentucky. In Tennessee, this species occurs in the western and central part of the state, but a broad contact zone with the Northern Dusky Salamander occurs running northwest to southeast from roughly Clarksville to east of Chattanooga. Distributions of the Dusky Salamanders within this zone remain unclear. Few populations are known from the Nashville Basin.

Habitat: Spotted Dusky Salamanders are found in a variety of habitats within forested areas, including seeps, springs, and in and along small to medium streams. They are rarely found more than a few meters away from water except during rainy weather at night. Individuals are often found within the same small stretch of stream for their entire lives. Juveniles and adults can be found underneath rocks, logs, moss, and other cover during the day.

Natural History: Breeding occurs in both autumn and spring. Females deposit 13–25 eggs in concealed areas in or near a stream, such as underneath rocks or logs, usually in June through August. Eggs are laid in globular or grapelike clusters typically suspended from the ceiling of a cavity or attached to roots, mosses, or other fibers. Females remain with the eggs until they hatch 5–8 weeks later. Larvae metamorphose in 10–13 months. Sexual maturity likely is reached in 3–4 years. Larvae feed on small aquatic invertebrates, while adults and juveniles feed many invertebrates, such as ants, beetles, earthworms, spiders, amphipods, isopods, springtails, and snails. Predators have not been reported but likely include birds, small mammals, snakes, and larger salamanders.

Conservation Status: While secure across its range, many populations are affected by stream degradation and urbanization. Spotted Dusky Salamanders are not listed in Tennessee.

George R. Wyckoff and
Matthew L. Niemiller

Northern Dusky Salamander adult, Carter County. (Photo by Matthew L. Niemiller)

Northern Dusky Salamander

Desmognathus fuscus

Description: The Northern Dusky Salamander is a medium-sized, robust salamander, with adults measuring 60–140 mm TL. The head is relatively flat and broad with large bulging eyes. A distinct light line extends on each side of the head from the eye to the angle of the jaw. The dorsal ground color is light brown to grayish often with the appearance of a relatively uniform, lighter middorsal stripe extending onto the tail. However, dorsal patterning is quite variable depending on the degree of retention of larval spotting. Older individuals often are melanistic. The venter is cream colored with scattered darker melanophores forming a weakly reticulate or "peppered" appearance that becomes more noticeable with age. The tail is triangular in cross section anteriorly, while the posterior

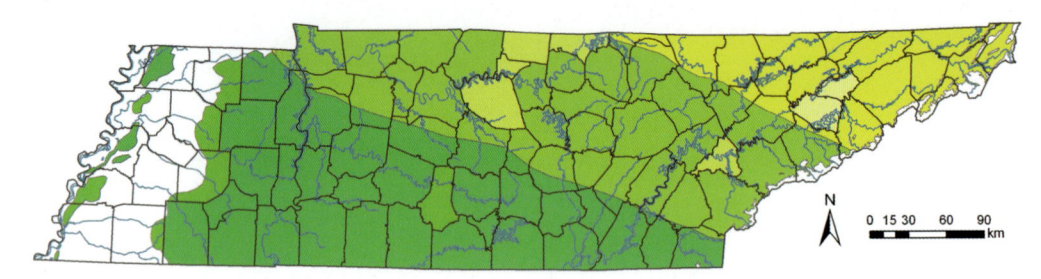

The Northern Dusky Salamander range is in yellow, while the Spotted Dusky Salamander (*D. conanti*) range is in green. A large contact zone between these two species occurs and is represented by light green and light yellow. See the text for details.

third is laterally compressed and keeled. There are usually 14 costal grooves and nasolabial grooves are present. The front limbs have four toes and are noticeably more slender than the hind limbs, which have five toes. The toe tips are not cornified. Sexually active males have a small, inconspicuous mental gland on the chin and papillose cloacal lips. The dorsum of hatchlings and small larvae is beige-yellow to light brown with five to eight pairs of even or alternative light spots on the dorsum between the limbs that continue onto the tail. As larvae grow, these spots often fade and coalesce to form a straight to wavy, darker dorsolateral stripe. The gills are white. Hatchlings are 12–20 mm TL. No subspecies are recognized.

Northern Dusky Salamander larvae, Ohio. (Photo by Carl R. Brune)

Etymology: The specific epithet *fuscus* is Latin, meaning "dark" or "dusky."

Similar Species: Spotted Dusky Salamanders (*Desmognathus conanti*) and Santeetlah Dusky Salamanders (*D. santeetlah*) are morphologically similar to Northern Dusky Salamanders, although with slight coloration differences. Santeetlah Dusky Salamanders are found at higher elevations and have a narrow geographic distribution. Santeetlah Dusky Salamanders have a drab brown to greenish dorsum with inconspicuous dorsolateral stripes, a slightly less keeled tail, and a yellowish wash occurs on the undersurfaces of the limbs and tail. However, hybridization is known to occur between Santeetlah Dusky Salamanders and Northern Dusky Salamanders, making identification of some specimens difficult. Spotted Dusky Salamanders typically have more pronounced red to golden spots and blotches on the dorsum which tend to be more evident in older individuals. However, dorsal patterning and coloration are highly variable in both Northern and Spotted Dusky Salamanders, and there is a large contact zone between the two species in Tennessee. Until a detailed analysis of this contact zone is conducted, it might be almost impossible to distinguish between these two species. Larvae also are nearly impossible to differentiate, although larval Santeetlah Dusky Salamanders tend to have fewer dorsal spots. Seal Salamanders (*D. monticola*) also are similar but are slightly larger as adults, with a boldly patterned dorsum, a distinct separation between the dorsal and ventral coloration, and cornified toe tips. Location is important when differentiating between these four species, though differentiation might not be possible in the contact zone without resorting to molecular methods.

Distribution: Northern Dusky Salamanders range throughout much of northeast North America from Maine and Nova Scotia southwest following the Appalachians into Kentucky, Tennessee, and North Carolina. In Tennessee, this species occurs in the northeastern part of the state but a broad contact zone with the Spotted Dusky Salamander occurs running northwest to southeast from roughly Clarksville to east of Chattanooga.

Habitat: Northern Dusky Salamanders are found in a variety of habitats within forested areas, including seeps, springs, and in and along small to medium streams generally below 1,200 m. They are rarely found more than a few meters away from water at lower elevations, except during rainy weather at night. Individuals are often found within the same small stretch of stream for their entire lives. Juveniles and adults can be found underneath rocks, logs, moss, and other cover during the day.

Natural History: Breeding occurs in both autumn and spring. Females deposit 22–33 eggs in concealed areas in or near a stream, usually from June to late August. Eggs are laid in globular or grapelike clusters typically suspended from the ceiling of a cavity or attached to roots, mosses, or other fibers. Females remain with eggs until they hatch 6–8 weeks later. Larvae metamorphose in 10–12 months. Sexual maturity is reached in 3–4 years. Larvae feed on small aquatic invertebrates, while adults and juveniles feed on terrestrial, semiterrestrial, and aquatic invertebrates, such as ants, beetles, earthworms, spiders, amphipods, and snails. Predators include watersnakes, gartersnakes, Spring Salamanders (*Gyrinophilus porphyriticus*), Black-Bellied Salamanders (*D. quadramaculatus*), and likely raccoons, skunks, and birds.

Conservation Status: Northern Dusky Salamanders are also commonly collected for fishing bait. Stream disturbance is the primary threat to the species. Currently the species is listed as secure and not in need of additional conservation measures.

George R. Wyckoff and
Matthew L. Niemiller

Imitator Salamander adult, Sevier County. (Photo by Nathan Haislip)

Imitator Salamander

Desmognathus imitator

Description: The Imitator Salamander is a medium-sized member of the Allegheny Mountain Dusky Salamander (*D. ochrophaeus*) complex, with adults measuring 70–110 mm TL. The tail is round in cross section, slightly longer than the length of the body, and is unkeeled. A light stripe runs from the eye to the rear angle of the jaw. Dorsal coloration and patterning is highly variable. The dorsum of adults often is a wavy dorsolateral stripe that can be varying shades of brown, yellow, and red. Prominent yellow, orange, or red patches are often present on the cheeks and sometimes on the upper surfaces of the legs that mimic the coloration found in Jordan's Red-Cheeked Salamanders (*Plethodon jordani*). However, some individuals lack these embellishments, while older individuals often are melanistic. The venter is usually unmarked and becomes light gray to grayish black with age. Fourteen costal grooves are present and the toe tips are not cornified.

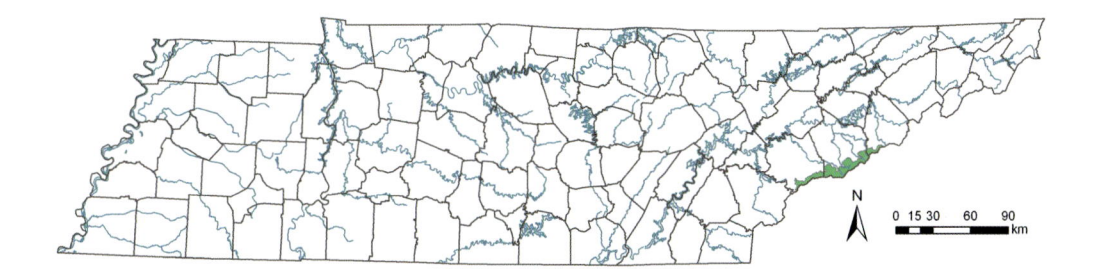

Left: Imitator Salamander adult, Sevier County. (Photo by Matthew L. Niemiller) *Right:* Imitator Salamander larva, Sevier County. (Photo by Matthew L. Niemiller)

Nasolabial grooves are present. Males possess small mental glands. Hatchlings and larvae typically have a dark ground color with distinct alternating orange to chestnut spots on the dorsum, rounded snouts, and white gills. Hatchlings measure 13–18 mm TL. No subspecies are recognized.

Etymology: The specific epithet, *imitator,* is Latin for "one who mimics," which of course refers to the color similarity and purported mimicry in this species of the unpalatable Jordan's Red-Cheeked Salamander (*Plethodon jordani*).

Similar Species: As a member of the Allegheny Mountain Dusky Salamander (*D. ochrophaeus*) complex, this species closely resembles other species in the complex. Identification of species within this complex is generally based on distribution, although individuals from adjacent or overlapping ranges might be extremely difficult to identify without using molecular data. Ocoee Salamanders are easily confused with dark phase Imitator Salamanders that lack obvious cheek spots in the Smoky Mountains; however, Ocoee Salamanders typically have straight-edged dorsal stripes, whereas Imitator Salamanders do not. In addition, where the two species co-occur above 900 m elevation, Ocoee Salamanders are generally confined to more terrestrial habitats, while Imitator Salamanders are more common closer to streams and seeps. In areas where Jordan's Red-Cheeked Salamander occurs, Imitator Salamanders can be found with red or yellow cheek patches. Although very similar in coloration, Imitator Salamanders can quickly be distinguished from Jordan's Red-Cheeked Salamanders by their larger hind limbs.

Distribution: The Imitator Salamander is narrowly distributed in western North Carolina and east-central Tennessee along the Smoky and Balsam mountains, with the majority of the range contained within the Great Smoky Mountains National Park.

Habitat: Imitator Salamanders are common in seeps, wet rock faces and on the forest floor in vicinity of water (streams and seeps) at higher elevations of 900–2,020 m. Both adults and juveniles typically are found under surface cover such as rocks and logs in forested areas. Salamanders can be found on the forest floor at night during favorable weather in large numbers and are most active on the surface in summer. Larvae are common in small seeps and streams at higher elevations in Great Smoky Mountains National Park.

Natural History: Imitator Salamanders imitate members of the noxious Red-Cheeked Salamander (*P. jordani*) complex. Jordan's Red-Cheeked Salamander has noxious skin secretions that serve to deter predation and bright red patches on their cheeks that warn predators that they are not palatable. Imitator Salamanders, on the other hand, are perfectly tasty salamanders as far as predators are concerned, but if they appear similar to the *Plethodon* then predators might leave them alone. This is thought to be an example of classical Batesian mimicry, where a palatable species imitates a noxious one in order to gain safety from predators.

Not much is known about the reproductive biology of the Imitator Salamander. Imitator Salamanders probably mate from late spring to autumn, and females typically deposit 13–30 eggs in hollowed cavities at or slightly above the water surface beneath rocks and decaying logs near springs, seeps, and streams during June and July. Females guard their nests and eggs probably hatch within 8–10 weeks. Length of the larval period is unknown but probably isn't more than one year. Adults probably reach sexual maturity in 3–4 years and live up to 10 years. Imitator Salamanders likely are generalists and feed on a variety of small invertebrates. Major predators include birds, snakes, small mammals, and large salamanders, including Spring Salamanders (*Gyrinophilus porphyriticus*) and Black-Bellied Salamanders (*D. quadramaculatus*).

Conservation Status: Since most populations of Imitator Salamanders occur within the Great Smoky Mountains National Park, it is thought that they are more or less protected from the destructive human activities that affect other populations of salamanders. However, the park is not immune to all activities, especially air pollution and climate change.

R. Graham Reynolds and
Matthew L. Niemiller

Shovel-Nosed Salamander adult, Blount County. (Photo by Matthew L. Niemiller)

Shovel-Nosed Salamander

Desmognathus marmoratus

Description: The Shovel-Nosed Salamander is a medium-sized salamander (80–152 mm adult TL) with a head that is relatively flat, tapering from a greatest height behind the eyes to the lowest point at the tip of the snout (hence shovel-nosed). The eyes are large and bulging. As with most species of *Desmognathus,* a pale line or spot occurs on the side of the head, located just behind the eye and extending to the angle of the jaw. The ground color of the dorsum and sides in juveniles and adults are various shades of brown or black, with two rows of irregularly shaped yellow, red, or gray blotches. The paler colored blotches on the dark background is reminiscent of marble. A white spot typically demarcates each lateral line pore of the trunk; consequently, many individuals have two rows of small white spots on each side of the body, one row where the dorsum meets the

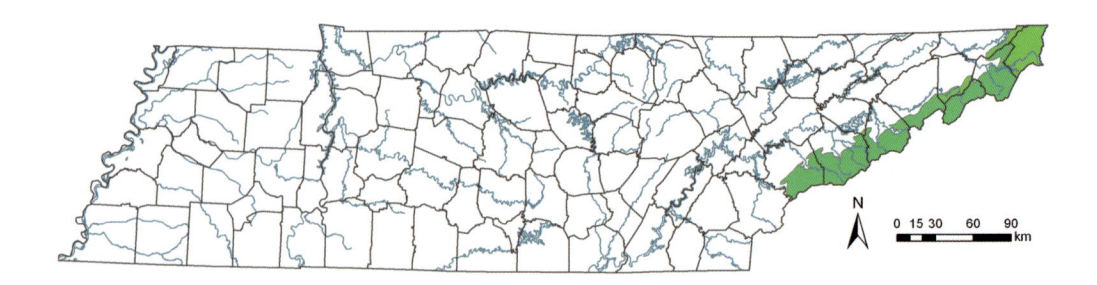

Left: Shovel-Nosed Salamander adult showing slope of snout, Blount County. (Photo by Matthew L. Niemiller) *Right:* Shovel-Nosed Salamander larva, Lumpkin County, Georgia. (Photo by Matthew L. Niemiller)

sides and the other row near where the sides meet the venter. The ground color of the venter is white or pale yellow in young salamanders but darkens with age to gray or black as pigment cells migrate into this region. There are usually 14 costal grooves and nasolabial grooves are present. The tail is laterally compressed with a dorsal keel. The front limbs are slender with four toes, whereas the hind limbs are stouter than the front limbs and have five toes. The tip of each toe is cornified and usually heavily pigmented, appearing black. The paired internal nares appear as slits, rather than circular pores. Adults typically have five or fewer vomerine teeth, and often they lack vomerine teeth entirely. The sexes look similar, but a series of morphological features can be used to distinguish males from females. For example, compared to females, males grow larger and have wider heads, larger teeth on the upper jaw, and a rougher surface to the lining of the cloacal vent. The dorsum of hatchlings and small larvae is beige-yellow to pale brown; two longitudinal rows of lighter colored flecks or spots occur on the sides. The overall coloration darkens as the larvae age. Larger larvae have cornified toe tips.

The gills are bright white. Hatchlings measure 10–12 mm SVL. No subspecies are recognized.

Etymology: The specific epithet *marmoratus* is Latin, meaning "marbled," and refers to the dorsal pattern of this species.

Similar Species: Shovel-Nosed Salamanders are closely related to and strongly resemble Black-Bellied Salamanders (*D. quadramaculatus*). Hatchlings and larvae of these two species are nearly indistinguishable from each other. Adults can also be difficult to distinguish, but the shape of internal nares (slit-like in Shovel-Nosed Salamanders versus round in Black-Bellied Salamanders) is useful in species identification. Unfortunately, the internal nares are difficult to view in living salamanders. The coloration of the abdomen can also be used: the venter of adult Black-Bellied Salamanders usually is an intense black, whereas in Shovel-Nosed Salamanders the venter is usually dark gray (never intense black). This characteristic is subjective, particularly when salamanders from different regions are compared. Furthermore, the systematics of these species is in a state of flux and additional species are likely to be described, further complicating identification of dark-bellied desmognathine salamanders in eastern Tennessee.

Distribution: Shovel-Nosed Salamanders range within the Blue Ridge Mountains from southwestern Virginia south and west into western North Carolina, eastern Tennessee, northeastern Georgia, and extreme northwestern South Carolina. In Tennessee, this species occurs in all of the counties bordering North Carolina except Monroe and Polk counties.

Habitat: Shovel-Nosed Salamanders typically inhabit second- and third-order woodland streams but are also found in some low-gradient, low-order streams at elevations of 300–1,680 m. Hatchlings are poor swimmers and are often washed downstream into areas with low current. They seek refuge in the interstices of the rock substrate, at least during daylight. Following metamorphosis, juveniles and adults remain in the streams, particularly in the riffle areas with high current and little silt, where they hide beneath rocks during the day. Adults occasionally wander a few meters from the streams during rainy nights and have been reported to climb creekside vegetation, but streamside terrestrial regions are not a significant aspect of Shovel-Nosed Salamander habitat.

Natural History: The Shovel-Nosed Salamander is the most aquatic of the desmognathine species and all life stages are aquatic. Breeding activities are poorly documented in Tennessee but likely do not differ significantly from that reported in neighboring states. Females lay eggs from late spring to early summer. The number of eggs a female lays is associated with her body size—larger females lay more eggs than smaller females. The eggs are white (unpigmented) and are attached to the undersurface of rocks in flowing water. Reported clutch size ranges from 20 to 65 eggs. Females remain with their eggs through hatching 10–12 weeks after oviposition, and hatchlings are found in the streams from August to late September. Hatchling and larval Shovel-Nosed Salamanders are opportunistic in feeding and eat a variety of aquatic invertebrate prey, including zooplankton and the larvae of stoneflies, mayflies, caddisflies, and beetles. Metamorphosis occurs when larvae are 26–38 mm TL. Sexual maturity is reached in 4–5 years. Juveniles and adults are also opportunistic in feeding and eat most invertebrates that they encounter, including worms, snails, crustaceans, millipedes, arachnids, and insects. Salamanders have also been found in the stomachs of Shovel-Nosed Salamanders. Interestingly, most metamorphosed salamanders that feed in water use suction feeding to capture prey; however, metamorphosed Shovel-Nosed Salamanders project their tongue to capture prey, even in water. Predation has seldom been reported, but predators likely include other salamanders, frogs, fishes, crayfish, snakes, birds, and mammals.

Conservation Status: Shovel-Nosed Salamanders are associated with well-oxygenated fast-flowing streams with rocky substrates. Consequently, this species is vulnerable to factors that degrade stream quality, including modifications to the terrestrial habitat that could result in increase siltation, decrease in aquatic insect community, or decrease in flow. Dams have eliminated populations from some regions, and chemical runoff has been found to be responsible for loss of other populations.

Brian T. Miller

Seal Salamander adult, Blount County. (Photo by Matthew L. Niemiller)

Seal Salamander

Desmognathus monticola

Description: The Seal Salamander is a medium-sized, robust salamander, with adults measuring 75–150 mm TL. The head is relatively flat and broad with large bulging eyes. A distinct light line extends on each side of the head from the eye to the angle of the jaw. The dorsal ground color is light brown to grayish often with darker wormlike markings, mottling, or reticulations, yet in some populations the dorsal patterning is reduced or absent. The venter is pale to whitish in younger individuals but can turn to light gray in older individuals without any discernable mottling. The demarcation from dorsal to ventral coloration is often distinct. A row of white spots often is present along the sides between the limbs. The tail is rounded anteriorly, while the posterior two-thirds is laterally compressed

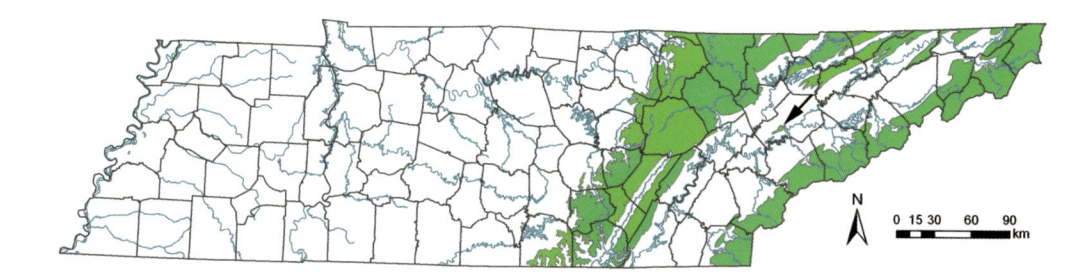

Left: Seal Salamander adult, Morgan County. (Photo by Matthew L. Niemiller) *Right:* Seal Salamander larva, Polk County. (Photo by Matthew L. Niemiller)

and keeled. There are usually 14 costal grooves and nasolabial grooves are present. The front limbs have four toes and are noticeably more slender than the hind limbs, which have five toes. The tip of each toe is heavily pigmented black and cornified. Sexually active males have an inconspicuous mental gland on the chin and papillose cloacal lips. The dorsum of hatchlings and small larvae is beige-yellow to pale brown with four to five pairs of light spots typically red in color on the dorsum between the limbs. As larvae grow, these spots often fade and coalesce into reticulate dorsal patterning found in adults. Larger larvae have cornified toe tips. The gills are white. Hatchlings are 11–12 mm SVL. No subspecies are recognized.

Etymology: The specific epithet, *monticola,* is Latin for "mountain dweller," referencing the fact that this species is often found in the mountains.

Similar Species: Seal Salamanders can be confused with several other species of *Desmognathus* salamanders, including Spotted Dusky Salamanders (*D. conanti*), Northern Dusky Salamanders (*D. fuscus*), Santeetlah Dusky Salamanders (*D. santeetlah*), Ocoee Salamanders (*D. ocoee*), Black-Bellied Salamanders (*D. quadramaculatus*), Shovel-Nosed Salamanders (*D. marmoratus*), and Black Mountain Dusky Salamanders (*D. welteri*). Spotted Dusky, Northern Dusky, Santeetlah Dusky, and Ocoee Salamanders all lack cornified toe tips, typically do not have a distinct demarcation between the dorsal and ventral coloration along the sides, and have mottled venters. Black-Bellied and Shovel-Nosed Salamanders have cornified toe tips but have much darker venters. The Black Mountain Dusky Salamander also has cornified toe tips but has a stippled venter and lacks a distinct demarcation between the dorsal and ventral coloration. Larval *Desmognathus* can be very difficult to tell apart. Larval Black-Bellied and Shovel-Nosed Salamanders do not have reddish spots on the dorsum.

Distribution: Seal Salamanders range throughout the Appalachian Highlands from southwestern Pennsylvania southwest to central Alabama. In Tennessee, this species is found in the Blue Ridge Mountains, Cumberland Mountains, and scattered localities along the Cumberland Plateau.

Habitat: Seal Salamanders are associated with small to medium fishless streams, springs, and seeps in mesic, hardwood forests generally below 1,500 m. Adults and juveniles can be found under cover adjacent to aquatic habitats, such as rocks, logs, and moss during the day, but can be found out on the surface on moist, humid nights. Seal Salamanders have been found climbing trees up to 1–2 m high while foraging.

Natural History: Breeding occurs in autumn and spring. Females lay 13–39 eggs typically attached as a monolayer to the undersurfaces of rocks or moss or in loose groups. Nests have been found in seepages, streambeds, and leaf clumps. Females brood eggs until hatching 4–8 weeks later. Larvae typically overwinter and metamorphose in spring to early summer 8–13 months later. Sexual maturity is reached at 4–7 years, and some individuals are known to live at least 11 years. Larvae probably feed on aquatic invertebrates, while juveniles and adults feed on a variety of aquatic and terrestrial invertebrates, such as millipedes, ants, flies, and beetles, and occasionally other salamanders. Predators have not been studied but presumably include larger salamanders, woodland snakes, small mammals, and birds. Seal Salamanders defend territories from other conspecifics.

Conservation Status: Most populations appear stable in Tennessee, but some are threatened by overcollection for fish bait and incompatible silviculture techniques, such as clear-cutting or timber harvesting.

George R. Wyckoff and
Matthew L. Niemiller

Allegheny Mountain Dusky Salamander adult, Morgan County. (Photo by Matthew L. Niemiller)

Allegheny Mountain Dusky Salamander

Desmognathus ochrophaeus

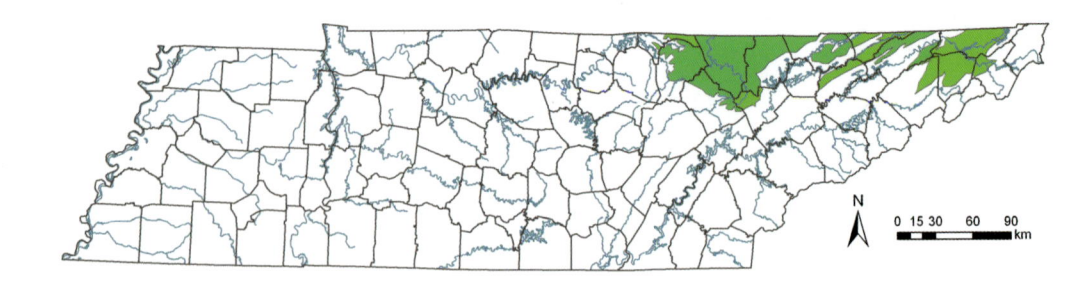

Description: The Allegheny Mountain Dusky Salamander is a medium-sized member of the Allegheny Mountain Dusky Salamander complex, with adults measuring 70–110 mm TL. The tail is round in cross section. A light stripe runs from the eye to the rear angle of the jaw. Dorsal coloration and patterning is highly variable. The dorsum of adults is typically brown in coloration and either a brownish, yellowish, or reddish straight-edged stripe or wavy, blotched patterning; however, most individuals have a straight-edged stripe that often encloses dark spots. Some individuals develop a row of chevron-shaped patches running along the dorsum. The venter lacks mottling and becomes light gray to grayish black with age. Fourteen costal grooves are present and the toe tips are not cornified. Nasolabial grooves are present. Males possess small mental glands. Hatchlings and larvae typically are dark with straight dorsolateral stripes and either lack the alternating spots found in other species in the complex or have them confined to the posterior region of the trunk. Hatchlings are 13–18 mm TL. Larvae also have rounded snouts and white gills. No subspecies are recognized.

Etymology: The specific epithet, *ochrophaeus*, is from the Greek *ochros* "yellow" and *phaeos* "light." This is in reference to the bright coloration of some individuals of this species.

Similar Species: A member of the Allegheny Mountain Dusky Salamander complex, this species closely resembles others in this group. Identification of species within this complex is generally based on distribution, although individuals from adjacent or overlapping ranges might be extremely difficult to identify without using molecular data. Allegheny Mountain Dusky Salamanders closely resemble Cumberland Dusky Salamanders (*D. abditus*) and might hybridize in Morgan County. The Cumberland Dusky Salamander differs from the Allegheny Mountain Dusky Salamander by having a dorsal pattern in which the positions of larval spots are nearly always evident in adults. In addition, the dorsal pattern of the Allegheny Mountain Dusky Salamander consists of nearly straight-edged dorsolateral stripes and indistinct larval spots with reddish or yellowish pigmentation not necessarily confined to the distinct larval spots.

Allegheny Mountain Dusky Salamander juvenile, Morgan County. (Photo by Matthew L. Niemiller)

Distribution: The Allegheny Mountain Dusky Salamander occurs in highland areas from the Adirondack Mountains in Quebec, Canada, southward to southwest Virginia and Tennessee. In Tennessee, this species is confined to northern sections of the Cumberland Plateau, the Cumberland Mountains, and the northern Ridge and Valley. However, the extent of its range in Tennessee is poorly delineated. The Allegheny Mountain Dusky Salamanders hybridizes with the Cumberland Dusky Salamander (*D. abditus*) around Frozen Head State Park in Morgan County.

Habitat: Allegheny Mountain Dusky Salamanders are common in and around seeps, first-order streams, and wet rock faces in hardwood forests. However, some individuals can be found underneath cover far away from water at higher elevations. Adults and juveniles are found in the same habitat typically underneath rocks and fallen logs during the day. Salamanders can be found on the forest floor at night during favorable weather and are most active on the surface in summer.

Natural History: Allegheny Mountain Dusky Salamanders mate from late spring to autumn and females typically deposit 8–37 eggs in late spring to early summer in small, grapelike clusters in crevices and cavities beneath rocks and decaying logs sometimes a considerable distance from water. Females guard their nests, and eggs hatch within 8–10 weeks. However, females are known to cannibalize their own eggs. Larvae typically inhabit seeps and pools in streams. The larval period is dependent upon on timing of oviposition and hydroperiod and is therefore quite variable, ranging from 2 weeks to up to 8 months. Males and females reach sexual maturity in 3–4 years and are known to live up to 20 years in captivity. Allegheny Mountain Dusky Salamanders feed on a variety of prey, including earthworms, snails, mites, and several orders of insects. Major predators include birds, snakes, and large salamanders, including Spring Salamanders (*Gyrinophilus porphyriticus*), Seal Salamanders (*D. monticola*), and Black Mountain Dusky Salamanders (*D. welteri*).

Conservation Status: Allegheny Mountain Dusky Salamanders are one of the most common salamanders throughout Appalachian Mountains and are in minimal need of protection. However, isolated populations should be monitored.

Matthew L. Niemiller

Ocoee Salamander adult, Monroe County. (Photo by Matthew L. Niemiller)

Ocoee Salamander

Desmognathus ocoee

Description: The Ocoee Salamander is a medium-sized member of the Allegheny Mountain Dusky Salamander (*D. ochrophaeus*) complex, with adults measuring 70–110 mm TL. The tail is round to triangular in cross section but might exhibit a low but distinct keel, especially toward the tail tip. A pale stripe runs from the eye to the rear angle of the jaw. Dorsal coloration and patterning is highly variable. The dorsum of adults is typically brown in coloration and shows evidence of four to six pairs of larval spots between the limbs that fuse to varying degrees with age to form a wavy to straight-edged dorsal stripe that also varies in color from brown to grayish green to yellow and red. Juveniles typically have red to brown, wavy dorsal stripes. The venter is usually unmarked and becomes light gray to

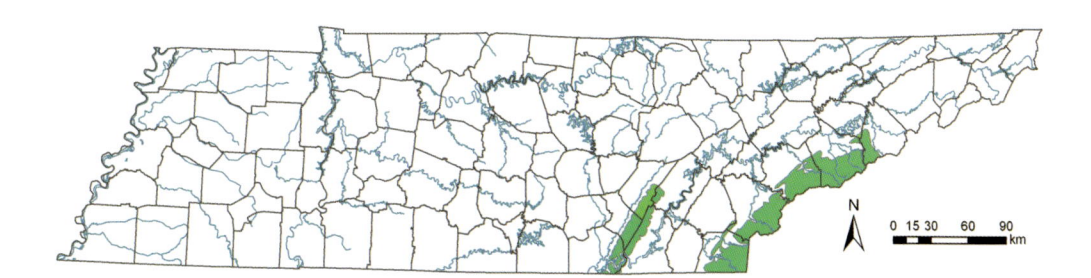

Left: Ocoee Salamander adult, Sevier County. (Photo by Matthew L. Niemiller) *Right:* Ocoee Salamander larva, Rhea County. (Photo by Matthew L. Niemiller)

grayish black with age. Fourteen costal grooves are present and the toe tips are not cornified. Nasolabial grooves are present. Males possess small mental glands. Hatchlings and larvae typically are dark with four to seven alternative light spots on the dorsum, have rounded snouts, and white gills. Hatchlings measure 13–18 mm TL. However, at least some larvae in the Smoky Mountains have the stripe patterning of adults. No subspecies are recognized.

Etymology: The specific epithet, *ocoee*, refers to the discovery of this species in the Ocoee Gorge in Polk County, Tennessee.

Similar Species: A member of the Allegheny Mountain Dusky Salamander (*D. ochrophaeus*) complex, this species closely resembles other species in the complex. Identification of species within this complex is generally based on distribution, although individuals from adjacent or overlapping ranges might be extremely difficult to identify without using molecular data. Ocoee Salamanders closely resemble Cumberland Dusky Salamanders and might hybridize along the northern extent of Walden's Ridge. Adult Cumberland Dusky Salamanders typically have a dorsal pattern in which the positions of larval spots are nearly always evident, whereas larval spotting is obscured by ontogenetic darkening in Ocoee Salamanders. In addition, the tails of Ocoee Salamanders on Walden's Ridge have a low but distinct keel, especially toward the tip of the tail, whereas Cumberland Dusky Salamanders lack a keel. Ocoee Salamanders are also easily confused with dark phase Imitator Salamanders (*D. imitator*) that lack obvious cheek spots in the Smoky Mountains; however, Ocoee Salamanders typically have straight-edged dorsal stripes, whereas Imitator Salamanders do not. In addition, where the two species co-occur above 900 m elevation, Ocoee Salamanders are generally confined to more terrestrial habitats. Ocoee Salamanders also can be confused with melanistic Santeetlah Dusky (*D. santeetlah*) and Spotted Dusky Salamanders (*D. conanti*). Santeetlah Dusky Salamanders usually have a yellow wash on the undersurfaces of the limbs and tail that is absent in Ocoee Salamanders. The venter of Spotted Dusky Salamanders usually is not very dark gray to black and often has a salt-and-pepper appearance. Additionally, Ocoee Salamanders typically occur at higher elevations than Spotted Dusky Salamanders.

Distribution: Ocoee Salamanders occur in two allopatric regions: a larger area in the southwestern Blue Ridge Mountains and adjacent Piedmont physiographic provinces and a smaller region to the west in the southern Cumberland Plateau in northeastern Alabama and south-central Tennessee. In Tennessee, the main region includes high-elevation populations in the Balsam, Great Smoky, and Unicoi mountains south of the Pigeon River as well as lower elevation populations in the Hiwassee and Ocoee river gorges. This region lies in Cocke, Sevier, Blount, Monroe, and Polk counties. This second region includes populations on the southern section of Walden Ridge of the Cumberland Plateau from Hamilton, Marion, Rhea, and Sequatchie counties.

Habitat: Ocoee Salamanders are common in seeps, wet rock faces, and on the forest floor in vicinity of water (streams and seeps) at higher elevations typically under surface cover such as rocks and logs. At lower elevations, Ocoee Salamanders are more abundant in the vicinity of streams and seeps in hardwood forests. This species occupies a greater elevational span than any other *Desmognathus* species. Within Great Smoky Mountains National Park, Ocoee Salamanders are found most often at elevations above 1,400 m but also occupy the lower elevation gorges of the Ocoee and Hiwassee rivers. Adults and juveniles are found in the same habitat typically underneath rocks and fallen logs during the day in forested areas. Salamanders can be found on the forest floor at night during favorable weather and are most active on the surface in summer.

Natural History: Ocoee Salamanders mate from late spring to autumn and females typically deposit 8–20 eggs in small, grapelike clusters in hollowed cavities at or slightly above the water surface beneath rocks and decaying logs near springs, seeps, and streams in July through early September. Females guard their nests and eggs hatch within 8–10 weeks, though females are known to cannibalize their own eggs as well as conspecific hatchlings. Larvae metamorphose in 9–10 months at 11–15 mm SVL. Males and females reach sexual maturity in 3–4 years and live up to 10 years. Ocoee Salamanders are generalists and feed on a variety of small invertebrates. Major predators include birds, snakes, and large salamanders, including Spring Salamanders (*Gyrinophilus porphyriticus*), Black-Bellied Salamanders (*D. quadramaculatus*), and Seal Salamanders (*D. monticola*).

Conservation Status: Ocoee Salamanders are one of the most common salamanders in the Southern Appalachians, though populations associated with Cumberland Plateau have not been studied in depth and merit attention. This species seems fairly resilient to logging operations.

Matthew L. Niemiller and
R. Graham Reynolds

Blue Ridge Dusky Salamander adult, Carter County. (Photo by Matthew L. Niemiller)

Blue Ridge Dusky Salamander

Desmognathus orestes

Description: The Blue Ridge Dusky Salamander is a medium-sized member of the Allegheny Mountain Dusky Salamander (*D. ochrophaeus*) complex, with adults measuring 70–110 mm TL. The tail is round in cross section, longer than the body, and lacks a keel. A pale stripe runs from the eye to the rear angle of the jaw. Dorsal coloration is highly variable but ranges from a straight-edged stripe to wavy blotches in varying shades of brown, yellow, and red. As individuals age, they often accrue melanistic deposits, making them appear darker in color. The venter is usually unmarked and gray to grayish black. Fourteen costal grooves are present and the toe tips are not cornified. Nasolabial grooves are present. Males possess small mental glands. Hatchlings and larvae have not been described, but hatchlings likely measure

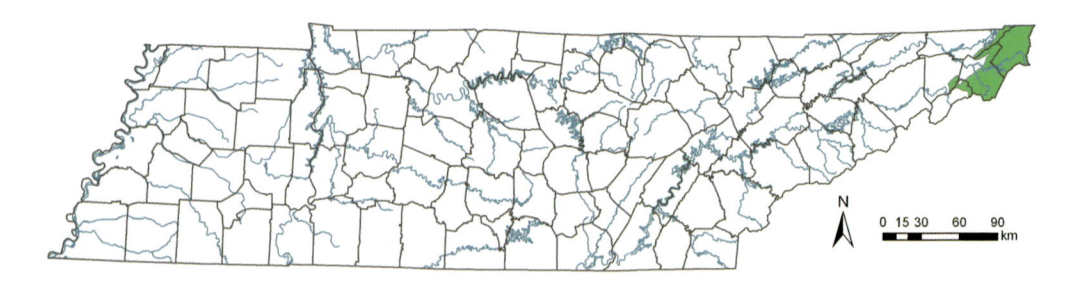

13–18 mm TL and have small, whitish gills. No subspecies are recognized.

Etymology: The specific epithet, *orestes,* honors the mythological Greek character Orestes, who was the son of Agamemnon and a mountaineer.

Similar Species: A member of the Allegheny Mountain Dusky Salamander (*D. ochrophaeus*) complex, this species closely resembles others in the complex. Identification of species within this complex is generally based on distribution, although individuals from adjacent or overlapping ranges might be extremely difficult to identify without using molecular data. Blue Ridge Dusky Salamanders can be confused with some species in the genus *Plethodon,* such as Northern Red-Backed Salamanders (*P. cinereus*). However, Blue Ridge Dusky Salamanders, like all desmognathine salamanders, have larger hind limbs relative to the fore limbs and a light stripe running from the eye to the rear angle of the jaw.

Distribution: The Blue Ridge Dusky Salamander occurs in the Blue Ridge Mountains of southwestern Virginia, northeastern Tennessee, and northwestern North Carolina. In Tennessee, this species is found east of Greeneville in Washington, Sullivan, Unicoi, Carter, and Johnson counties, where it can be locally abundant. We have found very dense populations in the Cherokee National Forest near the Appalachian Trail in Unicoi County, usually near or in small mountain springs.

Habitat: Blue Ridge Dusky Salamanders are associated with wet rock faces, seeps, springs, and forest floor habitats in the vicinity of first-order streams in mountainous, forested areas. They can be common in secondary growth,

Blue Ridge Dusky Salamander adult, Carter County. (Photo by Matthew L. Niemiller)

provided a closed canopy keeps the forest floor moist and some surface water exists. They are frequently found by turning rocks, logs, leaf mats, and moss near streams, seeps, springs, and other moist areas, although they are occasionally found in the forest litter well away from water. Blue Ridge Dusky Salamanders are nocturnal and remain hidden during the day. On rainy nights, they can be seen in large numbers moving about the forest floor and around streams.

Natural History: Blue Ridge Dusky Salamanders are active year round but will retreat underground during especially cold weather. This species mates from late spring through early autumn and females typically deposit 14–16 eggs in small, grapelike clusters in hollowed cavities at or slightly above the water surface beneath rocks, decaying logs, and within or under moss near springs, seeps, and streams in late May to early July. Females guard their nests and eggs hatch within 8 weeks. Larvae metamorphose in 8–9 months at 10–12 mm SVL. Adults reach sexual maturity in 3–5 years and live up to 10 years. No information is available on the diet of Blue Ridge Dusky Salamanders, but this species likely is a generalist feeder consuming a variety of small invertebrates. Few predators have been documented but likely include woodland birds, snakes, small mammals, and larger salamanders.

Conservation Status: Blue Ridge Dusky Salamanders are generally abundant in good forest habitat, but they are sensitive to disturbance. Like most salamanders, clear-cutting, stream siltation and eutrophication, and loss of forest cover will greatly impact populations of this species, which might take decades to recover.

R. Graham Reynolds and Matthew L. Niemiller

Northern Pygmy Salamander adult, Carter County. (Photo by Matthew L. Niemiller)

Northern Pygmy Salamander

Desmognathus organi

Description: The Northern Pygmy Salamander is a tiny woodland salamander distinguished by its small size and brown to bronze dorsal stripe, marked with a dark herringbone or chevron pattern down the midline of the dorsum. Adults typically measure just 40–60 mm TL and have a tail that is shorter than the body and round in cross section. Females have longer tails relative to body length than males. The dorsal surface of the head and snout are wrinkled, and the eyelids are often coppery in color. The venter is tan and unmottled. A light stripe runs from the eye to the rear angle of jaw. Costal grooves number

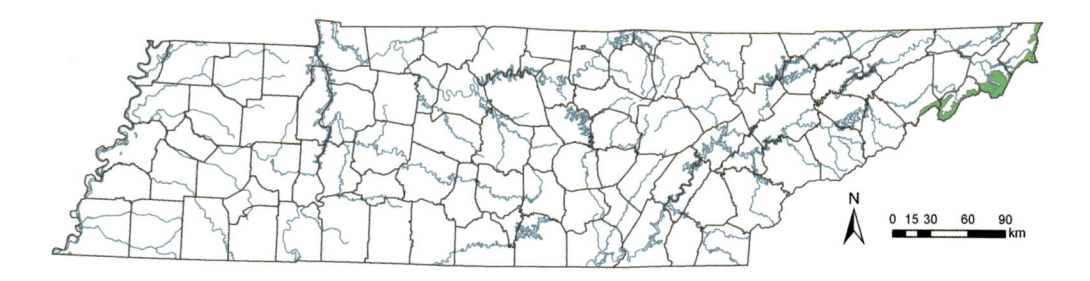

13–14. Nasolabial grooves are present. Four toes are found on the fore limbs and five toes on the hind limbs. The toe pads lack cornifications. There is not an aquatic larvae stage and 10–11 mm TL hatchlings have four to five pairs of light dorsal spots and very short tails. The gills are lost either before or within a few days of hatching. Juveniles resemble adults. Sexually active males can be differentiated during the breeding season by the presence of a U-shaped mental gland under the chin. No subspecies are recognized.

Etymology: The specific epithet, *organi*, honors James Organ, who wrote the first article describing the life history of populations of this species in 1961.

Similar Species: The Northern Pygmy Salamander is nearly indistinguishable from the Pygmy Salamander and is best distinguished by range. Both male and female Northern Pygmy Salamanders tend to be larger and have broader heads than Pygmy Salamanders. Northern Pygmy Salamanders are sympatric with Carolina Mountain Dusky Salamanders (*D. carolinensis*) and Blue Ridge Dusky Salamanders (*D. orestes*) but can be distinguished from juveniles of the these two species by their smaller body size, more rounded tails, and tails that are shorter than their body length.

Distribution: Characterized as a high-elevation species of hardwood and spruce-fir forests, Northern Pygmy Salamanders are distributed in the Blue Ridge Mountains north of the French Broad River in Unicoi, Greene, and Carter counties.

Habitat: Northern Pygmy Salamanders are the most terrestrial of *Desmognathus* species and are often found far from water. This species is generally associated with high-elevation spruce-fir forests generally above 1,100 m in elevation, although many populations are found in mature cove forests at lower elevations. Denizens of the forest floor, Northern Pygmy Salamanders readily climb vegetation when foraging. They may be located on humid nights in the leaf litter or on the bases of trees, or during the day beneath logs or stones. Heavily rotten logs with plenty of moisture seem to be a favorite refuge.

Natural History: Northern Pygmy Salamanders breed during autumn and spring, although little is know about nesting habits. Adults can be found on the forest floor from late spring through autumn but move underground in aggregations in winter. Females nesting away from water presumably nest in underground retreats. Females lay 3–10 eggs in a grape-like cluster in underground cavities in late summer. Females guard the eggs until hatching. Embryos are direct developing and hatch without entering a larval feeding stage. Hatchlings emerge from the egg as miniature versions of adults, though some hatchlings may have gills that are quickly lost. Sexually maturity is reached in 4–5 years. When foraging Northern Pygmy Salamanders are often found climbing vegetation to avoid larger predatory salamanders. This species is the most recent to be described in Tennessee.

Conservation Status: Northern Pygmy Salamanders occur in isolated populations and are restricted by habitat, making them vulnerable to incompatible land management and climate change. Accordingly, this species is listed as "Deemed in Need of Management" in Tennessee.

Comments: The Northern Pygmy Salamander was recently described by Crespi et al. (2010).

Matthew L. Niemiller

Black-Bellied Salamander adult, Monroe County. (Photo by Matthew L. Niemiller)

Black-Bellied Salamander

Desmognathus quadramaculatus

Description: The Black-Bellied Salamander is a relatively large salamander (90–210 mm TL) and is the largest of the desmognathine species. The head is relatively flat and broad with large bulging eyes. A distinct light line extends on each side of the head from the eye to the angle of the jaw. The ground color of the dorsum and sides in juveniles and adults are various shades of olive, reddish brown, brown, or black, with two rows of irregularly shaped yellow, red, or gray blotches. Some individuals have an irregular network of black markings on the dorsum, and in some populations in the Great Smoky Mountains the dorsum of some individuals is riddled with a series of small yellow or gold flecks. A white spot typically demarcates each

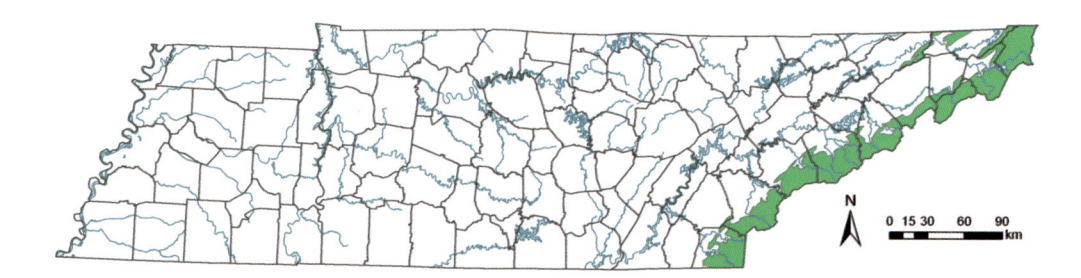

Left: Black-Bellied Salamander adult showing slope of snout and bulbous eyes, Blount County. (Photo by Matthew L. Niemiller) *Right:* Black-Bellied Salamander larva, Polk County. (Photo by Matthew L. Niemiller)

lateral line pore of the trunk; consequently, two rows of white spots on each side of the body are usually apparent, one row where the back meets the sides and the other row near where the side meets the venter. The ground color of the venter is white or pale yellow in newly metamorphosed salamanders but darkens with age to gray in older juveniles and to an intense black in adults as the density of pigment cells of the abdomen increases with age. There are usually 14 costal grooves. The tail is laterally compressed with a distinct dorsal keel. The front limbs have four toes and are noticeably more slender than the hind limbs, which have five toes. The enlarged hind limbs of this and other species of *Desmognathus* allow the salamanders to hop, a behavior they use frequently when confronted with capture. The tip of each toe is heavily pigmented black and is cornified. Nasolabial grooves are present. The sexes look similar, but a series of morphological features can be used to distinguish males from females. For example, compared to females, males grow larger, have wider heads, possess larger teeth on the upper jaw, and have a rougher surface to the lining of the cloacal vent. The dorsum of hatchlings and small larvae is beige-yellow to pale brown; two longitudinal rows of lighter colored flecks or spots occur on the sides. The overall coloration darkens as the larvae age. Larger larvae have cornified toe tips. The gills are bright white. Hatchlings measure 11–16 mm SVL. No subspecies are recognized.

Etymology: The specific epithet *quadramaculatus* is from the Latin *quadrus* "fourfold" and *maculatus* "spotted." This refers to the four rows of pale colored spots on the sides (two rows on each side) of individuals of this species.

Similar Species: Black-Bellied Salamanders are closely related to and strongly resemble Shovel-Nosed Salamanders. Hatchlings and larvae of these two species are nearly indistinguishable from each other. In some areas, larval Black-Bellied Salamanders have a reddish stripe on the dorsum of the tail. Unfortunately, this trait is not found in all populations of Black-Bellied Salamanders. Adults can also be difficult to distinguish, but the shape of internal nares (slit-like in Shovel-Nosed Salamanders versus round in Black-Bellied Salamanders) is useful in species identification. Unfortunately, the internal nares are difficult to view in living salamanders. The coloration of the abdomen can also be used: the venter of adult Black-

Bellied Salamanders usually is an intense black, whereas in Shovel-Nosed Salamanders the venter is usually dark gray (never intense black). This characteristic is subjective, particularly when salamanders from different regions are compared. Furthermore, the systematics of these species is in a state of flux and additional species are apt to be described further complicating identification of dark-bellied desmognathine salamanders in eastern Tennessee.

Distribution: The Black-Bellied Salamander ranges throughout the highlands of the Southern Appalachians from southeastern West Virginia through southwestern Virginia into eastern Tennessee, western North Carolina, northwestern South Carolina, and northern Georgia. In our state, the species is limited in distribution to extreme eastern Tennessee in the Bays Mountain region of the Ridge and Valley and in the Blue Ridge Mountains.

Habitat: Black-Bellied Salamanders typically inhabit fast-flowing, well-oxygenated, low-order woodland mountain streams. The fast-flowing current limits silt build up in the rocky substrate of these streams. Hatchlings are poor swimmers and are often washed downstream into areas with low current where they seek refuge in the interstices of the rock substrate, at least during daylight. Following metamorphosis, juveniles and adults remain near the streams and can be abundant under rocks and logs along the stream margins. Adults occasionally wander 5–10 m from the streams during rainy nights and have even been observed crossing roads.

Natural History: The Black-Bellied Salamander is the one of the more aquatic of the desmognathine species. Breeding activities are poorly documented in Tennessee or elsewhere. Breeding is thought to occur in late summer or early fall. Courtship is thought to resemble that described for other large desmognathine species but has never been observed. Females presumably lay eggs from late spring to early summer. The number of eggs a female lays is often, but not always, associated with her body size: larger females typically lay more eggs than smaller females. The eggs are white (unpigmented) and attached to the undersurface of rocks in flowing water. Reported clutch size ranges from 20 to 80 eggs. Females remain with their eggs through hatching in 10–12 weeks, and hatchlings are found in the streams from July through September. The larval period is long lasting 3–4 years, and individuals undergo metamorphosis when they are 34–44 mm SVL. Furthermore, the juvenile period is long, lasting 3–5 years. Individuals can live at least 15 years. Hatchlings and larvae are opportunistic in feeding and eat a variety of aquatic invertebrate prey, including zooplankton, and larvae of stoneflies, mayflies, caddisflies, and beetles. Juveniles are also opportunistic in feeding and eat most invertebrates that they encounter, including worms, snails, crustaceans, millipedes, arachnids, and insects. Much of their diet is aquatic prey, but they often forage on land during rainy nights, leaving the safety of their burrow beneath rocks and logs. However, the foraging behavior changes with age. Larger, and hence older individuals, have a decreased proclivity to wander from their secluded burrows. Rather than actively foraging for food, large individuals remain partially within their burrows with only their heads sticking out. From this position, they ambush passing prey. The diet of adults consists largely of terrestrial invertebrates, including the groups reported for juveniles. As with many large desmognathine salamanders, Black-Bellied Salamanders are occasionally cannibalistic and will also eat various species of *Eurycea* and *Plethodon*. Predation has seldom been reported, but predators include other salamanders, frogs, fishes, crayfish, snakes, birds, and mammals.

Conservation Status: Black-Bellied Salamanders are associated with well-oxygenated fast-flowing streams with rocky substrates. Consequently, this species is vulnerable to factors that degrade stream quality, including modifications to the terrestrial habitat that could result in increase siltation, decrease in aquatic insect community, or decrease in flow.

Brian T. Miller

Santeetlah Dusky Salamander adult, Monroe County. (Photo by Matthew L. Niemiller)

Santeetlah Dusky Salamander

Desmognathus santeetlah

Description: The Santeetlah Dusky Salamander is a medium-sized, robust salamander, with adults measuring 60–100 mm TL. The head is relatively flat and broad with large bulging eyes. A distinct light line extends on each side of the head from the eye to the angle of the jaw. The dorsal ground color is light brown to yellowish brown to greenish brown, occasionally with small reddish spots bordered with dark pigment. Other individuals have poorly defined dorsolateral stripes or lack any patterning. The venter is light gray with apparent mottling but is washed with yellow. The tail is triangular in cross section anteriorly, while the posterior third is laterally compressed and keeled. The undersurface of the tail and limbs also is washed with yellow. There are usually 14 costal grooves and nasolabial grooves are present. The front limbs have four toes and are noticeably more slender than the hind limbs, which have five toes. The toe tips are not cornified. Sexually active males have a small, inconspicuous mental gland on the chin and papillose cloacal lips. Juveniles resemble adults but have four to five pairs of chestnut-colored spots or blotches on the dorsum between the limbs that often fuse to form a middorsal stripe that fades with age. The dorsum of hatchlings and small larvae is beige-yellow to pale brown with four to five pairs of even or alternative light spots between the limbs that continue onto the tail. As larvae grow, these spots can fade and coalesce to form a wavy, darker dorsolateral stripe or become absent. The gills are white. Hatchlings are 12–20 mm TL. This species was formerly considered a subspecies of the Northern Dusky Salamander (*D. fuscus*). No subspecies are recognized.

Etymology: The specific epithet, *santeetlah*, refers to Santeetlah Creek, North Carolina.

Similar Species: Santeetlah Dusky Salamanders are very similar to Northern Dusky Salamanders and Spotted Dusky Salamanders (*D. conanti*). See the Northern Dusky Salamander account for characters to distinguish between these species.

Santeetlah Dusky Salamander adult, Sevier County. (Photo by Matthew L. Niemiller)

Distribution: The Santeetlah Dusky Salamander is narrowly distributed in just the Great Smoky, Balsam, and Unicoi mountains of eastern Tennessee and western North Carolina. In Tennessee, this species is known from Monroe, Blount, Sevier, and Cocke counties.

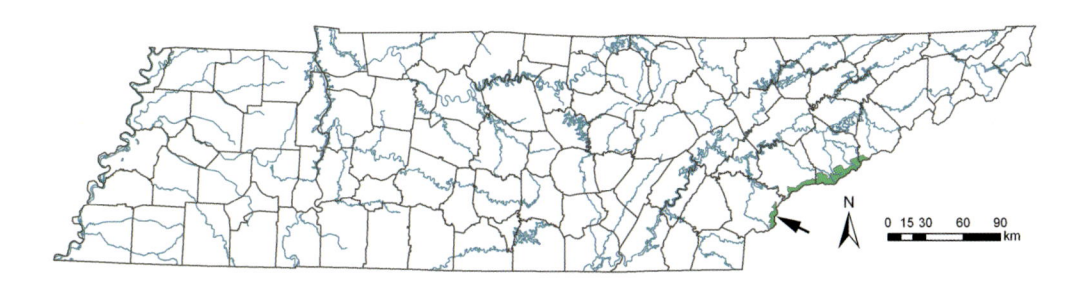

Habitat: The Santeetlah Dusky Salamander is a high-elevation species, generally found in small streams and seepages of 400–1,800 m elevation in mesic, hardwood forests. Usually found within a few meters of water, adults and juveniles inhabit streams with abundant cover, though occasionally might be found under rocks in exposed seeps at higher elevations. These salamanders are often observed on the surface during rainy nights feeding and under cover, such as rocks, logs, and leaf litter, during the day.

Natural History: Breeding occurs in both autumn and spring. Females deposit 17–21 eggs in cavities excavated in moss, rotting logs, and soil close to shallow areas in streams or seeps during summer. Eggs are laid in globular or grapelike clusters typically suspended from the ceiling of a cavity or attached to roots, mosses, or other fibers. Females remain with the eggs until hatching a few weeks later. Larvae metamorphose in 10–12 months. Sexual maturity is reached in 2–3 years. Larvae likely feed on small aquatic invertebrates, while adults and juveniles feed predominately on terrestrial invertebrates. Predators are unknown but likely include larger salamanders, birds, snakes, raccoons, and skunks.

Conservation Status: Populations of the Santeetlah Dusky Salamander appear secure, and much of the range of the species is contained within Great Smoky Mountains National Park. However, due to its restricted distribution, this species is state listed as "Imperiled/Vulnerable."

George R. Wyckoff and
Matthew L. Niemiller

Black Mountain Dusky Salamander adult, Morgan County. (Photo by Matthew L. Niemiller)

Black Mountain Dusky Salamander

Desmognathus welteri

Description: The Black Mountain Dusky Salamander is a large, robust salamander with adults measuring 75–170 mm TL. The tail is triangular in cross section at the base with a distinct keel on the posterior half toward the tail tip. A light stripe runs from the eye to the rear angle of the jaw. The dorsum typically is light brown in color with irregular dark markings with the dorsum of the tail lighter in color in many individuals. The venter is heavily mottled with light gray to brownish blotches. Fourteen costal grooves are present and the toe tips are cornified. Nasolabial grooves are present. The front limbs have four toes and are noticeably more slender than the hind limbs, which have five toes. Males possess small mental glands. Hatchlings,

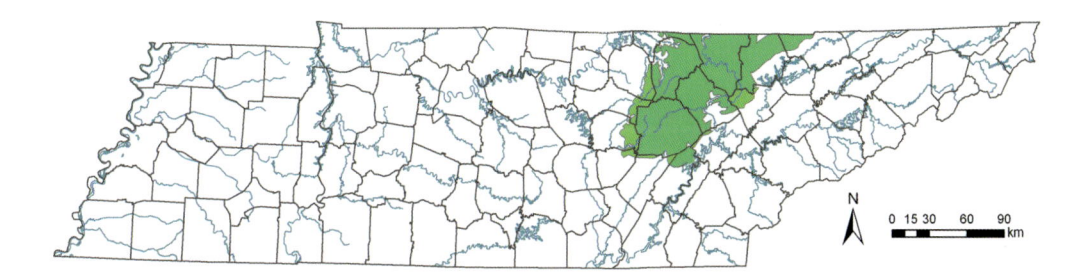

Left: Black Mountain Dusky Salamander adult, Morgan County. (Photo by Matthew L. Niemiller) *Right:* Black Mountain Dusky Salamander juvenile, Morgan County. (Photo by Matthew L. Niemiller)

larvae, and young juveniles typically are brown with five to eight pairs of light spots between the limbs that disappear after metamorphosis as the spots turn into blotches and later fuse and are obscured with age. The venter in larvae is light colored or lightly mottled and the toe tips are cornified like adults. Larvae also have rounded snouts and white gills. Hatchlings are 11–13 mm SVL. No subspecies are recognized.

Etymology: The specific epithet, *welteri*, honors Wilfred August Welter, professor of biology and department head (1932–1939) at Morehead College in Kentucky.

Similar Species: The Black Mountain Dusky Salamander closely resembles three species that it co-occurs with: The Spotted Dusky Salamander (*D. conanti*), Northern Dusky Salamander (*D. fuscus*) and Seal Salamander (*D. monticola*). Black Mountain Dusky Salamanders can be distinguished from both Spotted and Northern Dusky Salamanders by the presence of dark cornified toe tips. Seal Salamanders also have cornified toe tips, but the venter lacks the conspicuous mottling found in Black Mountain Dusky Salamanders. Additionally, the base of tail is rounded or oval in cross section in Seal Salamanders rather than triangular in Black Mountain Dusky Salamanders. Juveniles and larvae are particularly difficult to identify to species. Larval Seal Salamanders typically have reddish spots.

Distribution: The Black Mountain Dusky Salamander is found in the Cumberland Plateau and Cumberland Mountains of Tennessee, eastern Kentucky, and southwestern Virginia. In Tennessee, this species occurs in the northern part of the Cumberland Plateau and Cumberland Mountains from Cumberland County northward into Campbell, Claiborne, Fentress, Morgan, Pickett, and Scott counties.

Habitat: Black Mountain Dusky Salamanders are most common in permanent first- and second-order streams in upland hardwood forests. These streams lack fish and typically have moderate to steep gradients with coarse gravel to rocky substrates. Both adults and juveniles can be found underneath rocks and other cover objects in and along streams and within the splash zones of waterfalls.

Natural History: Little is known about the natural history of the Black Mountain Dusky Salamander. Females deposit 18–33 eggs in grapelike clusters in late spring and early summer inside leaf packs and underneath rocks just above the water line. Females guard their nests and eggs hatch in 12–14 weeks. The larval period is long, lasting 20–24 months, and most larvae metamorphose when they are around 20 mm SVL. Males and females reach sexual maturity in 4–5 years and are known to live up to 20 years in captivity. The diet and predators of the Black Mountain Dusky Salamander are unknown.

Conservation Status: Black Mountain Dusky Salamanders are negatively affected by habitat destruction and degradation caused by logging and mining operations. This species has experienced population declines in other states but the status of Tennessee populations is unknown. The Black Mountain Dusky Salamander is state listed as "Vulnerable" and is "Deemed in Need of Management" in Tennessee.

Matthew L. Niemiller and R. Graham Reynolds

Pygmy Salamander adult, Monroe County. (Photo by Matthew L. Niemiller)

Pygmy Salamander

Desmognathus wrighti

Description: The Pygmy Salamander is a tiny woodland salamander distinguished by its small size and reddish brown to bronze dorsal stripe, marked with a dark herringbone or chevron pattern down the midline of the dorsum. Adults typically measure just 36–52 mm TL and have a tail that is shorter than the body

Left: Pygmy Salamander adult, Monroe County. (Photo by Matthew L. Niemiller) *Right:* Pygmy Salamander adult, Cocke County. (Photo by Matthew L. Niemiller)

and round in cross section. The dorsal surface of the head and snout are wrinkled, and the eyelids are often coppery in color. The venter is tan and unmottled. A light stripe runs from the eye to the rear angle of jaw. Costal grooves number 13–14. Nasolabial grooves are present. Four toes are found on the fore limbs and five toes on the hind limbs. The toe pads lack cornifications. There is not an aquatic larvae stage and 10–11 mm TL hatchlings have four to five pairs of light dorsal spots and very short tails. The gills are lost either before or within a few days of hatching. Juveniles resemble adults. Sexually active males can be differentiated during the breeding season by the presence of a U-shaped mental gland under the chin. No subspecies are recognized.

Etymology: The specific epithet, *wrighti*, honors George Wright, chief of the Wildlife Division of the National Park Service in the early twentieth century.

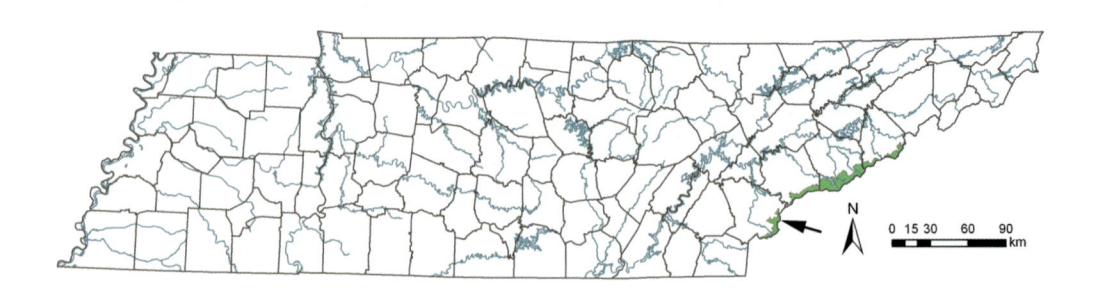

Similar Species: The Pygmy Salamander is nearly indistinguishable from the Northern Pygmy Salamander and is best distinguished by range. Both male and female Pygmy Salamanders tend to be smaller and have narrower heads than Northern Pygmy Salamanders. Pygmy Salamanders can often be differentiated from Seepage Salamanders (*D. aeneus*) by location; in Tennessee the two species distributions overlap only slightly in northern Monroe County and extreme southern Blount County. In areas where both species are found, the wrinkled top of the head, conspicuous dorsal herringbone pattern, and a U-shaped mental gland in breeding males can identify Seepage Salamanders. Even experts may have a hard time distinguishing these species, as a museum record from Monroe County remains ambiguous due to an apparent combination of the above traits.

Distribution: Characterized as a high-elevation species of hardwood and spruce-fir forests, Pygmy Salamanders are distributed in the Blue Ridge Mountains, primarily in Great Smoky Mountains National Park south of the French Broad River. In eastern Tennessee, this species is found in Monroe, Blount, Sevier, and Cocke counties.

Habitat: Pygmy Salamanders are the most terrestrial of *Desmognathus* species and are often found far from water. This species is generally associated with high-elevation spruce-fir forests of 800–2,000 m in elevation, although many populations are found in mature cove forests at lower elevations. Denizens of the forest floor, Pygmy Salamanders readily climb vegetation when foraging. They may be located on humid nights in the leaf litter or on the bases of trees, or during the day beneath logs or stones. Heavily rotten logs with plenty of moisture seem to be a favorite refuge.

Natural History: Pygmy Salamanders breed during autumn and spring, although little is know about nesting habits. Only six nests have been reported and a single pedicel under a stream bank in all nests suspended the eggs. Females remain coiled around the eggs until hatching. Females nesting away from water presumably nest in underground retreats. Embryos are direct developing and hatch without entering a larval feeding stage. Hatchlings emerge from the egg as miniature versions of adults, though some hatchlings may have gills that are quickly lost. Sexually maturity is reached in 3–5 years. When foraging Pygmy Salamanders are often found climbing vegetation to avoid larger predatory salamanders. The diet includes spiders, mites, beetles, flies, moths, and springtails. Known predators include Spring Salamanders (*G. porphyriticus*) and ground beetles; other presumed predators include congeneric salamanders, woodland snakes, small mammals, and birds.

Conservation Status: Pygmy Salamanders occur in isolated populations and are restricted by habitat, making them vulnerable to incompatible land management and climate change. Accordingly, this species is listed as "Deemed in Need of Management" in Tennessee.

George R. Wyckoff and
Matthew L. Niemiller

Brownback Salamander young adult, Alabama. (Photo by Pierson Hill)

Brownback Salamander

Eurycea aquatica

Description: The Brownback Salamander is a small plethodontid salamander that measures 62–95 mm TL, with the length of the tail accounting for less than half of the total length. The general body shape is short and stout with a shortened trunk, limbs, and tail. As their common name indicates, Brownback Salamanders have a medium to dark brown dorsum, which tapers into a thin stripe down to the tip of the yellowish tail, and dark brown or dusky black sides with no distinct lateral stripe. However, individuals can be the more typical yellow color of their relatives and some have the capacity to change color from dark brown to a lighter yellowish brown after capture. Reddish to orange specimens are found in northern Alabama and could be found in adjacent areas of Tennessee. The venter ranges in color from pale yellow to cream and is unpigmented. Costal grooves

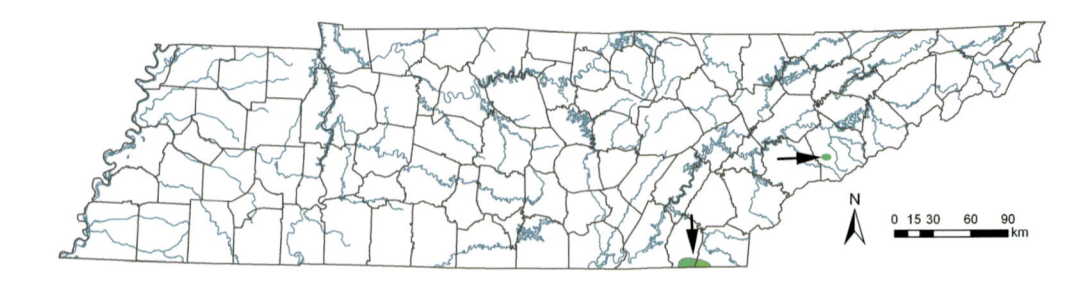

Left: Brownback Salamander small larva, Bradley County. (Photo by Matthew L. Niemiller) *Right:* Brownback Salamander neotenic adult, Bradley County. (Photo by Matthew L. Niemiller)

number 13–15 and nasolabial grooves are present. Four toes are present on the fore limbs and five on the hind limbs. There are no significant differences in TL between male and females; however, sexual dimorphism is present with males usually possessing robust (wide) heads. It is unknown at this time whether males show seasonal variation in this characteristic. Unlike most males of other *Eurycea* species, sexually active male Brownback Salamanders typically do not possess noticeably elongate cirri. Larvae reach a maximum size of 30 mm SVL and are remarkably similar to Southern Two-Lined Salamander (*E. cirrigera*), Blue Ridge Two-Lined Salamander (*E. wilderae*), and Junaluska Salamander (*E. junaluska*) larvae. At least one population in Tennessee appears to contain neotenic individuals, so larger larvae may be encountered. No subspecies are recognized.

Etymology: The specific epithet, *aquatica*, is from the Latin *aqua* "water" and *-ica* "belonging to."

Similar Species: The Brownback Salamander closely resembles the widely distributed Southern Two-Lined Salamander (*E. cirrigera*) and Blue Ridge Two-Lined Salamander (*E. wilderae*), as well as the less common and more geographically restricted Junaluska Salamander (*E. junaluska*). Brownback Salamanders can be differentiated from Southern Two-Lined Salamanders and Blue Ridge Two-Lined Salamanders, however, as Brownback Salamanders are generally more robust with wider heads, thicker trunks, and shorter tails. Brownback Salamanders are usually darker in coloration with a brown dorsum and dark brown or dusky black sides, whereas Southern Two-Lined Salamanders and Blue Ridge Two-Lined Salamanders have a dorsal orange, pale yellow, or tan ground coloration bordered with definitive black or dark brown dorsolateral stripes and dark dorsal speckling. Difficulty can arise distinguishing these species when Brownback Salamanders are found outside of their typical spring habitat where they might not appear very dark or brown, and females of these species are very similar in body proportions. Southern Two-Lined Salamanders and Brownback Salamanders have only been found together at one site in Alabama, although similar sites might occur elsewhere. Similar to the Brownback Salamander, the Junaluska Salamander is a robust *Eurycea* possessing a short tail. However, Junaluska Salamanders have a yellow-orange, red-orange, or cream-colored dorsum with black flecking. These two species are not known to co-occur in the same streams but according to recent molecular analyses, individuals of both species have been found in the same county (Sevier County). It can be difficult to differentiate between larvae of all members of the Two-Lined Salamander complex.

Distribution: Brownback Salamanders were originally described to be endemic to springs in north-central Alabama and northwestern Georgia. Since its formal description, molecular and morphological analyses have been used to show that Brownback Salamanders inhabit springs in Tennessee (Bradley and Sevier counties) as well. An older record from Davidson County was determined to be conspecific with Southern Two-Lined Salamanders, although additional sampling at this site might reveal this to be a valid record. More extensive sampling of *Eurycea* from springs in the Cumberland Plateau and Ridge and Valley of Tennessee, Kentucky, and Virginia are currently being conducted to determine the northern limits of its geographical distribution. There is significant genetic variation corresponding to geographical breaks between populations that are assignable to Brownback Salamanders. Further molecular studies will determine species and/or subspecies boundaries, and might be used in the description of at least two additional Brownback Salamander lineages.

Habitat: Brownback Salamanders typically inhabit springheads and spring runs in karst regions of the Ridge and Valley, Cumberland Plateau and Eastern Highland Rim in northern Alabama, northwestern Georgia, and eastern Tennessee. However, Brownback Salamanders have also been found occupying first- and second-order streams at several localities in the Cumberland Plateau of Alabama. Adult Brownback Salamanders can be found under rocks, logs, and mats of watercress (*Nasturtium officinale*) along springs, while larvae are commonly found in the cover provided by thick watercress carpets and under submerged rocks. It is unknown whether these salamanders remain in springs or retreat to nearby forests during the nonbreeding season.

Natural History: Since this species has historically been considered conspecific with Southern Two-Lined Salamanders, little is known about its natural history. They probably breed in winter prior to the nesting period. Males with grossly enlarged heads are found in springs January–March, and females are gravid during this time. Males are often found with bite scars, indicating male-male combat might occur for access to breeding females. In March and April, females and males can often be found together under cover objects (logs, rocks, and artificial cover objects) attending nests of approximately 80–100 eggs. Occasionally female or male-only nests are found, as well as nests without an attending adult. It is presumed that when males and females are found together with a clutch this represents biparental care, although studies are needed to confirm this behavior. Eggs hatch in April, and at least two size classes of larvae are generally found sympatrically, indicating that the Brownback Salamander might have a two-year larval period. Larvae are by far the most common life history phase encountered at a given site, and watercress beds are often writhing with scores of them. Larvae probably feed on tiny spring insects, worms, and crustaceans. Metamorphosing larvae have been found in April, but the terrestrial ecology of this species is practically unknown. There is evidence that Brownback Salamanders spend the nonbreeding season as terrestrial adults feeding in surrounding forests, and migrate back to springs for breeding. At least one population in Bradley County contains neotenic adults.

Conservation Status: Little is known regarding the status of the Brownback Salamander. This species is almost exclusively found in springs, a habitat that is extremely vulnerable to anthropogenic pressures, such as agriculture, urban development, dewatering of aquifers, and contamination. Although Brownback Salamanders are found in healthy numbers in pristine habitat elsewhere, they are secretive and of limited distribution and hence not commonly encountered in Tennessee.

Elizabeth K. Timpe and
Sean P. Graham

Southern Two-Lined Salamander adult, Cannon County. (Photo by Brian T. Miller)

Southern Two-Lined Salamander

Eurycea cirrigera

Description: The Southern Two-Lined Salamander is a slender plethodontid species. Adults are 60–100 mm in TL but have been recorded to reach 120 mm TL. This species exhibits considerable variation in coloration throughout its range in Tennessee. Typically the dorsal coloration is yellow but it can range from greenish yellow to bright orange or even red. Two distinct black or dark brown dorsolateral stripes running from the eye onto the tail are present. Between these two lines and on the remainder of the dorsum are numerous black spots or flecks. Some individuals might be dusky brown with darker pigmentation on the sides that accent small, light circles that run the length of the body. The venter ranges in coloration from white to yellow to red and lacks mottling. The tail is slightly laterally compressed and usually

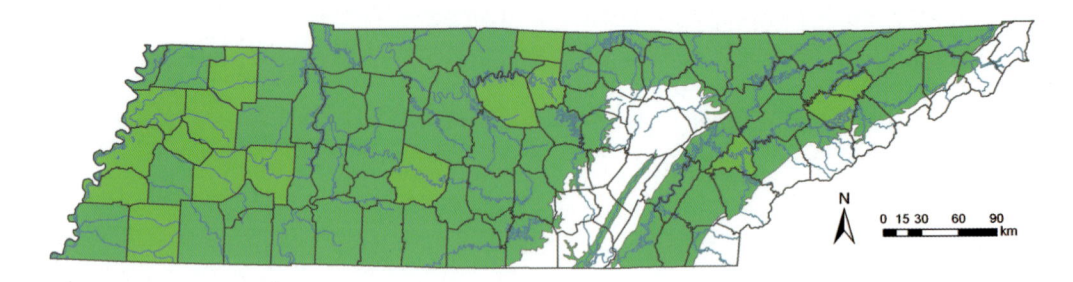

Top left: Southern Two-Lined Salamander adult, Morgan County. (Photo by Matthew L. Niemiller) *Top right:* Southern Two-Lined Salamander egg mass, Rutherford County. (Photo by Matthew L. Niemiller) *Bottom right:* Southern Two-Lined Salamander larva, Grundy County. (Photo by Matthew L. Niemiller)

accounts for half or more of the total length. Costal grooves number 13–16 and nasolabial grooves are present. Four toes are present on the fore limbs and five on the hind limbs. Males in many populations develop a pair of fleshy nasal cirri that extend downward from the upper lip and conspicuous mental glands on the chin. Larvae have a stream-type morphology with a streamlined body, short, bushy, red gills, and a tail fin that extends to the insertion of the hind limbs. Coloration varies but generally larvae are dusky brown on the dorsum with 6–9 pairs of lighter dorsolateral spots. The two dorsolateral lines are most often present though might not be as distinct as in the adults. The border of these lines is typically wavy. The venter usually is a light-colored yellow to brown although some populations have much darker pigmentation. The snout is blunt and the eyes appear large relative to size of the head in larger larvae. Hatchlings are 11–14 mm TL. This species was once considered a subspecies of the Northern Two-Lined Salamander (*E. bislineata*). No subspecies are recognized.

Etymology: The specific epithet, *cirrigera,* is from the Latin *cirrus,* meaning "lock or curl of hair," and *gera,* meaning "bearing." This refers to the prominent nasolabial cirri used in courtship by sexually active males.

Similar Species: The Southern Two-Lined Salamander closely resembles other members of the Two-Lined Salamander complex in Tennessee, including the Blue Ridge Two-Lined Salamander (*E. wilderae*), Brownback Salamander (*E. aquatica*), and Junaluska Salamander (*E. junaluska*). The Blue Ridge Two-Lined Salamander typically is more brightly colored and the dark dorsolateral stripes are broken and do not extend to the tail tip, whereas the dorsolateral stripes in the Southern Two-Lined

Salamander usually are unbroken and extend to the tail tip. Both the Brownback Salamander and the Junaluska Salamander have shorter tails that account for about 50% of the TL. Also, Brownback Salamanders are usually darker in coloration with a brown dorsum and dark brown or dusky black sides. Junaluska Salamanders typically have a mottled brown dorsum and if the dorsolateral stripes are present, they often are broken appearing as a series of wavy lines. Larvae of these species are very similar in appearance and can be very difficult to distinguish between. Likewise, Southern Two-Lined Salamander larvae are similar to larvae of both the Long-Tailed Salamander (*E. longicauda*) and Cave Salamander (*E. lucifuga*), but these two species usually lack the pair of longitudinal rows of pale dorsal spots. Larval *Desmognathus* might be confused with larval Southern Two-Lined Salamanders, but the heads of the *Desmognathus* are more rounded and their gills are white, not red as in the *Eurycea*.

Distribution: The Southern Two-Lined Salamander occurs from southern Indiana, Ohio, and West Virginia south between the Mississippi River and the Atlantic Coast to the Gulf Coast. In Tennessee, this species traditionally was thought to range throughout much of the state with the exception of the Blue Ridge Mountains in East Tennessee. Recent molecular studies of the Two-Lined Salamander complex have shown that several independent lineages exist, with at least six occurring in Tennessee. Populations traditionally considered Southern Two-Lined Salamanders from the southern Cumberland Plateau including Walden's Ridge are more similar to populations of Blue Ridge Two-Lined Salamanders in the southern Blue Ridge Mountains. Based on both morphological and genetic evidence, we tentatively recognized these populations as Blue Ridge Two-Lined Salamanders but expect the description of several other lineages in the future.

Habitat: Southern Two-Lined Salamanders occur in a variety of habitats up to 1,200 m in elevation. Both adults and juveniles are common along and in streams, seeps, and springs in mesic forests. Salamanders can be found underneath rocks, logs, leaf litter, and other debris both adjacent to and within aquatic habitats. However, during wetter periods salamanders can be found far away from water. Adults also can be found underneath moss and within crevices on moist rock faces. Larvae are typically found in shallow pools with considerable cover. Larvae and adults also have been reported from caves.

Natural History: Adult Southern Two-Lined Salamanders migrate to streams to breed in late winter and early spring, although small fall migrations can occur. Eggs, which are white to yellow in color and 2.5–3 mm in diameter, are deposited along streams and in other areas characterized by running water in streams, springs, and even caves; however, occasionally eggs have been found in pools of water. Eggs are normally attached one at a time to the undersurfaces of rocks, moss, and other objects. Females brood their nests of around 50 eggs until hatching 4–10 weeks later. Larvae live in slow-moving areas of the stream and are primarily benthic foragers, feeding on a variety of aquatic insects and zooplankton. Larvae metamorphose in 1–2 years. Adults and juveniles feed year round on a variety of terrestrial invertebrates and occasionally on aquatic invertebrates. Larval predators include fishes and other salamander species. A variety of fishes, birds, and reptiles are known to prey upon adults. Adults exhibit a defensive posturing, which consists of coiling the body, tucking the head, and undulating the tail. When faced with a predator they will also often flip-flop. Both of these behaviors probably reduce the risk of predation.

Conservation Status: The Southern Two-Lined Salamander is both widespread and abundant in Tennessee. As is the case with most salamanders, habitat destruction, acid rain, and pollution are among the top concerns to the preservation of this species. Interestingly, this species has been known to thrive in areas where the water is contaminated.

Stesha A. Pasachnik and Matthew L. Niemiller

Three-Lined Salamander adult, Monroe County. (Photo by Matthew L. Niemiller)

Three-Lined Salamander

Eurycea guttolineata

Description: The Three-Lined Salamander is medium-sized salamander ranging 100–180 mm TL with a bold, dark stripe running down the center of the mustard-colored dorsum. Dark stripes also run along each side of the body, which extend to the tail where they might degrade to vertical bands. The tail elongates as juveniles mature and becomes longer than the body size in adults, accounting for 60–65% of the total length. The venter is heavily speckled with gray, black, or white spots. Costal

Left: Three-Lined Salamander adult, Polk County. (Photo by Matthew L. Niemiller) *Right:* Three-Lined Salamander larva, Polk County. (Photo by Matthew L. Niemiller)

grooves number 13–14. The front limbs are slender with four toes, whereas the hind limbs are stouter than the front limbs and have five toes. Nasolabial grooves are present, and the tissue around these grooves swell in males during the breeding season and the cirri become evident. Furthermore, in males the area around the cloaca is swollen during the breeding season and a round mental gland is present on the undersurface of their heads. The teeth of the upper and lower jaws occur in single rows. The tongue is boletoid. Hatchlings are 16–19 mm TL, with short, red gills, and cream colored with uniformly distributed melanophores. Within one to two months, larvae develop dark dorsolateral stripes and a more narrow mid-dorsal stripe. The venter is immaculate. The snout is blunt and eyes appear large relative to the size of the head in larger larvae. Recent metamorphs are dark with almost black sides, dark chins, and an olive green–gray dorsum; however, the adult coloration and patterning typically develops within a few months. This species was formerly considered a subspecies of the Long-Tailed Salamander (*E. longicauda*). No subspecies are recognized.

Etymology: The specific epithet, *guttolineata,* is from the Latin *gutta* "spot" and *lineata* "marked with lines" and refers to the spots on the dorsum which form dark lines.

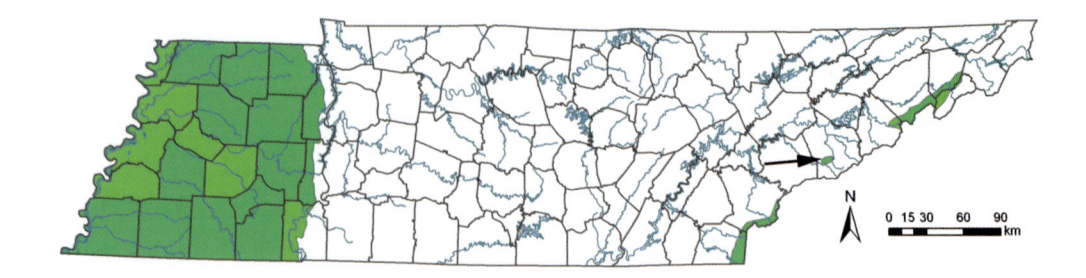

Similar Species: Three-Lined Salamanders are most similar in appearance to Long-Tailed Salamanders and Cave Salamanders (*E. lucifuga*). Three-Lined Salamanders have a distinct, dark mid-dorsal stripe that is lacking in Long-Tailed Salamanders. The spotting pattern of the tail is the most reliable feature that distinguishes Cave and Three-Lined Salamanders. In the Three-Lined Salamander, the spots on the sides of the tail often coalesce into a vertical chevron or herringbone pattern or dark stripe, whereas the spots on the sides of the tail in the Cave Salamander do not coalesce and remain apart from each other. Furthermore, the head is more slender in Three-Lined Salamanders compared to Cave Salamanders in which the head is flattened and broad. Larvae can be very difficult to distinguish. Larval Long-Tailed and Three-Lined Salamanders are best differentiated by geographic distribution. Cave Salamander larvae are similar but have pigmentation on the gular region that extends medially in front of the first gill and have pigmentation on the ventral surfaces of the hind feet. In Three-Lined Salamanders, the gular pigmentation does not extend medially in front of the first gill and the ventral surfaces of the hind lack or are only lightly pigmented. Likewise, larger Three-Lined Salamander have the mid-dorsal stripe apparent. Southern Two-Lined (*E. cirrigera*) and Blue Ridge Two-Lined Salamander (*E. wilderae*) also are similar to Three-Lined Salamander larvae but typically have six to nine pairs of light spots on the dorsum.

Distribution: Three-Lined Salamanders occur from northeast Virginia south to the panhandle of Florida, west across the Gulf Coast to the Mississippi River, and north into western Tennessee and Kentucky. In Tennessee, this species occurs in the western quarter of the state roughly west of the Tennessee River in the Mississippi Alluvial Valley, Mississippi Valley Loess Plains, and Southeastern Plains. However, isolated populations exist in the Blue Ridge Mountains near the North Carolina border in Monroe and Polk counties. The Three-Lined Salamander and Long-Tailed Salamander are largely allopatric in our state. In most of the eastern part of the state, the Long-Tailed Salamander occurs up to the North Carolina state line, where it is replaced at lower elevations on the other side of the highland divide by the Three-Lined Salamander. In addition to Polk and Monroe counties, Three-Lined Salamanders also are known from Greene, Washington, and Sevier counties. In extreme southeast Tennessee, Three-Lined Salamanders and Long-Tailed Salamanders might be micro-allopatric, as they occur in very close proximity though have not yet been found sympatrically.

Habitat: In Tennessee, this species is found near the margins of slow-moving streams, swamps, bogs, and ephemeral ponds in forested habitat. They are frequently encountered by flipping rotten logs in floodplain forests but might also be found under debris, though rarely very far from water or seasonally flooded habitats. Adults and juveniles can also be encountered while foraging on rainy nights. In the Blue Ridge Mountains, Three-Lined Salamanders are generally found at lower elevations. They seem to prefer bottomland forests below 800–1,000 m in elevation.

Natural History: The reproductive biology of Three-Lined Salamanders is poorly documented. Females deposit eggs in winter presumably in sluggish streams, bogs, seeps, springs, and backwater areas. Nests have rarely been found, but clutch sizes are probably small. Larvae metamorphose in 4–16 months depending on whether larvae overwinter. Sexual maturity is reached in two years after metamorphosis.

Larvae likely feed on zooplankton, amphipods, isopods, and worms. Adults feed on the usual assortment of terrestrial invertebrates, including ants, millipedes, isopods, worms, snails, and springtails. Predators likely include woodland snakes and small mammals, aquatic snakes, and other salamanders, such as large *Desmognathus* salamanders.

Conservation Status: Three-Lined Salamanders are common to abundant in appropriate habitat throughout their range and hence are of no specific management or conservation concern.

R. Graham Reynolds and Matthew L. Niemiller

Junaluska Salamander adult male, Monroe County. (Photo by Matthew L. Niemiller)

Junaluska Salamander

Eurycea junaluska

Description: The Junaluska Salamander is a robust member of the Two-Lined Salamander complex. Adults are 75–100 mm TL, with the length of the tail accounting for less than half of the total length. The general body shape is robust with a shortened trunk and tail. The dorsum is dark brown to greenish yellow to yellow-orange in color with black to dark brown flecks, spots, or wavy lines that extend along the sides onto the tail. The venter is light and immaculate. Costal grooves number 13–15. Nasolabial grooves are present. Four toes are present on the fore limbs and five on the hind limbs. Sexu-

Top left: Junaluska Salamander adult male, Monroe County. (Photo by Matthew L. Niemiller) *Top right:* Junaluska Salamander adult female, Monroe County. (Photo by Matthew L. Niemiller) *Bottom right:* Junaluska Salamander larva, Graham County, North Carolina. (Photo by Bill Peterman)

ally active males possess enlarged but short cirri, mental glands on the chin, and swollen vents. Larvae are robust with an olive green to brown dorsum with darker pigmentation along the sides of the body that is straight-edged. Well-defined cheek patches are present and iridophores are lacking on the venter. Hatchlings are 11–13 mm TL and older larvae might exceed 34 mm SVL. No subspecies are recognized.

Etymology: The specific epithet, *junaluska*, honors Junaluska, a Cherokee chief, who survived the Trail of Tears and returned to western North Carolina and was granted land in Graham County, which encompasses much of the range of this species.

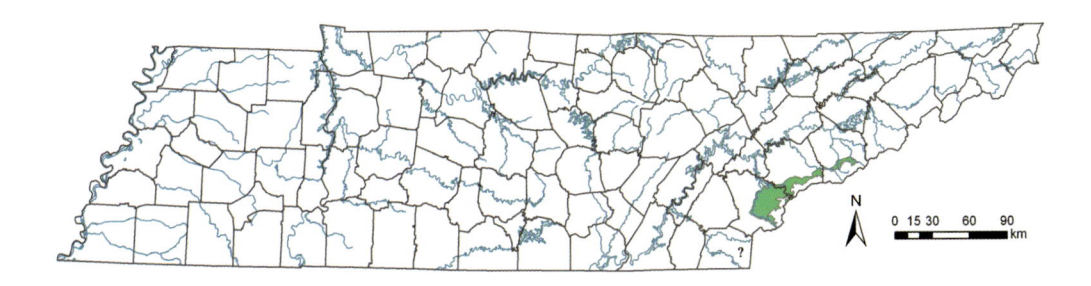

Similar Species: The Junaluska Salamander is a member of the Two-Lined Salamander (*E. bislineata*) complex and bears a resemblance to other species within this group. Adults may be distinguished from the Southern Two-Lined (*E. cirrigera*) and Blue Ridge Two-Lined (*E. wilderae*) Salamanders by measuring the length of the intact tail relative to the body length. Junaluska Salamanders are more robust and have a tail that is shorter than the body length, while the other two species have a tail longer than the body length. Moreover, the dorsolateral stripes, when present, in Junaluska Salamanders are diffuse, broken, and consist of a series of wavy lines compared to the prominent and bold dorsolateral stripes in Southern and Blue Ridge Two-Lined Salamanders. Larval Junaluska Salamanders are more difficult to differentiate from other *Eurycea,* and multiple characters must be used. In general, Junaluska Salamanders have darker pigmentation, a straight-line margin where the dorsal color intersects with the ventral color, dense cheek patches, and no iridophores on the venter compared to other members of the Two-Lined Salamander complex. Larvae larger than 34 mm SVL are almost always Junaluska Salamanders.

Distribution: The Junaluska Salamander is narrowly distributed in southwestern North Carolina and southeastern Tennessee. In our state, populations have been located in Blount, Sevier, and Monroe counties, including within the Great Smoky Mountains National Park at elevations below 525 m. There is an unconfirmed report from Polk County.

Habitat: A mostly riparian species, the Junaluska Salamander can primarily be found in association with high-order rocky streams. Adults can be found under rocks along the stream edge during autumn and spring, within the streams during cold weather, and in the surrounding forest underneath cover objects during the summer. Adults are found crossing roads near streams on warm rainy nights. Larvae are by far more commonly encountered and easily found. They frequently occur underneath large flat rocks within the stream in areas with some current and low sedimentation, and less frequently under cover in side pools and in riffles. Many larvae have also been taken by dip netting leaf mats during late autumn.

Natural History: Little is known about the reproductive biology of this species. Adults apparently migrate to breeding streams from surrounding forests in late winter and early spring. Females lay and brood 30–50 eggs attached to the undersurfaces of rocks in streams. Larvae metamorphose in 2–3 years. Diet of larvae and adults are mostly unreported, though their dietary habits are probably similar to other Two-Lined Salamanders and undoubtedly include aquatic and terrestrial macroinvertebrates. Predators likely include fish, such as trout, other salamanders, birds, small mammals, and snakes.

Conservation Status: Junaluska Salamanders are rare within their range, and as such, population status is difficult to assess. In Tennessee, populations appear stable, but their rarity, restricted distribution, and apparent sensitivity to human disturbance, as evidenced by extirpated populations in North Carolina, should indicate that this species deserves attention from landowners and conservation planners. As such, it is state listed as "Imperiled" and is "Deemed in Need of Management." Care should be taken to leave habitat undisturbed, and novel populations should be reported to conservation authorities.

R. Graham Reynolds and
Matthew L. Niemiller

Long-Tailed Salamander adult, Rhea County. (Photo by Matthew L. Niemiller)

Long-Tailed Salamander

Eurycea longicauda

Description: The Long-Tailed Salamander is a medium-sized slender salamander ranging 100–200 mm TL with a body that is slightly dorsoventrally compressed. The head is also flat and the eyes are protruding. The tail is laterally compressed and very long, typically accounting for > 60% of TL. The ground color of the dorsum and sides in juveniles and adults are various shades of yellow-brown, yellow-orange, orange, or red, with irregularly shaped and spaced black spots. Along each side, these black spots often coalesce, forming a broad, irregular stripe. On the sides of the tail, the spots also coalesce and form a vertical herringbone or chevron pattern. The ground color of the belly is white or pale yellow and lacks the spotting characteristic of the dorsum and sides. Costal grooves number 13–14, and nasolabial grooves are present. The front limbs are slender with four toes, whereas the hind limbs are stouter than the front limbs and have five toes. The tissues around the

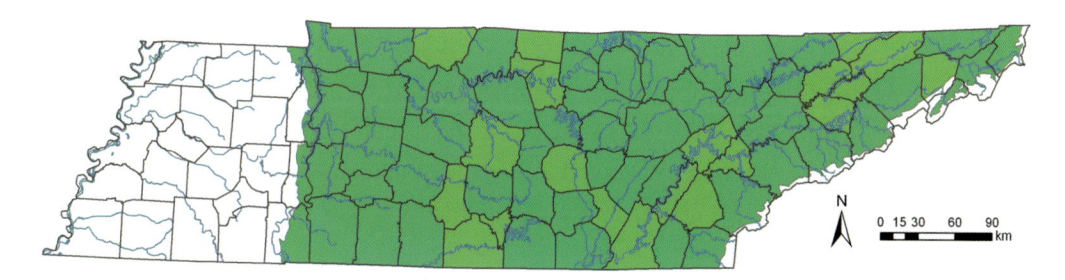

Top left: Long-Tailed Salamander adult, Blount County. (Photo by Matthew L. Niemiller) *Top right:* Long-Tailed Salamander larva, Ohio. (Photo by Carl R. Brune) *Bottom:* Long-Tailed Salamander metamorph, Monroe County. (Photo by Matthew L. Niemiller)

nasolabial grooves swell in males during the breeding season and the cirri become evident. Furthermore, in males the area around the cloaca is swollen during the breeding season and a round mental gland is present on the undersurface of their head. The teeth of the upper and lower jaws occur in single rows. The tongue is boletoid. The larvae are stream-type such that the tail fin is low and does not extend onto the body. Hatchlings are 17–19 mm TL with short red gills and cream colored with uniformly distributed melanophores. Within 1–2 months, larvae develop dark mottling on the sides and mottling is also usually present on the underside of the throat. In some individuals, a weakly defined middorsal stripe might develop. The snout is blunt and eyes appear large relative to the size of the head in larger larvae. Recent metamorphs are dark with almost black sides, dark chins, and an olive green–gray dorsum; however, the adult coloration and patterning typically develops within a few months. Two subspecies are recognized, and only the Long-Tailed Salamander (*E. l. longicauda*) occurs in Tennessee.

Etymology: The specific and subspecific epithet, *longicauda,* is from the Latin *longus* "long" and *cauda* "tail."

Similar Species: Long-Tailed Salamanders are most similar in appearance to Three-Lined Salamanders (*E. guttolineata*) and Cave Salamanders (*E. lucifuga*). Three-Lined Salamanders have a distinct, dark mid-dorsal stripe that is lacking in Long-Tailed Salamanders. The spotting pattern of the tail is the most reliable feature that distinguishes Cave and Long-Tailed Salamanders. In the Long-Tailed Salamander, the spots on the sides of the tail coalesce into a vertical chevron or herringbone pattern, whereas the spots on the sides of the tail in the Cave Salamander do not coalesce and remain apart from each other. Furthermore, the head is more slender in Long-Tailed Salamanders compared to Cave Salamanders in which the flattened head is broad. Larvae can be very difficult to distinguish. Larval Long-Tailed and

Three-Lined Salamanders are best differentiated by geographic distribution. Cave Salamander larvae are similar but have pigmentation on the gular region that extends medially in front of the first gill and have pigmentation on the ventral surfaces of the hind feet. In Long-Tailed Salamanders, the gular pigmentation does not extend medially in front of the first gill and the ventral surfaces of the hind lack or are only lightly pigmented. Southern Two-Lined (*E. cirrigera*) and Blue Ridge Two-Lined Salamander (*E. wilderae*) also are similar to Long-Tailed Salamander larvae but typically have six to nine pairs of light spots on the dorsum.

Distribution: Long-Tailed Salamanders are distributed from southern New York southwest throughout the Appalachians and Interior Low Plateau into Tennessee, northern Alabama, and northwestern Georgia then west into Missouri, Arkansas, and eastern Oklahoma. In Tennessee, this species is found in appropriate habitats in the eastern two-thirds of the state east of the north-flowing Tennessee River in western Tennessee. The Three-Lined Salamander replaces it to the west.

Habitat: Adults and juveniles are commonly found beneath rocks in and along creeks and also in the neighboring forest floor in mesic forests. Larval Long-Tailed Salamanders are common inhabitants of the subterranean streams, springs, headwater streams, and seeps. Long-Tailed Salamanders also inhabit the seasonal wetlands and associated forests in the Barrens region of Middle Tennessee. Adults and juveniles often can be found crossing roads on rainy nights.

Natural History: The reproductive biology of Long-Tailed Salamanders is poorly documented in Tennessee. Courtship occurs on land and presumably occurs from late summer through fall, with oviposition extending through early spring. The eggs of Long-Tailed Salamanders have rarely been found, and all reports of nesting sites are from subterranean habitats or seepages (e.g., caves, mines, and cisterns). All reports of egg clutches have described relatively small clusters of eggs attached singly by a slender stalk to the top, sides, or undersurface of rocks or boards in water, or suspended by the stalks above pools. The reported number of mature ova (60–100), counted by dissection of preserved specimens, far exceeds the number reported in natural clutches found; consequently, females are thought to scatter their eggs in several locations, rather than depositing them all in one location. Furthermore, this behavior of scattering eggs precludes females from brooding their eggs after depositing them. Eggs hatch in 4–12 weeks and larvae metamorphose in 6–12 months. Sexual maturity is reached 1–2 years after metamorphosis. Larvae are opportunistic in feeding and eat a variety of aquatic invertebrate prey, including zooplankton, amphipods, isopods, and worms. Adults are also opportunistic in feeding and eat most small invertebrates that they encounter, including worms, snails, crustaceans, millipedes, arachnids, and insects. Predation has seldom been observed, but likely predators include frogs, fishes, crayfish, snakes, birds, and mammals. Sculpins and sunfishes are known to prey upon larvae.

Conservation Status: The Long-Tailed Salamander is widespread and locally abundant in appropriate habitat in Tennessee.

Brian T. Miller and
Matthew L. Niemiller

Cave Salamander adult male, Wilson County. (Photo by Matthew L. Niemiller)

Cave Salamander

Eurycea lucifuga

Description: The Cave Salamander is a medium-sized, slender salamander 100–200 mm TL. The body is dorsoventrally compressed and the head also is flat and broad with large, bulging eyes. The ground color of the dorsum and sides in juveniles and adults are various shades of yellow-orange, orange, or red with irregularly shaped and spaced black spots. The venter is white or pale orange and lacks the spotting characteristic of the dorsum and sides. Costal grooves usually number 13–14, and nasolabial grooves are present. The tail is laterally compressed and very long, typically accounting for > 60% of TL. The front limbs are slender with four toes, whereas the hind limbs are stouter with five toes. The tissues around the nasolabial grooves swell in males during the breeding season and cirri become prominent. Furthermore, in males the area around the cloaca is swollen

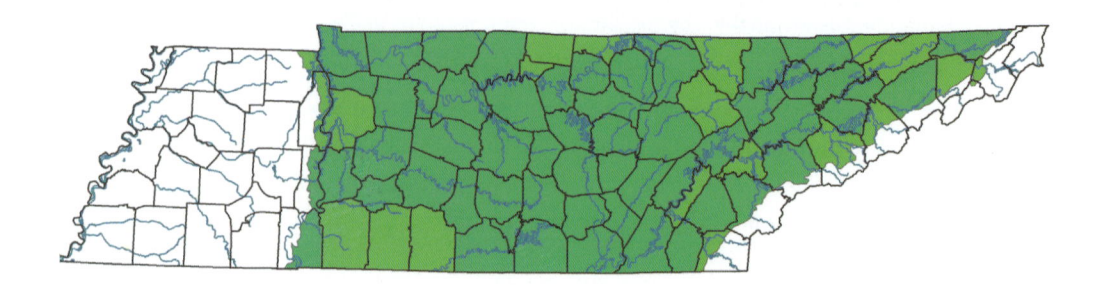

Top left: Cave Salamander adult, Grundy County. (Photo by Matthew L. Niemiller) *Top right:* Cave Salamander hatchling, Cannon County. (Photo by Matthew L. Niemiller) *Bottom right:* Cave Salamander late-stage larva, Roane County. (Photo by Matthew L. Niemiller)

during the breeding season and a round mental gland is present on the chin. The tongue is boletoid, and the teeth of the upper and lower jaws occur in single rows. The larvae are of the stream type with reddish gills and a tail fin stops near the hind limbs. Hatchlings are 11–17 mm TL and whitish but quickly assume the darker pigmentation of small larvae. Younger larvae also have three longitudinal series of lighter spots along the sides. Larger larvae are yellowish and begin to develop the black spotting found in metamorphosed individuals. The snout is blunt and the eyes appear large relative to size of the head in larger larvae. Gular pigmentation is present that extends medially in front of the first gill and the ventral surface of the hind feet is pigmented in larger larvae. No subspecies are recognized.

Etymology: The specific epithet, *lucifiga,* is from the Latin *lucis* "light" and *fuga* "flee." This refers to this species preference for dark habitats, such as caves and interstices.

Similar Species: Cave Salamanders are most similar in appearance to Long-Tailed Salamanders (*E. longicauda*) and Three-Lined Salamanders (*E. guttolineata*). The spotting pattern of the tail is the most reliable character that distinguishes Cave Salamanders from these two species. In Long-Tailed and Three-Lined Salamanders, the spots on the sides of the tail coalesce into a vertical chevron or herringbone pattern, whereas the spots on the sides of the tail in Cave Salamanders do not coalesce, remaining separated from each other. Furthermore, the head of Cave Salamanders is relatively broad with large bulging eyes, whereas the heads of Long-Tailed and Three-Lined Salamanders are more slender with smaller protruding eyes. Larvae can be difficult to distinguish between; however, larger Cave

Salamander larvae have pigmentation on the gular region that extends medially in front of the first gill and have pigmentation on the ventral surfaces of the hind feet. In Long-Tailed and Three-Lined Salamanders, the gular pigmentation does not extend medially in front of the first gill and the ventral surfaces of the hind feet lack or are only lightly pigmented. Southern Two-Lined (*E. cirrigera*) and Blue Ridge Two-Lined Salamander (*E. wilderae*) also are similar to Cave Salamander larvae but typically have six to nine pairs of light spots on the dorsum.

Distribution: Cave Salamanders are associated with limestone and karst regions of the Ozark Highlands, Interior Plateau, and Ridge and Valley from northeastern Oklahoma, northern Arkansas, and southern Missouri east into southern Indiana, Kentucky, Tennessee, northern Alabama, northwestern Georgia, western Virginia, and southeastern West Virginia. In Tennessee, these salamanders are found in the eastern two-thirds of the state and are not found in the Mississippi Alluvial Valley, Mississippi Valley Loess Plains, and Southeastern Plains of West Tennessee.

Habitat: Cave Salamanders are associated with limestone and, therefore, karst regions. Adults and juveniles are commonly found on the floors and walls of caves, particularly near entrances; however, during late winter and early spring, metamorphosed Cave Salamanders are frequently encountered beneath rocks and logs near or in small streams, and under rocks in the cedar glades of Middle Tennessee. Less frequently, Cave Salamanders are found wandering through woods, lawns, and fields in more urban areas. Larval Cave Salamanders inhabit subterranean streams, rimstone pools of caves, springs, seeps, and small streams.

Natural History: Breeding activities of Cave Salamanders are poorly documented. Courtship occurs on land and presumably occurs during summer and early fall. The eggs of Cave Salamanders rarely have been found, but limited evidence suggests that females deposit their eggs in subterranean passages. All reports of eggs have been from caves with small clusters of individual eggs found lying on the floor of small water-filled depressions, attached singly by a slender stalk to the sides of small rimstone pools, and attached to the sides or undersurface of submerged rocks in streams. Oviposition occurs during periods of low stream flow (June to early January), with peak activity during late summer and early fall. The number of eggs a female can oviposit is positively correlated with her body size and is, therefore, highly variable. Average number of mature ova, determined by dissection of preserved specimens, far exceeds the number reported in natural clutches. This is an indication that females scatter their eggs in several locations, rather than depositing them all in one location. Perhaps in association with this behavior, female Cave Salamanders abandon their eggs after depositing them. Larvae metamorphose in 12–15 months and sexual maturity is reached in 2–4 years. Larval Cave Salamanders are opportunistic in feeding and eat a variety of aquatic invertebrate prey, including zooplankton, amphipods, isopods, and worms. Adults are also opportunistic in feeding and eat most invertebrates that they encounter, including worms, snails, crustaceans, millipedes, arachnids, and insects. Predation has seldom been observed, but likely predators include frogs, fishes, crayfish, snakes, birds, and mammals. Furthermore, because of their association with subterranean streams, larval Red,

Spring, Berry Cave, and Tennessee Cave Salamanders are potential predators of larval Cave Salamanders.

Conservation Status: The Cave Salamander is widespread and locally abundant throughout its range in Tennessee.

*Brian T. Miller and
Matthew L. Niemiller*

Blue Ridge Two-Lined Salamander adult, Sevier County. (Photo by Matthew L. Niemiller)

Blue Ridge Two-Lined Salamander

Eurycea wilderae

Description: The Blue Ridge Two-Lined Salamander is a slender plethodontid salamander. Adults are 60–100 mm in TL but have been recorded to reach 120 mm TL. This species exhibits considerable variation in coloration throughout its range in Tennessee. Typically the dorsal coloration is yellow, but it can range from greenish yellow to bright orange or red. Two distinct black or dark brown dorsolateral stripes running from the eye onto the tail are present. The stripes typically begin to break up into a series of dots around the middle of the tail. Between these two lines and on the remainder of the dorsum are numerous black spots or flecks. The venter ranges in coloration from white to yellow to red and lacks mottling. The tail is slightly laterally compressed and usually accounts for > 50% TL. Costal grooves number 14–16 and nasolabial grooves are present. Four toes are present on the fore limbs and five on the

Left: Blue Ridge Two-Lined Salamander adult, Monroe County. (Photo by Matthew L. Niemiller) *Right:* Blue Ridge Two-Lined Salamander larva, Polk County. (Photo by Matthew L. Niemiller)

hind limbs. Males in many populations develop a pair of fleshy nasal cirri that extend downward from the upper lip and conspicuous mental glands on the chin. Males in some populations do not develop pronounced cirri; instead, they have enlarged heads. Larvae have a stream-type morphology with a streamlined body, short, bushy, red gills, and a tail fin that extends to the insertion of the hind limbs. Larvae can reach 60 mm TL before metamorphosis. Coloration varies, but generally larvae are dusky brown on the dorsum with six to nine pairs of lighter dorsolateral spots. The two dorsolateral lines are most often present though might not be as distinct as in adults. The border of these lines is typically wavy. The venter usually is a light-colored yellow to brown although some populations have much darker pigmentation. The snout is blunt and the eyes appear large relative to size of the head in larger larvae. Hatchlings are 11 to 14 mm TL. This species was once considered a subspecies of the Northern Two-Lined Salamander (*E. bislineata*). No subspecies are recognized.

Etymology: The specific epithet, *wilderae*, honors Inez Wilder, a turn-of-the-twentieth-century biologist and professor at Smith College in Massachusetts.

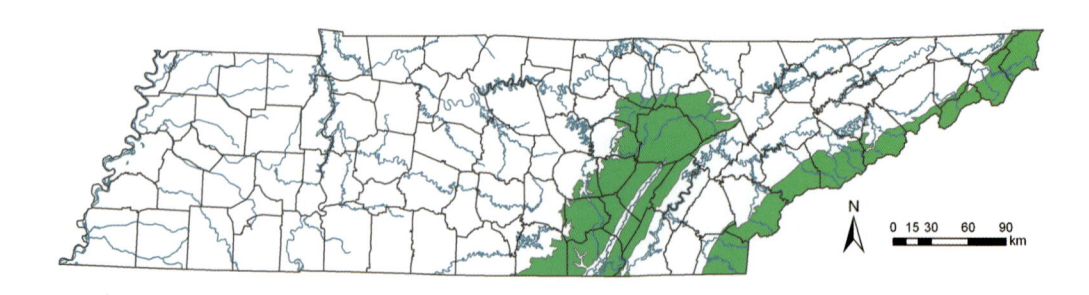

Similar Species: The Blue Ridge Two-Lined Salamander closely resembles other members of the Two-Lined Salamander complex in Tennessee, including the Southern Two-Lined Salamander (*E. cirrigera*), Brownback Salamander (*E. aquatica*), and Junaluska Salamander (*E. junaluska*). The Blue Ridge Two-Lined Salamander typically is more brightly colored and the dark dorsolateral stripes are broken and do not extend to the tail tip, whereas the dorsolateral stripes in the Southern Two-Lined Salamander usually are unbroken and extend to the tail tip. Both the Brownback Salamander and the Junaluska Salamander are more robust and have shorter tails that account for about 50% of the total length. Also, Brownback Salamanders are usually darker in coloration with a brown dorsum and dark brown or dusky black sides. Junaluska Salamanders typically have a mottled brown dorsum and if the dorsolateral stripes are present, they often are broken appearing as a series of wavy lines. Larvae of these species are very similar in appearance and can be very difficult to distinguish between. Junaluska Salamander larvae are more robust, are green to brown in dorsal coloration, and have distinct cheek patches without ventral iridophores. Likewise, Blue Ridge Two-Lined Salamander larvae are similar to larvae of both the Long-Tailed Salamander (*E. longicauda*) and Cave Salamander (*E. lucifuga*), but these two species lack the light pairs of dorsal spots. Larval *Desmognathus* might be confused with larval Blue Ridge Two-Lined Salamanders, however, the heads of the *Desmognathus* are more rounded and their gills are white, not red as in the *Eurycea*.

Distribution: The Blue Ridge Two-Lined Salamander occurs throughout the Blue Ridge Mountains of eastern Tennessee, western North Carolina, northwestern Georgia, and southwestern Virginia. In Tennessee, this species is found in the Blue Ridge Mountains; however, recent morphological and genetic evidence suggests that populations of Southern Two-Lined Salamanders from the southern Cumberland Plateau are in fact Blue Ridge Two-Lined Salamanders.

Habitat: This species occurs over a wide range of elevations, from lower elevation forests to the highest peaks of the Blue Ridge Mountains up to 2,000 m. Both adults and juveniles are common along and in streams, seeps, and springs in mesic forests. Salamanders can be found underneath rocks, logs, leaf litter, and other debris both adjacent to and within aquatic habitats. However, during wetter periods salamanders can be found far away from water. Adults also can be found underneath moss and within crevices on moist rock faces.

Natural History: Adult Blue Ridge Two-Lined Salamanders migrate to streams to breed in late winter and early spring, although small autumn migrations can occur. Eggs that are white to yellow in color and 2.5–3 mm in diameter are deposited along streams and in other areas characterized by running water, such as in streams and springs. Occasionally eggs have been found in pools of water, however. Eggs are normally attached one at a time to the undersurfaces of rocks, logs, moss, and other objects. Females brood their nests of 10–80 eggs until hatching 4–12 weeks later. Larvae live in slow-flowing areas of the stream and are primarily benthic foragers, feeding on a variety of aquatic insects and zooplankton. Larvae metamorphose in 1–2 years. Sexual maturity is reached in 3–4 years. Adults and juveniles feed on a variety of terrestrial invertebrates and occasionally on aquatic invertebrates. Larval predators include fishes and other salamander species. A variety of fishes, birds, and reptiles are known to prey upon adults. Adults exhibit a defensive posturing, which consists of coiling the body, tucking the head, and undulating the tail. When faced with a predator they will also often flip-flop. Both of these behaviors probably reduce the risk of predation.

Conservation Status: The Blue Ridge Two-Lined Salamander is both widespread and abundant throughout its range in Tennessee. This species is still common in areas that have been recently developed and in which other salamander species have declined.

Stesha A. Pasachnik and
Matthew L. Niemiller

Berry Cave Salamander adult, Roane County. (Photo by Matthew L. Niemiller)

Berry Cave Salamander

Gyrinophilus gulolineatus

Description: The Berry Cave Salamander is a large, permanently aquatic species found only in caves. Adults are 130–195 mm TL but can reach lengths up to 230 mm. Individuals rarely undergo metamorphosis in nature and retain gills and other larval features throughout their lives (e.g., are neotenic). Berry Cave Salamanders have broad heads with a spatulate snout and reduced eyes that lack eyelids. Conspicuous unpigmented dots marking the lateral line system on the snout and sides of the head and body are present. The tail is laterally compressed like an oar and has a distinct caudal fin. Adults are pigmented brown to dark purple with small, scattered brown to black spots dorsally and on the upper part of the sides. The venter and undersurface of the tail and limbs are typically flesh colored and lack spotting. In some individuals, a distinctive dark stripe or elongate

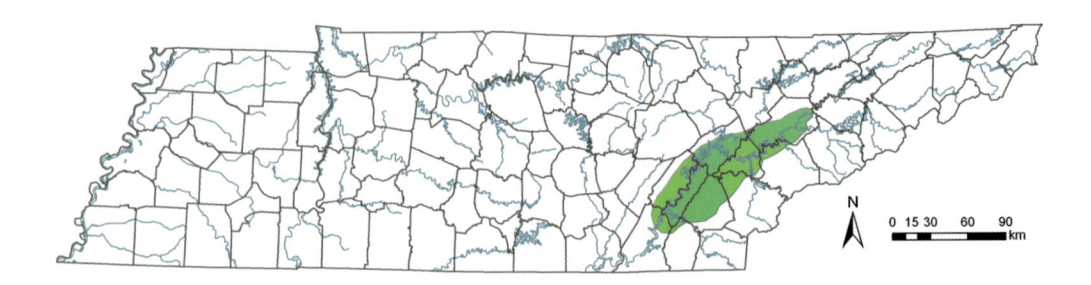

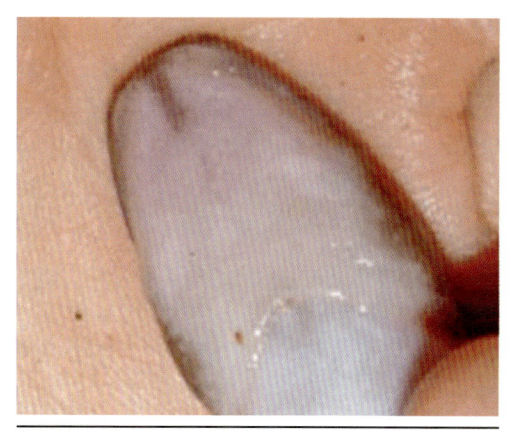

Top left: Gular stripe in an adult Berry Cave Salamander, Roane County. (Photo by Matthew L. Niemiller) *Top right:* Berry Cave Salamander metamorphosed adult, Knox County. (Photo by Matthew L. Niemiller) *Bottom right:* Berry Cave Salamander juvenile with parasitic infection, Roane County. (Photo by Matthew L. Niemiller)

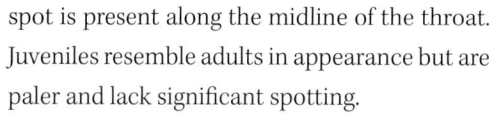

spot is present along the midline of the throat. Juveniles resemble adults in appearance but are paler and lack significant spotting.

Etymology: The specific epithet, *gulolineatus,* is from the Latin *gula* "throat" and *lineatus* "marked with lines" and refers to the dark stripe on the throat present on some adults.

Similar Species: Berry Cave Salamanders closely resemble Tennessee Cave Salamanders (*G. palleucus*) and larval Spring Salamanders (*G. porphyriticus*). See the Tennessee Cave Salamander account to distinguish Berry Cave Salamanders from other similar species.

Distribution: This species is only known from a few scattered caves within the Ridge and Valley of East Tennessee in Knox, McMinn, Meigs, and Roane counties in the Upper Tennessee and Clinch river watersheds. Its distribution however, likely is greater than currently known.

Habitat: The Berry Cave Salamander is found in subterranean streams. Salamanders typically inhabit calm, mud-bottomed stream pools and rimstone pools but are also found within interstices of gravel and cobble in riffles. Most individuals are encountered in the aphotic zone, but a few salamanders have been observed within the twilight zone close to a cave entrance. Three salamanders were collected from a flooded roadside ditch in McMinn County in 1953. Most individuals are found resting at the bottom of a pool but often will seek refuge underneath rocks or within cavities in the streambed when disturbed.

Natural History: Because of their subterranean existence and reclusive nature, the habits, life history, and ecology of the Berry Cave

Salamander are poorly understood. Eggs have never been discovered and little is known about reproduction, although oviposition is thought to occur from autumn to early winter. Berry Cave Salamanders feed on a variety of prey, including amphipods, isopods, worms, and other invertebrates. Adults also prey on younger conspecifics. Predators are unknown but likely include frogs, some fishes, and large crayfish. Salamanders will seek refuge underneath rocks and other cover when alarmed. Naturally metamorphosed individuals have been found in two cave systems. The fate of metamorphosed individuals (i.e., ability to survive), however, is unknown and metamorphosed individuals frequently appear emaciated. Like Tennessee Cave Salamanders, Berry Cave Salamanders are thought to have long life spans, but no data exist to verify this assumption.

Conservation Status: Seldom do surveys produce more than six individuals, and most caves are thought to have small populations. Access to suitable habitat during surveys, however, is very limited in most Ridge and Valley caves. Salamanders likely inhabit subterranean passages inaccessible to humans and likely are more widespread than previously thought. Because of the suspected small population size, limited distribution, and subterranean habitat, Berry Cave Salamanders are thought to be particularly vulnerable to habitat degradation caused by agricultural and logging practices, urbanization, and overcollecting. Some populations might be threatened by hybridization with Spring Salamanders. The Berry Cave Salamander is listed as "Threatened" in Tennessee and "Endangered" by IUCN but currently is not afforded protection by the U.S. Fish and Wildlife Service. This species is also state listed as "Critically Imperiled" and is the subject of a current petition for listing as an endangered species with the federal government.

Matthew L. Niemiller and
Brian T. Miller

Big Mouth Cave Salamander adult, Coffee County. (Photo by Brad M. Glorioso)

Tennessee Cave Salamander

Gyrinophilus palleucus

Description: The Tennessee Cave Salamander is a moderately large, neotenic, and permanently aquatic species confined to cave streams. Presumed adults are 70–105 mm SVL (135–190 mm TL) but can reach lengths exceeding 120 mm SVL (210 mm TL). The paired gills are relatively large and typically pale in coloration; consequently, they might go unnoticed when a salamander is first found. The gills, however, are bright red in stressed or disturbed salamanders and most photographs of this species depict distressed salamanders. The head is broad and the snout shovel-shaped. The eyes are small (reduced in size) and lack eyelids. Conspicuous unpigmented dots marking the lateral line system on the snout and sides of the head and body are present. The tail is laterally

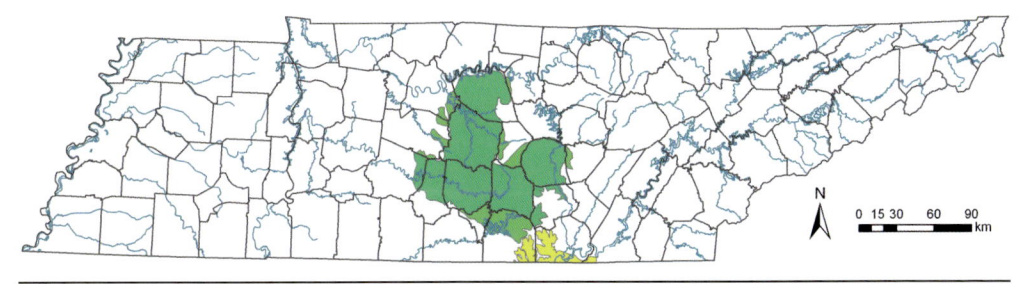

Two subspecies of Tennessee Cave Salamander are recognized: the Big Mouth Cave Salamander (*G. p. necturoides*), whose range appears in green, and the Pale Salamander (*G. p. palleucus*), whose range appears in yellow.

Left: Big Mouth Cave Salamander adult, Grundy County. (Photo by Matthew L. Niemiller) *Right:* Pale Salamander adult, Franklin County. (Photo by Matthew L. Niemiller)

compressed like an oar and the fin is distinct. Two subspecies of Tennessee Cave Salamanders are recognized: the Pale Salamander (*G. p. palleucus*) and Big Mouth Cave Salamander (*G. p. necturoides*). Pale Salamanders are a uniform pale pink or fleshly in color and lack prominent darker spotting. In contrast, Big Mouth Cave Salamanders are red to purple to beige to brown in color with conspicuous dark flecks, spots, or blotches on the dorsum and sides. Additionally, eyes are slightly larger relative to the length of the snout in Pale Salamanders than in Big Mouth Cave Salamanders. The venter and undersurface of the tail and limbs of both subspecies are pale and typically lack any darker flecks or spots. Smaller larvae (< 40 mm SVL) of both subspecies morphologically resemble adults but are paler and lack obvious flecks of dark pigment.

Etymology: The specific and subspecific epithets, *palleucus,* are from the Greek *palleucus* "white," indicating the pale coloration of this subspecies. The subspecific epithet, *necturoides,* is from the Greek *nektos* "swimming" *oura* "tail" and *-oides* "similar to," indicating that this subspecies is similar in appearance to Necturus, the mudpuppies.

Similar Species: Tennessee Cave Salamanders are most similar in appearance to Berry Cave Salamanders (*G. gulolineatus*) and larval Spring Salamanders (*G. porphyriticus*). A suite of morphological features can be used to distinguish Tennessee Cave Salamanders from larval Spring Salamanders; however, relative eye size (large with a discernible iris in Spring Salamanders, small and lacking a discernible iris in Tennessee Cave Salamanders) is the most obvious distinguishing feature. Both obligate cave species have longer, more spatulate snouts with small eyes that are one-quarter to one-fifth the length of the snout, whereas Spring Salamander larvae have slightly shorter snouts and larger eyes one-third the length of the snout. Some populations of Berry Cave Salamanders typically have a chin spot or line, which is lacking in Tennessee Cave Salamanders. Also, Berry Cave Salamanders grow to a larger size and have a broader snout than Tennessee Cave Salamanders. These differences notwithstanding, distinguishing among these three species can be difficult in some drainage systems, even for experts.

Distribution: Tennessee Cave Salamanders are found in subterranean waters of the

Left: Big Mouth Cave Salamander juvenile, Warren County. (Photo by Matthew L. Niemiller) *Right:* Pale Salamander juvenile, Franklin County. (Photo by Matthew L. Niemiller)

Inner Nashville Basin, Eastern Highland Rim, and escarpments of the southern Cumberland Plateau. The Pale Salamander inhabits subterranean waters within the Crow Creek drainage of southern Middle Tennessee and northeast Alabama and is associated with caves of the eastern escarpment of the Cumberland Plateau, whereas the Big Mouth Cave Salamander inhabits caves associated with the Collins, Elk, Duck, and Stones river drainages associated with the Inner Nashville Basin, Eastern Highland Rim, and western escarpment of the Cumberland Plateau.

Habitat: The Tennessee Cave Salamander is associated with subterranean waters. They are most commonly found inhabiting calm, shallow pools in subterranean streams but are also found in rimstone pools, phreatic zones, and beneath rocks and other cover objects, including the small spaces among gravel of streambeds. Tennessee Cave Salamanders typically are inhabitants of the dark zone of caves, but occasionally they are washed or wander out into the twilight zones and have even been found in springs.

Natural History: The habits, life history, and ecology of the Tennessee Cave Salamander are poorly understood. Eggs have never been discovered and little is known about reproduction. Based on studies of the reproductive tracts of females, presence of spermatophores in males, and discovery of hatchlings, mating and egg laying are thought to occur from autumn to early winter, with hatching occurring several months after laying. Females presumably remain with their eggs until hatching. The diet includes a variety of prey, including amphipods, isopods, worms, and other invertebrates. Adults might also prey on small salamander larvae, including those of Tennessee Cave Salamanders. Predation is poorly documented but likely includes frogs, fishes, crayfish, and other salamanders. Metamorphosis is readily induced in the lab, and naturally metamorphosed individuals have been found in several drainage systems. The fate of metamorphosed individuals (i.e., ability to survive) is unknown, and metamorphosed individuals frequently appear emaciated. Tennessee Cave Salamanders are thought to have long life spans, but no data exists to verify this assumption.

Conservation Status: The Tennessee Cave Salamander is the State Amphibian of Tennessee and is listed as "Threatened" and "Imperiled" in Tennessee and "Vulnerable" by IUCN. Recent surveys have shown that Tennessee Cave Salamanders are more widespread and abundant than previously recognized. However, like other cave organisms, Tennessee Cave Salamanders are vulnerable to a number of threats, including inundation by dams, increased water flow and siltation from deforestation and urbanization, pollution from surface runoff, and dumping of trash and other waste into sinkholes.

*Brian T. Miller and
Matthew L. Niemiller*

Blue Ridge Spring Salamander adult, Polk County. (Photo by Matthew L. Niemiller)

Spring Salamander

Gyrinophilus porphyriticus

Description: The Spring Salamander is one of the largest species of plethodontid salamanders measuring 110–220 mm TL but reaching 232 mm TL. The tail is laterally compressed with a distinct keel. A distinct ridge called the canthus rostralis runs from the eye to the nostril. Costal grooves number 17–19 and nasolabial grooves are present. There are four toes on the fore limbs and five on the hind limbs. Two subspecies occur in Tennessee: the Northern Spring Salamander (*G. p. porphyriticus*) and Blue Ridge Spring Salamander (*G. p. danielsi*). Northern Spring Salamanders are typically more drab and variable in coloration ranging from reddish orange or yellowish brown to purplish brown with distinct black or brown flecks, spots, or chevrons on the dorsum. These darker pigments often form a mottled or reticulate pattern in adults. The venter can be unpigmented to heavily mottled in some older adults. The canthus rostralis is not nearly as distinct as in Blue Ridge Spring Salamanders and might be outlined with yellowish gray to black pigmentation. Adult Blue Ridge Spring Salamanders are a more brightly colored reddish orange to salmon

Left: Blue Ridge Spring Salamander adult, Monroe County. (Photo by Matthew L. Niemiller) *Right:* Northern Spring Salamander adult, Morgan County. (Photo by Matthew L. Niemiller)

color with distinct dark flecks or spots on the dorsum that do not extend onto the venter. The canthus rostralis is distinctly outlined with yellowish gray or white to black pigmentation and the chin and lower jaw often have distinct black and white mottling. Juveniles resemble adults. Males and females are not sexual dimorphic. Hatchlings and larvae have stream-type morphology with large dorsal fins that extend near the insertion of the hind limbs, long, truncated snouts and relatively small eyes. Gills are large and often appear red because of the stress of handling. Body coloration of larvae varies with age but generally is a uniform light yellowish brown to gray or lavender that becomes darker with age. Larger larvae (up to 95 mm SVL) often have the small spots or flecks found in adults. The venter of larvae is light colored.

Etymology: The specific and subspecific epithets, *porphyriticus*, are from the Greek *porphyros* "reddish-brown or purple" and *-icus* calling attention to the color. The subspecific epithet, *danielsi*, honors Lewis E. Daniels, a turn-of-the-century doctor who collected some of the original specimens of this subspecies.

Similar Species: Spring Salamanders closely resemble Red Salamanders (*Pseudotriton ruber*) and Mud Salamanders (*P. montanus*), but these two species lack a canthus rostralis and have shorter, more rounded snouts. Larval Red Salamanders do not grow as large as larval Spring Salamanders and often have darker pigmentation running from the eye to the snout that is absent in larval Spring Salamanders. In addition, the snout of larval Red Salamanders is shorter and more rounded than

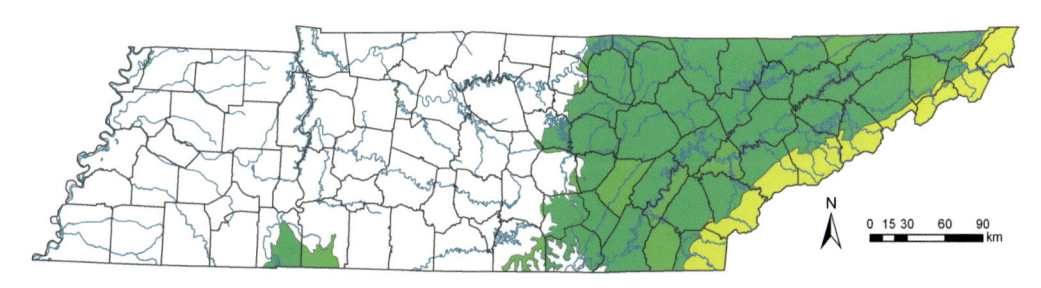

Two subspecies of Spring Salamanders are recognized in Tennessee: the Northern Spring Salamander *(G. p. porphyriticus)*, whose range appears in green, and the Blue Ridge Spring Salamander *(G. p. danielsi)* in yellow.

Left: Northern Spring Salamander larva from a cave, Knox County. (Photo by Brad M. Glorioso) *Right:* Blue Ridge Spring Salamander larva, Polk County. (Photo by Matthew L. Niemiller)

Spring Salamander larvae. Spring Salamander larvae in caves also might be confused with the closely related Tennessee Cave Salamander (*G. palleucus*) and Berry Cave Salamander (*G. gulolineatus*). Both obligate cave species have longer, more spatulate snouts with small eyes that are one-quarter to one-fifth the length of the snout, whereas Spring Salamander larvae have slightly shorter snouts and larger eyes one-third the length of the snout.

Distribution: Spring Salamanders are associated with the highlands of eastern North America from southern Quebec in Canada south to central Alabama. In Tennessee, Spring Salamanders are found throughout the Eastern Highland Rim, Cumberland Plateau, Ridge and Valley, and Blue Ridge Mountains in the eastern third of the state. Spring Salamanders have also been documented from southern Hardin County in West Tennessee. The Northern Spring Salamander occurs throughout most of the state but might intergrade with the Kentucky Spring Salamander (*G. p. duryi*). Populations in the Blue Ridge Mountains are assigned to the Blue Ridge Spring Salamander. However, this species likely is comprised of several cryptic taxa and further study is needed to delineate specific and subspecific boundaries.

Habitat: Spring Salamanders are most common in around springs, seepages, and first-order streams in mesic hardwood forests, and are particularly abundant in caves throughout their range in the state. Both adults and juveniles can be found underneath rocks and other cover objects in and along streams. On the surface, adults are most easily encountered on trails and roads near streams and seeps on wet, rainy nights. Larvae are most active at night and have been collected from gravel beds and underneath rocks and logs in springs, seepages, spring runs, and cave streams. In the Ridge and Valley, Spring Salamanders are found predominately in caves, but few records exist from the southern Ridge and Valley in Tennessee.

Natural History: Spring Salamanders likely breed in spring and autumn. Females deposit up to 100 eggs attached singly to the undersurfaces of rocks and logs deep within springs and caves in late summer and early autumn. Females guard eggs that hatch in 10–12 weeks. The larval period is considerable, ranging from up to 4–5 years for surface populations to up to 10 years for some subterranean populations. Males and females reach sexual maturity within a year of metamorphosis. Spring Salamanders feed on a variety of invertebrates in addition to other salamanders. Adults also are known to cannibalize smaller conspecifics. Spring Salamanders are known prey of Northern Watersnakes and Eastern Gartersnakes.

Conservation Status: Spring Salamanders are difficult to find because of their secretive nature and tendency to inhabit subterranean haunts, but they are by no means uncommon. Deforestation and urbanization likely are detrimental to surface populations, but large subterranean populations are known to exist in the Knoxville metropolitan area.

Matthew L. Niemiller

Four-Toed Salamander adult, Campbell County. (Photo by Matthew L. Niemiller)

Four-Toed Salamander

Hemidactylium scutatum

Description: The Four-Toed Salamander is a small, slender salamander with adults ranging 50–100 mm TL. Individuals are most easily identified by the presence of only four toes on both the fore and hind limbs and a distinct constriction at the base of the tail. The dorsum typically has a distinct chevron or herringbone pattern that is reddish brown, transitioning to gray laterally, whereas the venter is bright white with conspicuous black spots or blotches. Costal grooves number 13–14, and nasolabial grooves are present. Males are smaller on average and have longer tails relative to their body. Sexual active males have truncated snouts and enlarged premaxillary teeth that are visible when the mouth is shut. Females have rounded snouts. Juveniles generally have the same

Left: Four-Toed Salamander larva, Coffee County. (Photo by Matthew L. Niemiller) *Right:* Venter of the Four-Toed Salamander, Coffee County. (Photo by Brad M. Glorioso)

appearance as adults. Hatchlings are 11–15 mm TL. Larvae have a mottled yellow to brown dorsum, large eyes and gills, and a tail fin that extends almost to the head. No subspecies are currently recognized.

Etymology: The specific epithet, *scutatum,* is Latin meaning "armed with a shield," referring to the shield-like plates appearing to cover the costal grooves.

Similar Species: In Tennessee, no other salamander can be confused with the Four-Toed Salamander because of its unique combination of four toes on the hind limbs, basal constriction of the tail, and white venter with bold black spots. Larvae could potentially be confused with larval Mudpuppies (*Necturus maculosus*). However, Mudpuppies grow to a much larger sizes and do not have a tail fin that extends well onto the dorsum.

Distribution: The Four-Toed Salamander is widely distributed throughout eastern North America from Ontario, Canada, to the Gulf Coast. However, this species is characterized by many disjunct populations throughout its range. In Tennessee, this species is known from the Western Highland Rim east to the lower elevations of the Blue Ridge Mountains, though the exact extent of its range in the state is poorly known.

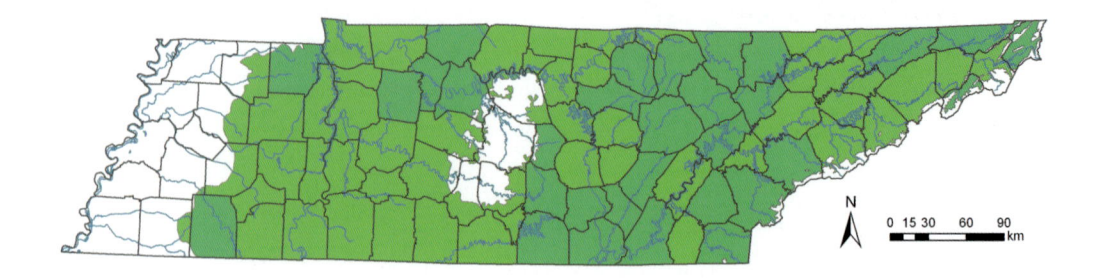

Habitat: Four-Toed Salamanders are found near fishless springs, vernal ponds, bogs, streams, and seeps in mesic forests. During the breeding season, females are most often found under moss mats (usually sphagnum) or under debris on the outskirts of these aquatic habitats. When not breeding this species is most often found in forests surrounding the breeding areas underneath rotting logs, rocks, and within leaf litter.

Natural History: Although information on Tennessee populations is unavailable, Four-Toed Salamanders likely mate prior to migrating to breeding ponds in late autumn and winter. A spring migration to nesting sites follows in most populations, but autumn migrations are known to occur in some Arkansas populations. Oviposition most likely occurs in February, when eggs are deposited in a loose cluster in crevices just above the water line under moss mats located at the edge of or on raised moss mats within bogs, swamps, vernal ponds, and even slow-moving streams. Eggs are less commonly found under a variety of debris on the forest floor. Eggs are slightly pigmented and have two envelopes, the outer of which is sticky. Communal nests of up to 1,110 eggs (30–35 females) have been reported. In these instances, only a couple of females remain to brood the nests. Eggs hatch in 6–9 weeks. After hatching larvae move into the adjacent water and forage on a variety of small invertebrates for a short period. Metamorphosis usually occurs within just 3–5 weeks at 17–25 mm TL. Juveniles disperse from the ponds, thriving in adjacent forests until reaching sexual maturity in 2 years. Adults tend to be found in large aggregations, foraging on beetles, caterpillars, spiders, mites, and other invertebrates. Predators are not well documented but likely include small mammals, snakes, and birds. Defensive posturing, noxious tail secretions, and tail autotomy all decrease predation risk for this species.

Conservation Status: The Four-Toed Salamander is state listed as "Vulnerable" and is "Deemed in Need of Management" in Tennessee. This species is highly specialized in its breeding biology. Thus, recent declines are thought to be due to a lack of suitable habitat for breeding, such as bogs, wetlands and vernal ponds that have moss mats associated with them. In order to preserve this species it is recommended that the above areas be protected as well as surrounding forests.

Stesha A. Pasachnik and
Matthew L. Niemiller

Tellico Salamander adult, Monroe County. (Photo by Matthew L. Niemiller)

Tellico Salamander

Plethodon aureolus

Description: The Tellico Salamander is a smaller member of the Slimy Salamander (*P. glutinosus*) complex with adults ranging 90–140 mm TL and reaching a maximum of 72 mm SVL (151 mm TL). Both adults and juveniles are pigmented slate gray to bluish black with abundant brassy spotting on the dorsum. The sides of the body have numerous yellowish to whitish spots, but higher elevation populations might lack much of this spotting. The venter is gray and lacks any discernable spotting or mottling. The tail is distinctly rounded in cross section. Sixteen costal grooves are present and nasolabial grooves are present. There are four toes on the fore limbs and five on the hind limbs. Sexually active males have conspicuously round mental glands on the chin. No subspecies are recognized.

Etymology: The specific epithet, *aureolus*, is Latin meaning "golden" or "splendid," referring to the brassy colored spots on the dorsum,

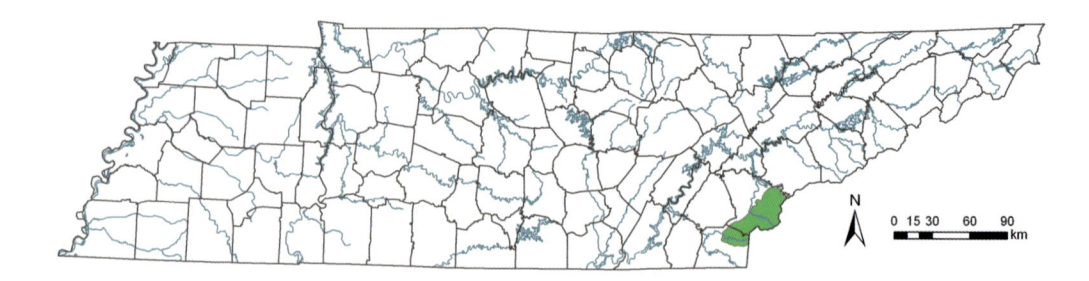

Left: Tellico Salamander adult, Monroe County. (Photo by Matthew L. Niemiller) *Right:* Tellico Salamander adult, Monroe County. (Photo by Matthew L. Niemiller)

which make this species a very attractive—indeed, splendid—one.

Similar Species: Tellico Salamanders co-occur with Southern Appalachian Salamanders (*P. teyahalee*) but can be distinguished by size and coloration. Southern Appalachian Salamanders have white spotting rather than brassy spotting on the dorsum and attain a larger size, reaching up to 90 mm SVL. Some allopatric populations of the Northern Slimy Salamander (*P. glutinosus*) are morphologically indistinguishable from Tellico Salamanders and are best differentiated based on distribution. Tellico Salamanders are known to hybridize over a wide zone with Red-Legged Salamanders (*P. shermani*) along Sassafras Ridge in Monroe County, making species determination of some individuals difficult. Generally, Tellico Salamanders can be distinguished from Red-Legged Salamanders based on coloration. Red-Legged Salamanders possess red patches on the legs and lack white spotting on the sides, whereas Tellico Salamanders lack and red coloration (but see the Red-Legged Salamander account).

Distribution: Tellico Salamanders have a limited distribution on the western slopes and adjacent lowlands of the Unicoi Mountains between the Little Tennessee and Hiwassee rivers in northeastern Polk and eastern Monroe counties in southeastern Tennessee, as well as a slight overlap into northwestern Graham and Cherokee counties in southwestern North Carolina.

Habitat: Tellico Salamanders are found in cool, moist, mountainous forests primarily at lower elevations but occurring up to 1,620 m. Adults and juveniles are found in the same habitat typically underneath rocks and fallen logs during the day in forested areas. Salamanders can be found on the surface at night during favorable weather and are most active on the surface during moist summer nights. Many individuals are found at the base of rocky outcrops, where they presumably hide in the rocks during unfavorable conditions. During periods of drought and cold, salamanders retreat deeper underground.

Natural History: Little published information exists on the life history and ecology of this species. Females likely brood terrestrial eggs. Sexual maturity probably is reached in two to three years. Like other species of *Plethodon*, this species produces noxious skin secretions from the tail to deter potential predators.

Conservation Status: Much of the distribution of this species occurs on state and federal properties. Tellico Salamanders also seem to be fairly resilient to logging operations. However, since this species has an extremely limited range in Tennessee, efforts should be made to monitor and protect existing populations. The Tellico Salamander is state listed as "Imperiled."

Matthew L. Niemiller and
R. Graham Reynolds

Eastern Red-Backed Salamander adult, Carter County. (Photo by Matthew L. Niemiller)

Eastern Red-Backed Salamander

Plethodon cinereus

Description: The Eastern Red-Backed Salamander is a small, terrestrial woodland salamander. Adults are 65–125 mm TL, although sexually mature individuals as small as 57 mm TL have been documented. Most individuals have 18–20 costal grooves and legs that appear somewhat short and stubby relative to overall body size. Eastern Red-Backed Salamander populations are often polymorphic, containing individuals of both a striped redback phase, with a distinct, straight-edged red to orange to tan longitudinal dorsal stripe extending from the head onto the tail, and an unstriped leadback phase, displaying a uniformly dark brown to blackish dorsum. The venter is similarly marked in both morphs, mottled with approximately equal amounts of both black and white, giving the belly a salt-and-pepper appearance, with little to no hints of red pigmentation. Interestingly, some populations also contain individuals with intermediate phenotypes, displaying conspicuous striping only anteriorly or posteriorly, as well as broken or dashed striping. Albinistic and erythristic (extensively red-pigmented) individuals have been documented from populations as well. The tail is distinctly rounded in cross section. Nasolabial grooves are present. Four toes are found on the fore limbs and five toes on the hind limbs. Sexually active males have small, slightly oval-shaped mental glands on the chin. No subspecies are recognized.

Etymology: The specific epithet, *cinereus,* is from the Latin *ciner* "ashes" and with the suffix means "ashy colored." This is in reference to the dorsal color of the leadback phase in this species.

Similar Species: The Eastern Red-Backed Salamander is quite similar to several other small, polymorphic eastern *Plethodon* salamanders found in Tennessee, including the Southern Red-Backed Salamander (*P. serratus*) and Zigzag Salamander complex (*P. dorsalis* and *P. ventralis*). Though the redback forms of both the Eastern and Southern Red-Backed Salamanders are extremely similar, distinguishing between these two species is easily accomplished via geography alone. Eastern Red-Backed Salamanders occur north and east of the French Broad River, while Southern Red-Backed Salamanders occur to the south and west. Striped individuals of Eastern Red-Backed Salamanders are also easily distinguishable from redback Zigzag Salamanders by their much more uniform and straighter edged dorsal stripe as compared to the wavy, sinuous borders of the stripe in Zigzag Salamanders. Unstriped morphs of Eastern Red-Backed Salamanders can also be distinguished from unstriped Zigzag Salamanders by their shorter limbs, with Eastern Red-Backed Salamanders typically having 8–10 costal folds between adpressed limbs, compared to 6–7 costal folds between adpressed limbs for Zigzag Salamanders.

Distribution: Eastern Red-Backed Salamanders range from the Northeast and Great Lakes regions southward into West Virginia, Virginia, portions of North Carolina, and northeastern Tennessee. This species occurs in the northern sections of the Ridge and Valley and Blue Ridge Mountains in northeastern Tennessee,

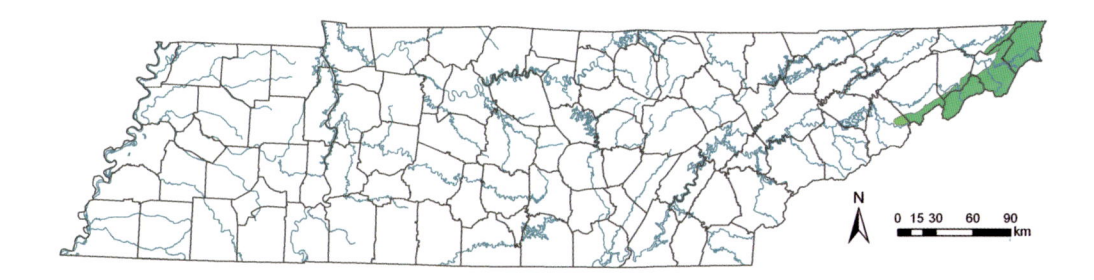

Eastern Red-Backed Salamander leadback phase adult, Steuben County, Indiana. (Photo by Todd Pierson)

north and east of the French Broad River with verified records from Greene, Washington, Unicoi, Carter, Sullivan, and Johnson counties.

Habitat: The Eastern Red-Backed Salamander occupies a wide variety of terrestrial forest habitats and can be found in deciduous, mixed, and sometimes conifer forests. Individuals typically are encountered under cover objects, such as rocks and logs, which they might actively defend as feeding territories. Salamanders can also be found within leaf litter, rotting logs, and in cavities in the soil or other cool, moist locations where risks of exposure to extreme temperatures or desiccation are reduced. Individuals seem to prefer areas of near-neutral soil pH (approximately 6.0–6.8), seemingly exclusively avoiding regions of acidic soil (pH < 3.7) and extremely rocky substrates.

Natural History: Eastern Red-Backed Salamanders are often extremely abundant in parts of their range. For instance, biomass estimates of individuals in New Hampshire exceed that of nesting birds, and are comparable to that of mammals, even when based only on individuals that were active on the surface at the time of sampling. Such great abundance is probably a major factor underlying the wealth of studies on this salamander, about which much is known regarding its life history and ecology. Like all members of the genus *Plethodon,* the Eastern Red-Backed Salamander has a completely terrestrial life cycle. Courtship occurs from fall to early spring, and is a highly chemical affair. In late spring to early summer (sometimes as late as early autumn), 1–14 (typically 6–9) pale yellow eggs are deposited in damp cavities or crevices within leaf litter, burrows, or rotting logs, typically suspended from above by thin gelatinous stalks. Eggs are typically guarded by the female, which defends her nest against conspecific females. Females might occasionally cannibalize their own eggs, however. The direct-developing hatchlings emerge about six weeks later appearing as miniature versions of the adults but occasionally still possessing three embryonic gills, which are lost shortly thereafter. Eastern Red-Backed Salamanders feed on a wide variety of small invertebrate prey, typically consuming any available prey item they can capture, sometimes even conspecific juveniles, although this is rare. Both males and females aggressively defend territories against conspecifics, as well as other congeners, which might represent defense of feeding areas or mates. Predators include several snakes, small mammals, leaf litter–foraging birds, and large predatory invertebrates.

Conservation Status: Populations of the Eastern Red-Backed Salamanders appear stable and secure in Tennessee. Habitat quality and forest patch size have both been positively associated with abundance of this species. Therefore, clear cutting and forest fragmentation both pose substantial risks for possible population declines.

Jason R. Jones and
Matthew L. Niemiller

Eastern Zigzag Salamander leadback phase adult, Rutherford County. (Photo by Matthew L. Niemiller)

Zigzag Salamander Complex

Northern Zigzag Salamander
Plethodon dorsalis

Southern Zigzag Salamander
Plethodon ventralis

Description: Zigzag Salamanders are small, terrestrial woodland salamanders that exhibit dorsal color polymorphism occurring in both a striped and unstriped morph in most populations. Adults are 65–100 mm TL but can reach 111 mm TL. The striped morph has an undulating ("zigzag") stripe yellowish brown to dark red in color on the dorsum extending from the head to the tail tip. However, this stripe might become obscured by darker pigmentation, such that the stripe appears to extend only to the middle of the dorsum or only a faint outline of the stripe remains. The unstriped or lead morph lacks evidence of a dorsal stripe. Instead the ground color of the dorsum is grayish black. Both morphs have numerous silvery white to brassy flecks on the sides and dorsum that often

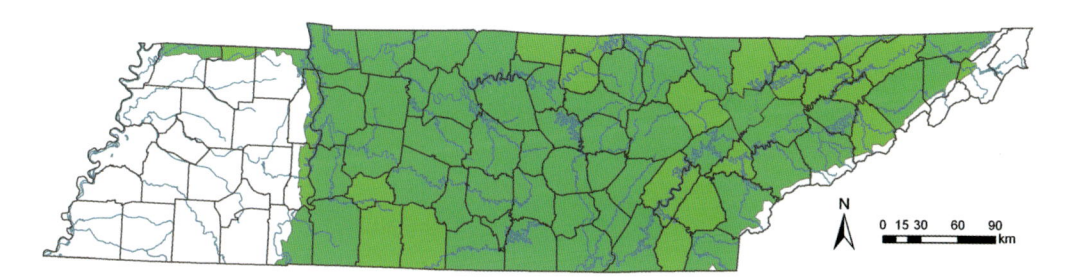

Left: Northern Zigzag Salamander adult, Putnam County. (Photo by Matthew L. Niemiller) *Right:* Southern Zigzag Salamander adult, Blount County. (Photo by Matthew L. Niemiller)

can produce a frosted appearance, particularly in the unstriped morph. Likewise, the venter in both morphs is mottled with black, white, gray, and orange to red pigmentation. Orange to red pigmentation is often present at the insertion of the limbs, particularly in the unstriped morph. In some populations in central Tennessee, this pigmentation is more extensive forming a conspicuous orange to red shoulder patch at the insertion of the fore limbs. The tail is distinctly rounded in cross section. Costal grooves number 18–21. Nasolabial grooves are present. Four toes are found on the fore limbs and five toes on the hind limbs. Sexually active males have small, oval-shaped mental glands on the chin and nasolabial swellings. No subspecies are recognized; however, based on allozyme data the Southern Zigzag Salamander (*P. ventralis*) was considered conspecific with the Northern Zigzag Salamander (*P. dorsalis*) until recently. These two species cannot be distinguished morphologically, and their distributions have not yet been thoroughly examined in Tennessee. Therefore, we treat these two species in a single account.

Etymology: The specific epithet, *dorsalis,* is from the Latin for "back," referring to the distinct pattern on the dorsum that distinguishes this species from other similar plethodontids. The specific epithet, *ventralis,* is Latin for "of the belly" and refers to the coloration of the venter of this species, consisting of nearly equal amounts of red, black, and white pigmentation.

Similar Species: Both species of Zigzag Salamanders can be confused with both the Eastern and Southern Red-Backed Salamander. The striped morph of both Red-Backed Salamander species has a more uniform and straighter-edged dorsal stripe compared to the wavy, sinuous stripe of Zigzag Salamanders. Unstriped morphs of the Red-Backed Salamander species can also be distinguished from unstriped Zigzag Salamanders by their shorter limbs, with Eastern Red-Backed Salamanders typically having 8–10 costal folds between adpressed limbs, compared to 6–7 costal folds between adpressed limbs for Zigzag Salamanders. Zigzag Salamanders are sometimes confused with round-tailed *Desmognathus* salamanders (e.g., Cumberland Dusky Salamanders and

Ocoee Salamanders); however, *Desmognathus* salamanders have much larger hind limbs than fore limbs and possess a light line that runs from the eye to the posterior angle of the jaw.

Distribution: The Zigzag Salamander Complex is associated with karst limestones in the Interior Low Plateau of southern Indiana and Illinois, Kentucky, Tennessee, northern Alabama, northwest Georgia, and portions of the Ridge and Valley and Blue Ridge Mountains in eastern Tennessee and western North Carolina. The complex occurs throughout much of Tennessee but is noticeably absent from the Mississippi Alluvial Plain, Mississippi Valley Loess Plains, and the Southeastern Plains. However, Zigzag Salamanders have been reported from Obion and Henry counties. The complex also is noticeably absent from much of the Cumberland Mountains. The Southern Zigzag Salamander is thought to range southward from south-central Kentucky and southwestern Virginia into eastern Tennessee, northwestern Georgia, northern Alabama, and northeastern Mississippi, whereas the Northern Zigzag Salamander ranges south from southern Indiana into central and western Kentucky, small portions of east-central and south Illinois, and central Tennessee. However, the ranges of both species in Tennessee have not been thoroughly examined.

Habitat: Zigzag Salamanders occur in a variety of habitats below 760 m in elevation, typically in rocky areas in mixed hardwood forests, along the banks of streams and springs, and in caves, with both species seeming to prefer moister habitats than Red-Backed Salamanders. During the day, individuals can often be located beneath rocks and logs, as well as in most packs of leaf litter. Both adults and juveniles are surface active during autumn and winter and move underground in burrows and crevices in limestone from April through October. However, salamanders can be found on the surface at night during rainy weather.

Natural History: The reproductive biology of Zigzag Salamanders in poorly documented, as few nests have ever been found. Oviposition occurs in summer after females retreat from the surface because of increasing temperatures. All known nests are from caves, where females lay small clutches of 2–5 eggs attached to the substrate in crevices in mud banks, cave walls, or in cave formations. Females brood their eggs, which presumably hatch in 9–12 weeks as miniature adults. Sexual maturity is reached in 2–3 years. The diet consists of small invertebrates, including beetles, mites, and spiders. Predators are poorly documented but likely include birds, woodland snakes, and small mammals. Unlike other species of *Plethodon,* Zigzag Salamanders apparently show little aggression toward conspecifics, as multiple individuals are often found under the same cover object.

Conservation Status: Both species of Zigzag Salamander are secure with stable populations in Tennessee. Urbanization and conversion of hardwood forest habitat to agricultural use are likely the largest threats to populations of both species.

Jason R. Jones and
Matthew L. Niemiller

Northern Slimy Salamander adult, Coffee County. (Photo by Brad M. Glorioso)

Slimy Salamander Complex

White-Spotted Slimy Salamander
Plethodon cylindraceus

Northern Slimy Salamander
Plethodon glutinosus

Mississippi Slimy Salamander
Plethodon mississippi

Description: These three members of the Slimy Salamander complex are large lungless salamanders measuring 120–190 mm TL. The ground color of the dorsum and sides are dark bluish gray to black with brassy, yellow, or white flecks or spots. The spots migrate to the sides of the body as an individual ages, often coalescing into a broad pale side stripe in older individuals. The ground color of the venter is grayish black and usually paler than, and lacks the spotting characteristic of, the dorsum and sides. There are usually either 16 or 17 (occasionally 15) costal grooves and nasolabial grooves are present. The tail is round in cross section, often paler in coloration than the trunk, and relatively long. The front limbs are slender with four toes, whereas the hind limbs are stouter than the front limbs and have five toes. Sexually active

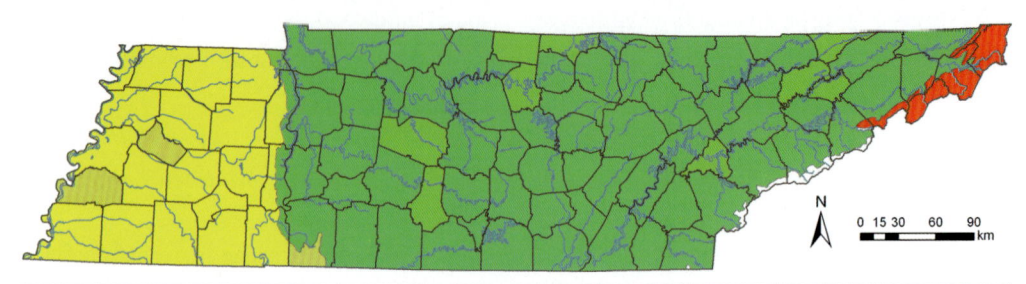

Three species of Slimy Salamanders are recognized in Tennessee: the White-Spotted Slimy Salamander (*P. cylindraceus*), whose range appears in red; the Northern Slimy Salamander (*P. glutinosus*), whose range appears in green; and the Mississippi Slimy Salamander (*P. mississippi*), whose range appears in yellow.

Left: White-Spotted Slimy Salamander adult, Carter County. (Photo by Matthew L. Niemiller) *Right:* Northern Slimy Salamander adult, Morgan County. (Photo by Brad M. Glorioso)

males have a prominent, round mental gland under the chin and small, round yellow to orange glands on the venter. Hatchlings are 18–30 mm TL and uniformly gray to black on the dorsum and lack pigmentation on the venter. The dorsum also has unpigmented areas that appear as light spots. Members of this complex were once considered a single species, but several species are currently recognized based on molecular analyses. These three species are all very similar in morphology and are best differentiated based on distribution or using molecular data.

Etymology: The specific epithet, *glutinosus,* is Latin for "full of glue," referring to the sticky white secretions produced as a defense mechanism in the tail. The specific epithet, *cylindraceus,* is from the Latin *cylindrus* "cylinder" and *-aceus* "resembles," probably referring to the shape of the body. The specific epithet, *mississippi,* refers to the state, where the type locality was obtained. Originally from the Chippewa words *mici zibi* "great river" and Algonquin *messipi.*

Similar Species: Members of the Slimy Salamander complex are most similar in appearance to each other. Distinguishing among members of the complex by morphology is very difficult and geography is often the best way to determine species. Northern Slimy Salamanders are easily confused with Southern Appalachian Salamanders (*P. teyahalee*); however, Northern Slimy Salamanders typically have larger and more numerous white or brassy spotting on the dorsum and sides and also have a darker chin than Southern Appalachian Salamanders. Northern Slimy Salamanders also are very similar to Tellico Salamanders (*P. aureolus*) but the latter generally have brassy rather than white spots or flecks on the dorsum. Some allopatric populations of the Northern Slimy Salamander are morphologically indistinguishable from Tellico Salamanders and are best differentiated based on distribution. Northern Slimy Salamanders also closely resemble Cumberland Plateau Salamanders (*P. kentucki*). Cumberland Plateau Salamanders generally are smaller, have fewer and smaller white spots or flecks on the dorsum, have a paler colored chin and throat, and the males have smaller mental glands. Northern Slimy Salamanders often cannot be distinguished from Cumberland Plateau Salamanders, however. Northern Slimy Salamanders resemble Red-Cheeked Salamanders

Left: Mississippi Slimy Salamander, Chester County. (Photo by Matthew L. Niemiller) *Right:* White-Spotted Slimy Salamander hatchling, Carter County. (Photo by Matthew L. Niemiller)

(*P. jordani*) and Red-Legged Salamanders (*P. shermani*) but lack the diagnostic reddish cheek patches and reddish leg patches found in these two species, respectively. Another member of the Red-Cheeked Salamander complex, the Northern Gray-Cheeked Salamander (*P. montanus*) also resembles the White Spotted Slimy Salamander but lacks conspicuous white spotting. Northern Slimy Salamanders are known to hybridize with Southern Appalachian Salamanders, Tellico Salamanders, and members of the Red-Cheeked Salamander complex. Species identification of some individuals can be extremely difficult in some areas. Northern Slimy Salamanders and Mississippi Slimy Salamanders are also often confused with Small-Mouthed (*Ambystoma texanum*) and Streamside Salamanders (*A. barbouri*). Members of the complex can be distinguished from the ambystomatid species by the presence of nasolabial grooves (lacking in ambystomatids) and white to brassy flecking or spotting pattern.

Distribution: The Slimy Salamander complex is distributed across all of Tennessee. Mississippi Slimy Salamanders are found in the western third of the state, roughly west of the north-flowing Tennessee River in the Coastal Plain ecoregions (Mississippi Alluvial Valley, Mississippi Valley Loess Plains, and the Southeastern Plains). The Northern Slimy Salamander is found in the eastern two-thirds of the state throughout the Interior Plateau, Cumberland Plateau, Cumberland Mountains, Ridge and Valley, and the southern and central Blue Ridge Mountains. The White-Spotted Slimy Salamander is found in extreme eastern Tennessee in the northern sections of the Ridge and Valley and Blue Ridge Mountains.

Habitat: Members of the Slimy Salamander complex in Tennessee are associated with mesic, deciduous forests generally below 1,500 m, where they inhabit moist environments on the forest floor often beneath rocks, logs, and other cover. Slimy Salamanders also inhabit the twilight zones of caves where they can be found beneath rocks on the cave floor and in crevices of the walls and ceilings. Salamanders can be found on the forest floor at night during favorable weather and are most active on the surface in summer. During periods of drought and cold, salamanders retreat underground.

Natural History: Breeding activities of Slimy Salamanders are poorly documented in Tennessee. Courtship is elaborate and occurs on land presumably from spring through early autumn. Relatively few nests have been discovered, but female Slimy Salamanders deposit 8–18 white to pale yellow eggs in moist subterranean cavities or, more rarely, underneath or within rotting logs or other surface debris. Ovipositon occurs from late spring through late summer. Females remain with their eggs until they hatch 2–3 months later; occasionally females are found coiling around their egg cluster. As with all members of the genus *Plethodon,* the larval stage is bypassed in the egg. Hatchlings resemble adults, but some individuals hatch with gill remnants that are quickly (1–2 days) reabsorbed. Hatchlings often remain in the nest site for 2–3 weeks, and the female often continues to brood her young during this time. Individuals are sexually active one (males) to two (females) years after hatching. Mississippi Slimy Salamanders have been documented to reach at least 11 years of age. Slimy Salamanders are opportunistic in feeding; their diets include a variety of small invertebrates, such as insects, spiders, millipedes, phalangids, and earthworms. A few accounts of Slimy Salamanders ingesting other salamanders have been reported. Members of this complex produce copious secretions from the skin, particularly from the tail, when threatened or handled. These secretions are particularly sticky (hence the specific epithet *glutinosus* for the Northern Slimy Salamander) and function to deter predation. Nonetheless, Slimy Salamanders are eaten by a variety of predators, including several species of snakes, other salamanders, birds, and mammals.

Conservation Status: These species are widespread and locally abundant throughout their respective ranges in Tennessee. We have found members of this complex to be particularly abundant in the twilight zones of caves in Middle Tennessee. In some caves we documented 100-plus individuals within the twilight zone. Caves are often used as nesting sites. Consequently, protecting the forest habitat associated with caves and sinks will benefit the Slimy Salamander complex.

Brian T. Miller and
Matthew L. Niemiller

Field Notes

Jordani by the Hundreds

The weather was perfect, a warm and rainy October night in the Great Smoky Mountains. Matt and I loaded up our gear—headlamps and boots—and headed for the mountains with Dylan Dittrich-Reed and Jennifer, a short 45-minute drive from our home base in Knoxville. There is nothing quite like the Smoky Mountains on a rainy night. For one thing, there is no one else there. No long lines of cars, drivers honking through the tunnels, or people splashing in the creeks—just silence, Nature, and the scents of a moist forest. For those who pay attention to these things, the Smokies have a unique smell. It is a spicy olfactory signature that those who are familiar with this region can recognize, and the smell on a rainy night is enchanting. It is a mixture of mountain streams, thick humus, rotten logs, fungi, and plants—a rich, palpable smell that instantly transports you to a place away from anthropocentrism. It is on these nights, enriched by scent, sound, and moisture, that amphibians are perhaps best appreciated.

We began this evening like most others, by cruising the park road from Cades Cove to Sugarlands. We found the usual assortment of herptiles crossing the pavement: *Desmognathus*, *Eurycea*, and *Gyrinophilus* salamanders; *Lithobates*, *Hyla*, and *Anaxyrus* frogs; and the obligatory (and ubiquitous!) Northern Copperheads (*Agkistrodon contortrix*) out chasing prey. We eventually arrived at one of our favorite spots for amphibians, a place where the true abundance of salamanders can only be appreciated on nights like this. We geared up and headed into the forest along a stream, very close to a popular diurnal picnic area. Within seconds we began to realize how special this night was to be. "Hey, I got a *jordani!*" said Matt. "Me too!" answered Dylan. "There are dozens!" announced Jen.

I began to scan the ground and nearly lost my breath. There, scattered across the leaf litter, on shrubs and grass stems, at the bases of trees and climbing rocks, were more Red-cheeked Salamanders than all I had previously seen combined. Hundreds, perhaps thousands, of these incredibly beautiful animals were cavorting on the surface, enjoying that magical night. In hours of rock turning during the day a fair number of this species might be found, but this was truly mind-blowing. Their red cheek patches glowed back at us from our headlamps like hundreds of dayglo paint splotches. To add to our delight, other salamanders were there as well—*Pseudotriton ruber*, *Eurycea wilderae*, *Plethodon serratus*, and *Desmognathus imitator*, in nearly equal numbers. We enjoyed, photographed, and appreciated the diversity and abundance of amphibians in the park and returned to Knoxville much richer for the experience. This was a magical evening indeed.

R. Graham Reynolds

Jordan's Red-Cheeked Salamander adult, Sevier County. (Photo by Matthew L. Niemiller)

Jordan's Red-Cheeked Salamander

Plethodon jordani

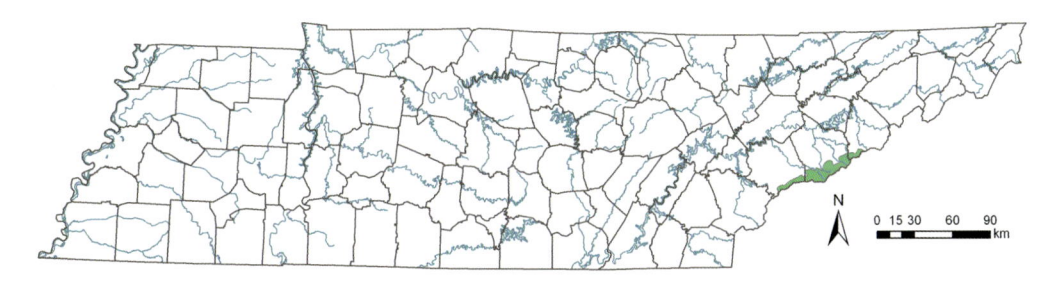

Description: Jordan's Red-Cheeked Salamander is arguably the most attractive salamander in the Great Smoky Mountains. Adults have a gunmetal gray dorsal coloration which lacks obvious spots or pattern, a lighter gray venter, and large protuberant pink to bright red to orange cheek patches which extend from behind the eye to above the lateral extension of the gular fold. The top of the head might be a dull brown color and there are usually 15–16 costal grooves and nasolabial grooves are present. Adults can be quite large averaging about 112 mm TL, with a record size of about 180 mm TL. The tail accounts for about half of the body length, and is round in cross section. The fore and hinds limbs are similar in size with four toes on the fore limbs and five on the hind limbs. Males develop prominent mental glands during the breeding season but otherwise can be distinguished by the presence of prominent cloacal lips. Juveniles resemble adults but have red spots on the dorsum instead of red cheeks, which will develop later. No subspecies are recognized.

Etymology: The specific epithet *jordani*, honors David S. Jordan, president of Indiana University (1885–1891) and Stanford University in California (1900–1931). He coined Jordan's Law, which states that a species' closest relative must be found just across a distributional barrier.

Similar Species: Jordan's Red-Cheeked Salamander is quite distinct from other plethodontid species due to the presence of bright red cheek patches. Slimy Salamanders (*P. glutinosus* complex) usually have white spots or flecks and lack red embellishments. Jordan's Red-Cheeked Salamanders are closely mimicked by the Imitator Salamander (*Desmognathus imitator*), which also has red cheek patches. The Imitator Salamander can be distinguished readily by having hind limbs that are larger in proportion to the front limbs and a pale line that runs from the eye to the posterior angle of the jaw.

Distribution: The range of Jordan's Red-Cheeked Salamander is contained entirely within Great Smoky Mountains National Park. In Tennessee, these salamanders can be found at middle to high elevations (870–2,020 m) in Blount and Sevier counties, as well as part of Cocke County.

Habitat: Jordan's Red-Cheeked Salamander is a locally common species, usually found associated with spruce-fir forest and mixed deciduous hardwood forest in areas with plenty of moss and cover objects. They take refuge in burrows underneath cover objects during the hottest and coldest periods of the year. During the day they seek shelter under cover and can be readily discovered by turning and replacing

Jordan's Red-Cheeked Salamander adult, Sevier County. (Photo by Matthew L. Niemiller)

cover objects, such as rocks and logs. We have walked altitudinal transects and have found no individuals in some areas and many in other areas just a short distance down a trail. Like some other members of the genus *Plethodon*, to truly appreciate the density of this species, you must be out in the forest on a warm rainy or misty night, when hundreds of these salamanders blanket the forest floor—a magical spectacle that we highly recommend to all amphibian enthusiasts (see "*Field Notes: Jordani* by the Hundreds").

Natural History: Most aspects of the reproductive biology of Jordan's Red-Cheeked Salamander are unknown. Mating likely occurs in August or September, with oviposition occurring in underground cavities in spring. Juveniles emerge in May and mature in 3–5 years. Adults and juveniles feed on a variety of forest floor invertebrates. Predators include other salamanders, such as Black-Bellied Salamanders (*Desmognathus quadramaculatus*) and Spring Salamanders (*Gyrinophilus porphyriticus*), woodland snakes, and small mammals. It is hypothesized that the red cheeks of this species serve to advertise their noxious tail secretions to potential predators. The slimy secretions are much like glue and are probably foul tasting (we haven't yet tried it). The Imitator Salamander is thought to be mimicking the red cheek patches of Jordan's Red-Cheeked Salamander in order to take advantage of this aposematic trait to disguise their own palatability. Both of these species might be found in close proximity, sometimes under the same cover object.

Conservation Status: No conservation guidelines exist for this species, which enjoys the protection afforded by having nearly its entire range within a national park. Some monitoring is recommended, however, as even national parks are not immune to adverse human activity.

R. Graham Reynolds

Cumberland Plateau Slimy Salamander, Bell County, Kentucky. (Photo by Matthew L. Niemiller)

Cumberland Plateau Salamander

Plethodon kentucki

Description: The Cumberland Plateau Salamander is one of the larger *Plethodon* species measuring 100–170 mm TL. Both adults and juveniles have a slate gray to bluish black dorsal ground color. Small white spots, which can occasionally be slightly brassy, are present, scattered on the dorsum. These spots often coalesce on the sides and the legs. The venter is dark gray with the throat and chin lighter than the rest of the venter. The tail is distinctly rounded in cross section. Sixteen costal grooves are present and nasolabial grooves are present. There are four toes on the fore limbs and five on the hind limbs. Sexually active males have conspicuously round mental glands on the chin. Hatchlings are 14–15 mm SVL and resemble adults but lack much of the characteristic white dorsal spotting. This species was originally thought to be a junior species of *P. glutinosus,* but both morphological and molecular work has found it to be distinct. No subspecies are currently recognized.

Etymology: The specific epithet, *kentucki,* refers to the major range of this species in Kentucky and the location from which the type specimen was obtained.

Cumberland Plateau Slimy Salamander, Bell County, Kentucky. (Photo by Matthew L. Niemiller)

Similar Species: Adult Cumberland Plateau Salamanders resemble Northern Slimy Salamanders (*P. glutinosus*) very closely and might be indistinguishable in the field. Cumberland Plateau Salamanders are generally smaller, have fewer and smaller spots on the dorsum, the chin and throat are often lighter, and adult males have a smaller mental gland. It should be noted that extreme variation does occur in all of these traits in both species. Adult Cumberland Plateau Salamanders might also resemble Wehrle's Salamander (*P. wehrlei*), which has large yellow spots, a dark gray or brown background, and small pale spots on the sides.

Distribution: Cumberland Plateau Salamanders occur in the Cumberland Plateau and Cumberland Mountains from western West Virginia and southwestern Virginia into eastern Kentucky south to the Kentucky-Tennessee border. This species has only been recorded from Scott County in Tennessee near the Kentucky state line. It is likely that populations exist in other parts of the Cumberland Mountains in Tennessee. The editor (RGR) found this species in Bell County, Kentucky, just a couple of miles across the state line, and it is hypothesized that Cumberland Plateau Salamanders might occur in Claiborne County north and west of Harrogate.

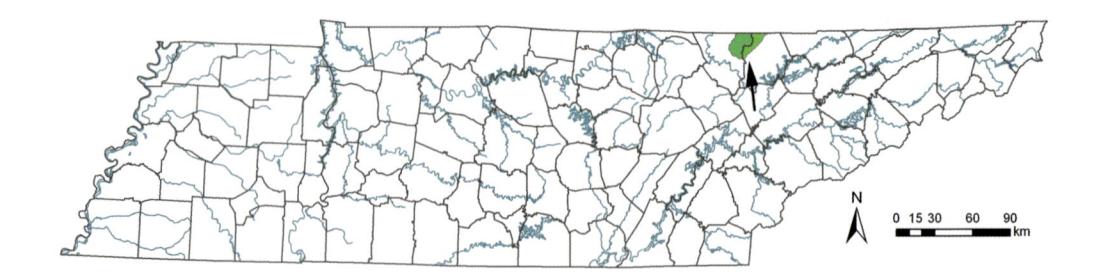

Habitat: Cumberland Plateau Salamanders are associated with mesic, deciduous forests where adults and juveniles inhabit moist environments on the forest floor often beneath rocks, logs, and other cover. In Tennessee, this species was found in a shale outcropping that bordered a gravel road. Throughout its range this species prefers mature hardwood forests that have developed on top of sandstone or shale deposits. In Kentucky Cumberland Plateau Salamanders can be common in closed canopy forest underneath rocks and rotten logs. They can also be found within crevices in the sandstone and shale itself. This species is most active on warm wet nights just after dusk in March and April.

Natural History: Adults breed from late July to late October. Females are thought to oviposit only every other year or less often, whereas males most likely reproduce annually. Females oviposit in underground retreats, laying 9–12 eggs in a grapelike cluster, and guarding them through and often after hatching. Clutch size ranges from 9 to 12 eggs. Hatchlings typically emerge from underground the following summer in June and July. Males reach sexual maturity in 3–4 years and females in 4–5 years. The diet includes springtails, spiders, snails, mites, flies, and beetles. Predators are unknown but likely include small mammals, birds, and snakes.

Conservation Status: The Cumberland Plateau Salamander is state listed as "Critically Imperiled/Imperiled" because of its extremely restricted distribution in our state and apparent low abundance. Habitat destruction and fragmentation could be detrimental to this species. Mature forests are ideal for Cumberland Plateau Salamanders and thus they should be protected in order to guarantee the preservation of this species.

Stesha A. Pasachnik

Northern Gray-Cheeked Salamander adult, Carter County. (Photo by Matthew L. Niemiller)

Northern Gray-Cheeked Salamander

Plethodon montanus

Description: A small- to medium-sized member of the Red-Cheeked Salamander (*P. jordani*) complex, the Northern Gray-Cheeked Salamander measures 85–180 mm TL. The dorsum is slate gray to bluish black and lacks any discernable lighter spotting or flecking. Lighter gray patches are present on the cheeks. The venter is gray and lacks any discernable spotting or mottling, while the chin usually is considerably lighter in coloration. The tail is distinctly rounded in cross section. There are usually 16 costal grooves present, and the fore and hind limbs are of similar diameter. Nasolabial grooves are present. Four toes are present on the fore limbs and five on the hind limbs. Like other *Plethodon* species, sexually active males have conspicuous rounded mental glands on the chin. Hatchlings and juveniles resemble adults.

Etymology: The specific epithet, *montanus,* is Latin for "belonging to a mountain," in reference to this species' proclivity for high-elevation mountainous habitats.

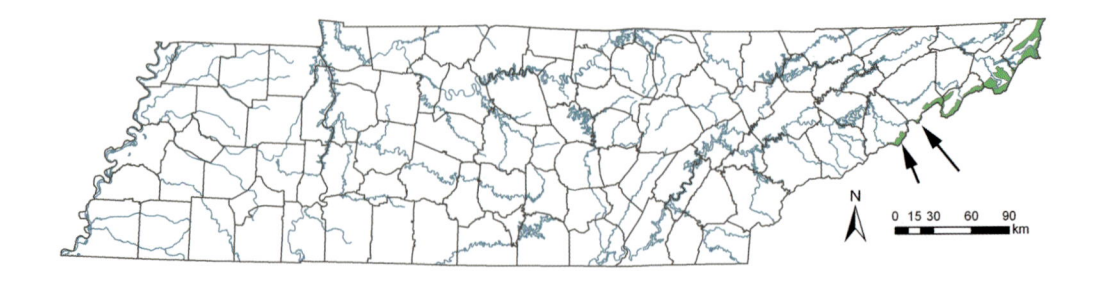

Similar Species: Northern Gray-Cheeked Salamanders resemble other members of the Red-Cheeked Salamander (*P. jordani*) complex. All species in this complex are virtually identical except for coloration. Northern Gray-Cheeked Salamanders lack any red or orange pigmentation on the upper surfaces of the legs or cheeks. Northern Gray-Cheeked Salamanders also resemble members of the Slimy Salamander (*P. glutinosus*) complex, with which they might interbreed, thus complicating identification. In general, distribution and absence of white to brassy spots or flecking should identify Northern Gray-Cheeked Salamanders from Slimy Salamanders.

Distribution: The Northern Gray-Cheeked Salamander is distributed from southwestern Virginia south along the border of North Carolina and Tennessee roughly north of Interstate 40. Within this range, populations are fragmented, occurring on only 11 higher elevation peaks along the spine of the Appalachian Mountains. In Tennessee, populations occur in the vicinity of Roan Mountain in Carter County, the Max Patch Mountains in Cocke County, and the Bald Mountains in Greene and Unicoi counties. This species also occurs in eastern Johnson County.

Habitat: Northern Gray-Cheeked Salamanders are restricted to higher elevations within their range generally above 800 m. Like some other highland plethodontids, this species is usually found in mixed deciduous closed-canopy forest or occasionally in spruce-fir forest. Moist, sloped hillsides with plenty of cover, including rotten and fallen logs, are undoubtedly the preferred habitat. Both adults and juveniles can be found underneath rocks, logs, and other cover on the forest floor.

Northern Gray-Cheeked Salamander adult, Carter County. (Photo by Matthew L. Niemiller)

Natural History: Most aspects of the reproductive biology of the Northern Gray-Cheeked Salamander are unknown. Females likely brood eggs in underground cavities. Developing embryos are direct-developing. Adults and juveniles feed on the usual assemblage of forest litter invertebrates, including springtails, ants, mites, spiders, earthworms, and many others. In Tennessee, they are found in sympatry with other salamander species, such as White-Spotted Slimy Salamanders (*P. cylindraceus*), Eastern Red-Backed Salamanders (*P. cinereus*), Weller's Salamanders (*P. welleri*), and Yonahlossee Salamanders (*P. yonahlossee*). Adults are usually surface active during mild seasons, retreating underground during the coldest parts of the winter and the warm and dry periods of the summer. Predators are undocumented but most likely include forest snakes, small mammals, and birds.

Conservation Status: Northern Gray-Cheeked Salamanders appear to be common to abundant in appropriate habitat within their range. Northern Gray-Cheeked Salamanders are not specifically protected within their range, though many of the populations occur within protected forested areas. Although they are wide-ranging compared to other members of the Red-Cheeked Salamander complex, the populations appear to be isolated on mountaintops and hence are not continuous. There are conflicting opinions about this species' ability to cope with harmful forestry practices, but like other plethodontids, they most likely require closed canopy forest.

R. Graham Reynolds

Southern Ravine Salamander adult, Carter County. (Photo by Matthew L. Niemiller)

Southern Ravine Salamander

Plethodon richmondi

Description: Southern Ravine Salamanders are small- to medium-sized lungless salamanders measuring 65–145 mm TL, half of which is tail length. The body is elongate and the legs short relative to body size, superficially giving this species a wormlike appearance. A particularly handsome species, adults have a dark grayish brown to black dorsal ground coloration with abundant metallic silver and gold flecking. The venter is uniformly dark gray to black, while the throat might have some patterning and is generally a lighter shade than the venter. The tail is distinctly rounded in cross section. Costal grooves number 19–23, and nasolabial grooves are present. There are four toes on the fore limbs and five on the hind limbs. Hatchlings are 14–15 mm SVL and light gray on the dorsum with an immaculate venter. Juveniles resemble adults but have longer legs and shorter tails relative to the size of the body. Sexually active males have crescent-shaped mental glands on the chin and enlarged cloacal papillae. Males also tend to be slightly smaller than females, though distinguishing the sexes is difficult outside the breeding season.

Etymology: The specific epithet, *richmondi*, honors Neil Richmond, curator of amphibians and reptiles at Carnegie Museum, 1955–1971.

Similar Species: Though similar to many small woodland plethodontid salamanders, such as the Northern Red-Backed Salamander (*P. cinereus*), the Southern Ravine Salamander can be distinguished by its elongate body and long tail, 19–23 costal grooves, and the presence of both dorsal gold flecking and a black unspotted venter. Eastern Red-Backed Salamanders are more robust and have a salt-and-pepper mottled venter.

Distribution: Southern Ravine Salamanders are distributed from Ohio and southwestern Pennsylvania southward into eastern Kentucky, western West Virginia, southwestern Virginia, northwestern North Carolina, and northeastern Tennessee. In our state, this species occurs in the Cumberland Mountains, Ridge and Valley and Blue Ridge Mountains near the borders of Kentucky and Virginia, including Campbell, Claireborne, and Hawkins counties, as well as most of northeastern Tennessee east of Greeneville.

Southern Ravine Salamander adult, Carter County. (Photo by Matthew L. Niemiller)

Habitat: Southern Ravine Salamanders seem to favor steeply sloped, forested habitats with plenty of rock cover, especially ravines. Deciduous upland forest with plenty of leaf litter, rocks, and logs, and talus slopes with forest cover appear to be a favored habitat. They might occasionally be found in rocky outcrops, and occasionally on ridge tops. This species appear to be quite common in appropriate habitat, and we have found them in numbers on moist forested ridge tops. They are generally active in the fall and spring, though they might remain active throughout the winter if the weather remains somewhat mild. Southern Ravine Salamanders retreat to burrows and interstices during the heat of summer, generally from May to September, and are only occasionally found until they reemerge in autumn.

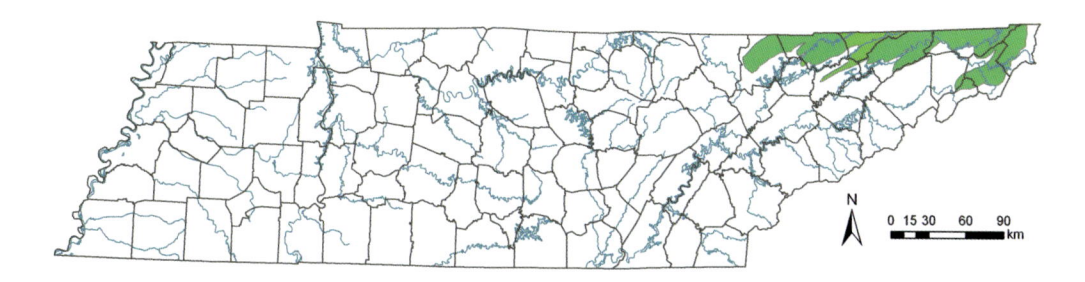

Natural History: Adults breed from autumn through early spring. Females lay around eight eggs in underground cavities or beneath rocks buried in soil in from late May to late June. Females likely brood their eggs, which hatch in early autumn as miniature adults. Maturing in their third or fourth year, adults feed on most of the small invertebrate fauna of the forest floor, including springtails, earthworms, beetles, snails, and spiders. Predators include the usual suite of woodland salamander hunters, including Ring-Necked (*Diadophis punctatus*) and Gartersnakes (*Thamnophis sirtalis*), small mammals, and woodland birds. Adult Southern Ravine Salamanders are not territorial, and might be found in association with many other species of woodland salamanders, including most of the plethodontid species that they share their range with in Tennessee. As such, searching for salamanders in these areas might yield a number of species in the same habitat.

Conservation Status: Southern Ravine Salamanders appear to be common throughout their range, though their narrow distribution in the state has prompted some to call for further study of Tennessee populations to determine their status. Like many salamanders, Southern Ravine Salamanders are sensitive to deforestation and human activity.

R. Graham Reynolds

Southern Red-Backed Salamander adult, Blount County. (Photo by Matthew L. Niemiller)

Southern Red-Backed Salamander

Plethodon serratus

Description: The Southern Red-Backed Salamander is a small, terrestrial woodland salamander. Adults are 65–105 mm TL. Most individuals have 18–21 costal grooves and legs that appear somewhat short and stubby relative to overall body size. Like the Eastern Red-Backed Salamander (*P. cinereus*), this species exhibits two distinct morphs: a redback phase consisting of individuals possessing an easily discernible red to orange stripe on the dorsum, and a leadback, or unstriped, phase where individuals have a relatively uniformly colored, brownish dorsum. Both morphs have brownish lateral coloration, often marked with white or silvery spotting, which might vary in intensity and a salt-and-pepper venter with little to no reddish pigmentation. Although dorsal pigmentation varies, most individuals typically possess some degree of red pigmentation at the bases of the limbs. The tail is distinctly rounded in cross section. Nasolabial grooves are present. Four toes are found on the fore limbs and five toes on the hind limbs. Sexually active males have small, slightly oval-shaped mental glands on the chin.

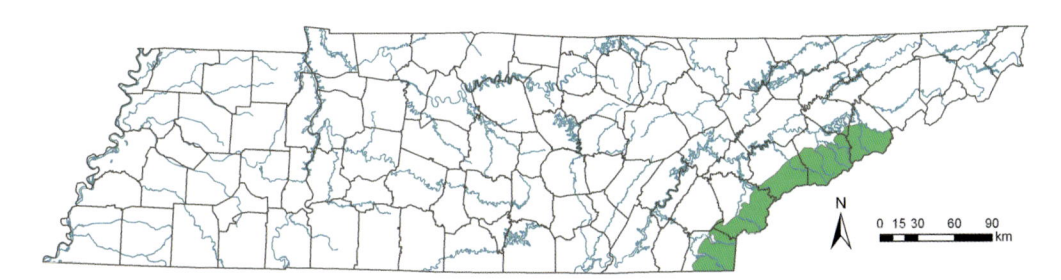

Left: Southern Red-Backed Salamander adult in defensive posture, Sevier County. (Photo by Matthew L. Niemiller) *Right:* Southern Red-Backed Salamander adult, Monroe County. (Photo by Matthew L. Niemiller)

This species once was considered a subspecies of the Eastern Red-Backed Salamander. No subspecies are recognized.

Etymology: The specific epithet, *serratus,* is Latin for "serrated," which refers to the jagged edges of the dorsal stripe in the redback phase.

Similar Species: The Southern Red-Backed Salamander bears a marked similarity to the Eastern Red-Backed Salamander but can be distinguished based on distribution. Eastern Red-Backed Salamanders occur north and east of the French Broad River, while Southern Red-Backed Salamanders occur to the south and west. Striped individuals of Southern Red-Backed Salamanders are also easily distinguished from redback Zigzag Salamanders by their much more uniform and straighter-edged dorsal stripe as compared to the wavy, sinuous borders of the stripe in Zigzag Salamanders. Unstriped morphs of Southern Red-Backed Salamanders can also be distinguished from unstriped Zigzag Salamanders by their shorter limbs, with Southern Red-Backed Salamanders typically having 8–10 costal folds between adpressed limbs, compared to 6–7 costal folds between adpressed limbs for Zigzag Salamanders.

Distribution: The distribution of the Southern Red-Backed Salamander consists of several distinct isolates: one major group of populations in the Salem Plateau of southeastern Missouri extending partially into southeastern Illinois, another in the Ouachita Mountains of Arkansas and Oklahoma, a "Piedmont and Blue Ridge group" extending from southwestern North Carolina and partially into southeast Tennessee and southward into northwest Georgia and northeast Alabama, and a small region of isolated populations in the Red River Valley and Upper Delta regions of central Louisiana. In Tennessee, this species is associated with the southern Blue Ridge Mountains in Cocke, Sevier, Blount, Monroe, and Polk counties.

Habitat: Southern Red-Backed Salamanders are found in a variety of habitats throughout their range, including mesic to moderately xeric pine-oak and mixed hardwood forests, particularly in the Smoky Mountains. Salamanders can be found on rocky slopes as well as near moist leaf litter around streams. Individuals can typically be found under cover, such as logs, rocks, and leaf litter, during the day and out on the forest floor on rainy nights foraging.

Natural History: Southern Red-Backed Salamanders are thought to be very similar in terms of ecology and life history to Eastern Red-Backed Salamanders, although much of the reproductive biology remains unknown. Females lay small clutches averaging 5–7 eggs attached to the ceiling of small cavities and crevices in rotten logs, moss, or rocks during summer. Females brood their eggs, which hatch 6–8 weeks later. Sexual maturity is reached in 2–3 years. The diet consists of a variety of invertebrates, including ants, beetles, snails, and earthworms. Predators have not been document but presumably include small mammals, snakes, and birds.

Conservation Status: Populations of the Southern Red-Backed Salamander are stable and secure in Tennessee. However, logging of mature hardwoods poses a threat to this species, after which populations typically recover quite slowly compared to Eastern Red-Backed Salamanders.

Jason R. Jones and
Matthew L. Niemiller

Red-Legged Salamander adult, Macon County, North Carolina. (Photo by R. Graham Reynolds)

Red-Legged Salamander

Plethodon shermani

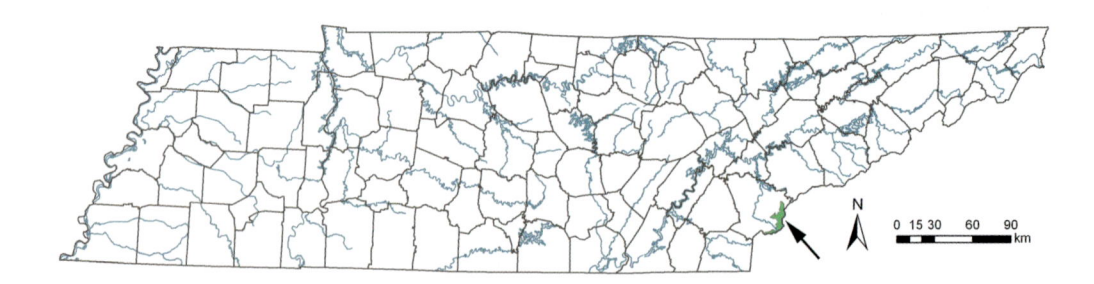

Description: The Reg-legged Salamander is a large terrestrial member of the Red-Cheeked Salamander (*P. jordani*) complex. Adults typically are 85–185 mm TL and have 16 costal grooves. Nasolabial grooves are present. In the bulk of their range in North Carolina, both adults and juveniles are pigmented slate gray to bluish black with distinctive reddish to pinkish coloration on the dorsal surface of the legs. Some Unicoi Mountain populations, including the only known population that occurs in Tennessee, rarely (perhaps never) exhibit this red coloration. Rather, some white spotting is present on the sides but not on the dorsum. The venter is gray and lacks any discernable spotting or mottling. The tail is distinctly rounded in cross section. Four toes are found on the fore limbs and five toes on the hind limbs. Like other *Plethodon* species, sexually active males have conspicuous rounded mental glands on the chin. Juveniles resemble adults in appearance but younger individuals might have paired red spots situated along the back.

Etymology: The specific epithet, *shermani*, honors Franklin Sherman Jr., professor of zoology and entomology at Clemson University in South Carolina.

Similar Species: In North Carolina, Red-Legged Salamanders can be distinguished from closely related members of the Red-Cheeked Salamander complex by coloration and distribution. The species differs from Red-Cheeked Salamanders (*P. jordani*) by generally lacking conspicuous reddish cheek patches. Red-Legged Salamanders can be distinguished from nearby populations of the Tellico Salamander (*P. aureolus*) and Southern Appalachian Salamander (*P. teyahalee*) by possessing red patches on the legs and lacking white spotting on the sides. In Tennessee, however, high-elevation populations of the Tellico Salamander lack much of the dorsal spotting, though Southern Appalachian Salamanders usually have white dorsal spotting. Populations of Red-Legged Salamanders in Tennessee closely resemble both Tellico and Southern Appalachian Salamanders, and are likely the result of past hybridization with either Tellico Salamanders, which occur down the mountain from Tennessee Red-Legged Salamanders, or Southern Appalachian Salamanders. Hybridization between these species likely has been aggravated by extensive logging activities at the turn of the century. Red-Legged Salamanders in Tennessee are best identified by their narrow range and coloration, specifically, a lack of dorsal spotting, some lateral spotting, and little to no red on the legs.

Red-Legged Salamander x Southern Appalachian Salamander hybrid, Monroe County. (Photo by Matthew L. Niemiller)

Distribution: Red-Legged Salamanders are found in four disjunct isolates in the Unicoi and Nantahala Mountains of North Carolina, northern Georgia, and extreme southeastern Tennessee. In Tennessee, this species has only been confirmed from the eastern extension of Sassafras Ridge in eastern Monroe County above Stratton Gap. The probable range in Tennessee is likely bounded by Sassafras Ridge to the North, Rough Ridge to the south, and the state line to the east along the extension of Sassafras Ridge to John's Knob and Big Junction. However, we include the area south of the Tellico River to at least Jenks Knob and Little Bald as potential range of this species. Populations in Tennessee likely represent a hybrid swarm with the Southern Appalachian Salamander (*P. teyahalee*) and/or the Tellico Salamander (*P. aureolus*).

Habitat: Red-Legged Salamanders are found in cool, moist, mountainous forests at elevations from 850 to 1,500 m. During the day, adults and juveniles can be found underneath rocks and fallen logs and within rotten logs on forested hillsides. Salamanders can be found on the surface at night during favorable weather.

Red-Legged Salamanders, unlike some other plethodontid species, are frequently active on the surface in summer. During periods of drought and cold, this species retreats deeper underground.

Natural History: Individuals are most active at night while foraging during periods of favorable weather and can be found crossing roads during nighttime rains. Little is known about the reproductive biology of this species. Females likely brood terrestrial eggs. Sexual maturity is reached in three years. Red-Legged Salamanders feed on a variety of invertebrates, including millipedes, earthworms, and several groups of insects. Known predators include Spring Salamanders (*G. porphyriticus*). When threatened, Red-Legged Salamanders will become immobile, and, like other species of *Plethodon*, this species produces noxious skin secretions from the tail to deter potential predators.

Conservation Status: In Tennessee, Red-Legged Salamanders receive protection as populations are located on federal and state properties. This species also appears fairly resilient to logging operations as robust populations have been found in secondary-growth forests and small, fragmented forest stands in North Carolina. Since this species has an extremely limited range in Tennessee, however, efforts should be made to locate, monitor and protect any existing populations. Although not afforded state protection, the Red-Legged Salamander is justly listed as "Rare" and "Imperiled" in Tennessee because of its limited distribution in the state.

Comments: It is the opinion of the editors, who have extensively searched the known range of Red-Legged Salamanders in Tennessee, that pure *P. shermani* do not occur in our state. Individuals on Sassafras Ridge in Cherokee National Forest (Monroe County) lack red on the legs and usually have a few white spots on the lateral sides of the dorsum. These individuals are known to possess mitochondrial DNA haplotypes consistent with *P. shermani* from North Carolina populations (Unicoi isolate; Weisrock et al. 2005). Southern Appalachian Salamanders from this area generally have a few white dorsal spots, while Tellico Salamanders tend to have larger, brassy spots on the dorsum. Populations in Tennessee appear to be hybrids of at least Red-Legged Salamanders and Southern Appalachian Salamanders, and perhaps Tellico Salamanders as well. Further study is certainly warranted.

Matthew L. Niemiller and
R. Graham Reynolds

Southern Appalachian Salamander adult, Monroe County. (Photo by Matthew L. Niemiller)

Southern Appalachian Salamander

Plethodon teyahalee

Description: The Southern Appalachian Salamander is a large member of the Slimy Salamander (*P. glutinosus*) complex, with adults ranging 120–210 mm TL. Both adults and juveniles are pigmented slate gray to bluish black with scattered tiny white spots on the dorsum. The sides of the body have numerous larger, whitish spots, and small red spots are occasional present on the legs. The venter is gray and lacks any discernable spotting or mottling. The chin is lighter in color than the venter. The tail is distinctly rounded in cross section. Sixteen costal grooves are present and nasolabial grooves are present. Four toes are found on the fore limbs and five on the hind limbs. Sexually active males have conspicuously round mental glands on the chin. No subspecies are recognized.

Etymology: The specific epithet, *teyahalee*, possibly refers to the mountain summit known as Teyahalee Bald in Graham County, North Carolina.

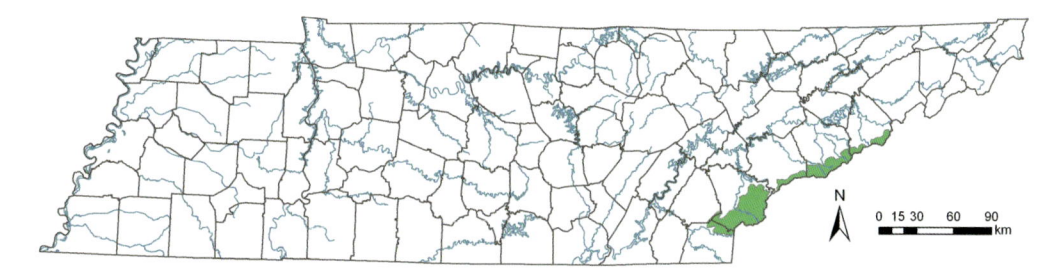

Similar Species: Southern Appalachian Salamanders coexists with Tellico Salamanders (*P. aureolus*) but can be distinguished by size and coloration. Southern Appalachian Salamanders have white spotting rather than brassy spotting on the dorsum and attain a larger size reaching up to 90 mm SVL. Southern Appalachian Salamanders also are easily confused with Northern Slimy Salamanders (*P. glutinosus*). Northern Slimy Salamanders typically have larger and more numerous white or brassy spotting on the dorsum and sides and also have a darker chin than Southern Appalachian Salamanders. Likewise, Southern Appalachian Salamanders resemble Red-Cheeked Salamanders (*P. jordani*) and Red-Legged Salamanders (*P. shermani*), with which they co-occur, but lack the diagnostic reddish cheek patches and reddish leg patches found in these two species, respectively. However, the Southern Appalachian Salamander hybridizes with Northern Slimy Salamanders in a narrow zone in Blount, Monroe, and Sevier counties, with Red-Cheeked Salamanders in a narrow zone in the Great Smoky Mountains, and with Red-Legged Salamanders at all known contacts between the two species. Therefore, species identification of some individuals can be extremely difficult in several areas.

Distribution: Southern Appalachian Salamanders are found within the Blue Ridge Mountains of southeastern and east-central Tennessee, southwestern North Carolina, northwestern South Carolina, and extreme northeastern Georgia. In Tennessee, this species is known from the Unicoi Mountains in Monroe and Polk counties and from the Great Smoky Mountains in Blount, Cocke, and Sevier counties.

Habitat: Southern Appalachian Salamanders are found in cool, moist, mountainous forests. In the Great Smoky Mountains, this species

Southern Appalachian Salamander juvenile, Monroe County. (Photo by Matthew L. Niemiller)

is typically found at middle elevations ranging from 640 to 910 m but reaching elevations as high as 1,520 m. Adults and juveniles are found in the same habitat typically underneath rocks and fallen logs during the day in forested areas. Salamanders can be found on the forest floor at night during favorable weather and are most active on the surface in summer. During periods of drought and cold, salamanders retreat underground.

Natural History: Little published information exists on the life history and ecology of this species. Breeding probably occurs from July to late October. Females likely nest underground and brood terrestrial eggs in late spring to early summer. Females reach maturity within five years. The diet is diverse and includes ants, caterpillars, harvestmen, spiders, crickets, slugs, centipedes, millipedes, beetles, and earthworms. Predators have not been documented for this species but likely include Spring Salamanders (*Gyrinophilus porphyriticus*), Black-Bellied Salamanders (*Desmognathus quadramaculatus*), shrews, small snakes, and forest-dwelling birds. Like other species of *Plethodon,* this species produces noxious skin secretions from the tail to deter potential predators.

Conservation Status: Much of the distribution of this species occurs on state and federal properties and is afforded protection. This species also seems fairly resilient to logging operations. Since this species has a limited distribution in Tennessee efforts should be made to monitor and protect existing populations.

Matthew L. Niemiller and
R. Graham Reynolds

Wehrle's Salamander adult, Campbell County. (Photo by Matthew L. Niemiller)

Wehrle's Salamander

Plethodon wehrlei

Description: A larger plethodontid, Wehrle's Salamander adults are usually 100–170 mm TL and slender to moderately robust. The dorsal ground color is dark brown to black and frequently punctuated by bluish white to yellow spots. These spots tend to be larger along the flanks and often fuse to form irregular bands or blotches. The venter is a uniform gray, but the throat and upper chest might have some flecks of lighter pigment and usually are much lighter in color. Some populations, including those found in Tennessee, have individuals with medium-sized yellow or gold spots running along the dorsum. The tail is distinctly rounded in cross section. Seventeen costal grooves usually are present. Nasolabial grooves are present. There are four toes on the fore limbs and five on the hind limbs. Hatchlings and juveniles are similarly colored, although they might have paired reddish spots running along the dorsum that sometimes are retained in adults. Sexually active males have enlarged mental glands and cloacal papillae. Males also tend to be slightly smaller than females, though distinguishing the sexes is difficult outside the breeding season.

Left: Wehrle's Salamander adult, Campbell County. (Photo by Matthew L. Niemiller) *Right:* Wehrle's Salamander juvenile, Campbell County. (Photo by Matthew L. Niemiller)

Etymology: The specific epithet, *wehrlei*, honors Richard W. Wehrle, who collected most of the original examples of this species.

Similar Species: Wehrle's Salamanders closely resemble members of the Slimy Salamander (*P. glutinosus*) complex in Tennessee. Slimy Salamanders generally have white to brassy spots or flecking on the dorsum and not just on the sides. Slimy Salamanders also usually have just 16 costal grooves and grayish throats.

Distribution: Wehrle's Salamander occurs from southern New York south to the border of Virginia and North Carolina. Disjunct populations occur in southwestern Virginia and on the Cumberland Plateau of Kentucky and Tennessee. In Tennessee, this species can be found in the Cumberland Mountains along the Kentucky border exclusively in Campbell County. However, the range of Wehrle's Salamander in Tennessee is not well known, and fewer than 20 specimens have been found in Tennessee. The editors have only been able to locate two individuals of this species in our state.

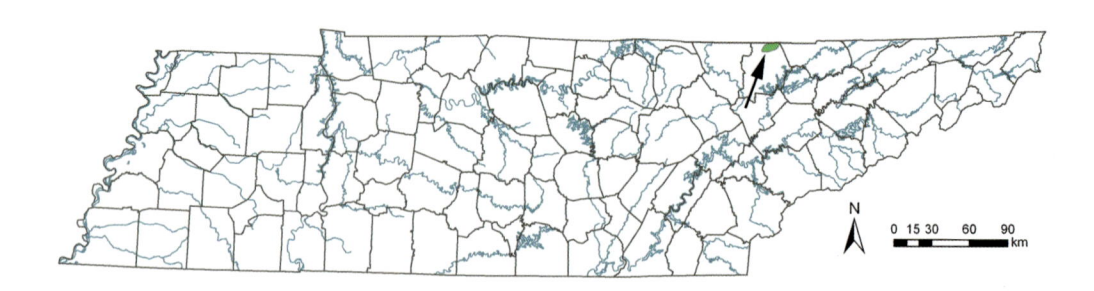

Habitat: Throughout their range, Wehrle's Salamanders inhabit a variety of upland habitats up to 1,450 m, including both deciduous and coniferous forest. Closed canopy forest with plenty of rocks and logs for hiding places is preferred. Adults and juveniles often occupy burrows, particularly during aestivation, and can be found in very high densities in appropriate habitat. Surface activity is usually between March and September, depending on elevation. In Tennessee, these salamanders are much more rare and appear to have a surface activity pattern similar to Green Salamanders (*Aneides aeneus*). They appear to be exclusively encountered on hillsides and slopes. The single known population in Campbell County inhabits rock faces, rocky interstices, and the twilight zone of caves and deep fissures. Few individuals have been reported from this population. A single individual was found on a rock outcrop on a rainy night in May, two individuals have been found in a shallow overhang, and a juvenile has been found underneath a rock at the base of the rock outcrop.

Natural History: Not much is known about Wehrle's Salamander in Tennessee, but populations in other parts of the range have been well studied. This species is frequently the most abundant salamander where it occurs, with some populations exceeding 1,000 individuals per hectare. Little is know about the reproductive biology of this species, however. Mating occurs in autumn. Females presumably nest in underground cavities laying 6–20 eggs in late spring. Females likely brood their direct-developing eggs. Wehrle's Salamanders mature at around 4 or 5 years of age, and as adults they feed on a wide variety of small forest floor invertebrates, including spiders, millipedes, springtails, beetles, mites, flies, and ants. Wehrle's Salamanders are territorial and might defend their home range against conspecifics and heterospecifics. In Tennessee, this species occurs in association with Green Salamanders (*Aneides aeneus*) on rocky outcrops. Predators most likely include the Ring-Necked Snake (*Diadophis punctatus*), which is a salamander-eating specialist, as well as other forest floor snakes, small mammals, and birds.

Conservation Status: Outside of Tennessee, this is one of the most abundant salamanders where it occurs and populations appear to be secure. Population status in Tennessee is unknown and this species is state listed as "Critically Imperiled" and is "Deemed in Need of Management." Like many upland forest salamanders, this species is undoubtedly negatively impacted by forest clearing and pollution such as acid rain. Protection in Tennessee is especially important, as few populations occur in a narrow range within our state.

R. Graham Reynolds and Matthew L. Niemiller

Weller's Salamander adult, Unicoi County. (Photo by Matthew L. Niemiller)

Weller's Salamander

Plethodon welleri

Description: Weller's Salamander is a small species of *Plethodon* measuring 64–92 mm TL. Adults are pigmented slate gray to black on the dorsum that is also heavily pigmented with gold to brassy flecks and blotches. The sides of the body have numerous larger, whitish spots and small red spots are occasional present on the legs. The venter is dark gray with numerous tiny whitish spots. Hatchlings lack the distinctive brassy patterning of adults but develop pairs of brassy spots along the anterior part of the dorsum within a few days of hatching. The tail is distinctly rounded in cross section. Four toes are found on the fore limbs and five toes on the hind limbs. Sixteen costal grooves are present and nasolabial grooves are present. Sexually active males have small, slightly oval-shaped mental glands on the chin and have papillose vent linings. No subspecies are recognized.

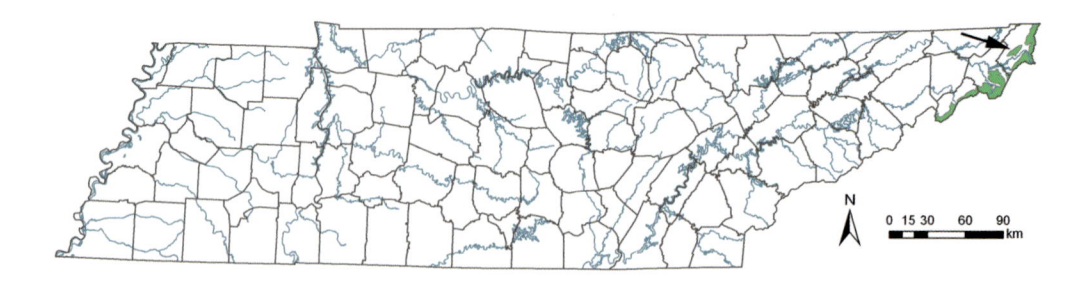

Left: Weller's Salamander adult, Unicoi County. (Photo by Matthew L. Niemiller) *Right:* Weller's Salamander juvenile, Unicoi County. (Photo by Matthew L. Niemiller)

Etymology: The specific epithet, *welleri,* honors Worth H. Weller, a young man who collected the type specimen for this species. He was killed in a fall just after his high school graduation while collecting additional specimens.

Similar Species: Weller's Salamanders resemble the leadback phase of the Northern Red-Backed Salamander (*P. cinereus*) with which it coexists but can easily be distinguished by coloration. Northern Red-Backed Salamanders lack the characteristic gold to brassy pigmentation found on the dorsum of Weller's Salamanders. Additionally, the venter of Northern Red-Backed Salamanders is mottled, with black and white (sometimes yellow) pigmentation producing a salt-and-pepper effect, rather than the dark venter with numerous white spotting of Weller's Salamanders. Weller's Salamanders also occur with Southern Ravine Salamanders (*P. richmondi*) in Johnson County. Southern Ravine Salamanders grow to a larger size (75–145 mm TL), have 20–23 costal grooves, and have a longer tail that accounts for about 50% of the total length.

Distribution: Weller's Salamanders are found within the Blue Ridge Mountains of northwestern North Carolina, northeastern Tennessee, and southwestern Virginia. In Tennessee, this species is known from the Unaka Mountains in eastern Unicoi County as well as from Carter and Johnson counties.

Habitat: Weller's Salamanders are found in cool, high-elevation spruce-fir forests typically occurring above 1,500 m. However, individuals are occasionally found at elevations as low as 700 m in coves with limestone or mixed hardwood forests. Adults and juveniles are found in the same habitat, typically underneath rocks and fallen logs and are often found in or near talus during the day in forested areas. Salamanders can be found on the forest floor at night during favorable weather and are most active on the surface in summer. During periods of drought and cold, salamanders retreat underground.

Natural History: Breeding probably occurs in spring and fall. Females likely nest underground and brood up to 11 terrestrial eggs in late spring to early summer with hatching occurring 2–3 months later. Nests have been found in rotten conifer logs and under moss mats. Juveniles reach maturity in three years.

The diet is diverse and includes spiders, mites, slugs, earthworms, beetles, springtails, caterpillars, and flies. Predators have not been documented for this species but likely include shrews, snakes, and woodland birds. Like other species of *Plethodon,* this species produces noxious skin secretions from the tail to deter potential predators.

Conservation Status: Most populations likely are isolated to suitable habitat on mountaintops and hence are separated from one another. However, several mountain peaks throughout the range of this species are on state or federal property and are afforded protection. Since this species has a limited distribution in Tennessee, efforts should be made to monitor and protect existing populations. Weller's Salamanders are state listed as "Imperiled" and are "Deemed in Need of Management" in Tennessee.

Matthew L. Niemiller and
R. Graham Reynolds

Yonahlossee Salamander adult, Carter County. (Photo by Matthew L. Niemiller)

Yonahlossee Salamander

Plethodon yonahlossee

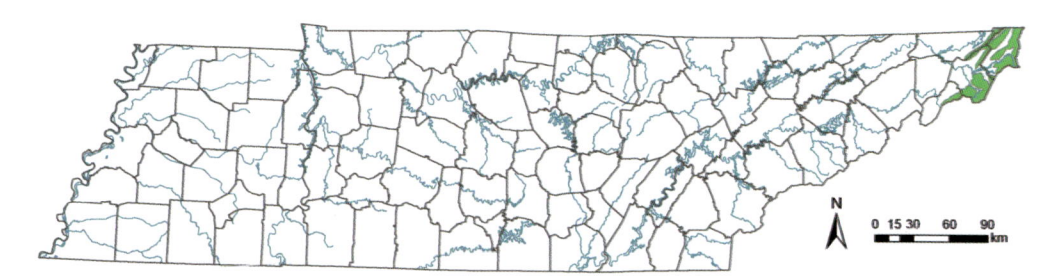

Description: The largest of the *Plethodon* salamanders in Tennessee, the Yonahlossee Salamander can reach total lengths of 110–220 mm as an adult. This is a large and robust salamander with a strikingly handsome coloration. Adults have a black to grayish dorsal ground color, often with small gray to silvery white spots or flecks distributed on the flanks, sides of the tail, and upper limbs. A large, paintbrush-like swath of solid reddish brown or chestnut color covers most of the dorsum from the neck to just posterior of the cloacal opening on the tail. The shape of this color patch is irregular and appears as though someone has swabbed the animal with a brush of deep brick red paint, creating an attractive pattern contrasting with the more neutral, dark-colored background. The lateral surfaces and limbs of adults are usually lighter gray, while the venter is similar to the dorsal background black to dark gray color and often is flecked with lighter spots. Sixteen costal grooves are present and nasolabial grooves are present. Four toes are present on the fore limbs and five on the hind limbs. Juvenile coloration is less dramatic, with a similar dark background color dorsally, often with paired red spots that fuse with age to form the swath found in adults, and a lighter colored venter.

Etymology: The specific epithet, *yonahlossee*, refers to Yonahlossee Road in Avery County, North Carolina, and is a Cherokee word meaning "trail of the bear."

Similar Species: This is the only large salamander in northeastern Tennessee with a large red or chestnut swath of color on the dorsal surface and lighter colored flanks. Individual Yonahlossee Salamanders with reduced red pigment on dorsum might be mistaken for other sympatric plethodontids, such as White-Spotted Slimy Salamanders. Some species of *Desmognathus* (Dusky Salamanders) resemble the Yonahlossee Salamander in coloration but have a light line running from the eye to the posterior angle of the jaw and larger hind limbs than fore limbs.

Distribution: Yonahlossee Salamanders have a limited range in the Blue Ridge Mountains of southwestern Virginia, northeastern Tennessee, and western North Carolina. In Tennessee, Yonahlossee Salamanders are found in and around the Cherokee National Forest along the North Carolina border north of the Great Smoky Mountains National Park to the Virginia Border in the extreme northeastern part of the state.

Habitat: Though occasionally difficult to locate, Yonahlossee Salamanders are apparently common throughout their range and are surface active during the summer months. Adults and juveniles are usually found in deciduous forest with plenty of hiding places, such as fallen logs, boulders, rocks, and talus at elevations of 450–1,750 m; however, individuals in the Iron Mountains of Johnson County are also found on rocky road embankments, near seasonal streams, and in pastures. They are most often located by turning rocks, logs, and bark in appropriate habitat, although their use of burrows can complicate facile capture of this species.

Yonahlossee Salamander subadult, Carter County. (Photo by Matthew L. Niemiller)

Natural History: Little information is available on the natural history of the Yonahlossee Salamander. Females probably oviposit underground in late spring or early summer. Females probably brood their nests of 15–30 eggs through hatching, which is 2–3 months later. Sexual maturity is reached in three years. Populations in Johnson County have been found to feed on a wide variety of invertebrates, including springtails, beetles, isopods, caterpillars, and dipteran larvae. Predators most likely include birds, snakes, and small forest mammals. Like other species of *Plethodon*, Yonahlossee Salamanders can produce copious sticky and noxious secretions to deter predation. This species is often part of a diverse salamander community, though it appears to be more elevationally restricted than other salamanders.

Conservation Status: While not specifically protected in their range, Yonahlossee Salamanders are undoubtedly sensitive to destructive forestry practices and pollution at high elevations. They do appear to tolerate secondary growth and fragmentation, as they do not require migration corridors to breeding grounds and generally have small home ranges. Additionally, much of their range in Tennessee and elsewhere is within National and State Forest, which confers a certain level of protection to populations. Regardless, this species is state listed as "Imperiled."

R. Graham Reynolds

Midland Mud Salamander adult, Ohio. (Photo by Carl R. Brune)

Mud Salamander

Pesudotriton montanus

Description: The Mud Salamander is a medium-sized lungless salamander measuring 75–200 mm TL. The ground color of the dorsum and sides in juveniles and adults is various shades of brown or red, with sparse, widely spaced, and sharply defined black spots. The ground color of the venter is a light brown or beige and lacks the spotting characteristic of the back and sides. There are usually 16 or 17 costal grooves and nasolabial grooves are present. The head is large with a short and blunt snout, and the eyes do not appear to bulge. The irises of the eyes are usually dark brown. The tail is short, typically accounting for about 40% of the TL. Furthermore, the tail is rounded near the base, but the distal half is laterally compressed and keeled above and below. The fore

Left: Midland Mud Salamander juvenile, Coffee County. (Photo by Matthew L. Niemiller) *Right:* Midland Mud Salamander larva, Ohio. (Photo by Carl R. Brune)

and hind limbs are stout but short; there are four toes on the fore limbs and five toes on the hind limbs. Nasolabial grooves are present, and the tongue is boletoid. The teeth of the upper and lower jaws occur in single rows. Females grow to larger sizes than males, but otherwise, sexual dimorphism is not apparent. Hatchlings are 12–18 mm TL. Both hatchlings and larvae have a stream morphology and are light brown dorsally and immaculate on the venter. Small, faint spots might be present on the dorsum that form light flecks, streaks, or reticulations along the sides. Larvae can reach 75 mm TL before undergoing metamorphosis. Four subspecies are recognized, and only one occurs in Tennessee, the Midland Mud Salamander (*P. montanus diasticus*).

Etymology: The specific epithet, *montanus*, is Latin for "belonging to a mountain," while the subspecific epithet, *diasticus*, is from the Greek *dia* "throughout" and *stiktos* "dotted," which refers to the spotted dorsal patterning.

Similar Species: Mud Salamanders are most similar in appearance to Red Salamanders (*Pseudotriton ruber*); however, the spotting pattern of the sides and backs are different in these two species. In Mud Salamanders the relatively fewer spots have a sharply defined border and are spaced relatively far apart from each other, whereas in Red Salamanders the numerous spots have a diffuse border and are spaced relatively close together, often touching. Furthermore, the iris in Mud Salamanders is usually dark brown, whereas the iris in Red Salamanders is golden. The Mud Salamander superficially resembles the Spring Salamander (*Gyrinophilus porphyriticus*), but Spring Salamanders possess a canthus rostralis, which is lacking in Mud Salamanders.

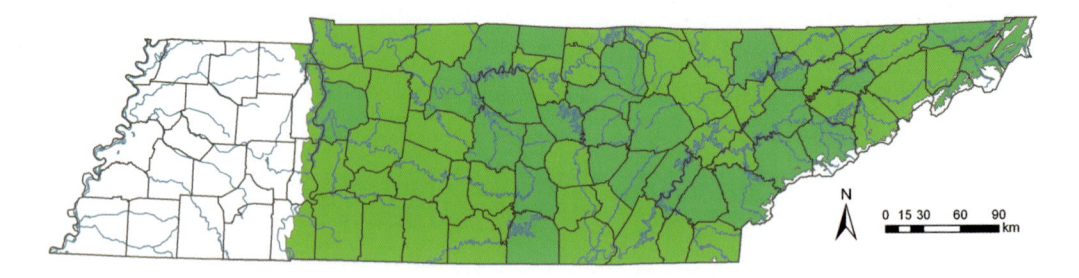

Distribution: Mud Salamanders are found in two disjunct groups. The Midland Mud Salamander is found west of the Appalachian Mountains in southern Ohio, southwestern West Virginia, southwestern Virginia, central and eastern Tennessee, and eastern and central Kentucky. Mud Salamanders are found in appropriate habitat in the Nashville Basin, Eastern Highland Rim, Cumberland Plateau, Cumberland Mountains, Ridge and Valley, and Blue Ridge Mountains ecoregions of central and eastern Tennessee.

Habitat: Mud Salamanders are fossorial and, therefore, spend most of their life in moist burrows, primarily in areas with lowland springs, floodplain creeks, or swampy, forested lands adjacent to these areas up to 550 m in elevation. Adults and juveniles are occasionally found beneath rocks and logs in and along drying creeks and forest floor. However, most individuals are encountered in muddy or mucky areas at the margins of aquatic habitats, whereas larvae are found within these waters.

Natural History: Very little is known about the reproductive biology of this species. Courtship and breeding presumably occur from late fall through winter. Eggs have rarely been found, perhaps because females lay them in secluded areas, such as attached to roots and leaves in springs or bogs. Although dissections have revealed up to 192 ova, clutches with over 30 eggs have not been reported. The larval period lasts 1.5–2.5 years. Sexual maturity is reached in 2–5 years and individuals can live at least 15 years. Larval Mud Salamanders are opportunistic in feeding and eat a variety of aquatic invertebrate prey, including zooplankton, amphipods, isopods, and worms. Adults are also opportunistic in feeding and eat most types of small invertebrates that they encounter, including worms, snails, crustaceans, millipedes, spiders, and insects. Additionally, they eat smaller salamanders. Predation has seldom been observed, but likely predators of Mud Salamanders include frogs, fishes, crayfish, snakes, birds, and mammals.

Conservation Status: Because they are fossorial, Mud Salamanders are rarely encountered even during surveys of amphibians. For example, only two individuals were found during a two-year inventory of amphibians and reptiles of Arnold Air Force Base in the Barrens of the Eastern Highland Rim in Coffee and Franklin counties. Consequently, little is known about the relative abundance or population trends of this species in Tennessee.

Brian T. Miller and
Matthew L. Niemiller

Northern Red Salamander adult, Campbell County. (Photo by Matthew L. Niemiller)

Red Salamander

Pesudotriton ruber

Description: The Red Salamander is a moderately large and robust salamander measuring 110–150 mm TL (record 181 mm TL). The ground color of the back and sides in juveniles is various shades of beige, pink, or red, whereas in adults the ground color is various shades of brown, orange, or red. The sides and backs of juveniles and adults are peppered with irregularly shaped and spaced black spots. Some spots coalesce with age, and old individuals can be a very dark purplish brown, a condition known as ontogenetic melanism. The ground color of the venter is pink or red and lacks the spotting characteristic of the back and sides. There are usually 16 or 17 costal grooves and nasolabial grooves are present. The head is relatively large and the snout rounded. The eyes are relatively small compared to the head size and do not appear to bulge. The irises of the eyes

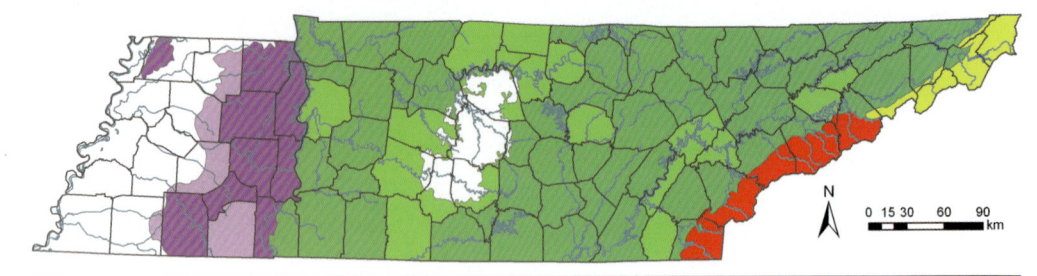

Four subspecies of Red Salamanders are recognized in Tennessee: the Northern Red Salamander (*P. r. ruber*), whose range appears in green; the Southern Red Salamander (*P. r. vioscai*), whose range appears in purple; the Black-Chinned Red Salamander (*P. r. schencki*), whose range appears in red; and the Blue Ridge Red Salamander (*P. r. nitidus*), whose range appears in yellow.

Top left: Southern Red Salamander adult, Liberty County, Florida. (Pierson Hill) *Top right:* Black-Chinned Red Salamander adult, Polk County. (Photo by Matthew L. Niemiller) *Bottom right:* Blue Ridge Red Salamander adult, Unicoi County. (Photo by Matthew L. Niemiller)

are yellow or golden. The tail is short, typically accounting for < 40% of TL. Furthermore, the tail is rounded near the base, but the distal half is laterally compressed and keeled above and below. The front and hind limbs are stout but short; there are four toes on the front limbs and five toes on the hind limbs. A pair of nasolabial grooves is present. The tongue is boletoid. The teeth of the upper and lower jaws occur in single rows. Females grow to larger sizes than males; otherwise, sexual dimorphism is not apparent. Red Salamander larvae are adapted for stream life; consequently, the tail fin terminates at the hind limbs. The dorsal coloration of the larvae is a light brown and pores associated with the lateralis system are obvious on the head and trunk. Younger larvae are usually uniformly colored, however, the back and sides of larger larvae are typically spotted, with the spots often organized into a mottled or streaked pattern. Additionally, darker pigment often is present running from the eye to the snout. Size at metamorphosis varies geographically, from 34 to 50 mm SVL. Hatchlings are 15–20 mm TL. Four subspecies are recognized and all four occur in Tennessee. The Northern Red Salamander (*P. r. ruber*) is the largest subspecies with conspicuous black flecking on the margin of the chin and spots or flecking throughout the length of the tail. The Black-Chinned Red Salamander (*P. r. schencki*) closely resembles the Northern Red Salamander but has heavy black flecking on the margin of the chin that is broader than that in the Northern Red Salamander. The Blue Ridge Red Salamander (*P. r. nitidus*) is the smallest subspecies reaching only 120 mm TL. This subspecies is similar to the Northern Red Salamander but largely lacks black spotting or flecks on the top of the posterior half of the tail and little or no black pigmentation on the chin. The Southern Red Salamander (*P. r. vioscai*) usually is purplish brown with the dark spotting on the dorsum fusing to form a herringbone pattern. White flecks are also present on the snout and

Top left: Northern Red Salamander larva, DeKalb County. (Photo by Matthew L. Niemiller) *Top right:* Northern Red Salamander egg mass, DeKalb County. (Photo by Matthew L. Niemiller) *Bottom left:* Northern Red Salamander hatchlings, Cannon County. (Photo by Brad M. Glorioso)

sides of the head. This subspecies likely intergrades with the Northern Red Salamander.

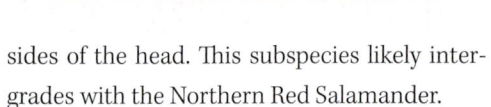

Etymology: The specific and subspecific epithets, *ruber,* are Latin for "red," which is certainly a prominent coloration in this species. The subspecific epithet, *nitidus,* is Latin for "bright," which refers to the bright orange color of this subspecies. The subspecific epithet, *schencki,* honors Carl A. Schenck, founder of the Biltmore Forest School on the property owned by George Vanderbilt, known as Biltmore Estate and Forest. The subspecific epithet, *vioscai,* honors Percy Viosca Jr., who collected the type specimen.

Similar Species: Red Salamanders are most similar in appearance to Mud Salamanders (*P. montanus*); however, the spotting pattern of the sides and dorsum are different in these two species. In Red Salamanders the numerous spots have a diffuse border and are spaced relatively close to each other, often touching, whereas in Mud Salamanders the relatively fewer spots have a sharply defined border and are spaced relatively far apart from each other. Furthermore, the iris in Red Salamanders is golden or yellow, whereas the iris in Mud Salamanders is brown. The Red Salamander superficially resembles the Spring Salamander, but Spring Salamanders possess a canthus rostralis, which is lacking in Red Salamanders.

Distribution: Red Salamanders are distributed throughout much of the eastern United States from southern New York southwest to Indiana then south to the Gulf Coast. Although found throughout much of Tennessee, Red Salamanders are absent from the Mississippi Alluvial Valley and Mississippi Valley Loess Plains ecoregions in West Tennessee and absent from or uncommon in the Nashville Basin of Middle Tennessee. Southern Red Salamanders occur in the Southeastern Plains of West Tennessee. Northern Red Salamanders are found in the Interior Low Plateau, Cumberland Plateau, Cumberland Mountains, and Ridge and Valley. Black-Chinned Red Salamanders are found in the Blue Ridge Mountains west and south of the French Broad River, whereas the Blue Ridge Red Salamander is found north and east of the French Broad River.

Habitat: The Red Salamander is associated with low-order streams, springs, seeps, and neighboring terrestrial habitat up to 1,500 m. Adults and juveniles are commonly found beneath rocks in and along creeks and neighboring forest floor. In the Eastern Highland Rim and Cumberland Plateau, adult Red Salamanders are frequently found in cave streams that they apparently use for breeding activities. Larval Red Salamanders are common inhabitants of the subterranean streams, springs, headwater streams, and seeps.

Natural History: Red Salamanders breed during late summer and early fall. Courtship occurs on land, presumably during summer and early fall. The eggs of Red Salamanders have rarely been found, but females are known to attach 30–130 eggs to the undersurface of rocks deep in springs or subterranean streams or to the margins of rim stone pools. Females remain with their eggs until they hatch in late winter, but they might briefly abandon the eggs to forage. The larval period is long lasting 1.5–3.5 years. Sexual maturity is reached in 3–5 years and adults can live in excess of 20 years. Larval Red Salamanders are opportunistic in feeding and eat a variety of aquatic invertebrate prey, including zooplankton, amphipods, isopods, and worms. Adults are also opportunistic in feeding and eat most types of small invertebrates that they encounter, including worms, snails, crustaceans, millipedes, arachnids, and insects. Additionally, they eat smaller salamanders. Predation has seldom been observed, but likely predators include frogs, fishes, crayfish, snakes, birds, and mammals. Anecdotally, many fishermen in Middle and East Tennessee suggest that Red Salamanders are much better bait than the more common brown (= desmognathine) salamanders, indicating that perhaps game fish prefer this species.

Conservation Status: The Red Salamander is widespread and locally abundant throughout its range in Tennessee.

Brian T. Miller and
Matthew L. Niemiller

13
Family Proteidae (Waterdogs and Mudpuppies)

Waterdogs and Mudpuppies are fairly large, permanently aquatic salamanders with conspicuous plume-like external gills and reaching lengths of 30–40 cm TL. Adults possess lungs, have well-developed caudal fins, and have only four toes on each hind foot rather than the typical five toes found in most other salamanders. Proteids occur in eastern North America and Europe. Six species occur in North America, and only one is found in Tennessee. Fossils of this family date to the Late Paleocene in North America. Proteids occur in lakes, rivers, and larger streams throughout their distribution in North America. A European species, the Olm, is found in caves. In Tennessee, Mudpuppies are primarily association with larger streams and rivers. The family name, Proteidae, is from the mythological Greek character Proteus, a servant of Poseidon (hence associated with water) capable of shape changing. The generic epithet, *Necturus,* is from the Greek *nektos* "swimming" and *oura* "tail."

Common Mudpuppy

Necturus maculosus

Description: The Mudpuppy is a large permanently aquatic salamander with adults ranging 200–300 mm TL but reaching up to 490 mm TL. Adults have large, conspicuous gills and a very blunt snout. The body is robust and cylindrical. The gills generally are bushy and floppy in appearance, superficially resembling a dog's ears (hence the common name). The tail is heavily keeled and accounts for just 30–35% of the total length. The dorsum varies from grayish black to reddish brown and has irregular black spotting that might form a dorsolateral line in rare instances. A stripe runs through the eye to the gills. The venter is white or gray and might have some spotting. Usually 15–16 indistinct costal grooves are present. All four feet have four toes. Males have swollen cloacae during the breeding season. Juveniles have a bold black stripe down the dorsum, bordered on each side by a striking yellow stripe. When juveniles reach 130–150 mm TL, they begin to assume the adult coloration and patterning. Hatchlings are 22–23 mm TL and look very similar to juveniles though the stripes might appear more faded. Albinos have been observed but rarely. Two subspecies are currently recognized and only one, the Common Mudpuppy (*N. m. maculosus*) is thought to occur in Tennessee.

Etymology: The specific epithet, *maculosus,* is from the Latin and means "full of spots."

Similar Species: Salamander larvae with conspicuous gills often are confused with Mudpuppies. However, all species in Tennessee, with the exception of the Four-Toed Salamander (*Hemidactylium scutatum*), have five toes on the hind limbs. Four-Toed Salamander larvae are significantly smaller than even juvenile

Common Mudpuppy adult, Polk County. (Photo by Matthew L. Niemiller)

Mudpuppies. Younger Mudpuppies are distinctive because of their bold black and yellow coloration and the presence of four toes on all feet. Lesser Sirens (*Siren intermedia*) also are confused with Mudpuppies but lack hind limbs.

Distribution: Mudpuppies are found from the Great Lakes region and upper Mississippi River basin from southern Canada southward into northern Georgia, Alabama, and Mississippi. This species probably is found statewide, but records are lacking from northwestern Tennessee.

Habitat: Mudpuppies thrive in a variety of permanently aquatic habitats, including streams, rivers, reservoirs, and lakes. Within these habitats individuals spend most of their time beneath tree roots, boulders, ledges and large debris piles. However, some individuals can be found at considerable depths up to 27 m deep. Juveniles can often be found in or underneath leaf packs.

Natural History: Detailed information on the breeding behavior of the Mudpuppy is lacking. Breeding and egg deposition occurs in au-

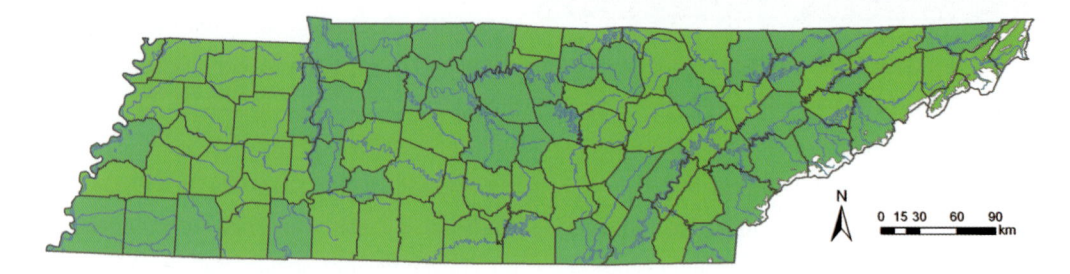

Left: Common Mudpuppy adult, Polk County. (Photo by Matthew L. Niemiller) *Right:* Common Mudpuppy juvenile, Cannon County. (Photo by Matthew L. Niemiller)

tumn and winter throughout its range but extends into the spring throughout the southern portion of its range. Females create depressions under rocks, logs, and other cover 10–60 cm below the water surface and attach 30–150 eggs singly to the undersurfaces of such objects. Females remain with their nests until hatching 6–10 weeks later. Sexual maturity is reached in 5–8 years and this species is known to live as long as 34 years or more. Mudpuppies forage on a variety of prey, including crustaceans, fish, insects, worms, mollusks, and amphibians. There is even a record of a Mudpuppy consuming a small turtle. Juveniles consume smaller prey, such as snails, mayflies, and caddisflies. This species will also eat larvae and eggs of other Mudpuppies. Predation on this species is poorly known. Crayfishes, fishes, turtles, and watersnakes likely prey upon Mudpuppies.

Conservation Status: The Mudpuppy is not currently listed with any agency as threatened. It is generally agreed that this species is doing well throughout its range, although declines in Ohio have been recorded and are thought to be due to pollution and increases in silt. In some locations in the Great Smoky Mountain National Park its abundance appears to be low, and it is thought that this might be due to the use of fish poison used in the rainbow trout introduction project during the 1950s. Humans are also known to greatly increase the mortality of this species because fishermen often catch, discard, or kill Mudpuppies. This species also has been recorded in the pet trade.

Stesha A. Pasachnik and
Matthew L. Niemiller

14
Family Salamandridae (Newts)

The family name, Salamandridae, comes from the Persian *samandar,* referring to a mythical creature that lived in fire. The generic name for the single species found in Tennessee, *Notophthalmus,* is from the Greek *noto* "mark" and *opthalmus* "eye," which refers to the spots on the dorsum. Unlike other salamanders, newts have rough skin and lack distinct costal grooves. Over 50 species of newts are described, with the greatest diversity occurring in Asia, Europe, and northern Africa. Just seven species occur in North America—four species in the western United States and three in the eastern United States. A single species occurs in Tennessee. Fossil newts date back to the Late Oligocene, 25 million years ago. Some newt species are viviparous giving birth to live young, however, most lay eggs and have aquatic larvae. Newts of eastern North America have a complex life cycle with three distinct life stages. Aquatic larvae metamorphose into a terrestrial juvenile known as an eft, and then metamorphose into an aquatic adult. Efts inhabit a variety of habitats in close proximity to the ponds and wetlands where larvae and adults can be found. All newts have toxic skin secretions throughout all developmental stages and many species exhibit aposomatic coloration.

Eastern Newt

Notophthalmus viridescens

Description: Eastern Newts have a complex life cycle with most populations exhibiting four distinct life stages: egg, larva, eft, and aquatic adult. Aquatic adults measure 60–140 mm TL, lack gills, and generally are olive green to yellowish brown on the dorsum. Some populations are neotenic with gilled adults. Up to 45 red spots are usually scattered on the dorsum; however, the largest spots usually form a distinct row on each side of the dorsum. The venter is yellowish with numerous black spots. The tail accounts for 50% of the total length, and a conspicuous tail fin is present. The skin is slightly granular and costal grooves are absent. Four toes are present on the fore limbs and five on the hind limbs. During the breeding season, males develop broadly keeled tails, swollen cloacae, enlarged hind limbs, dark, cornified toe tips, and horny, black ridges on the inner surfaces of the thighs. Outside the breeding season, males generally have larger hind limbs than females. The terrestrial eft (juvenile) stage is typically bright orange to red in coloration but can also be a drab yellowish brown to dark reddish brown. Efts measure 35–85 mm TL and have rough, granular skin with red spots similar to those of the aquatic adults. The tail is triangular and lacks a distinct tail fin. Hatchlings are 7–9 mm TL with prominent external gills, a yellowish green coloration, and smooth skin. Larvae frequently have a dark-colored stripe running along the side of the rounded head through the eye to the gills. Four subspecies are recognized, two of which occur in Tennessee. The Red-Spotted Newt (*N. v. viridescens*) has red dorsal spots present that are encircled by

Red-Spotted Newt adult, Campbell County. (Photo by Matthew L. Niemiller)

black pigment. The Central Newt (*N. v. louisianensis*) is more slender and normally does not have red dorsal spots. If they are present, however, the dorsal spots are small and are not completely outlined in black.

Etymology: The specific and subspecific epithet, *viridescens,* is Latin for "slightly green," referring to the aquatic adult stage coloration. The subspecific epithet, *louisianensis,* means "belonging to the state of Louisiana," referring to the type locality of this subspecies near New Orleans.

Similar Species: Eastern Newts resemble other species of salamanders in Tennessee but can easily be distinguished by their lack of costal grooves and granular skin. Terrestrial efts can be confused with Mud Salamanders (*Pseudotriton montanus*), Red Salamanders (*P. ruber*), and Spring Salamanders (*Gyrinophilus porphyriticus*), as these three species often

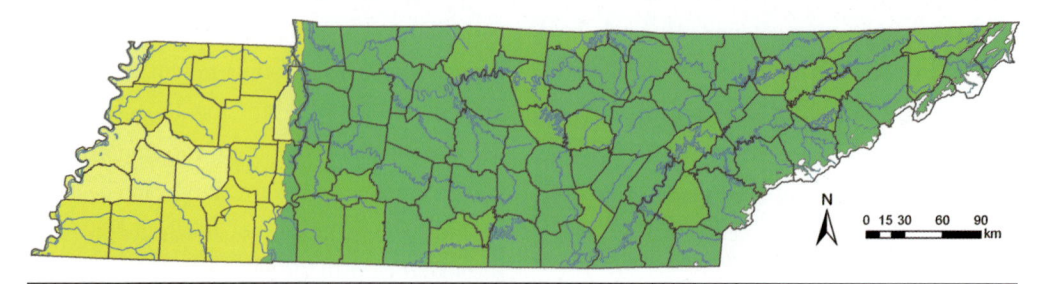

Two subspecies of Eastern Newts are recognized in Tennessee: the Red-Spotted Newt (*N. v. viridescens*), whose range appears in green, and the Central Newt (*N. v. louisianensis*), whose range appears in yellow.

Top left: Red-Spotted Newt eft, Cumberland County. (Photo by Matthew L. Niemiller) *Top right:* Red-Spotted Newt larva, Knox County. (Photo by Nathan Haislip) *Bottom right:* Central Newt larva, St. Martin Parish, Louisiana. (Photo by Matthew L. Niemiller)

mimic the eft stage in coloration. Efts can, however, be readily distinguished by their granular skin and lack of costal grooves.

Distribution: A widely ranging species, Eastern Newts occur throughout eastern North America from southern Canada to south Florida and Texas. They are present nearly throughout all of our state in appropriate habitats below 1,000 m. The Red-Spotted Newt occurs in the eastern two-thirds of the state east of the north-flowing Tennessee River, whereas the Central Newt occurs to the west in the Coastal Plain ecoregions. However, there is evidence of hybridization between the two subspecies in Land Between the Lakes in Stewart County.

Habitat: Due to the unusual complex life cycle of this species, habitats vary for each stage of the life cycle. Eggs are laid in ponds, lakes, swamps, and ephemeral pools and larvae hatch into these habitats where they persist for 2–5 months. The larvae then metamorphose into efts and move into surrounding forested habitats, during which time they are exclusively terrestrial. Efts might be found in moist forested areas by turning rotten logs, and occasionally are seen in numbers moving about on rainy nights or even during the day. Interestingly, many summer camps have large densities of Eastern Newts, which breed readily in the recreational ponds and lakes. Seining or dipnetting the vegetated shorelines of lentic aquatic habitats where eggs and larvae are also found can yield aquatic adults.

Natural History: Unlike other salamanders, Eastern Newts have an intermediate juvenile stage of 2–3 years known as an eft, although this stage may last as long as 7 years. Efts are entirely terrestrial and are usually brightly colored. This is thought to be an example of aposematism, or possessing warning colors. Newts contain tetrodotoxin in their skin, which is a highly effective neurotoxin, and renders them unpalatable to most potential predators. By warning predators of their toxicity, newts might avoid repeated attacks by predators who have learned to associate the bright red or orange coloration with toxicity. Other bright red or orange salamanders, such as Mud or Spring Salamanders, might be imitating the color of the toxic newts to avoid predation. However, Eastern Newts do have a few predators that are apparently resistant to the toxins. Raccoons, Smallmouth Bass, Hog-Nosed and Gartersnakes, Snapping Turtles, American Bullfrogs, Tiger Salamanders, Common Mudpuppies, and leeches all feed on Eastern Newts. Adults and efts are active most of the year, except in the coldest parts of winter. Breeding in Tennessee occurs between late autumn and spring, and adults might often be found with ambystomatid salamanders awaiting spring rains in ephemeral aquatic habitats. Males likely breed annually, while females might skip a few years between reproductive events. Females deposit eggs singly on submerged vegetation, wrapping each egg in a folded leaf or in other detritus. Oviposition occurs in February through April. Females lay 200–375 eggs over several weeks. Eggs hatch in 3–5 weeks, and the larval period lasts 2–5 months, after which larvae metamorphose into terrestrial efts. The eft stage lasts 2–7 years. Neotenic adults and aquatic adults that bypass the terrestrial eft stage are sexually mature in as little as 7 months, while those that undergo the eft stage mature considerably later. Eastern Newts can live 15 years or more. Newts feed on aquatic and terrestrial invertebrates and will occasionally cannibalize hatchlings.

Conservation Status: Eastern Newts are widespread, locally abundant, and are efficient colonizers of new habitat due to the mobility of the terrestrial eft stage. As such, no conservation concerns are reported for this species.

R. Graham Reynolds and
Matthew L. Niemiller

15
Family Sirenidae (Sirens)

The name Sirenidae is derived from *seiren,* the mythological Greek mermaids—a sensible reference as we amphibian biologists consider these creatures attractive if not beautiful. Sirens are elongate, neotenic salamanders with large bushy gills and reaching lengths of nearly 1 m. Sirens also lack hind limbs and have greatly reduced fore limbs. Sirens constitute a small family of four species endemic to eastern North America. Siren fossils date to the Late Cretaceous, 71–84 million years ago in North America. A single species is found in Tennessee and is associated with the Coastal Plain in the western part of the state. These permanently aquatic salamanders live in swamps, sloughs, ditches, backwater areas, and slow-flowing streams. Fertilization in this group is poorly documented but is assumed to be external, as these salamanders lack the internal structures associated with internal fertilization found in other salamanders.

Lesser Siren

Siren intermedia

Description: The Lesser Siren is a large eel-like salamander with three pairs of large, bushy gills. Adults are 18–50 cm TL and lack rear limbs. Front limbs are present, each of which has four toes. Adults are olive green to brown to black, and small black spots are occasionally present on the dorsum. The venter is dark with light spots or flecks. White to yellowish spots or flecks also can be present on the sides. A horny sheath covers the jaw margins. Costal grooves number 33–37. Males are often slightly longer than females and have enlarged jaw muscles, causing the head to appear swollen behind the eyes. Hatchlings have conspicuous dorsal fins and partially developed front limbs. Hatchlings and juveniles are more colorful than adults and often have yellow or red stripes along the sides of the head and longitudinal stripes along the body. The venter and sides are light colored in hatchlings and juveniles. Toe tips might be cornified in juveniles. As juveniles develop, the dorsal fin and coloration on the head gradually disappears. Two subspecies are recognized, one of which, the Western Lesser Siren (*S. intermedia nettingi*), occurs in Tennessee.

Etymology: The specific epithet, *intermedia,* is from the Latin meaning "in between," referring to the intermediate size of this species. The subspecific epithet, *nettingi,* honors M. Graham Netting, a curator of herpetology and museum director at Carnegie Museum and professor at the University of Pittsburgh in the mid-twentieth century.

Similar Species: Western Lesser Sirens can be distinguished from all other salamanders in Tennessee by the lack of hind limbs. Three-Toed

Western Lesser Siren adult, Lake County. (Photo by Brad M. Glorioso)

Amphiumas (*Amphiuma tridactylum*) have a similar body form and habitat but have diminutive fore and hind limbs with three toes each and lack external gills. Mudpuppies (*Necturus maculosus*) typically inhabit permanent bodies of water and have hind limbs.

Distribution: The Western Lesser Siren occurs from the upper Mississippi and Ohio River drainages in Indiana, Illinois, and Missouri south to the Gulf Coast of Texas, Louisiana, and Mississippi. Western Lesser Sirens are known from slow-moving waters of the Coastal Plain in western Tennessee and from sluggish aquatic habitats near the Cumberland River in Middle Tennessee, including Stewart, Montgomery, and Davidson counties.

Habitat: Lesser Sirens are found in both permanent and ephemeral aquatic habitats, including swamps, marshes, ponds, and ditches. Slow sluggish waters with abundant aquatic vegetation and deep sediments are preferred. Ditches, sloughs, and small streams are typical

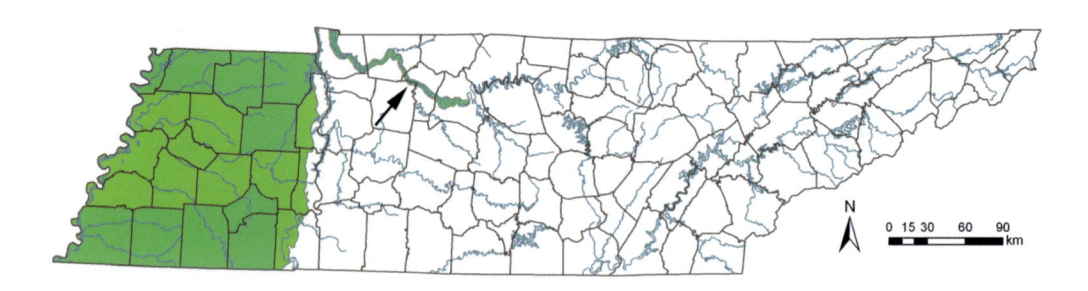

Left: Western Lesser Siren adult, Lake County. (Photo by Matthew L. Niemiller) *Right:* Western Lesser Siren hatchling, Union County, Illinois. (Photo by Andrew M. Durso)

habitats in West Tennessee, while marshes and swamps are preferred along the Cumberland River floodplain.

Natural History: A fully aquatic salamander, Lesser Sirens are nocturnal and spend the day buried in vegetation, sediment, or crawfish burrows. Breeding occurs in autumn and winter as adults become more active. Oviposition occurs in the late winter to early spring, when females lay 200–500 eggs in vegetation or on the substrate in muddy depressions. Eggs hatch in 6–10 weeks and larvae are around 11 mm TL. Sexual maturity is reached in 2 years and sirens can live for 7 years or more. Individuals are often found with bite marks from conspecifics, indicating that biting may be a part of courtship or aggression. Prey consists mainly of aquatic invertebrates, minnows, and earthworms, although cannibalization of eggs has been observed. Predators are not well documented but presumably include aquatic snakes, fish, and wading birds. When habitats dry, Lesser Sirens burrow into the sediment and secrete a mucus-like membrane that protects them from desiccation.

Conservation Status: Lesser Sirens are abundant in appropriate habitats in Tennessee but are threatened by the loss of wetlands and distribution corridors.

George R. Wyckoff and
Matthew L. Niemiller

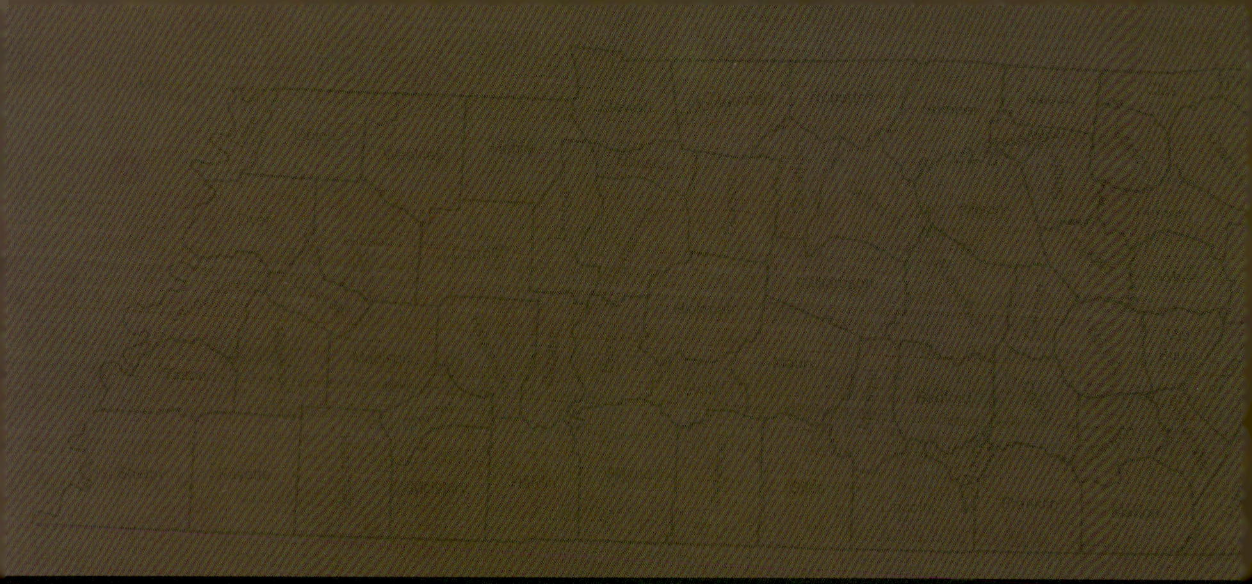

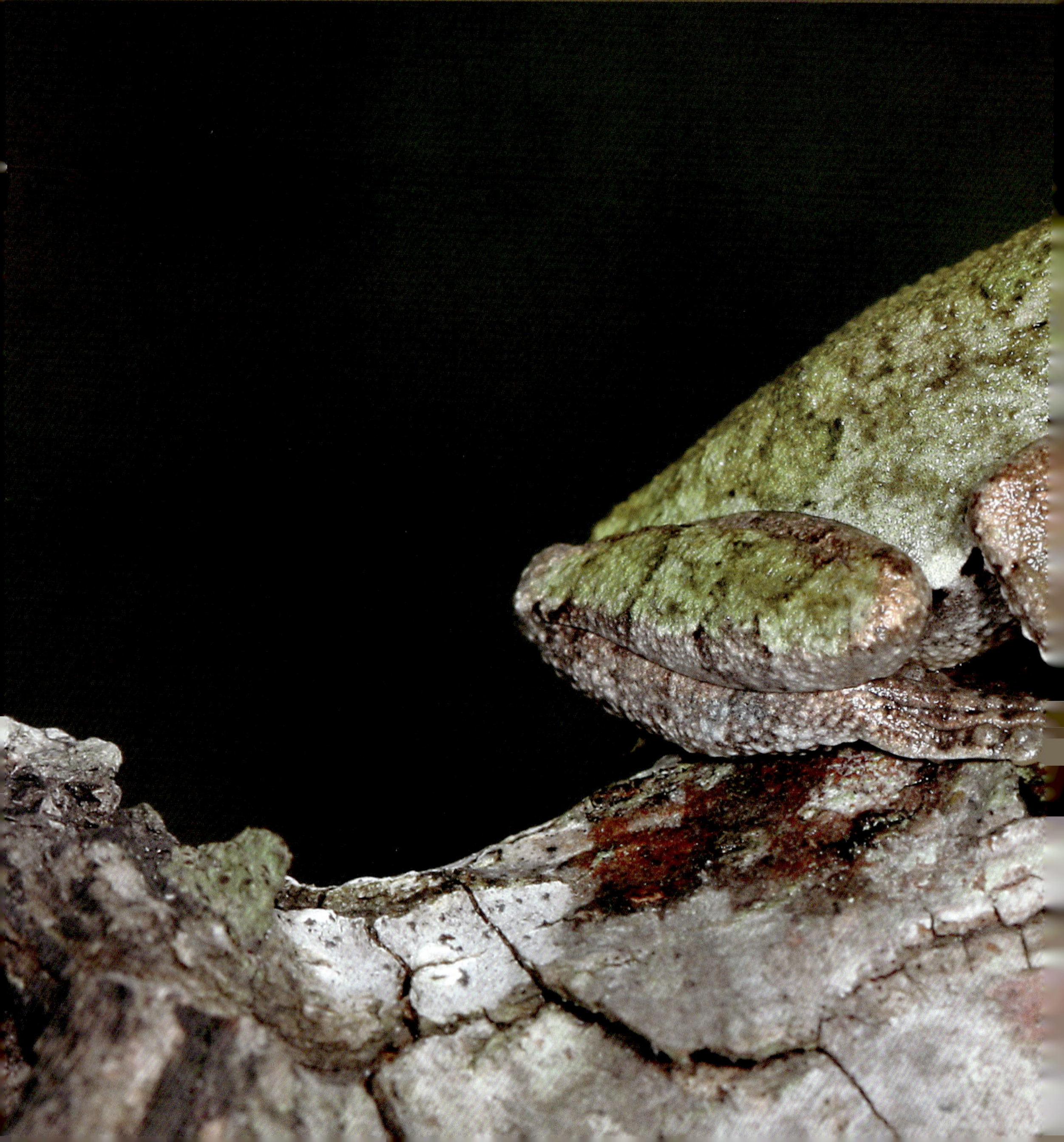

Part 3

Frogs

16
Key to the Adult Frogs of Tennessee

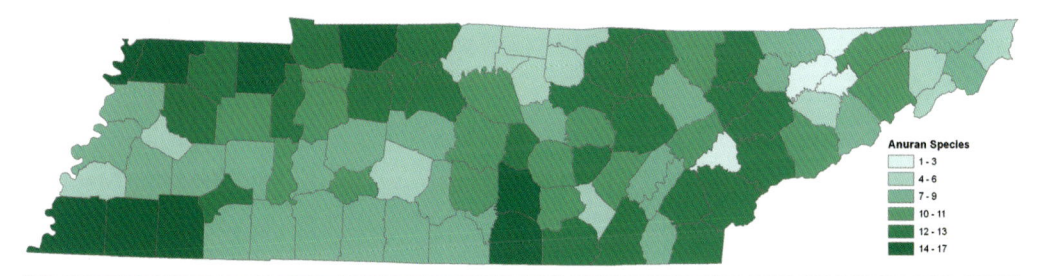

Diversity of anuran species in Tennessee based on county records. Note that low diversity in some counties (e.g., Loudon) is likely due to limited sampling.

1a. Hind feet with one or two spade-like tubercles; parotoid glands present behind eyes; skin typically dry and warty ➔ **2**

1b. Hind feet lacking spade-like tubercles; parotoid glands absent; skin typically smooth or slightly warty and moist ➔ **5**

2a. Pupil of eye vertical in orientation; parotoid glands round and less conspicuous; a single tubercle per hind foot present—**Eastern Spadefoot (*Scaphiopus holbrookii*) Family Scaphiopodidae**

2b. Pupil of eye horizontal in orientation; parotoid glands elongate and conspicuous; one large and one small tubercle per hind foot present ➔ **3 (Family Bufonidae)**

3a. Parotoid glands oval-shaped and connected to cranial crest; 3 or more warts per dark spot on dorsum; chest usually unspotted with dark pigment—**Fowler's Toad (*Anaxyrus fowleri*)**

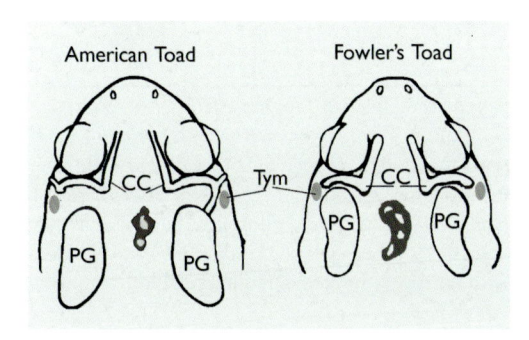

Parotoid glands (PG), cranial crests (CC), and dark dorsal spots of toads from Tennessee. American Toad (*Anaxyrus americanus*) on left, parotoid glands separated from cranial crest or connected by a spur and fewer than three warts per dark dorsal spot. Fowler's Toad (*A. fowleri*) on right, parotoid glands touching cranial crest and three or more warts per dark dorsal spot. Tympanum (Tym) also shown.

3b.   Parotoid glands kidney-shaped and either not connected to or connected to cranial crest by a short spur; 1–2 warts per dark spot on dorsum; chest usually spotted with dark pigment → **4**

4a.   Seldom exceeding 65 mm TL; often reddish in coloration; usually a single wart per dark spot on dorsum; from West Tennessee—**Dwarf American Toad (*Anaxyrus americanus charlesmithi*)**

4b.   Often exceeding 65 mm TL (up to 110 mm); ground coloration variable; 1–2 warts per dark spot on dorsum; from Middle and East Tennessee—**Eastern American Toad (*Anaxyrus americanus americanus*)**

5a.   Transverse fold of skin behind head present; robust body with short limbs and narrow, pointed head—**Eastern Narrow-Mouthed Toad (*Gastrophryne carolinensis*) (Family Microhylidae)**

5b.   Transverse fold of skin behind head absent → **6**

6a.   Intercalary cartilage present between last two phalanges of the toes; some toes with expanded toe tips forming adhesive pads, or if absent with a V-shaped or triangular marking between eyes present; dorsolateral fold absent → **7 (Family Hylidae)**

6b.   Intercalary cartilage absent; Tips of toes without adhesive pads; dorsolateral fold present or absent → **16 (Family Ranidae)**

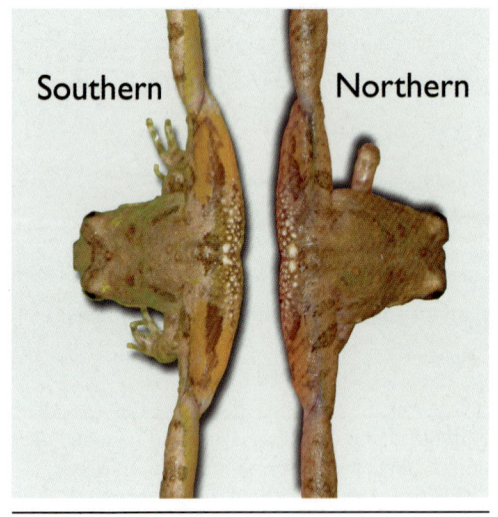

Hind limbs of Cricket Frogs from Tennessee. Southern Cricket Frogs (left) have a smooth-edged dark stripe on the rear of the thigh bordered by two pale yellow or green stripes. Northern Cricket Frogs (right) lack well-defined dark stripes and bordering pale stripes.

Dorsolateral folds of Tennessee frogs. A = American Bullfrog *(Lithobates catesbeianus)* with only a tympanal fold; B = Green Frog *(L. clamitans)* showing broken dorsolateral fold; C = Pickerel Frog *(L. palustris)* with wide and unbroken dorsolateral fold; and D = Southern Leopard Frog *(L. sphenocephalus)* with narrow unbroken dorso-lateral fold.

7a. Tips of toes without adhesive pads; warty in appearance; V-shaped or triangular marking between eyes present → **8**

7b. Tips of toes with adhesive pads; not warty in appearance; V-shaped or triangular marking between eyes usually absent → **9**

8a. Dark stripe of rear of thigh without ragged edges and bordered by two well-defined pale stripes; head pointed; hind limbs longer; webbing between hind toes less extensive with at least 2 1/2 joints of the longest toe free of webbing; from southwest or extreme southeast Tennessee—**Southern Cricket Frog (*Acris gryllus gryllus*)**

8b. Dark stripe on rear of thigh ragged and not bordered by two discernable pale stripes; head blunt; hind limbs shorter; webbing between hind toes more extensive with less than 2 1/2 joints of the longest toe free of webbing—**Northern Cricket Frog (*Acris crepitans*)**

9a. Adhesive toe pads small; webbing between toes less extensive; dorsal patterning in the form of longitudinal stripes, reverse parentheses, or X-shaped marking → **10**

9b. Adhesive toe pads medium to large; webbing between toes more extensive → **13**

10a. Dorsal patterning with three broken or continuous, longitudinal stripes → **11**

10b. Dorsal patterning with reverse parentheses or X-shaped marking → **12**

11a. Dorsal patterning with three broken, often weakly defined, longitudinal stripes—**Upland Chorus Frog (*Pseudacris feriarum*)**

11b. Dorsal patterning usually with three strongly defined, continuous, longitudinal stripes; from Western Pennyroyal Karst in Montgomery County—**Western Chorus Frog (*Pseudacris triseriata*)**

12a. Dorsal patterning often with reverse parentheses; pale-colored upper lip; from Cumberland Plateau, Cumberland Mountains, and southern Blue Ridge Mountains—**Mountain Chorus Frog (*Pseudacris brachyphona*)**

12b. Dorsal patterning usually with a distinct X-shape; tan to reddish brown ground coloration; upper lip not pale colored—**Spring Peeper (*Pseudacris crucifer*)**

13a. White spot beneath eye present → **14**

13b. White spot beneath eye absent → **15**

14a. Rear of thigh pale green to yellowish in coloration; from West Tennessee—**Bird-Voiced Treefrog (*Hyla avivoca*)**

14b. Rear of thigh yellow-orange in coloration—**Gray Treefrog Complex (*Hyla chrysoscelis/ Hyla versicolor*)**

15a. Skin smooth; body slender; ground color green with smooth-edged, white to yellow line running along body; dorsum often with a few small white or yellowish spots—**Green Treefrog (*Hyla cinerea*)**

15b. Skin granular; body robust; ground color ranging from gray to bright green often with small to medium brown spots—**Barking Treefrog (*Hyla gratiosa*)**

16a. Dorsolateral folds absent on trunk—**American Bullfrog (*Lithobates catesbeianus*)**

16b. Dorsolateral folds extending at least partially down trunk → **17**

17a. Dorsolateral folds extending only partway down trunk → **18**

17b. Dorsolateral folds extending completely down trunk → **19**

18a. Dorsum generally bronze without spotting; venter often marked with dark spots and vermiculations; from West Tennessee—**Bronze Frog (*Lithobates clamitans clamitans*)**

18b. Dorsum highly variable in color but usually green to brown with spots and blotches; venter often white with a few dark spots or mottling under limbs and head; from Middle and East Tennessee—**Green Frog (*Lithobates clamitans melanotus*)**

19a. Head with a dark mask on sides extending from snout to behind tympanum—**Wood Frog (*Lithobates sylvaticus*)**

19b. Head without prominent mask → **20**

20a. Pale line lacking along upper lip; body robust with short limbs → **21**

20b. Pale line present along upper lip; body more slender with longer limbs; conspicuous spots present on dorsum → **22**

21a. Venter largely unmarked; dorsal spots dark and encircled by pale pigment; from West Tennessee—**Northern Crawfish Frog (*Lithobates areolatus circulosus*)**

21b. Venter often heavily pigmented; dorsal spots inconspicuous; from Coffee County—**Gopher Frog (*Lithobates capito*)**

22a. Dorsum with two rows of rectangular spots positioned between dorsolateral folds; bright yellow to orange pigmentation on groin and undersurfaces of thighs—**Pickerel Frog (*Lithobates palustris*)**

22b. Dorsum with round (circular or oval) spots typically not positioned into two rows between dorsolateral folds; bright yellow to orange pigmentation lacking on groin and undersurfaces of thighs—**Southern Leopard Frog (*Lithobates sphenocephalus utricularius*)**

17
Key to the Tadpoles of Tennessee

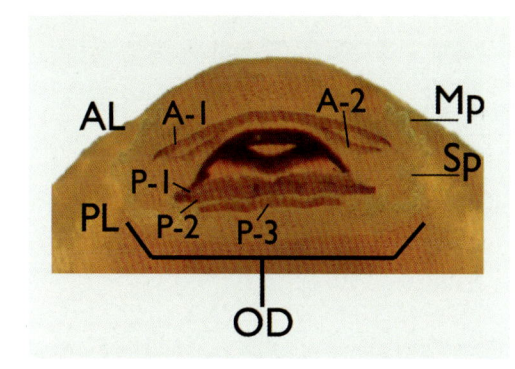

Larval American Bullfrog (*Lithobates catesbeianus*) mouthparts. AL = anterior labium; PL = posterior labium; A-1 = first anterior tooth row; A-2 = second anterior tooth row; Mp = marginal papilla; Sp = submarginal papilla; P-1 = first posterior tooth row; P-2 = Second posterior tooth row; P-3 = Third posterior tooth row; and OD = Oral disc.

1a. Mouthparts simple; oral disc absent; labial teeth absent; horny beak absent; labial papillae absent—**Eastern Narrow-Mouthed Toad (*Gastrophryne carolinensis*) (Family Microhylidae)**

1b. Mouthparts complex; oral disc present; labial teeth present; horny beak present; labial papillae present ➔ **2**

2a. Anus medial; eyes dorsal; submarginal papillae on lower lip absent; total length of largest tadpoles usually less than 40 mm ➔ **3**

2b. Anus opens on right side of lower tail fin; eyes dorsal or lateral; submarginal papillae present on lower lip; total length often exceeding 40 mm ➔ **6**

3a. Oral disc round and not emarginate; marginal papillae present along entire lip or absent from only a short medial gap on upper lip—**Eastern Spadefoot (*Scaphiopus holbrookii*) Family Scaphiopodidae**

3b. Oral disc emarginate at jaw edges; marginal papillae present only around sides of lips ➔ **4 (Family Bufonidae)**

4a. Dorsum mottled or frosted in life with abundant silver to brassy iridophores; small tadpoles often black; throat usually pale in coloration or with clear patch; dorsal tail musculature often with clear patches; snout rounded in lateral view; eyes large relative to head; tail height/musculature height 2.0 or greater—**Fowler's Toad (*Anaxyrus fowleri*)**

4b. Dorsum usually unicolored; golden iridophores often present on dark dorsal tail musculature; throat heavily pigmented; snout sloping in lateral view; eyes small relative to head; tail height/musculature height 2.0 or less ➔ **5**

5a. From West Tennessee—**Dwarf American Toad (*Anaxyrus americanus charlesmithi*)**

5b. From Middle and East Tennessee—**Eastern American Toad (*Anaxyrus americanus americanus*)**

6a. Oral disc oval and not emarginate; eyes dorsal or lateral; total length usually less than 60 mm ➔ **7 (Family Hylidae)**

6b. Oral disc emarginate; eyes dorsal; total length up to 170 mm ➔ **17 (Family Ranidae)**

7a. Two rows of teeth present on posterior labium ➔ **8**

7b. Three rows of teeth present on posterior labium ➔ **11**

8a. Eyes dorsolateral; A-2 gap on anterior labium wide; tail tip usually black; nostrils large; body slightly depressed with total length usually less than 45 mm ➔ **9**

8b. Eyes lateral; A-2 gap on anterior labium narrow; tail tip never black; nostrils typically small; total length up to 60 mm ➔ **10**

9a. Spiracle tube long and projecting as a tube free from body; dark band on chest often present; from southwest and southeast Tennessee—**Southern Cricket Frog (*Acris gryllus gryllus*)**

9b. Spiracle tube short and not projecting free from body; dark band on chest absent—**Northern Cricket Frog (*Acris crepitans*)**

10a. Dorsal tail musculature striped (younger stages), uniformly dark, or with irregular pale patches; tail fins clear or blotched; few submarginal papillae laterally; length of left or right side of A-2 row 3x the width of A-2 gap—**Spring Peeper (*Pseudacris crucifer*) (in part)**

10b. Dorsal tail musculature uniformly dark; few to no submarginal papillae present; left or right side of A-2 row less than 3x the width of A-2 gap—**Upland Chorus Frog (*Pseudacris feriarum*) and Western Chorus Frog (*Pseudacris triseriata*) (in part)**

11a. Body and tail musculature dark; dorsal tail musculature with white, silver, or red saddles; similarly colored interorbital and orbitonasal bands present; throat heavily pigmented; gut not visible; from West Tennessee—**Bird-Voiced Treefrog (*Hyla avivoca*)**

11b. Body and tail musculature dark or pale without saddles; interorbital and orbitonasal bands present or absent; gut visible or not visible ➔ **12**

12a. Length of P-2 row 1.3–1.6x the length of P-3 row; highly arched dorsal tail fin extending anteriorly to the eyes; dark saddle spot often present on the dorsal tail musculature—**Barking Treefrog (*Hyla gratiosa*)**

12b. Length of P-2 row greater than 1.8x the length of P-3 row; dorsal tail fin not extending anteriorly to the eyes ➔ **13**

13a.	Throat not pigmented; dorsum uniformly brown; length of P-2 row greater than 2.5x the length of P-3 row ➔ **14**
13b.	Throat with some pigmentation even if diffuse ➔ **15**
14a.	Length of P-2 row greater than 2.5x the length of P-3 row; left or right side of A-2 row less 3x the width of A-2 gap; lower jaw sheath narrow—**Mountain Chorus Frog (*Pseudacris brachyphona*)**
14b.	Length of P-2 row greater than 2.7x the length of P-3 row; left or right side of A-2 row less than 2.1x the width of A-2 gap; lower jaw sheath narrow to medium—**Upland Chorus Frog (*Pseudacris feriarum*) and Western Chorus Frog (*Pseudacris triseriata*) (in part)**
15a.	Length of P-3 long; length of P-2 row 1.0–1.3x the length of P-3 row; left or right side of A-2 greater than 3.4x the width of A-2 gap; coloration and patterning extremely variable; later developmental stages sometimes with reddish, yellowish, or orangish coloration in tail fin; tail fin with blotches—**Gray Treefrog Complex (*Hyla chrysoscelis/Hyla versicolor*)**
15b.	Length of P-3 short; length of P-2 row greater than 1.3x the length of P-3 row ➔ **16**
16a.	Length of P-2 row 3.0x or greater than the length of P-3 row—**Spring Peeper (*Pseudacris crucifer*) (in part)**
16b.	Length of P-2 row less than 3.0x the length of P-3 row; pale yellow stripe often present on either side of the head running from the nostril to the eye—**Green Treefrog (*Hyla cinerea*)**
17a.	Four rows of teeth present on posterior labium; body globular; dorsum uniformly dark; tail fins with few to no markings—**Wood Frog (*Lithobates sylvaticus*)**
17b.	Three rows of teeth present on posterior labium ➔ **18**
18a.	One, two (most common), or three rows of teeth on anterior labium; nostrils small; beak with narrow black edges; coloration and patterning highly variable; total length often greater than 70 mm and reaching 140 mm ➔ **19**
18b.	Usually just two rows of teeth on anterior labium; nostrils medium; beak with wider black edges; total length usually less than 70 mm ➔ **21**
19a.	Body unicolored brown to green, usually with many small black spots on body, dorsal fin, and dorsal tail musculature; venter cream to yellow in coloration; total length up to 140 mm—**American Bullfrog (*Lithobates catesbeianus*)**
19b.	Body typically dark to pale brown to gray without small, distinct black spots; spots that are present with fuzzy edges; spotting lacking in dorsal fin but distal third of dorsal fin often with irregular rectangular pigmentation; tail fins usually densely speckled; venter usually white with silvery iridophores in younger developmental stages; total length up to 90 mm ➔ **20**

20a. From West Tennessee—**Bronze Frog (*Lithobates clamitans clamitans*)**

20b. From Middle and East Tennessee—**Green Frog (*Lithobates clamitans melanotus*)**

21a. Medial gap in P-1 row present; length of P-2 row 1.5x the length of P-3 row; left or right side of A-2 0.2–0.5x the width of A-2 gap; often with a white line running between nostrils on snout—**Southern Leopard Frog (*Lithobates sphenocephalus*)**

21b. Medial gap in P-1 row absent; left or right side of A-2 0.5x or greater than the width of A-2 gap → **22**

22a. Length of P-2 row 1.5x the length of P-3 row; left or right side of A-2 0.7x the width of A-2 gap; white lip line faint to absent; tail fins usually heavily pigmented—**Pickerel Frog (*Lithobates palustris*)**

22b. Length of P-2 row 1.7x the length of P-3 row; left or right side of A-2 0.5x the width of A-2 gap; white lip line usually present; tail fins usually clear but can have bold markings → **23**

23a. From Coffee County in central Tennessee—**Gopher Frog (*Lithobates capito*)**

23b. From West Tennessee—**Northern Crawfish Frog (*Lithobates areolatus circulosus*)**

18

Family Bufonidae (True Toads)

Toads are often unfair subjects of tall tales, considered by some to be ugly wart-spreading creepy-crawlies—a shameful characterization of a fascinating group of amphibians (which do not spread warts, by the way). Over 400 species are recognized in the family that are native to every continent but Australia (where they have since been introduced) and Antarctica. Two species occur in Tennessee, both of them widespread and occupying a variety of natural and disturbed habitats. Toads are known from the upper Tertiary and Quaternary of North America but date to the upper Paleocene of South America. The genus name, *Anaxyrus*, is Greek meaning "a king or chief." Toads are of average size and have rough, dry skin, covered with warts. Toads possess poison glands called parotoid glands, which are used to defend against potential predators. When the toad is sufficiently disturbed, a thick white liquid will ooze from these glands, located just behind the eyes, and irritate whatever organism is threatening it. The liquid is potent, and rubbing your eyes or nose after handling a toad can cause an unpleasant burning sensation. Toads are terrestrial as adults and have horny protuberances on their hind feet for digging.

American Toad

Anaxyrus americanus

Description: The American Toad is a medium- to large-sized toad with conspicuous paired parotoid glands and cranial crests. Adults measure 50–111 mm TL and have dry, warty skin. Ground color varies from dull grayish brown to greenish tan to brick red. Darker spots and blotches sometimes are present on the dorsum and typically are yellow to dark brown to black in color. Additionally, these spots and blotches seldom contain more than one or two warts. Warts can be yellow to red to dark brown and are especially prominent on the tibia. A pale line is occasionally present running along the center of the dorsum. The kidney-shaped parotoid glands are prominent and located behind the eyes. These glands are either separated from the cranial crests located behind the eyes or connected by a short spur. The venter is white to cream in color with the chest usually spotted or blotched with darker pigment, but this can be absent in some individuals. Males have dark gray throat pouches and enlarged horny pads on the inside of their forelimbs during the breeding season. Females typically are larger than males. Four toes are present on the front feet and five toes on the hind feet. Tadpoles are 18–27 mm TL with round to oval bodies and small, dorsal eyes. Ground color is dark brown to black with scattered gold to copper flecks or spots, especially on the venter and along the dorsal tail musculature. The tail is bicolored with the dorsal tail musculature usually dark and the lower tail musculature pale. The tail fin typically is unpigmented and rounded at the tip. Newly metamorphosed toadlets are 7–14

Eastern American Toad adult, Blount County. (Photo by Matthew L. Niemiller)

mm TL. Two subspecies occur in Tennessee: the Eastern American Toad (*A. a. americanus*) and Dwarf American Toad (*A. a. charlesmithi*). Dwarf American Toads differ from Eastern American Toads by seldom exceeding 64 mm TL, they are usually reddish, and if dorsal spots are present, they typically contain only one wart.

Etymology: The specific and subspecific epithet, *americanus,* means "from America," likely referencing the large range of this species. The subspecific epithet, *charlesmithi,* honors Charles C. Smith, a biologist and professor from Kansas.

Similar Species: American Toads can easily be confused with Fowler's Toads (*A. fowleri*), especially small individuals, and the two species are known to hybridize. American Toads have larger cranial crests and more prominent

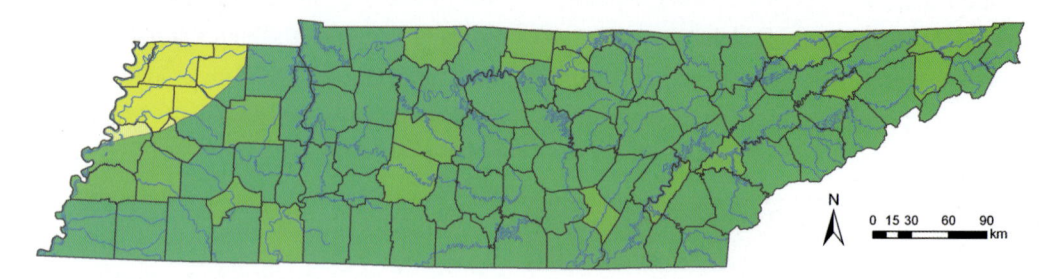

Two subspecies of American Toad are recognized in Tennessee: the Eastern American Toad *(A. a. americanus),* whose range appears in green, and the Dwarf American Toad *(A. a. charlesmithi),* whose range appears in yellow.

Left: Dwarf American Toads in amplexus, Lake County. (Photo by Matthew L. Niemiller) *Right:* Eastern American Toad tadpole, Coffee County. (Photo by Matthew L. Niemiller)

parotoid glands than those found in Fowler's Toads. Likewise, the parotoid glands in American Toads either are separated from or connected by a spur to the cranial crests located behind the eyes, whereas these glands directly touch the cranial crests in Fowler's Toads. Additionally, American Toads usually have only one or two warts in the largest dorsal spots and enlarged warts on the tibia, whereas Fowler's Toads have three or more warts and do not have enlarged warts on the tibia. Finally, the chest of Fowler's Toads usually is immaculate. Tadpoles of these two species also are similar. The tails are distinctly bicolored in American Toad tadpoles, whereas Fowler's Toad tadpoles do not have bicolored tails and usually have a pale or clear patch on the throat.

Distribution: The American Toad is found throughout eastern North America from the Maritime Provinces west to Manitoba in Canada and south to Louisiana, Mississippi, Alabama, and Georgia. The American Toad is found statewide in Tennessee. The Eastern American Toad occurs throughout most of the state, except in the northwestern counties where the Dwarf American Toad replaces it.

Habitat: American Toads occurs in a variety of habitats and can be quite ubiquitous. Typical habitats include forests, open fields, pastures, and suburban areas with a preference for sandy to loamy soil with accumulated leaf litter where individuals have an easier time burrowing. American Toads are most abundant in terrestrial habitats surrounding breeding sites that include roadside ditches, water-filled vehicle ruts, ephemeral ponds, borrow pits, floodplain pools, and the margins of rivers and lakes. American Toads have been found up to 1650 m in elevation in Tennessee. American Toads are primarily nocturnal and can be found underneath rocks, logs, and other debris during the day. Both adults and metamorphs can be observed on roads at night during or after rains.

Natural History: Breeding occurs from late January into early April in Tennessee depending on elevation. Females are highly fecund, laying 2,000–20,000 eggs in a pair of long gelatinous strands freely on the bottom or on submerged vegetation in shallow water. Eggs hatch in 3–12 days and the larval period lasts 6–8 weeks. Metamorphs can be found from June through September depending on the timing of egg

Left: Eastern American Toad egg masses, Coffee County. (Photo by Matthew L. Niemiller) *Right:* Eastern American Toad toadlet, Coffee County. (Photo by Matthew L. Niemiller)

deposition. Sexual maturity usually is reached in three to four years and adults can live considerably longer. American Toads feed on a variety of insects and other invertebrates, including earthworms. Tadpoles feed on aquatic matter, including algae, dead fish, detritus, and dead tadpoles. Snakes, birds, raccoons, opossums, and skunks are known predators of adult American Toads. Diving beetles, giant water bugs, dragonfly naids, crayfish, and birds are predators of tadpoles and eggs. Adults produce thick and milky toxic skin secretions from the skin and parotoid glands that are noxious to many predators. Likewise, both eggs and tadpoles are toxic to some predators. When encountering a predator, an American Toad typically crouches and remains motionless first, then inflates its body and extends its hind limbs to appear larger.

Call: The call of the American Toad is a long, high-pitched, musical trill lasting 6–30 seconds in duration with a 30–40 per second trill rate. Males congregate in a breeding chorus and call while floating or sitting near the edge of water.

Conservation Status: American Toads are widespread and common throughout Tennessee and populations appear stable.

Matthew L. Niemiller and R. Graham Reynolds

Fowler's Toad adult, Blount County. (Photo by Matthew L. Niemiller)

Fowler's Toad

Anaxyrus fowleri

Description: Fowler's Toad is a medium-sized toad with conspicuous paired parotoid glands and cranial crests. Adults measure 50–75 mm TL but can reach lengths up to 95 mm. Ground coloration varies from pale brown to gray to red. Most individuals have six or so well-defined dark brown to black, irregular spots on the dorsum. The skin is dry and warty. The spots on the dorsum typically contain three or more warts per spot. A white stripe also might be present running down the center of the dorsum. Warts are typically red to dark brown and are not prominent on the tibia. The parotoid glands touch the distinct cranial crests located behind the eyes. The venter is white to cream in color without prominent spotting on the chest. Males have dark gray throat pouches and enlarged horny pads on the inside of their forelimbs during the breeding season. Females typically are

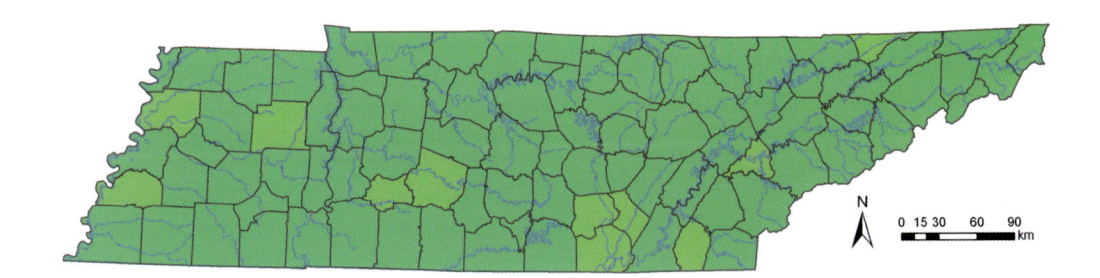

Left: Red morph of Fowler's Toad, Wilson County. (Photo by Matthew L. Niemiller) *Right:* Fowler's Toad adult, Rutherford County. (Photo by Matthew L. Niemiller)

larger than males. Four toes are present on the front feet and five toes on the hind feet. Tadpoles are 18–27 mm TL with round to oval bodies and small, dorsal eyes. Ground color is dark brown to black and usually mottled. The center of the tail musculature also is dark brown to black. The tail fin is narrow and typically unpigmented. Newly metamorphosed toadlets are 8–11 mm TL. No subspecies are recognized.

Etymology: The specific epithet, *fowleri*, honors S. P. Fowler, a Massachusetts naturalist.

Similar Species: Fowler's Toads can easily be confused with American Toads (*A. americanus*), especially small individuals, and the two species are known to hybridize. American Toads have larger cranial crests and more prominent parotoid glands than those found in Fowler's Toads. Likewise, the parotoid glands in American Toads are either separated from or connect by a spur to the cranial crests located behind the eyes, whereas these glands directly touch the cranial crests in Fowler's Toads. Additionally, American Toads usually have only 1–2 warts in the largest dorsal spots and enlarged warts on the tibia, whereas Fowler's Toads have three or more warts and do not have enlarged warts on the tibia. Finally, the chest of Fowler's Toads usually is immaculate. Tadpoles of these two species also are similar. The tails are distinctly bicolored in American Toad tadpoles, whereas Fowler's Toad tadpoles do not have bicolored tails and usually have a pale or clear patch on the throat.

Distribution: Fowler's Toads range from the Great Lakes and the Northeast south to the Gulf Coast and west into eastern Oklahoma and Texas. In Tennessee they occur statewide, although not much beyond 1,200 m in elevation.

Habitat: Fowler's Toads occupy a variety of habitats including urban areas, although they often seem to prefer more xeric areas than American Toads. They are common in well-drained soils, such as the cedar glades of the Inner Nashville Basin. Adults can be found far from water hiding under rocks, logs, and leaf litter during the day and emerging to feed at dusk. Fowler's Toads breed in ephemeral wetlands, such as tire ruts, the margins of lakes and swamps, and woodland pools. Tadpoles occupy the margins of ponds and pools often in great numbers.

Natural History: Fowler's Toads move to breeding areas with the arrival of warmer weather and spring rains, usually between February and May. Males call from the edges of most types of aquatic habitats, and amplexed couples lay in shallow water near vegetation. Many pool owners will find that toads are catholic in their choice of breeding sites, frequently ovipositing in the accumulated water above winter pool covers. Clutches contain 2,000–10,000 eggs, which are laid in twin strings, and the tadpoles hatch about one week later. Tadpoles are gregarious and feed on suspended organic detritus and metamorphose 1–2 months later, usually during the summer. Metamorphs can frequently be seen in great numbers around breeding localities as they disperse away from the water. Adults feed on many invertebrates, particularly beetles, and become sexually mature after 2 years. Adults can be found abroad at night, particularly on humid nights, and are frequently found underneath cover objects during the day. Adults avoid freezing by burrowing into loose soil. Fowler's Toads are chemically defended, producing noxious secretions in the parotoid glands to deter predators, an effective defense and certainly an irritant to human eyes and mucous glands. Some predators can defeat this formidable defense, including American Bullfrogs, raccoons, and Hog-Nosed Snakes, the latter of which specialize on toads.

Call: The male advertisement call of Fowler's Toad is a high-pitched, rapid *waaah* lasting for one or several seconds, though usually not more than four seconds. Both males and females can produce a short chirping sound when grasped by conspecifics, predators, and humans.

Conservation Status: Fowler's Toads appear stable throughout the state and no protective measures are in place, though they have been extirpated from several locations elsewhere in their range. However, hybridization with the American Toad, which might increase under current climate change scenarios, could threaten the genetic integrity of this species.

R. Graham Reynolds and
Matthew L. Niemiller

Field Notes

Swamps and Frogs

MATT AND I HAD COME TO WEST TENNESSEE one rainy summer evening in search of the euphonious Bird-Voiced Treefrog, and as usually happens with us, an adventure was in the works. We began by surveying the northern Southeastern Plains in Henry, Carroll, and Gibson counties, stopping frequently to check the legs of all the small gray hylids we came across on the roads. Bird-Voiced Treefrogs closely resemble members of the Gray Treefrog complex, except in two important respects. First, Bird-Voiced Treefrogs have a greenish wash on the thighs, which may be viewed by carefully extending the rear legs, while Cope's Gray Treefrogs generally have orangish thigh coloration. Second, Bird-Voiced Treefrogs have a melodic call resembling the soft, repeated whistles of a bird, while Cope's Gray Treefrogs have a decidedly brusque and raspy trill. Bird-Voiced Treefrogs are generally found by following their calls, which are emitted from trees above standing, stagnant water, such as swamps. Having had no luck on the roads, we donned headlamps and rain jackets and walked along the margins of various swamps and sloughs, hoping to hear that soft call. We failed to turn up our quarry, but we did encounter some other welcome amphibians, including several calling ranids, plenty of Cope's Gray Treefrogs, larval Mole and Small-Mouthed Salamanders, and calling American Toads. As midnight approached we had to make a decision—call it a night and try again tomorrow or head to a new area to take advantage of the warm and rainy conditions. We knew there had to be some calling Bird-Voiced Treefrogs on such a night, so we headed south toward Henderson and Chester counties, arriving well after midnight. We began to search for entrances to swampy areas near Pinson Mounds, driving slowly with the windows down. At last, a faint *whit, whit whit* repeated several times per second—we had found them! We found a pull-off on a lonely road, surrounded by miles of lowland swamp in each direction. Having donned our gear—headlamps, waders, and rain jackets—we descended into the swamp. As I attempted to locate a calling male, I began to reflect on the nature of our situation. How many people would willingly enter a vast and lonely swamp in the rain at two in the morning? Surely a lowly gray frog would not lure them to such a place in such conditions. But the scent of the swamp, the shadows of the great cypress trees, and the melodious calling of dozens of Bird-Voiced Treefrogs, punctuated with the occasional startling and guttural *baa-room* of a bullfrog, made me think that more people should suspend their aversion to dark swamps and try this—it was great fun! "Whoa!" I exclaimed out loud, shuffling backward in the waist-deep water and nearly submerging. In my reflections I had almost stepped onto a very large Western Cottonmouth, a venomous snake common in the swamps of West Tennessee; indeed, I had nearly taken a swim with it. Assuring it of my intention to withdraw the affront, I shooed it away and issued a warning to Matt: "Got a Mouth over here."

Matt, unconcerned about my nearly having ended the evening, as well as the trip, was intently tracking a calling Bird-Voiced Treefrog in a tree. Locating the frog, I shined my headlamp on it as Matt climbed well up into the tree and slowly eased his hand around it. Without a struggle, the small gray frog went along with the procedure, even enduring a fusillade of camera flashes electrifying the darkness and blinding all three of us. In all we found nearly a dozen male and female Bird-Voiced Treefrogs that night, dodged several more Cottonmouths, and gained an experience not to be soon forgotten. Though I may be scoffed at by those disinclined to adventure, I say that every naturalist should spend a night in a swamp, especially one with acoustic jewels of calling Bird-Voiced Treefrogs dotting the treetops.

R. Graham Reynolds

19

Family Hylidae (Treefrogs)

Treefrogs are charismatic amphibians, which range from very small to medium in size and frequently possess pads on the toes. These pads function in some species of the genus *Hyla* as sticky grippers, allowing them to climb readily, even up slick surfaces such as glass. While *Hyla* is an arboreal genus, others in this family, such as *Pseudacris* and *Acris,* are usually found on the ground or in low vegetation near water. The family name is from the Greek *Hylas,* a mythological companion of Heracles who disappeared into a spring and whose name Heracles called repeatedly as he searched for the missing Argonaut. This is referencing the aquatic affinities of hylids and the prominent repeated calls in these frogs. Over 700 species are recognized from North America, South America, Europe, Asia, Australia, and northern Africa. This family is represented by three genera (and 11 species) in Tennessee: *Acris, Hyla,* and *Pseudacris.* The etymology of these genera is as follows. *Acris* is from the Greek *akris* "locust," which refers to the insect-like call of advertising males; hence the common name cricket frog. *Pseudacris* is from the Greek *pseudes* "false" and *akris* "locust," referring to the superficial similarity of chorus frogs to cricket frogs. Hylid fossils are known from the Oligocene of North America. Treefrogs frequently thrive in the vicinity of humans, with Upland Chorus Frogs being common backyard neighbors in East Tennessee, while Green Treefrogs might be found on lighted exterior walls in West Tennessee. It is always a pleasure to wander into a chorus of hylids on warm moist evenings, and the editor (RGR) maintains a backyard specifically designed to attract Cope's Gray Treefrogs and Upland Chorus Frogs, though his neighbors might say that mosquitoes equally enjoy the habitat.

Northern Cricket Frog

Acris crepitans

Description: Northern Cricket Frogs are diminutive hylids achieving a TL of only 16–38 mm. The toes do not have enlarged pads like other hylid species and the hind feet are highly webbed. Small warts freckle the dorsal surface and upper legs, giving the skin a granular appearance. The dorsal color is highly variable, ranging from brown to gray usually with patches of paler color such as green or dull yellow and occasional black patches. There is often a dark triangle between the eyes pointing backward toward the posterior. A pale green stripe occasionally extends from the snout down the middle of the back. The hind legs generally have prominent ragged-edged black stripes running along the back of the thighs. Four toes are present

Northern Cricket Frog in water, Obion County. (Photo by Brad M. Glorioso)

on the front feet and five on the webbed hind feet. Females are slightly larger than males. Males have darker throats during the breeding season. Tadpoles reach 40 mm TL and have dorsal eyes. Ground coloration is pale to dark greenish brown with a distinctive black tail tip. The tail is long and the tail fin is generally translucent with slight spotting or speckling. Newly metamorphosed froglets are 13–15 mm TL. Traditionally, two subspecies were recognized in Tennessee. However, recent molecular work indicates that the two subpecies are actually distinct species, and only Northern Cricket Frogs occur in Tennessee. Blanchard's Cricket Frogs (*A. blanchardi*) are found west of the Mississippi River and to north in Indiana and Ohio.

Etymology: The specific epithet, *crepitans*, Latin for "rattling sound" or "crackling sound," refers to the rapid, high-pitched call of this species.

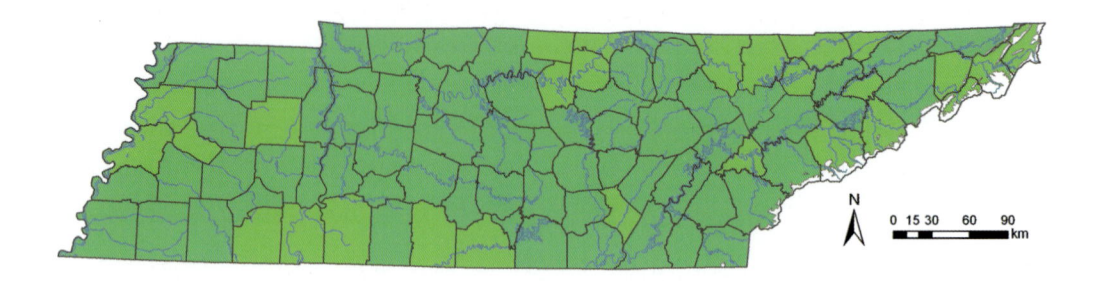

Similar Species: Northern Cricket Frogs closely resemble Southern Cricket Frogs (*A. gryllus*), although some individuals might be problematic to identify in the field, as the two species sometimes hybridize. In general, Northern Cricket Frogs are less slender and have a blunt snout, have more webbing on the hind feet, and shorter legs. In Southern Cricket Frogs, the fourth digit on the hind foot has at least two joints free of webbing, and the heel of the foot will reach the snout if the leg is manually extended forward toward the head. Additionally, the stripes on the back of the thighs of Northern Cricket Frogs have ragged edges, whereas these stripes are more sharply demarcated in Southern Cricket Frogs. Tadpoles also are very similar in appearance, but the spiracle is much shorter in Northern Cricket Frogs than in Southern Cricket Frogs.

Distribution: Northern Cricket Frogs are found from southern New York south into the Carolinas and Georgia, then south and west into the Gulf Coast of the panhandle of Florida, Alabama, and Mississippi, then north into Tennessee and Kentucky. This species is found statewide in Tennessee, except for the middle to high elevations of the Blue Ridge Mountains.

Habitat: Northern Cricket Frogs occur along the shore of permanent aquatic habitats with plenty of vegetation but with a decent amount of sunlight penetrating to the ground. They rarely leave this habitat and are most easily seen by walking along the banks of ponds, slow-moving rivers, and small lakes. Individuals are often seen jumping into the water, then immediately swimming back toward land on the surface.

Northern Cricket Frog adult, Henry County. (Photo by Matthew L. Niemiller)

Natural History: Breeding takes place in mid-spring to late summer with males calling prior to and after actual oviposition occurs. Eggs are laid in small groups of 2–20, but occasionally in larger clusters up to 400 eggs, along the margins of aquatic habitats in shallow water. Tadpoles hatch within days and metamorphose after 29–90 days. Metamorphs become sexually mature the following year. Tadpoles consume phytoplankton and adults feed on small invertebrates and occasional mollusks and crustaceans. Predators include other amphibians, snakes, birds, and small mammals.

Call: The advertisement call of male Northern Cricket Frogs is a high-pitched series of clicks similar to that of an insect (cricket or cicada), repeated continuously as short chirps or clicks. The call also has been described as hitting two marbles together repeatedly.

Conservation Status: Northern Cricket Frog populations appear stable in Tennessee, although documented declines in populations of the closely related Blanchard's Cricket Frog have been reported from northern states.

R. Graham Reynolds and
Matthew L. Niemiller

Southern Cricket Frog adult, Bradley County. (Photo by Matthew L. Niemiller)

Southern Cricket Frog

Acris gryllus

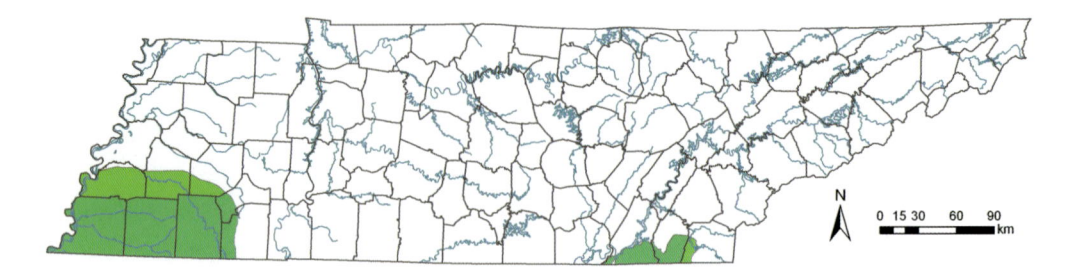

Description: Southern Cricket Frogs are diminutive hylids achieving a TL of only 16–33 mm. The toes do not have enlarged pads like other hylid species, and the hind feet are highly webbed. Small warts freckle the dorsal surface and upper legs, giving the skin a granular appearance. The dorsal color is highly variable, ranging from brown to gray to black, usually with patches of paler color, such as green or dull yellow, and occasional black patches. There is often a dark triangle between the eyes pointing backward toward the posterior. A pale green, yellow, or red stripe extends from the snout down the middle of the back that usually forks around the dark triangle atop the head. Many individuals also have a pale diagonal line located below the eye. The hind legs generally have one or two prominent well-defined black stripes running along the back of the thighs. Four toes are present on the front feet and five on the webbed hind feet. Females are slightly larger than males. Males have darker throats during the breeding season. Tadpoles reach 38 mm TL and have dorsal eyes. Ground coloration is pale to dark greenish brown with a distinctive black tail tip. The tail is long and the tail fin is generally translucent with slight spotting or speckling. Newly metamorphosed froglets are 10–15 mm TL. Two subspecies are recognized, and only the Costal Plain Cricket Frog (*A. g. gryllus*) occurs in Tennessee.

Etymology: The specific epithet, *gryllus,* Latin for "cricket" or "grasshopper," refers to the similarity of the male advertisement call to that of these insects.

Similar Species: Southern Cricket Frogs closely resemble Northern Cricket Frogs (*A. crepitans*), although some individuals might be problematic to identify in the field, as the two species sometimes hybridize. In general, Northern Cricket Frogs are less slender and have a blunt snout, have more webbing on the hind feet, and shorter legs. In Southern Cricket Frogs, the fourth digit on the hind foot has at least two joints free of webbing, and the heel of the foot will reach the snout if the leg is manually extended forward toward the head. Additionally, the stripes on back of the thighs of Northern Cricket Frogs have ragged edges, whereas these stripes are more sharply demarcated in Southern Cricket Frogs. Tadpoles also are very similar in appearance; however, the spiracle is much shorter in Northern Cricket Frogs than in Southern Cricket Frogs.

Distribution: Southern Cricket Frogs occur throughout much of the Coastal Plain of the southeastern United States. In Tennessee, Southern Cricket Frogs are mostly found in the southwestern counties in the Coastal Plain, including Shelby, Chester, Fayette, Hardeman, and McNairy counties. Populations have also recently been discovered in Hamilton and Bradley counties in extreme southeastern Tennessee.

Southern Cricket Frog adult, Hardeman County. (Photo by Matthew L. Niemiller)

Habitat: Southern Cricket Frogs occur along the shore of permanent or temporary aquatic habitats with plenty of vegetation but also with a decent amount of sunlight penetrating to the ground. They are frequently found away from water, though are most easily seen by walking along the banks of ponds, slow-moving rivers, swamps, ditches, and pools. Individuals are often seen jumping into the water, then immediately swimming back toward land on the surface.

Natural History: Breeding takes place from mid-spring to late summer with males calling prior to and after oviposition takes place. Eggs are laid in small groups of 7–12 eggs along the margins of shallow water, with a single female producing 200–300 eggs in total. Tadpoles hatch within days and metamorphose after 50–90 days. Metamorphs become sexually mature the following year. Tadpoles consume phytoplankton and algae, while adults feed on small invertebrates and terrestrial arthropods. Predators include other amphibians, fish, snakes, birds, and small mammals.

Call: The advertisement call of male Southern Cricket Frogs is high-pitched series of clicks (*gick gick gick*) similar to that of an insect (cricket or cicada), repeated continuously as short chirps or clicks. The call also has been described as hitting two marbles together repeatedly.

Conservation Status: Certain Southern Cricket Frog populations appear stable in Tennessee, although not much is known about recently discovered populations in Hamilton and Bradley counties. Nevertheless, this species is listed as "Imperiled/Vulnerable" in the state.

R. Graham Reynolds and Matthew L. Niemiller

Bird-Voiced Treefrog male, Chester County. (Photo by Matthew L. Niemiller)

Bird-Voiced Treefrog

Hyla avivoca

Description: Bird-Voiced Treefrogs are small hylids, with adults measuring 25–50 mm TL. Dorsal coloration is usually a mottled pale gray, dark gray, or even green with patterning that resembles lichen. Coloration varies with activity and ambient temperature. A pale white to yellow-green patch extends below the eye to the top of the upper lip. A distinctive pale green to yellow-green wash occurs on the groin and inner thigh region and can be viewed by gently extending a hind leg. Darker bars are often present on the hind limbs. Four toes are present on the front feet and five on the hind feet. The skin is slightly granular, but not warty, and the toes have large, expanded adhesive

Left: Bird-Voiced Treefrog female, Chester County. (Photo by Matthew L. Niemiller) *Right:* Bird-Voiced Treefrog female (left) and male (right), Chester County. (Photo by Matthew L. Niemiller)

discs. There is moderate webbing of the hind feet. Juveniles tend to be more greenish in dorsal coloration but otherwise resemble adults. Males are smaller than females and have a dark throat. Tadpoles are very distinctive, measuring up to 40 mm TL with red to orange saddles on the dorsal tail musculature separated by black bands. The head has a white to red line running between the eyes that extends from the eyes to the nostrils forming a triangle. The eyes are laterally positioned. The venter is dark making the intestinal coil invisible. Froglets are around 13 mm TL at metamorphosis. No subspecies are recognized.

Etymology: The specific epithet, *avivoca,* is from the Latin *avis* "bird" and *voca* "call." The call of males of this species resembles that of a bird.

Similar Species: The Bird-Voiced Treefrog is very similar to both Cope's Gray (*H. chrysoscelis*) and Gray Treefrogs (*H. versicolor*). Bird-Voiced Treefrogs are smaller with less granular skin and a green to yellowish color on the inner thighs and groin, as opposed to the warty skin and orange inner thigh color of Cope's Gray and Gray Treefrogs. Juveniles of all three species can be almost impossible to differentiate between until the groin coloration develops. The tadpoles of Bird-Voiced Treefrogs are very distinctive with the presence of the dorsal saddles.

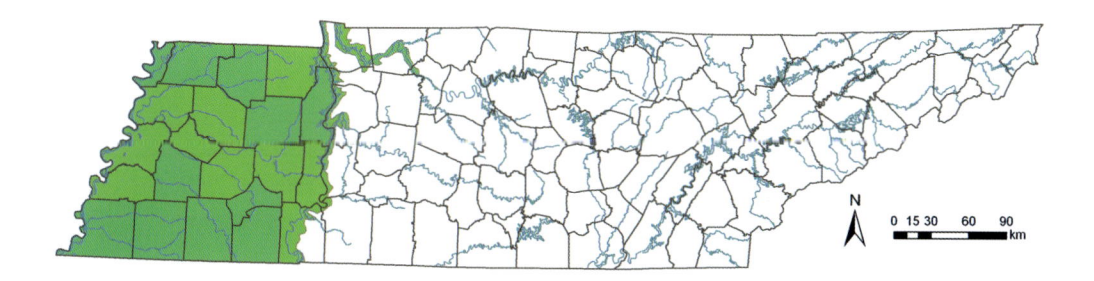

Distribution: Bird-Voiced Treefrogs occur along the Mississippi River drainage, roughly from southern Illinois and Missouri south to the Gulf Coast and then east through southern Alabama and Georgia to the Atlantic Coast. In Tennessee, they can be found throughout most of the Coastal Plain ecoregions west of the Tennessee River and along the Cumberland River in the Western Pennyroyal Karst ecoregion.

Habitat: Bird-Voiced Treefrogs are usually found in association with lowland areas prone to flooding, such as hardwood swamps and lowland forest. Cypress swamps are a preferred habitat in Tennessee. Adults and metamorphs are usually found in vegetation in the vicinity of breeding sites year-round, though they frequently ascend high into trees during the day. The editors have found both males and females at night in trees above flooded wetlands.

Natural History: Breeding in Tennessee usually coincides with the onset of warm weather (generally above 70°F) and rain, usually in late spring, and continues throughout the summer months. Males begin calling from treetops above breeding sites during the day and move to lower vegetation at night. Females lay about 400–800 eggs in small clusters while perched on vegetation overhanging the water. The eggs hatch within a few days, and the tadpole stage lasts about one month. Sexual maturity is reached in 1–2 years. Metamorphs and adults are primarily arboreal, and forage on arboreal invertebrates. Predators of tadpoles include watersnakes, fish, wading birds, and aquatic insects, while snakes, birds, and small mammals, such as raccoons, probably prey on adults. Their coloration aids in camouflage and likely decreases their risk of predation.

Call: The call of the Bird-Voiced Treefrog, perhaps not surprisingly, resembles that of a bird, although with a distinct whistling character. The advertisement call consists of a series of high-pitched and rapidly repeated *whits* that resembles the call of a Pileated Woodpecker.

Conservation Status: Bird-Voiced Treefrogs, while not listed in Tennessee, are dependant on specific habitats for survival and reproduction. Their preference for flooded areas and hardwood swamps means that they are limited to areas with these features. Preservation of bottomland cypress swamp should benefit this species in Tennessee.

R. Graham Reynolds

Cope's Gray Treefrog adult, Monroe County. (Photo by Matthew L. Niemiller)

Cope's Gray Treefrog

Hyla chrysoscelis

Gray Treefrog

Hyla versicolor

Description: Cope's Gray Treefrogs and Gray Treefrogs are medium-sized, robust treefrogs, with adults measuring 30–52 mm TL. Dorsal coloration is usually a mottled pale gray, dark gray, or even green with patterning that resembles lichen. Coloration varies with activity and ambient temperature. A pale white or green patch extends below the eye to the top of the upper lip. A distinctive yellow or bright orange coloration occurs on the groin and inner thigh region and can be viewed by gently extending a hind leg. Darker bars are often present on the hind limbs. The skin is granular, but not warty, and the toes have large, expanded adhesive discs. There is moderate webbing of the hind feet. Four toes are present on the front feet and five on the hind feet. Juveniles tend to be more

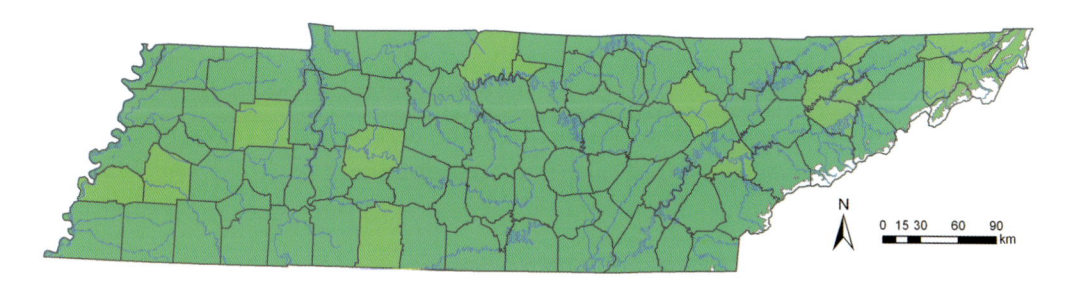

Left: Cope's Gray Treefrog adult, Lake County. (Photo by Matthew L. Niemiller) *Right:* Green and gray color morphs of the Cope's Gray Treefrog, Coffee County. (Photo by Matthew L. Niemiller)

greenish in dorsal coloration but otherwise resemble adults. Males are smaller than females and have a dark throat. Tadpoles measure up to 65 mm TL with lateral eyes and are yellowish brown to gray with a high and mostly translucent tail fin that also tapers to a prominent point. In some populations, the tail fin might contain red to orange pigment punctuated by dark spots or blotches. The venter is cream colored and the intestinal coil is visible. However, coloration and pattern of tadpoles is extremely variable. Younger tadpoles are grayish and tend to lack the brighter pigmentation of older individuals. Froglets are around 20 mm TL at metamorphosis. Cope's Gray Treefrogs and Gray Treefrogs are morphologically identical and can only be distinguished by examining their karyotypes (i.e., chromosome number). Cope's Gray Treefrogs are diploid and have 24 chromosomes, whereas Gray Treefrogs are tetraploid and have 48 chromosomes. Because of this difference in chromosome number, the two species are reproductively isolated. The cells of Cope's Gray Treefrogs are smaller than those of Gray Treefrogs when examined under a microscope. No subspecies are recognized in either species.

Etymology: The specific epithet, *chrysoscelis,* is from the Greek *chryso* "gold" and *kelis* "spot," referring to the color on the inside of the thighs. The specific epithet, *versicolor,* is from the Latin *versi* "variable" and *color* "color," referring to this species' ability to change dorsal coloration depending on temperature, activity, and time of day.

Similar Species: Cope's Gray and Gray Treefrogs are identical morphologically. Both species most closely resemble other hylids, especially the Bird-Voiced Treefrog (*H. avivoca*), which is slightly smaller in body size and has a greenish wash on the inner thighs instead of the orange or yellow wash in Cope's Gray and Gray Treefrogs. However, Cope's Gray Treefrogs are known to hybridize with Bird-Voiced Treefrogs. Juveniles of all three species can be nearly impossible to differentiate between until the groin coloration develops. The tadpoles Cope's Gray and Gray Treefrogs resemble the tadpoles of Green Treefrogs (*H. cinerea*), but Green Treefrog tadpoles typically have a pale yellow stripe on either side of the head that runs from the eye to the nostril.

Distribution: Cope's Gray and Gray Treefrogs are found throughout much of the eastern United States from southern Canada, the

Left: Cope's Gray Treefrog tadpole, St. Martin Parish, Louisiana. (Photo by Brad M. Glorioso) *Right:* Cope's Gray Treefrog eggs, Wilson County. (Photo by Matthew L. Niemiller)

Northeast, and the Great Lakes south to the Gulf Coast. Gray Treefrogs are more northern in their distribution and are found in the northeastern United States west through the Great Lakes region then south into Missouri, Arkansas, eastern Oklahoma, eastern Texas, and western Louisiana. Cope's Gray Treefrogs occur in the majority of forests east of the Great Plains with the exception of the northeastern United States and the southern peninsula of Florida. In Tennessee, Gray Treefrogs have been confirmed from around the Memphis area (Shelby County) in the southwestern part of the state, while Cope's Gray Treefrogs are found statewide.

Habitat: Cope's Gray and Gray Treefrogs are found in a variety of habitats from mountain forests to lowland cypress swamps to urban backyards. They are a frequent sight on the sides of homes and buildings at night near lights, where they wait for insects to land nearby. During the day they climb high into trees and sit motionless relying on their excellent camouflage to avoid predators. During the breeding season, adults frequent trees around breeding sites, such as ponds, woodland pools, roadside ditches, borrow pits, and swamps. During periods of heavy rain, they might be seen by the dozens moving from forest to breeding habitats, and are extremely common on roads during spring rains.

Natural History: Males of both species of Gray Treefrogs begin moving and calling at breeding sites during the first mild rains of the year, typically from March through August. Males call from treetops as they descend toward breeding sites, and then continue to call from vegetation around the site. Females lay up to 2,000 eggs in clusters of 30–40 eggs on the surface of the water, often attaching them to aquatic vegetation. Females appear catholic in their choice of breeding sites, often choosing unsuitable places, such as backyard pools or highly ephemeral puddles. Eggs hatch within five days and tadpoles develop for 1–2 months before metamorphosing. Tadpoles feed on aquatic detritus, whereas adults consume small arboreal invertebrates, especially lepidopteran larvae and beetles. Predators include birds, small mammals, and snakes; and tadpoles are prey for several aquatic invertebrates, including dragonfly nymphs and aquatic beetles, snakes, salamander larvae, and wading birds.

Call: The calls of Gray Treefrogs and Cope's Gray Treefrogs are similar but these species can be distinguished based on their advertisement call, although distinguishing between the two is difficult and might require a tape recorder and a stopwatch. Cope's Gray Treefrog has a loud, quick, musical trill of 30–65 notes per second that resembles the call of a Red-Bellied Woodpecker. Gray Treefrogs produce a slower, less harsh trill at 16–35 notes per second. When both species are calling at the same locality and temperature, the differences between the calls are readily apparent. Trill rates for both species are dependent on ambient temperature. Both species also produce other non-advertisement calls. For instance, males will produce a distinct call that sounds like a hen turkey when approached by a rival male.

Conservation Status: Populations of the Cope's Gray Treefrog are stable and this species appears to do well in urban areas. Little is known, however, about populations of Gray Treefrogs in the state.

R. Graham Reynolds

Green Treefrog adult, Lake County. (Photo by Brad M. Glorioso)

Green Treefrog

Hyla cinerea

Description: Green Treefrogs are one of the most attractive anurans in our state. Adults are large, 32–60 mm TL, and usually bright yellow-green dorsally with a pure cream underside. Dorsal coloration can fade to gray or brighten to neon depending on an individual's health, activity, and temperature. A white or pale yellow lateral stripe is usually present, extending from the upper lip down the sides nearly

Top left: Green Treefrog adult resting on vegetation, Lake County. (Photo by Brad M. Glorioso) *Top right:* Green Treefrog tadpole, Lafayette Parish, Louisiana. (Photo by Brad M. Glorioso) *Bottom right:* Calling Green Treefrog male, Obion County. (Photo by Brad M. Glorioso)

reaching the groin. Occasionally, small yellow or white spots freckle the dorsum. The skin is smooth. The toes are large and have large adhesive pads while the back feet are webbed. Four toes are present on the front feet and five on the hind feet. Males are similar in size to females but can sometimes be recognized by their dark, wrinkled throats where the vocal sacs are folded when not in use. Tadpoles measure up to 45 mm TL and are olive green with lateral eyes. A pale yellow stripe runs from the nostril to the eye. The tail musculature is mottled but lacks any stripes. The tail is long with a tail fin that is high and usually with dark spots or blotches. Sometimes red or orange pigment is present on the tail fin. Froglets are 12–18 mm TL at metamorphosis. No subspecies are recognized.

Etymology: The specific epithet, *cinerea*, is from the Latin *ciner* "ashes" and with the suffix means "ashy colored." This might be in reference to the color of preserved dead specimens of this species, which fade from green to gray postmortem. This is an unfortunate name, as their color in life is so incredibly brilliant.

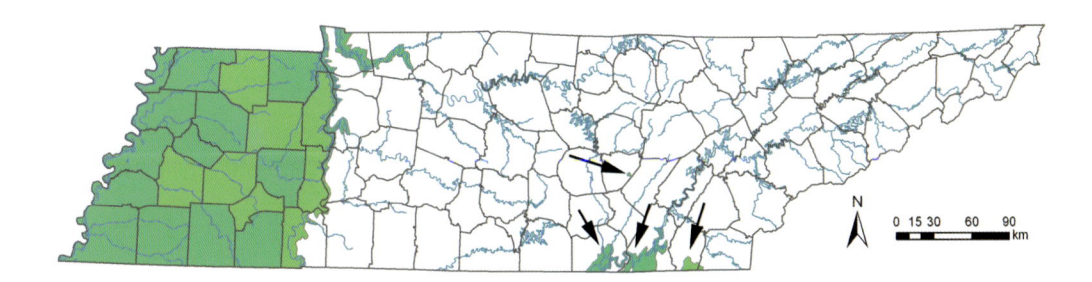

Similar Species: Green Treefrogs are similar in appearance to several other species of hylids, especially the Squirrel Treefrog (*H. squirella*), which might occur in Tennessee (see "Erroneous Species and Species of Possible Occurrence"). Squirrel Treefrogs can be distinguished by their smaller size (< 50 mm TL) and less well-defined lateral stripe. In Tennessee, Green Treefrogs are most frequently confused with Barking Treefrogs (*H. gratiosa*), which can be distinguished by a larger body size (50–70 mm TL), granular skin, wider proportions, and brownish spots. Barking Treefrogs also do not have a prominent, well-defined lateral stripe. Green Treefrogs are known to hybridize with Barking Treefrogs, however. Bird-Voiced Treefrogs (*H. avivoca*) and Gray Treefrogs (*Hyla chrysoscelis/ versicolor*) with a greenish wash on the dorsum can also be mistaken for Green Treefrogs, but the former are rarely predominantly bright green (usually gray with some green patches) and have either an orange or pale green wash on the groin and a pale colored patch under the eye.

Distribution: Green Treefrogs occur throughout much of the southeastern United States from Maryland south into Florida, west to eastern Texas, and north along the Mississippi River Valley into southeastern Missouri, western Tennessee, western Kentucky, and southern Illinois and Indiana. Green Treefrogs are most common west of the north-flowing Tennessee River in Tennessee within the Coastal Plain ecoregions. This species appears to be expanding its range in the state upstream along the Cumberland River as well as along the Tennessee River Valley west of Chattanooga in Hamilton and Marion counties. A single disjunct population occurs in Van Buren County, possibly representing an introduction from the pet trade. Other populations likely will be documented in the future.

Habitat: Green Treefrogs are frequently encountered and are easily found when in breeding aggregations. This species breeds around small ponds, ditches, and swamps and might be found at night when calling from vegetation above their aquatic environments. They are also frequently found in association with human habitations, frequenting the walls of buildings near external lighting and spending the day in irrigated vegetation or even in PVC pipes, gutters, and drains. In more natural environs, individuals can be located diurnally in thick vegetation along the margins of swamps and sloughs. This species is more likely to breed in habitats with fish present than other hylids.

Natural History: Breeding takes place in spring and summer, generally after temperatures rise above 18°C. Males position themselves on vegetation above or near water, establishing small territories but still generally associated with large choruses of other frogs, including conspecifics. Eggs are laid in small clusters in water near mats of vegetation, and clutches vary in size from 275 to 1,200 eggs. Females might produce two or three clutches during a single breeding season. Eggs hatch in 2–3 days and tadpoles metamorphose in 5–10 weeks. Tadpoles feed on detritus and other vegetation typically in shallow areas near the edges of their aquatic habitats. Tadpoles are particularly susceptible to aquatic insect predators, as well as turtles and fish, and hence have higher survival rates in smaller bodies of water with fewer predators. Adult Green Treefrogs consume a wide variety of small invertebrates, and will actively orient toward a prey item when movement is detected. Predators include aquatic and semi-aquatic snakes, wading birds, and large spiders.

Call: The advertisement call of the male Green Treefrog is very distinctive and quite loud. It consists of a very nasal, almost ducklike *honk, quonk,* or *quannk,* almost always heard in a chorus of several to hundreds of individuals. Calling typically reaches its peak shortly after sunset and gradually tapers throughout the night.

Conservation Status: The Green Treefrog is abundant where it occurs in the state and appears to be expanding its range in the state.

R. Graham Reynolds

Barking Treefrog adult, Coffee County. (Photo by Matthew L. Niemiller)

Barking Treefrog

Hyla gratiosa

Description: The Barking Treefrog is the largest native species of hylid in the United States, with adults measuring 50–70 mm TL. Adults are highly variable in color, ranging from pale green to brown. Typically, the dorsum is a bright, deep green with scattered dark brown or black spots and small flecks of gold or yellow. A pale yellow or white line runs from the upper lip toward the hip on each side of the body. The line is either incomplete or broken before reaching the hip. The inside of the hind legs, throat, and belly are usually a deep yellow color. Individual coloration can vary throughout the day in association with changes in light and temperature. Furthermore, the spotting pattern can fade or sharpen. Four

Left: Barking Treefrog adult, Coffee County. (Photo by Matthew L. Niemiller) *Right:* Barking Treefrog adult, Carroll County. (Photo by Brian T. Miller)

toes are present on the front feet and five toes on the hind feet. The tip of each toe is expanded into an adhesive disc that facilitates climbing in vegetation. The back is covered with a series of scattered small warts or bumps, which gives the body a granular appearance and texture. During the breeding season, the enlarged vocal sacs that extend from the angle of the mouth to halfway to the groin distinguish males from females. When not enlarged, the throat of males is typically dark, at least during the breeding season. Tadpoles grow up to 70 mm TL with round to oval bodies and lateral eyes. Ground color is olive to olive brown on the dorsum, while the venter has a yellowish wash. The tail fin is translucent, high, and extends almost even with the eyes on the dorsum. Smaller tadpoles often have four dark stripes on the dorsum, while larger individuals typically have a darker smudge on the anterior aspect of the dorsal tail fin. A dark saddle spot is present about midway down the dorsal tail musculature. Froglets are 14–20 mm TL just after metamorphosis. No subspecies are recognized.

Etymology: The specific epithet, *gratiosa*, is Latin for "favored" or "pleasurable," perhaps referring to the handsome coloration or interesting call of this species.

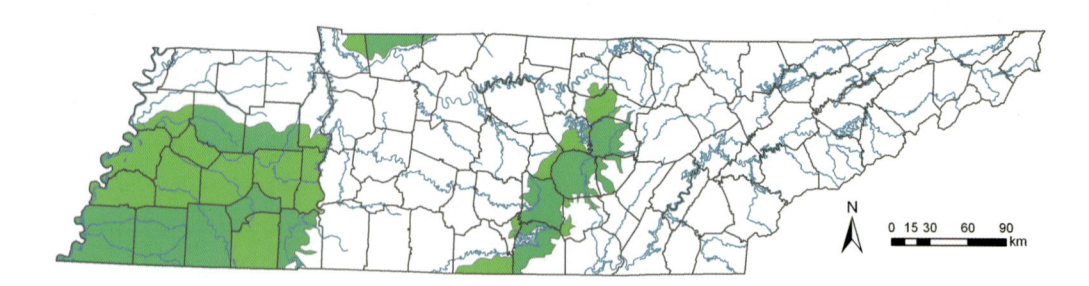

Similar Species: Barking Treefrogs are most similar in appearance to Green Treefrogs (*H. cinerea*). The spotting pattern of the back and the stripe on the sides can be used to distinguish between these species. The lateral stripe in Green Treefrogs runs interrupted from the upper jaw to the hip, whereas this stripe is interrupted or breaks down to a series of spots before reaching the hip in Barking Treefrogs. Furthermore, Green Treefrogs are more slender than and lack both the dark dorsal spots and granular skin found in Barking Treefrogs. Tadpoles can be extremely difficult to distinguish from other hylids; however, Barking Treefrog tadpoles reach a larger size than other hylids and the dorsal tail fin inserts more toward to the head than other species of treefrogs.

Distribution: Barking Treefrogs are distributed throughout much of the southeastern United States from the Coastal Plain of North Carolina south to south-central Florida, west to eastern Louisiana, and north into Tennessee and Kentucky. This species is found throughout much of the western third of Tennessee in the Coastal Plain ecoregions. However, smaller pockets of populations are located in the Western Pennyroyal Karst of north-central Tennessee and Eastern Highland Rim in the central part of the state.

Habitat: In Tennessee, adult Barking Treefrogs are inhabitants of forests in the vicinity of breeding wetlands. Outside of the breeding season, they are arboreal—living in trees and shrubs. During dry weather, Barking Treefrogs will burrow into the soil, particularly in association with tree roots and clusters of vegetation where they presumably are seeking moisture. During the breeding season, adults cluster around the breeding localities, such as ephemeral wetlands, floodplain wetlands, borrow pits, and roadside ditches. These water bodies are typically fish-free and generally have an open canopy allowing penetration of sunlight.

Natural History: Breeding activity generally coincides with heavy rains in late spring or summer. Males advertise their presence to females with a distinct series of barklike calls from the tops of trees as they approach the breeding site. Males also vocalize while floating on the surface of the pond. Females enter the breeding site after males and eventually amplexus ensues. Females typically breed only once per year, but males will breed with several females during a season. Fertilization is external, and females typically deposit about 2,000 eggs, but nearly 3,000 eggs have been reported in some clutches. The eggs hatch in about two days, and the tadpole stage lasts 6–10 weeks. Juveniles and adults are carnivorous and eat a variety of invertebrates. More is known about their diet when they are in vicinity of the breeding pond than outside of the breeding season when they are arboreal. Predators of larvae include dragonfly nymphs and ambystomatid salamanders, whereas adults are consumed by aquatic (watersnakes and cottonmouths) and semi-aquatic (ribbon and gartersnakes) snakes and likely other terrestrial vertebrates.

Call: The male advertisement call is a hollow, abbreviated *donk* note that is given every 1 to 2 seconds, used to attract females to a breeding pond. This call sounds much like a barking dog. Males also call from trees, sometimes called a rain call, which very much resembles the distant barking of a dog, though with a distinct nasal character.

Conservation Status: Barking Treefrogs are locally abundant in Tennessee, but their distribution and population trends are poorly understood. Consequently, this species is listed as "Deemed in Need of Management" and state listed as "Vulnerable." Furthermore, because of the association with forests and permanent ponds, any activities that reduce these habitats could jeopardize local populations.

Brian T. Miller

Mountain Chorus Frog adult, Franklin County. (Photo by Matthew L. Niemiller)

Mountain Chorus Frog

Pseudacris brachyphona

Description: The Mountain Chorus Frog is a small hylid frog (adults measuring 24–38 mm TL) with granular skin and small but evident expanded toe pads. Ground color is greenish-brown, tan, or gray but is quite variable. Typically, adults have two dark brown stripes that curve inward toward the midline to form two reverse parentheses. However, these stripes can be broken, absent, or form an "X." A dark brown triangle also is usually present between the eyes. A dark stripe runs from the snout through the eye and terminates just past the tympanum forming a masklike appearance. The upper lip is much paler in color. The venter is white with a few dark flecks and is paler in color in males. Yellow pigment is present on the hidden, inner surfaces of the thighs. Four toes are present on

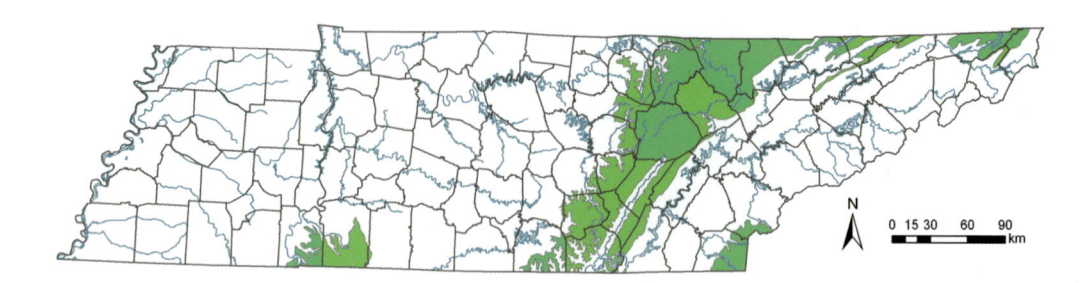

Left: Mountain Chorus Frog adult, Campbell County. (Photo by Matthew L. Niemiller) *Right:* Mountain Chorus Frog tadpole, Franklin County. (Photo by Nathan Haislip)

the fore feet and five are on the hind feet. Females typically are larger than males. Tadpoles grow up to 35 mm TL with round to oval bodies and lateral eyes. Ground color is pale brown to brassy on the dorsum that is often mottled with paler flecks or dots. The venter is considerably paler with darker pigment lacking on the throat. The tail fin is clear while the tail musculature is darkly mottled. Froglets are 8–10 mm TL just after metamorphosis. No subspecies are recognized.

Etymology: The specific epithet, *brachyphona,* from the Greek *brachys* "short" and *phone* "sound," refers to the short call of this species.

Similar Species: The Mountain Chorus Frog is easily confused with the three other *Pseudacris* species that occur in Tennessee, the Upland Chorus Frog (*P. feriarum*), Western Chorus Frog (*P. triseriata*), and Spring Peeper (*P. crucifer*). Upland Chorus and Western Chorus Frogs typically have three longitudinal stripes or rows of elongated spots running the length of the dorsum. Spring Peepers usually have a distinct "X" on the dorsum, lack paler pigmentation on the upper lip, and have more extensive webbing of the hind feet. The tadpoles of these four species can be very difficult to differentiate. Refer to the other *Pseudacris* species accounts for characters to distinguish between these species. Mountain Chorus Frogs also can be confused with Wood Frogs (*Lithobates sylvaticus*) because both share a masklike appearance. However, Wood Frogs grow much larger and have distinct dorsolateral folds running down the dorsum.

Distribution: Mountain Chorus Frogs are found in the Appalachians and associated uplands from southwest Pennsylvania southeast into Tennessee, Alabama, and Georgia. In Tennessee, Mountain Chorus Frogs are found throughout the Cumberland Plateau and Cumberland Mountains. Additional populations also are known from the southern Blue Ridge Mountains in Monroe and Polk counties in southeast Tennessee as well as Hardin County near the Mississippi-Tennessee state line in West Tennessee.

Habitat: Mountain Chorus Frogs are associated with forested uplands up to 1,100 m in elevation. Adults breed in small, shallow bodies of water, including roadside ditches, ephemeral pools, bogs, and ruts in dirt roads. Mountain Chorus Frogs are seldom seen outside the breeding season.

Natural History: Breeding occurs from early February through May when temperatures are above 4.5°C. Adults migrate from upland habitats to breeding sites. Females lay 300–1,500 eggs in small masses, each containing 10–50 eggs attached to aquatic vegetation. Eggs hatch in 7–14 days and the larval period lasts 4–8 weeks. Tadpoles feed on detritus. Sexual maturity usually is reached the following year. Little is known about the ecology of Mountain Chorus Frogs outside the breeding season. Adults feed on a variety of small insects and other invertebrates. Birds, snakes, mammals, and ranid frogs are all likely predators of adult Mountain Chorus Frogs. Aquatic invertebrates, such as dragonfly nymphs and beetles, eat tadpoles, as do salamander larvae.

Call: The call of the Mountain Chorus Frog is a short, raspy trill that trends upward in pitch. Some have described this call as a squeaky wagon wheel. It is short in duration (0.25 sec) but is repeated rapidly, up to 50–70 calls per minute. The call of the Mountain Chorus Frog is similar to that of the Upland Chorus Frog but is faster, more raspy, and repeated at a much faster rate.

Conservation Status: The status and overall distribution of the Mountain Chorus Frog is not well established in Tennessee, although it appears that most populations are fairly secure. However, deforestation and loss of wetlands associated with urbanization, logging, and mining operations are detrimental to this species.

Matthew L. Niemiller

Spring Peeper adult, Monroe County. (Photo by Matthew L. Niemiller)

Spring Peeper

Pseudacris crucifer

Description: The Spring Peeper is a small, slender hylid frog, adults measuring 18–35 mm TL (maximum 37 mm TL), with granular skin and small but evident expanded toe pads. Ground color is olive brown, tan, or gray and is quite variable. Typically, adults have two narrow dark stripes that form a characteristic "X" on the dorsum. However, in some individuals the left and right halves of the "X" do not actually touch. A dark stripe runs from the snout through the eye and down each side. The venter is white, cream, or yellow in color with occasional darker flecks of brown. Males have a black vocal sac. Four toes are present on the fore feet and five are on the hind feet. Tadpoles are small reaching up to 35 mm TL with round to oval bodies and lateral eyes. Ground color is dark brown, which can be mottled with brassy to gold flecks or dots in older tadpoles. The

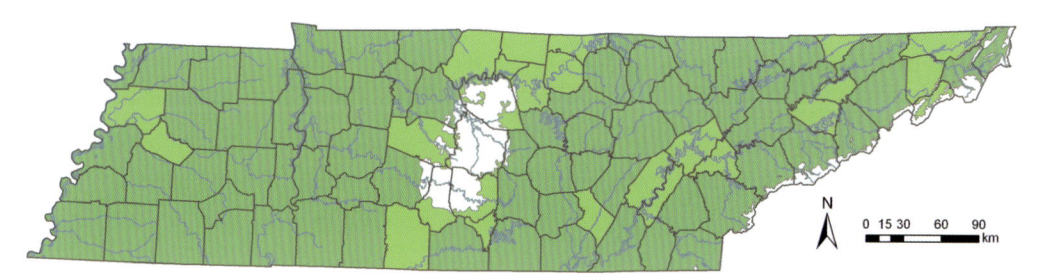

Top left: Calling Spring Peeper male, Coffee County. (Photo by Matthew L. Niemiller) *Top right:* Spring Peeper tadpole, Blount County. (Photo by Matthew L. Niemiller) *Bottom right:* Spring Peeper froglet, Blount County. (Photo by Matthew L. Niemiller)

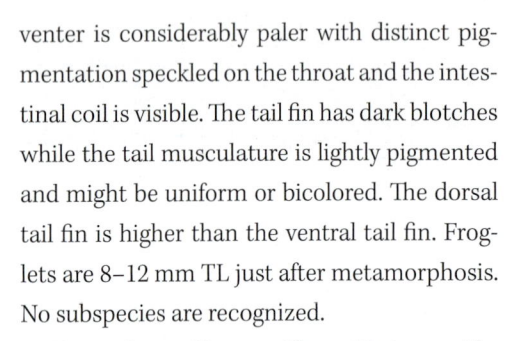

venter is considerably paler with distinct pigmentation speckled on the throat and the intestinal coil is visible. The tail fin has dark blotches while the tail musculature is lightly pigmented and might be uniform or bicolored. The dorsal tail fin is higher than the ventral tail fin. Froglets are 8–12 mm TL just after metamorphosis. No subspecies are recognized.

Etymology: The specific epithet, *crucifer,* from the Latin *crucis* "cross" and *-ifer* "bearer," refers to the X-shaped markings on the dorsum.

Similar Species: Spring Peepers can be confused with the other three *Pseudacris* species that occur in Tennessee, the Mountain Chorus Frog (*P. brachyphona*), Upland Chorus Frog (*P. feriarum*), and Western Chorus Frog (*P. triseriata*). Mountain Chorus Frogs have the two dark dorsal stripes that often curve inward forming a reverse-parentheses pattern rather than an X-shaped mark, and there usually is a prominent dark triangle between the eyes. Both Upland Chorus Frogs and Western Chorus Frogs have three stripes on the dorsum and a prominent pale upper lip. Spring Peeper tadpoles are very similar in appearance to other *Pseudacris* but have distinct pigmentation on the throat and blotching in the tail fin.

Distribution: Spring Peepers range throughout most of the eastern United States east of the Great Plains. In Tennessee, Northern Spring Peepers occur statewide up to 1,220 m in elevation but are notably absent from the Inner Nashville Basin in Middle Tennessee.

Habitat: Spring Peepers are associated with forested habitats in the vicinity of breeding locations. Adults breed in small, temporary, and shallow bodies of water with abundant vegetation, including marshes, swamps, bogs, flooded fields, roadside ditches, ephemeral pools, and ruts in dirt roads. However, this species is known to breed in more permanent bodies of water, including beaver and farm ponds. Spring Peepers are seldom observed outside the breeding season.

Natural History: Spring Peepers are one of the first frog species to breed in Tennessee as breeding occurs as early as mid-January into April, when temperatures climb above 2°C. During the peak of the breeding season, males will even call during the day. Adults migrate to breeding sites during rainy nights with males arriving before females. It is during this time period that adults are most frequently encountered. Throughout the rest of the year, adults are rarely found. Males typically call up to 2 m above the water surface. Females lay 500–1,000 eggs during a single breeding season, either singly or in small clusters attached to submerged vegetation. Eggs hatch in 5–10 days and the larval period lasts about 8–10 weeks. Tadpoles feed on detritus. Adults feed on a variety of small insects and other invertebrates. Birds, snakes, mammals, and ranid frogs are all likely predators of adult Spring Peepers. Aquatic invertebrates, such as dragonfly nymphs and beetles, eat tadpoles of this species, as do as salamander larvae.

Call: Spring Peepers get their common name from the sound of their advertisement call, a repeated high-pitched *peep* that lacks pulses or trills. However, males produce a rapid series of raspy trills similar to that of the other chorus frog species when other males invade their territories.

Conservation Status: Spring Peepers are extremely abundant and populations are stable in Tennessee.

Matthew L. Niemiller and
R. Graham Reynolds

Upland Chorus Frog adult, Coffee County. (Photo by Matthew L. Niemiller)

Upland Chorus Frog

Pseudacris feriarum

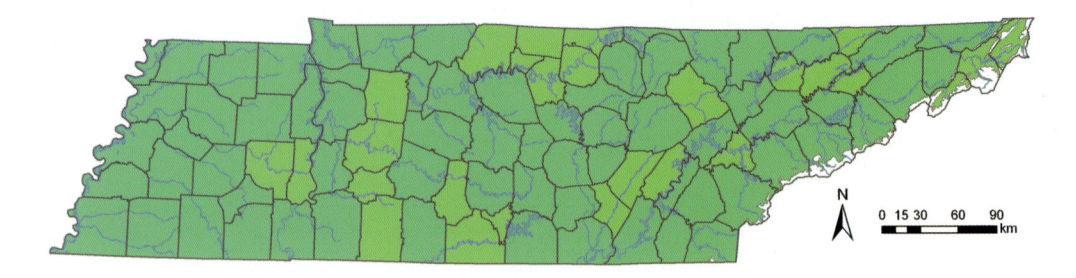

Description: The Upland Chorus Frog is a small, slender hylid frog, adults measuring 20–35 mm TL (maximum 38 mm TL), with granular skin and small but evident expanded toe pads. Ground color is greenish brown, tan, or gray but is quite variable. Typically, adults have three slender, dark brown parallel stripes running down the dorsum. However, these stripes are often broken into long spots or are completely absent. A dark stripe runs from the snout through the eye and down each side. A prominent pale stripe occurs on the upper lip below the dark stripe that runs through the eye. A triangular spot is often present between the eyes. The venter is white to cream in color with occasional darker markings on the chest and is paler in color in males. The length of the tibia is about half the total length. Four toes are present on the front feet and five toes on the hind feet. Females typically are larger than males. Tadpoles are small, reaching up to 35 mm TL, with round to oval bodies and lateral eyes. Ground color is dark brown that can be mottled with bronze to brassy flecks or dots in older tadpoles. The venter is considerably paler without darker pigment on the throat and the intestinal coil is visible. The tail fin is generally clear with some dark flecks while the tail musculature has a distinct darker stripe running its length. The dorsal tail fin is higher than the ventral tail fin. Froglets are 8–10 mm TL just after metamorphosis. No subspecies are currently recognized.

Upland Chorus Frog adult, Blount County. (Photo by Matthew L. Niemiller)

Etymology: The specific epithet, *feriarum*, is Latin for "holidays" or "leisure."

Similar Species: The Upland Chorus Frog is easily confused with the other three *Pseudacris* species that occur in Tennessee, the Mountain Chorus Frog (*P. brachyphona*), Spring Peeper (*P. crucifer*), and Western Chorus Frog (*P. triseriata*). Spring Peepers usually have a distinct "X" on the dorsum, lack paler pigmentation on the upper lip, and have more extensive webbing of the hind feet. Mountain Chorus Frogs have only two dark dorsal stripes that often curve inward forming a reverse-parentheses pattern. Western Chorus Frogs can be considerably difficult to distinguish from Upland Chorus Frogs because the two species are known to hybridize. Generally, however, the three dark dorsal stripes are unbroken in Western Chorus Frogs, whereas those in Upland Chorus Frogs are more slender and often broken. Likewise, the length of tibia is less than half the total length in Western Chorus Frogs. Upland Chorus Frogs also can be confused with Wood Frogs (*Lithobates sylvaticus*) because both share a masklike appearance. However, Wood Frogs grow much larger and have distinct dorsolateral folds running down the dorsum.

Distribution: Upland Chorus Frogs range from Pennsylvania east of the Appalachians south into Georgia, west to Alabama and east Mississippi, and north into Tennessee and Kentucky. In Tennessee, Upland Chorus Frogs occur throughout the state, except at the higher elevations of the Cumberland Plateau, where it is replaced by the Mountain Chorus Frog, and around the Clarksville area in Montgomery County, where the Western Chorus Frog presumably replaces it. Upland Chorus Frogs are generally absent above 760 m in the Blue Ridge Mountains.

Habitat: Upland Chorus Frogs are associated with forested areas in the vicinity of breeding locations. Adults breed in small, shallow bodies of water with abundant vegetation including marshes, swamps, bogs, flooded fields, roadside ditches, ephemeral pools, and ruts in dirt roads. Upland Chorus Frogs are seldom observed outside the breeding season.

Natural History: Upland Chorus Frogs are one of the first frog species to breed in Tennessee, as breeding occurs as early as the beginning of January into April, when temperatures get above 2°C. During the peak of the breeding season, males will even call during the day. Adults migrate to breeding sites during rainy nights with males arriving before females. It is during this time period that adults are most frequently encountered. Throughout the rest of the year, adults are rarely found. Females lay 500–1,500 eggs during a single breeding season in small, loose, and irregular clusters, each containing 40–100 eggs attached to aquatic vegetation. Eggs hatch in 5–10 days and the larval period lasts 8–12 weeks. Tadpoles feed on detritus. Adults feed on a variety of small insects and other invertebrates. Birds, snakes, mammals, and ranid frogs are all likely predators of adult Upland Chorus Frogs. Aquatic invertebrates, such as dragonfly nymphs and beetles, as well as salamander larvae, eat tadpoles.

Call: The call of the Upland Chorus Frog is a short trill, very similar to that of the Western Chorus Frog that trends upward in pitch lasting 0.5 to 1.25 sec in duration and containing 15–25 pulses. It is best described as the sound of running your thumbnail across the teeth of a comb, a regularly repeated *crreeekk* or ***prreeepp***. The duration of the call is dependent on temperature, as longer calls are produced at colder temperatures. The call of the Upland Chorus Frog is similar to that of the Mountain Chorus Frog but is slower, less raspy, and repeated at a much slower rate.

Conservation Status: Upland Chorus Frogs are abundant and populations are stable in Tennessee.

Matthew L. Niemiller and
R. Graham Reynolds

Western Chorus Frog adult, Jennings County, Indiana. (Photo by Todd Pierson)

Western Chorus Frog

Pseudacris triseriata

Description: The Western Chorus Frog is a small, slender hylid frog, adults measuring 20–35 mm TL (maximum 39 mm TL), with granular skin and small but evident expanded toe pads. Ground color is greenish brown, tan, or gray but is quite variable. Typically, adults have three prominent, dark brown parallel stripes running down the dorsum. However, these stripes can be broken into long spots or absent. A dark stripe runs from the snout through the eye and down each side. A prominent pale stripe occurs on the upper lip below the dark stripe that runs through the eye. A triangular spot is often present between the eyes. The venter is white to cream in color with occasional darker markings on the chest and is paler in color in males. The length of the tibia is less than half the total length. Four toes are present on the fore feet and five are on the hind

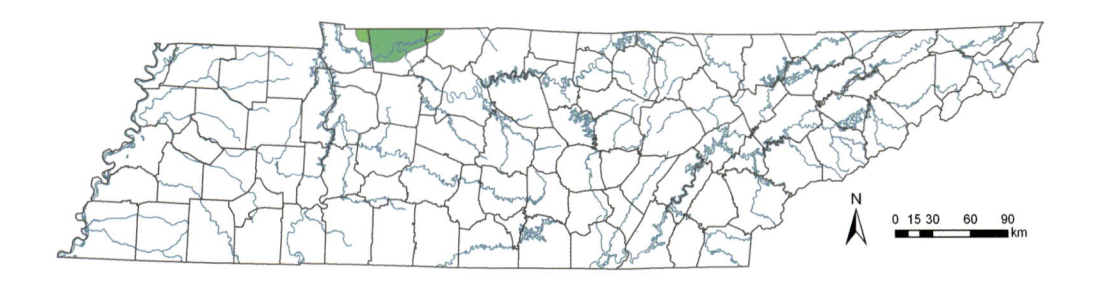

Western Chorus Frog tadpole, Michigan. (Photo by Nathan Haislip)

feet. Females typically are larger than males. Tadpoles are small reaching 30–35 mm TL with round to oval bodies and lateral eyes. Ground color is dark brown that can be mottled with bronze to brassy flecks or dots in older tadpoles. The venter is considerably paler without darker pigment on the throat and the intestinal coil is visible. The tail fin is generally clear with some dark flecks while the tail musculature has a distinct darker stripe running its length. The dorsal tail fin is higher than the ventral tail fin. Froglets are 8–10 mm TL just after metamorphosis. No subspecies are recognized.

Etymology: The specific epithet, *triseriata*, is from the Latin *tri* "three" and *seriata* "lines" or "serrations," referring to the three dark stripes present on the dorsum of this species.

Similar Species: The Western Chorus Frog is easily confused with the other three *Pseudacris* species that occur in Tennessee, the Mountain Chorus Frog (*P. brachyphona*), Spring Peeper (*P. crucifer*), and Upland Chorus Frog (*P. feriarum*). Spring Peepers usually have a distinct "X" on the dorsum, lack paler pigmentation on the upper lip, and have more extensive webbing of the hind feet. Mountain Chorus Frogs have only two dark dorsal stripes that often curve inward forming a reverse-parentheses pattern. Upland Chorus Frogs can be considerably difficult to distinguish from Western Chorus Frogs because the two species are known to hybridize. Generally, however, the three dark dorsal stripes are unbroken in Western Chorus Frogs, whereas those in Upland Chorus Frogs are more slender and often broken. Likewise, the length of tibia is less than half the total length in Western Chorus Frogs.

Distribution: Western Chorus Frogs range from the Lower Peninsula of Michigan and southwest New York south into Indiana, Ohio, southern Illinois, west-central Kentucky, and just into north-central Tennessee. In Tennessee, Western Chorus Frogs are currently known from a single population north of the Cumberland River near Clarksville in Montgomery County. However, other populations likely exist around this area.

Habitat: Western Chorus Frogs are associated with a variety of terrestrial habitats, including forests, prairies, and agricultural areas. Adults breed in small, shallow bodies of water with abundant vegetation including marshes, swamps, flooded fields, roadside ditches, and ephemeral pools. Western Chorus Frogs are seldom observed outside the breeding season.

Natural History: The life history and ecology of Tennessee populations of the Western Chorus Frog are unknown, as this species was just recently found in the state; however, the biology of this species likely is similar to that of the Upland Chorus Frog. Refer to the Upland Chorus Frog account for information on natural history.

Call: The call of the Western Chorus Frog is a short trill, very similar to that of the Upland Chorus Frog that trends upward in pitch lasting 0.5 to 1.0 sec in duration and containing 15–25 pulses. It is best described as the sound of running your thumbnail across the teeth of a comb, a regularly repeated *crreeekk* or ***prreeepp***. The duration of the call is dependent on temperature, as longer calls are produced at colder temperatures. Males call 20–45 times per minute.

Conservation Status: The status of the Western Chorus Frog in Tennessee is unknown since it was only discovered in the state in 2007. Studies are needed to determine the distribution of this species in the state and to investigate potential hybridization with the Upland Chorus Frog.

Matthew L. Niemiller

20
Family Microhylidae (Narrow-Mouthed Toads)

Microhylids are very small anurans, 10–80 mm TL. The family name is from the Greek *mikros* "small" and *Hylas*, a mythological companion of Heracles who disappeared into a spring and whose name Heracles called repeatedly as he searched for the missing Argonaut. This is referencing the aquatic affinities of hylids and the prominent repeated calls in these frogs. Narrow-Mouthed Toads are plump, with distinctly small heads, reduced toe webbing, and short limbs. They frequently spend much of their time underground or under cover, emerging during periods of heavy rain to breed, when they are most easily found. Fossil microhylids are known from the Miocene of Florida. Microhylidae is one of the largest anuran families, composed of many dozens of genera and more than 300 species, though we have but a sole representative in Tennessee. Most the diversity in this family occurs in tropical regions of North America, South America, Africa, Asia, and Australia. Our only genus, *Gastrophryne,* is from the Greek *gaster* "stomach" and *phrynos* "toad," referring to the bulging midsection relative to the small head in this genus.

Eastern Narrow-Mouthed Toad

Gastrophryne carolinensis

Description: The Eastern Narrow-Mouthed Toad is a small but plump frog with short limbs, a tiny head, and a pointed snout. Adults measure 20–38 mm TL, with females attaining slightly larger sizes than males. A distinctive transverse fold of skin occurs on the head just posterior to the eyes. The skin is generally smooth. The ground coloration is highly variable within populations but is usually a shade of gray, brown, or red. In many individuals, the center color of the dorsum, which tapers toward the head, is darker than the bordering dorsolateral stripes. The venter is grayish and lightly mottled. Males can be discerned from females during the breeding season by the presence of a deeply pigmented vocal sac on the throat. The Eastern Narrow-Mouthed Toad lacks a visible tympanum and is devoid of webbing between the toes of all limbs. Four toes are present on the front feet and five toes on the hind feet. A single tubercle is present on the heel of each hind limb, which assists in burrowing. Tadpoles have a pointed head, lateral eyes, and are dorsolaterally flattened, giving them a squarish appearance when viewed from above. The dorsal coloration is usually dark but paler in color than the venter. Whitish blotches are usually present on the lateral sides of the stomach region. A lateral white stripe bordered by black extends partway down the tail musculature. Unlike the tadpoles of other Tennessee frogs and toads, the Eastern Narrow-Mouthed Toad tadpole lacks keratinized mouthparts. Tadpoles typically are 15–30 mm TL but can reach 48 mm, with newly metamorphosed individuals 7–13 mm TL. No subspecies are recognized.

Eastern Narrow-Mouthed Toad adult, Cocke County. (Photo by Matthew L. Niemiller)

Etymology: The specific epithet, *carolinensis,* means "belonging to Carolina" and refers to the description of this species from Charleston, South Carolina.

Similar Species: The Eastern Narrow-Mouthed Toad is easily distinguished from all other frogs native to Tennessee by a combination of their small size, pointed snout, overall body shape, and lack of toe webbing.

Distribution: The native range of the Eastern Narrow-Mouthed Toad extends from southern Maryland to the Florida Keys, and west to southern Missouri, extreme southeastern Kansas, eastern Oklahoma and eastern Texas. It also has been introduced on Grand Bahama and New Providence Islands in the Bahamas, as well as Grand Cayman in the Cayman Islands. In Tennessee, the Eastern Narrow-Mouthed Toad can be found nearly statewide but is absent at high elevations of the Blue Ridge Mountains.

Habitat: The Eastern Narrow-Mouthed Toad is known to inhabit a wide variety of habitats from pine and hardwood forests to meadows and urbanized areas and even brackish

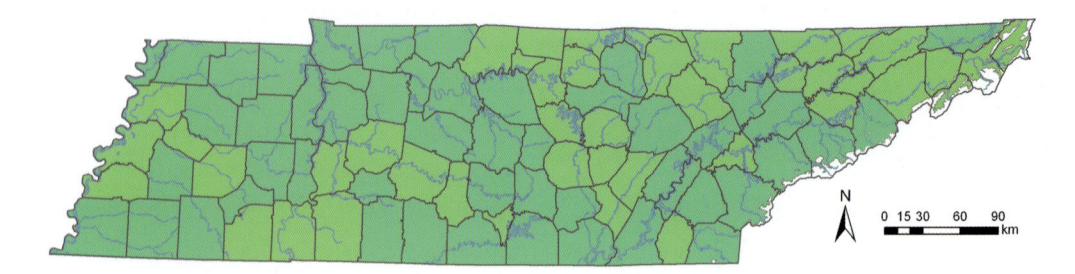

Top left: Eastern Narrow-Mouthed Toad adults, Grundy County. (Photo by Matthew L. Niemiller) *Top right:* Eastern Narrow-Mouthed Toad adult, Cannon County. (Photo by Brian T. Miller) *Bottom right:* Eastern Narrow-Mouthed Toad tadpole, St. Martin Parish. (Photo by Brad M. Glorioso)

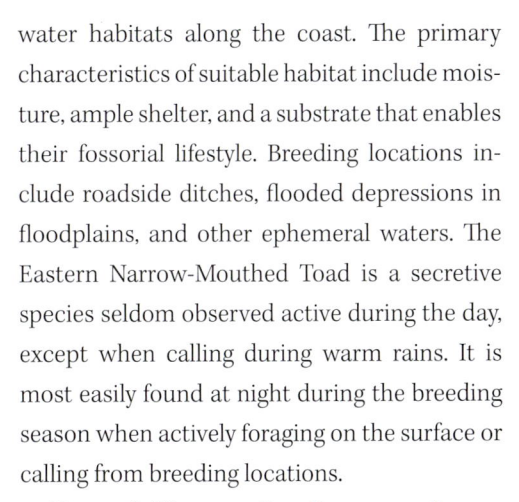

water habitats along the coast. The primary characteristics of suitable habitat include moisture, ample shelter, and a substrate that enables their fossorial lifestyle. Breeding locations include roadside ditches, flooded depressions in floodplains, and other ephemeral waters. The Eastern Narrow-Mouthed Toad is a secretive species seldom observed active during the day, except when calling during warm rains. It is most easily found at night during the breeding season when actively foraging on the surface or calling from breeding locations.

Natural History: Breeding generally occurs in explosive bursts associated with warm rains from late spring through early fall in shallow ephemeral waters amid vegetation. In Tennessee, the peak of breeding activity occurs in midsummer. Females are known to lay as many as 1,600 eggs in total, but usually less, and distribute them over several locations in batches of 10–150 eggs. The eggs are laid in a thin film on the water's surface as the male fertilizes them. Due to their overall body shape, males are unable to firmly clasp onto females like other frog species. Males overcome this obstacle by secreting a substance from special glands on their abdomen, which enables them to adhere to females during amplexus. Eggs hatch in 1–3 days and the larval period lasts 20–70 days across their range. In Tennessee, the larval period probably lies in the higher range, given the cooler water temperatures relative to more southern populations. After metamorphosis, males typically attain sexual maturity in 1 year, while females might take 1–2 years. Eastern Narrow-Mouthed Toads have been documented to live almost 7 years in captivity, but certainly the average lifespan in the wild is much shorter, though unknown. The Eastern Narrow-Mouthed Toad is a well-documented predator of ants and termites but also consumes small beetles and other small arthropods. The transverse skin fold is thought to aid in feeding on ants by moving forward, wiping away ants that might be attacking the eyes. The tadpoles, lacking keratinized mouthparts, typical of other tadpoles, are suspension feeders, eating plankton and other organic matter from the water column. The Eastern Narrow-Mouthed Toad affords itself some protection from predators by inhabiting subterranean haunts as well as by being primarily active only at night. Also, adults and later stage tadpoles deter many predators with a toxic skin secretion. Still, some birds and snakes are known predators of adults, while carnivorous aquatic insects, fish, and snakes presumably eat tadpoles.

Call: The advertisement call of the male Eastern Narrow-Mouthed Toad, usually given from well-concealed locations amid vegetation near or in the breeding pools, is a high-pitched, nasal blast lasting 0.5–4 seconds in length. This primary call is often preceded by a quick peep or whistle, audible only in close proximity. The primary call has been frequently described as sounding like the bleating of a lamb or an electric buzzer.

Conservation Status: The Eastern Narrow-Mouthed Toad appears stable throughout Tennessee.

Brad M. Glorioso

21
Family Ranidae (True Frogs)

True frogs are widespread, occurring on every continent but Antarctica. Over 600 species have been described, and seven species occur statewide in Tennessee. All ranid frogs in Tennessee belong to the genus *Lithobates,* which is from the Greek *litho* "stone" and *bates* "one who walks or haunts." Fossil ranids are known from the Tertiary and Quaternary of Europe and North America. These are the largest frogs in the state, with some species reaching sizes of 110–200 mm total length. The family name derives from the Latin *rana* "frog." These are long-legged, jumping frogs that are commonly found near aquatic habitats. They have smooth skin and their tadpoles have eyes positioned close to the top of their heads. Some species are utilized for food, especially the American Bullfrog, whose legs continue to grace many a table in Tennessee and around the world. As a culinary delicacy, American Bullfrogs have since been introduced well beyond their range and pose a threat to native wildlife due to their voracious appetites and possibly due to disease transmission.

Crawfish Frog

Lithobates areolatus

Description: The Crawfish Frog is a medium-sized ranid frog with relatively short but stout limbs, a robust build, and limited webbing of the hind feet. Adults measure 55–75 mm TL (maximum 92 mm TL) and have mostly smooth, moist skin. Ground color is variable but generally is a pale gray to tan with several dark spots on the dorsum and upper surfaces of the legs, each encircled by a pale border. These spots sometimes fuse to form elongate blotches. Two distinct dorsolateral folds run from behind the eyes to the groin. The venter usually is white without any dark markings on the throat and chin. A yellowish wash is present throughout the groin and undersurfaces of the thighs. Four toes are present on the fore feet and five are on the hind feet. Adult males generally are smaller than females. Tadpoles grow up to 64 mm TL with round to oval bodies. Ground color is greenish to brownish on the dorsum with scatter black flecks or dots. The venter is cream in color with the viscera visible. The tail fin is pale in color. Scattered dark flecks or dots are present on the tail. Metamorphs are just over 25 mm TL. Two subspecies are recognized, and only the Northern Crawfish Frog (*L. areolatus circulosus*) occurs in Tennessee.

Etymology: The specific epithet, *areolatus,* is Latin for "marked with small spaces," referring to the spots on the dorsum. The subspecific epithet, *circulosus,* from the Latin *circuli* "circles" or "rings" and *-osus* "full of," refers to the pale spots on the dorsum.

Similar Species: In Tennessee, Crawfish Frogs most closely resemble the Gopher Frog (*L. capito*), but Gopher Frogs have an often heavily

Northern Crawfish Frog adult male, Henry County. (Photo by Robert English, LEAPS)

pigmented venter and lack pale-bordered dark spotting on the dorsum. Crawfish Frogs also can be confused with Southern Leopard Frogs (*L. sphenocephalus*) and Pickerel Frogs (*L. palustris*). However, both of these species are slender with proportionally longer bodies and legs. Also, Pickerel Frogs can easily be distinguished by the yellowish to orangish wash on the undersurfaces of the thighs and groin and the squarish dark spots on the dorsum rather than the rounded spots found in Southern Leopard Frogs and Northern Crawfish Frogs. Tadpoles of Crawfish Frogs are difficult to distinguish from those of other ranids, including American Bullfrogs (*L. catesbeianus*), Green Frogs (*L. clamitans melanotus*), and Southern Leopard Frogs. However, the inner row of teeth on the upper jaw is bisected by a gap forming two distinct halves in Crawfish Frogs.

Distribution: The Northern Crawfish Frog has a sporadic distribution from western Indiana west to eastern Kansas and southeast into

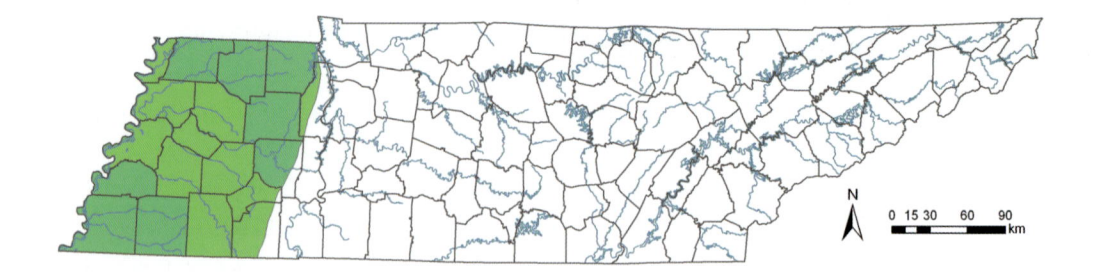

Left: Northern Crawfish Frog metamorph, Jefferson County, Indiana. (Photo by Todd Pierson) *Right:* Northern Crawfish Frog adult male, Henry County. (Photo by Robert English, LEAPS)

Mississippi. In Tennessee, Northern Crawfish Frogs are found exclusively in the Coastal Plain west of the Tennessee River.

Habitat: Crawfish Frogs spend the majority of their lives underground in crayfish and small mammal burrows in river floodplains, mixed hardwood and pine forests, and open pastures. Accordingly, adults are seldom observed except during the breeding season. Adults breed in isolated seasonal wetlands, flooded fields, ditches, and farm ponds.

Natural History: Breeding is explosive, occurring over a short time period, and occurs from February through early May. Males migrate to breeding locations several days before females during or after steady rainfall. Females lay 2,000–7,000 eggs on the surface or attached to vegetation in shallow water. Several females might deposit their eggs in a single large cluster. Eggs typically hatch in 4–10 days and the larval period lasts 8–12 weeks. Sexual maturity is reached within two years and adults can live up to five years. Crawfish Frogs feed on a variety of insects and other invertebrates. Tadpoles feed on algae and other microscopic plant matter. Predators are unknown but likely include birds, snakes, and raccoons. Tadpoles are prey for aquatic invertebrates and fishes.

Call: The call of the Crawfish Frog is a low-pitched, loud, guttural snore lasting 1–2 seconds in duration. This call carries well and can be heard over a half mile away.

Conservation Status: Although widespread, the Crawfish Frog is apparently uncommon throughout much of its range, including Tennessee. However, this might reflect their infrequency above ground rather than actual abundance. The editors have failed to find individuals in some historical populations located in the middle of agricultural fields, suggesting that local extirpation might be occurring. This species is not currently tracked by the state of Tennessee.

Matthew L. Niemiller

Gopher Frog juvenile, Coffee County. (Photo by Brian T. Miller)

Gopher Frog

Lithobates capito

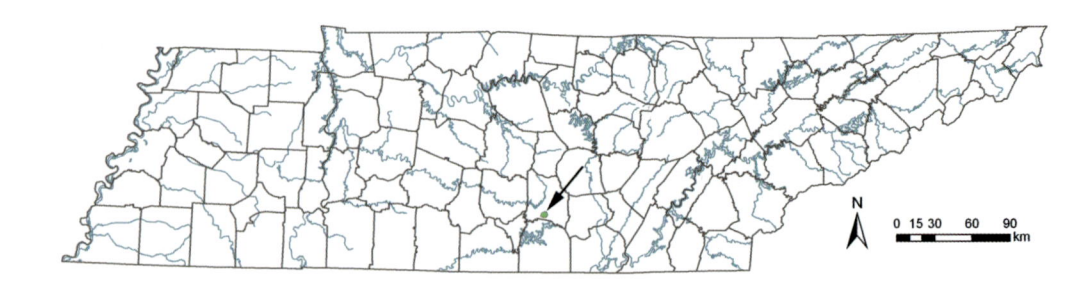

Description: The Gopher Frog is a stout, medium-sized frog with a relatively large head. The maximum TL reported is 112 mm, but most adults are smaller than this length, 65–90 mm TL. Dorsal and lateral coloration of the body and limbs is gray, brown, or creamy white with small, scattered brown to black spots. The texture of the skin varies from smooth to warty, but a pair of prominent dorsolateral folds extends from just behind each eye to the groin. These folds can be highlighted with yellow or brassy color. Darker, irregular blotches are present on the dorsum, sides, and legs. The venter is pale white, cream, or yellow with spotting or dark stippling on the belly. Often the posterior venter and undersurfaces of the hind limbs are washed in yellow. During the breeding season, the enlarged vocal sacs that extend from the angle of the mouth to halfway to the groin and enlarged thumbs distinguish males from females. Furthermore, male Gopher Frogs are generally smaller and paler than females. Metamorphs and juveniles cannot be sexed by use of external features, but this stage of development is of relatively short duration, at least for males. Tadpoles can grow up to 85 mm TL with an oval body and dorsal eyes. The body is deep with a dorsal coloration of greenish brown and typically lacking spots, but some individuals have scattered darker spots on the dorsum and tail. The venter is cream to yellow with spotting and the intestinal coil is not visible. The tail is long with a medium arch of the dorsal tail fin and with either a translucent or spotted tail fin. The snout also can be translucent and does not have a pale line extending from the corner of the jaw. Froglets are about 32 mm TL at metamorphosis. See the "Comments" section for subspecific information.

Etymology: The specific epithet, *capito*, is Latin for "big-headed," clearly referencing the size of the head relative to the body in this species.

Similar Species: Adult Gopher Frogs are most similar in appearance to Crawfish Frogs (*Lithobates areolatus*). Both species are stocky with heads that are relatively large compared to other members of the genus. The spotting pattern of the dorsum and stippling of the venter can be used to distinguish between these species. In Gopher Frogs, the venter is stippled with small dark flecks, whereas the belly of Crawfish Frogs is unpigmented. Furthermore, a pale ring borders the dark dorsal spots in Crawfish Frogs, whereas the dorsal spots in Gopher Frogs lack the pale ring. Tadpoles of the Gopher Frog most closely resemble that of the Southern Leopard Frog. However, Southern Leopard Frogs do not have a translucent snout and have a pale line extending from the each corner of the jaw.

Gopher Frog tadpole, Taylor County, Georgia. (Photo by Nathan Haislip)

Distribution: Gopher Frogs occur in the Coastal Plain of the southeastern United States from North Carolina south to Florida and west to Alabama. Disjunct populations occur in central Alabama and Tennessee. Only two individuals have been found in Tennessee, and both of these were collected in the northern section of Arnold Air Force Base in Coffee County, Tennessee.

Habitat: Gopher Frogs are secretive amphibians that inhabit moist meadows, prairies, woodlands, and pine scrub habitats within Coastal Plain ecosystems. Adults and juveniles are fossorial and therefore spend most of their lives in moist burrows. Although strongly associated with the Southeastern Coastal Plain upland longleaf pine forests, at least two populations of Gopher Frogs exist outside this region. Gopher frogs breed in fish-free ephemeral or semipermanent bodies of water, such as clear woodland ponds, swamps, and vernal pools. These ponds generally have an open canopy allowing penetration of sunlight, a water depth of > 2 feet, submergent vegetation available for attachment of egg masses, and a $pH \geq 4.3$. Habitat preference for Gopher Frogs in Tennessee can only be inferred from habitat surrounding the points of captures. Outside of Tennessee, Gopher Frogs are fossorial, often seeking refuge in the burrows of tortoises, small mammals, and crawfish, or the tunnels created from decaying root systems from toppled trees. Because of their secretive habits, Gopher Frogs are encountered rarely, except during the breeding season when adults leave subterranean retreats and travel overland to breeding ponds. These disjunct populations occur in Shelby County, Alabama, and Coffee County, Tennessee.

Natural History: Nothing is known about any aspects of the natural history (e.g., breeding period, breeding sites, diurnal retreats) of Gopher Frogs in Tennessee. Indeed, the natural habitat at Arnold Air Force Base is unlike that described as preferred by the species (e.g., xeric upland pine-dominated communities). Males arrive at the breeding sites prior to females and might remain in the pond for several weeks. In contrast, females generally spend less than a week at the breeding site. The timing of reproduction is highly variable from year to year, but breeding generally coincides with heavy rains during late winter and early spring. Occasionally, breeding occurs during the fall. Storms associated with hurricanes stimulate fall breeding of coastal populations in Alabama. Also, breeding has been reported during most months of the year at Eglin Air Force Base in Florida. Frequency of breeding among years apparently is site specific. For example, breeding occurs annually at many locations but is infrequent (known breeding activities are separated by several years) at peripheral, small populations in South Carolina. The egg mass produced by a female Gopher Frog typically contains 1,000 to 2,000 eggs, but over 6,000 eggs in a single mass have been reported. Each egg is surrounded by an individual set of "jelly" (mucopolysaccharides) membranes, and a relatively firm communal jelly coat holds the entire mass together. Gopher Frog egg masses typically are attached to vertical stems of aquatic vegetation. Although grass stems are often utilized and perhaps preferred, essentially any thin "stem," whether herbaceous, woody, or even metallic, is used. Eggs hatch within a few weeks and transformation of the tadpoles into juveniles occurs in 2–6 months. Juvenile and adult Gopher Frogs are carnivorous and are able to ingest large prey items, including frogs, and toads. Their diet also includes a variety of invertebrates, beetles, grasshoppers, spiders, and earthworms. Predators of southern populations include Banded Watersnakes (*Nerodia fasciata*) and possibly Florida Softshell Turtles (*Apalone ferox*).

Call: Males advertise their presence to females with a distinct, snore-like call. At many localities, males vocalize while floating on the surface of the pond and their call is directed aerially. With the proper climatic conditions, such calls travel relatively great distances overland (> 1/4 mi). Recent evidence suggests that many males, perhaps all at some sites, call while submerged in water. In contrast to the situation described for floating males, the muffled, distorted calls of submerged males travel only a few meters overland.

Conservation Status: Throughout their range, Gopher Frog populations are threatened by habitat loss resulting from conversion of natural forests to pine plantations, destruction of breeding ponds, fire suppression, introduction of fish to breeding ponds, and road mortality. Only two individuals have been found in Tennessee, and both of these were collected in the northern section of Arnold Air Force Base in

Coffee County, Tennessee. An intensive three-year survey for breeding sites was conducted at the base from 1998 to 2000 and failed to detect any evidence of Gopher Frog breeding activity. If Gopher Frogs are extant at the base, they are exceedingly rare, exceptionally secretive, or breed in an undiscovered or undersurveyed wetland. This species is "Deemed in Need of Management" by the state and state listed as "Critically Imperiled."

Comments: Gopher Frog taxonomy is currently in a state of flux, with various authors recognizing a single species (*L. captio*), two species (*L. captio* and *L. sevosus*), or a single species with three subspecies (*L. c. captio, L. c. sevosus,* and *L .c. aesopus*). Until further resolution is obtained, we refer to this complex as the single species *L. captio*. As only two specimens have ever been recorded from Tennessee, we have an extremely incomplete understanding of the affinities of our population. When additional individuals are found and tissue samples are obtained for DNA analysis, we will be better able to determine the taxonomy of Tennessee Gopher Frogs.

Brian T. Miller

American Bullfrog adult, Wilson County. (Photo by Matthew L. Niemiller)

American Bullfrog

Lithobates catesbeianus

Description: The American Bullfrog is the largest frog species native to the United States, with adults averaging 90–154 mm TL and achieving a maximum of 200 mm TL. Females attain larger sizes than males. Dorsal coloration is typically olive or green, with brown or black mottling sometimes forming a reticulum, though dorsal coloration and patterning can be quite variable. Ventral coloration is typically white to cream but usually yellowish in males, especially on the throat during the breeding season, with brown or black mottling. The skin is generally smooth but usually includes small, scattered tubercles throughout the dorsum. The toes on the rear feet are extensively webbed, with the tip of the longest toe extending beyond the webbing. Four toes are present on the front feet and five on the hind feet. Dorsolateral folds extend above and behind the tympanum and are not found on the trunk. The eyes are relatively large and prominent. The tympanum in adult females is similar

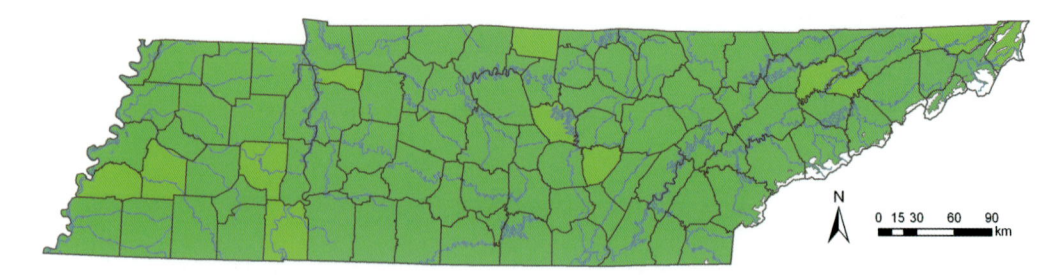

Top left: American Bullfrog adult, Polk County. (Photo by Brad M. Glorioso) *Top right:* American Bullfrog juvenile, Knox County. (Photo by Matthew L. Niemiller) *Bottom right:* American Bullfrog tadpole, North Carolina. (Photo by Nathan Haislip)

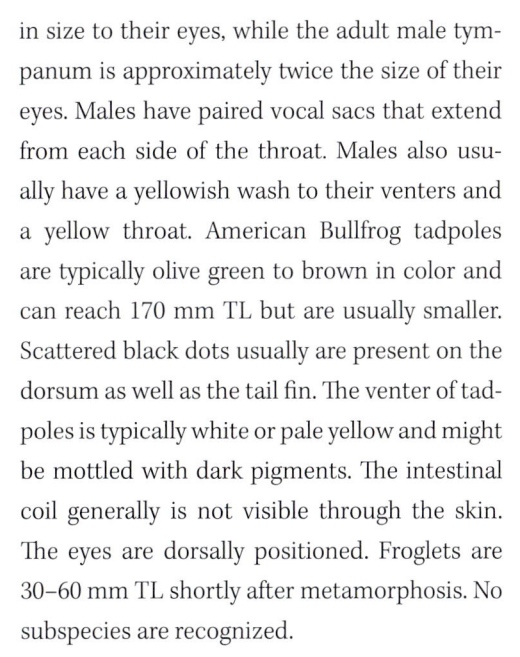

in size to their eyes, while the adult male tympanum is approximately twice the size of their eyes. Males have paired vocal sacs that extend from each side of the throat. Males also usually have a yellowish wash to their venters and a yellow throat. American Bullfrog tadpoles are typically olive green to brown in color and can reach 170 mm TL but are usually smaller. Scattered black dots usually are present on the dorsum as well as the tail fin. The venter of tadpoles is typically white or pale yellow and might be mottled with dark pigments. The intestinal coil generally is not visible through the skin. The eyes are dorsally positioned. Froglets are 30–60 mm TL shortly after metamorphosis. No subspecies are recognized.

Etymology: The specific epithet, *catesbeianus,* honors Mark Catesby, an eighteenth-century naturalist.

Similar Species: In Tennessee, only the Green Frog (*L. clamitans*) could be confused with the American Bullfrog. Both species occupy similar habitats and can be found statewide. However, unlike the American Bullfrog, Green Frogs have dorsolateral folds that extend roughly two-thirds down the length of the body. American Bullfrog tadpoles most closely resemble those of Green Frogs and Southern Leopard Frogs. Green Frog tadpoles do not grow as large and generally lack distinct black spots on the dorsum and tail. Southern Leopard Frog tadpoles usually have a vertical white stripe down the middle of the snout between the nostrils and do not have distinct black dots scattered on the dorsum and tail.

Distribution: The native range of the American Bullfrog extends from New Brunswick and Nova Scotia in Canada south to south-central Florida, west to Wisconsin and parts of Minnesota and across the Great Plains to the Rocky Mountains. The natural southwestern range limit is often reported to be through Veracruz, Mexico, but this is confounded by multiple introductions into parts of Mexico. The American

Bullfrog has been introduced throughout the western United States, British Columbia, and Hawaii, as well as several islands in the Caribbean, including Cuba, Hispaniola, Puerto Rico, and Jamaica. Southern Europe, Central and South America, Asia, and several oceanic islands also now have established populations of this frog. In Tennessee, the American Bullfrog can be found statewide, except the higher elevations of the Blue Ridge Mountains.

Habitat: The American Bullfrog typically inhabits permanent waters, including ponds, lakes, and reservoirs, as well as backwater swamps, marshes, and sloughs of larger rivers. Although they tend to prefer larger bodies of water than many frogs, they can be found in nearly any body of water that provides sufficient permanence for successful reproduction. The American Bullfrog is usually observed at the water's edge or in the water, amid snags and vegetation that provide hideouts. This species also does well in urban areas.

Natural History: Breeding generally occurs from late spring through early fall in shallow permanent waters amid vegetation. Males are very territorial and will call for females while defending a small range from other males. Females are known to lay 10,000–20,000 eggs per clutch in a thin film on the water's surface covering an area of 1 m across or more; the eggs are fertilized by the clasping male. Eggs hatch in 2–5 days and the tadpole stage lasts 5–36 months across their range. In Tennessee, the tadpole stage probably lasts 11–14 months. After metamorphosis, males typically attain sexual maturity in 1–2 years, while females might take 2–3 years. American Bullfrogs might live 7–10 years in the wild and are known to live 16 years in captivity. The American Bullfrog is a well-documented generalist predator consuming virtually anything it can swallow. In addition to the invertebrate prey items characteristic of many frog species, the American Bullfrog includes other frogs, snakes, turtles, fish, birds and mammals in their diet. Tadpoles and juveniles of the American Bullfrog are particularly vulnerable to predation by fish, snakes, turtles, birds and mammals, as well as some larger invertebrates. However, many predators find the eggs and tadpoles of American Bullfrogs to be distasteful, thus allowing them to thrive in permanent fish-filled waters. Larger birds, snakes and mammals take adults. American Bullfrogs are also known to prey on each other as tadpoles, as well as postmetamorphic life stages.

Call: The advertisement call of the male American Bullfrog, given day or night usually from shallow water near the shoreline, is a loud bass note about one second in length, often repeated in series. The call is frequently described as sounding like a deep *jug o'rum* or perhaps simply *brrrwooom*. The call carries well and is reputed to be audible half a mile away in ideal conditions. American Bullfrog also will produce a high-pitched and loud distress call when attacked or grabbed.

Conservation Status: American Bullfrogs are a game species in Tennessee and may be taken with a hunting license in all waters of the state except waters within state and federal wildlife refuges. The daily bag limit is 20 per person. The season is open year-round, except on TWRA-managed lakes where the season is 1–30 June. Despite this harvest, American Bullfrog populations appear stable throughout Tennessee.

Brad M. Glorioso

Bronze Frog adult, Lake County. (Photo by Matthew L. Niemiller)

Green Frog

Lithobates clamitans

Description: The Green Frog is a medium to large ranid, measuring 55–90 mm TL as adults with some northern females measuring over 100 mm TL. Females generally are larger than males. The dorsal coloration is highly variable ranging from dull brown or bronze to pale green. During colder temperatures, some individuals can be dark greenish black. The lower portion of the face is often green, even if the dorsum is brown. Spotting or mottling can be present on the dorsum, and the venter is usually white or cream and typically is mottled. The skin is generally smooth but with some small, wartlike bumps. The hind legs are long with strongly webbed feet, and a large tympanum is obvious behind the eye. Four toes are present on the front feet and five on the hind

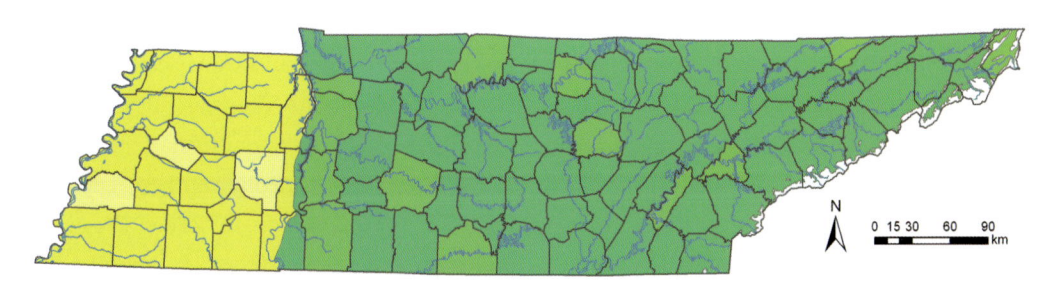

Two subspecies of Green Frog are recognized in Tennessee: the Northern Green Frog *(L. c. melanotus)*, whose range appears in green, and the Bronze Frog *(L. c. clamitans)*, whose range appears in yellow.

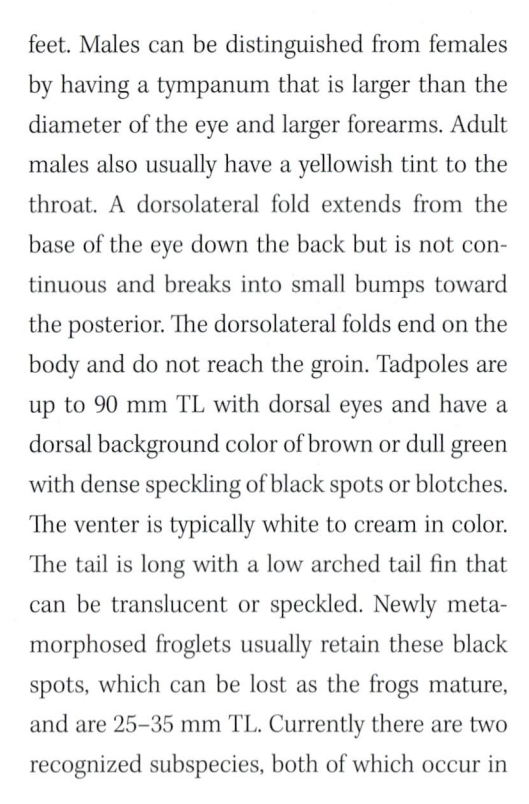

Top left: Green Frog adult, Cannon County. (Photo by Brian T. Miller) *Top right:* Green Frog tadpole, Bradley County. (Photo by Matthew L. Niemiller) *Bottom left:* Green Frog froglet, Blount County. (Photo by Matthew L. Niemiller)

feet. Males can be distinguished from females by having a tympanum that is larger than the diameter of the eye and larger forearms. Adult males also usually have a yellowish tint to the throat. A dorsolateral fold extends from the base of the eye down the back but is not continuous and breaks into small bumps toward the posterior. The dorsolateral folds end on the body and do not reach the groin. Tadpoles are up to 90 mm TL with dorsal eyes and have a dorsal background color of brown or dull green with dense speckling of black spots or blotches. The venter is typically white to cream in color. The tail is long with a low arched tail fin that can be translucent or speckled. Newly metamorphosed froglets usually retain these black spots, which can be lost as the frogs mature, and are 25–35 mm TL. Currently there are two recognized subspecies, both of which occur in Tennessee: the Green Frog (*L. c. melanotus*) and Bronze Frog (*L. c. clamitans*). Distinguishing between them morphologically is difficult and is usually accomplished based on distribution. Other field guides state that Green Frogs have markings on the dorsum in strong contrast to the dorsal ground color; however, coloration can be highly variable and this is not always diagnostic.

Etymology: The specific epithet, *clamitans,* is from the Latin *clamito* "to call loudly." The subspecific epithet, *melanotus,* is from the Greek *melaina* "black" and *notus* "mark," referring to the markings of some individuals.

Similar Species: Green Frogs superficially resemble other ranids, although the dorsolateral fold can be used to distinguish this species from others in the genus. American Bullfrogs (*L. catesbeianus*) lack dorsolateral folds that extend past the tympanum toward the groin. Wood Frogs (*L. sylvaticus*), Southern Leopard Frogs (*L. sphenocephalus*), Pickerel Frogs (*L. palustris*) and Gopher Frogs (*L. capito*) have dorsolateral folds that extend unbroken all the way to the groin. The latter three species also have well-defined spots or blotches between the dorsolateral folds on the dorsum. Tadpoles can be extremely difficult to differentiate between and is usually a process of elimination. American Bullfrog tadpoles grow larger than Green Frog tadpoles and have distinct black spots scattered on the dorsum and tail. Southern Leopard Frog tadpoles typically have a vertical white line running down the middle of the snout between the nostrils.

Distribution: Green Frogs are widely distributed throughout much of the eastern United States east of the Great Plains. They are found statewide in Tennessee up to 900 m in elevation. The Green Frog, *L. c. melanotus,* is found roughly east of the north-flowing Tennessee River, while the Bronze Frog, *L. c. clamitans,* is found in the Coastal Plain.

Habitat: Green Frogs are common inhabitants of most aquatic habitats in the state, from mountainous rivers and streams in the Blue Ridge Mountains to Coastal Plain lakes and swamps in West Tennessee. Both adults and juveniles are particularly abundant in permanent waters, such as farm ponds. They are frequently spooked from the shorelines of lakes and ponds, where they sit among vegetation during the day. They might be found abroad on rainy nights, including on roadways near water.

Natural History: Green Frogs breed from mid-spring to late summer in most permanent wetland habitat, usually preferring areas with some aquatic and shoreline vegetation. Eggs are laid in clumps of 3,000–5,000 along the shoreline among vegetation and individual eggs are roughly 1 to 1.5 mm in diameter. Females occasionally will produce more than one clutch during a single breeding season. Hatching occurs within a week and metamorphosis occurs after 2–3 months, although in some northern populations the tadpoles will overwinter and metamorphose the following spring. Sexual maturity is reached in 1–2 years. Tadpoles feed on aquatic detritus and diatoms and after metamorphosis they can disperse several kilometers away from natal wetlands. Adults feed on most moving organisms that will fit in their mouths, everything from mollusks to arthropods and other invertebrates, as well as large vertebrates, such as fish and other amphibians. Predators include aquatic snakes, wetland birds, and American Bullfrogs. Green Frogs let out a startling *squeek* when surprised by a potential predator and immediately jump into the water.

Call: The male advertisement call is usually described as similar to the plucking of a banjo string, a low-pitched *blung* or *clung* repeated one to four times in succession. Males will call both day and night typically from solitary locations. This call is known to carry over half a mile.

Conservation Status: Green Frog populations appear stable and this species is common throughout Tennessee.

Comments: The validity of the subspecies of Green Frogs has been called into question by some authors.

R. Graham Reynolds and Matthew L. Niemiller

Pickerel Frog adult, Campbell County. (Photo by Matthew L. Niemiller)

Pickerel Frog

Lithobates palustris

Description: The Pickerel Frog is a medium-sized ranid frog with large hind limbs and extensive webbing of the hind feet. Adults measure 44–87 mm TL and have smooth, moist skin. Ground color is greenish brown to greenish tan with two distinct dorsolateral folds than run from behind the eye to the groin. In between these folds are typically two rows of paired, square-shaped, brownish spots that often fuse to form long rectangles. The snout is pointed and a white line runs along the upper jaw. The hind limbs have black bars forming a banding appearance. Four toes are present on the front feet and five toes on the hind feet. The venter is variable, ranging from white to mottled gray. However, the undersurfaces of the hind limbs and groin are yellow to orange.

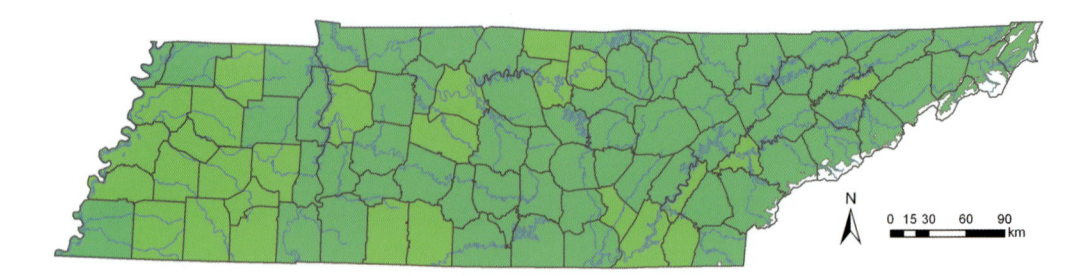

Top left: Pickerel Frog adult, Rutherford County. (Photo by Matthew L. Niemiller) *Top right:* Venter of Pickerel Frog showing yellow coloration, Coffee County. (Photo by Brad M. Glorioso) *Bottom right:* Pickerel Frog tadpole, Blount County. (Photo by Matthew L. Niemiller)

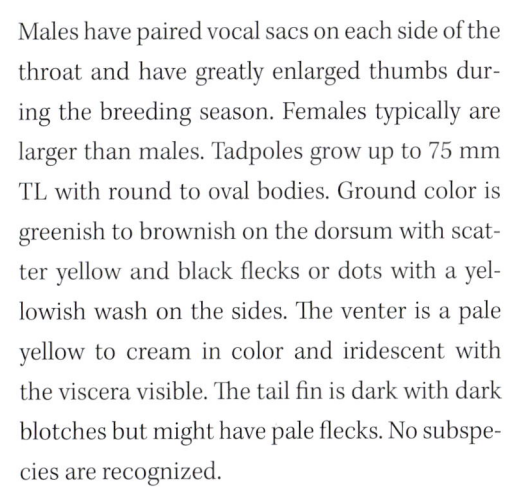

Males have paired vocal sacs on each side of the throat and have greatly enlarged thumbs during the breeding season. Females typically are larger than males. Tadpoles grow up to 75 mm TL with round to oval bodies. Ground color is greenish to brownish on the dorsum with scatter yellow and black flecks or dots with a yellowish wash on the sides. The venter is a pale yellow to cream in color and iridescent with the viscera visible. The tail fin is dark with dark blotches but might have pale flecks. No subspecies are recognized.

Etymology: The specific epithet, *palustris,* is Latin for "of the marsh," in reference to the habitat in which this species might be frequently found.

Similar Species: In Tennessee, Pickerel Frogs most closely resemble Southern Leopard Frogs (*L. sphenocephalus*). However, Pickerel Frogs can easily be distinguished by the yellowish to orangish wash on the undersurfaces of the thighs and groin. In addition, Pickerel Frogs have squarish dark spots on the dorsum rather than the rounded spots found in Southern Leopard Frogs. Tadpoles of Pickerel Frogs are difficult to distinguish from those of American Bullfrogs (*L. catesbeianus*), Green Frogs (*L. clamitans melanotus*), and Southern Leopard Frogs. Pickerel Frog tadpoles generally have a yellowish wash on the sides.

Distribution: The Pickerel Frog has a broad distribution throughout the eastern United States from Maine westward to the Great Lakes, southward into the Carolinas, northern Alabama, northern Georgia, Mississippi, Louisiana, and eastern Texas. In Tennessee, Pickerel Frogs can be found statewide but are less common in the Coastal Plain of West Tennessee and the Nashville Basin of Middle Tennessee.

Habitat: Pickerel Frogs are most abundant in and around the cool waters of springs, streams, and ponds in forested areas up to 850 m in elevation but can also be found in sphagnum bogs and floodplain swamps. Adults and metamorphs also can be quite common in and around caves, particularly in winter. Both adults and metamorphs can be observed on roads at night during or after rains.

Natural History: Breeding occurs from February through May in temporary woodland ponds or pools in springs and streams. Females lay 2,000–4,000 eggs in a round cluster up to 10 cm in diameter attached to debris and vegetation in shallower water. Eggs are bicolored—brownish above and yellowish below. Eggs hatch in about 10 days and the larval period lasts 12–14 weeks. Metamorphs can be found from June to late September, depending on the timing of egg deposition. Sexual maturity usually is reached in two years. Pickerel Frogs feed on a variety of insects and other invertebrates. Birds, snakes, raccoons, American Bullfrogs, and Green Frogs are all known predators of adult and metamorph Pickerel Frogs. However, adults produce toxic skin secretions that also are distasteful to many predators. These secretions are powerful enough to kill other amphibians if kept in the same container as a Pickerel Frog. Tadpoles are susceptible to aquatic invertebrates and fishes.

Call: The call of the Pickerel Frog is a low-pitched, croaking snore 1–2 seconds in duration and constant in tempo. This call is not very loud and does not carry well with distance. Males also often call underwater.

Conservation Status: Pickerel Frog populations appear stable throughout Tennessee.

Matthew L. Niemiller and
R. Graham Reynolds

Southern Leopard Frog adult, Rutherford County. (Photo by Matthew L. Niemiller)

Southern Leopard Frog

Lithobates sphenocephalus

Description: The Southern Leopard Frog is a medium-sized frog with adults measuring 51–90 mm TL but attaining a maximum of 127 mm TL. Females grow considerably larger than males. The head is pointed and the skin is generally smooth with a dorsal coloration typically a shade of olive, green, brown, or gray. The common name of this species refers to the irregularly scattered dark spots on the dorsum, which might be round or oblong-shaped. Well-developed dorsolateral folds, typically yellow in color, are present just posterior to the eye running down the trunk to the hind limbs. The hind limbs are extensively webbed, and at rest they have a vertically barred appearance. Four toes are found on the front feet and five on the hind feet. Ventral coloration is white or cream with no prominent markings. The tympanum typically has a white or yellow spot in the center. During the breeding season, males have swollen thumbs. Additionally, males have paired vocal

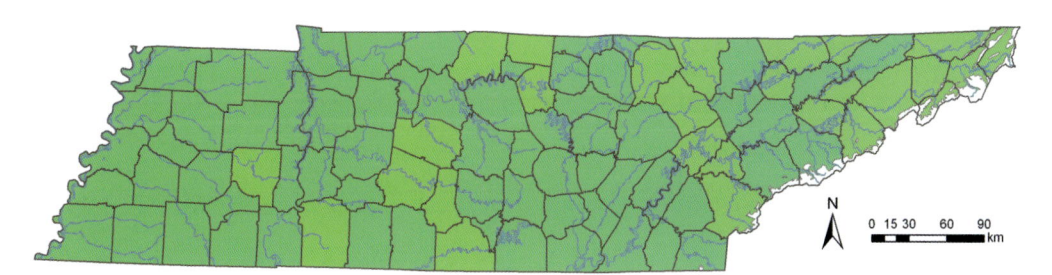

Top left: Aberrantly patterned Southern Leopard Frog, Coffee County. (Photo by Matthew L. Niemiller) *Top right:* Southern Leopard Frog tadpole, Gibson County. (Photo by Nathan Haislip) *Bottom left:* Southern Leopard Frog egg mass, Rutherford County. (Photo by Brad M. Glorioso)

sacs located on each side of the head between the tympanum and forelimb. Southern Leopard Frog tadpoles are highly variable with a body color ranging from green to brownish with or without darker markings. The tail fin has a low to medium arch and is sometimes translucent, while in other individuals might have brownish spots or mottling. The venter is white to pale pink and the intestinal coil is visible through the skin. A white line often is apparent on the snout at the nostrils. The eyes are dorsally positioned. Tadpoles can reach 83 mm TL but are usually smaller. Newly metamorphosed Southern Leopard Frogs are 20–33 mm TL. Two subspecies are recognized and only one, the Southern Leopard Frog (*Lithobates sphenocephalus utricularius*) occurs in Tennessee.

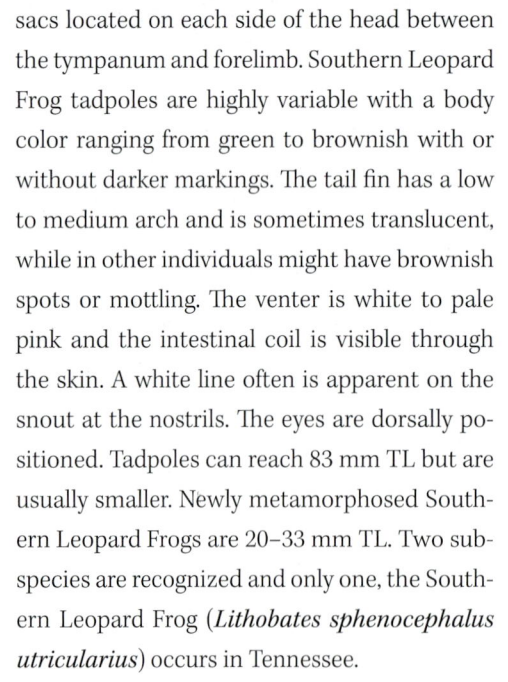

Etymology: The specific epithet, *sphenocephalus*, from the Greek *sphenos* "wedge" and *kephalos* "headed," referring to the shape of the head. The subspecific epithet, *utricularius,* is Latin for "bearing a little bag," referencing male throat pouches.

Similar Species: In Tennessee, only the Pickerel Frog (*L. palustris*) could be confused with the Southern Leopard Frog. Both species can occupy similar habitats and can be found nearly statewide. Pickerel Frogs have squarish spots on the dorsum arranged in two distinct rows, while the Southern Leopard Frog has round or oblong irregularly scattered spots on the dorsum. Also, the dorsolateral fold in the Southern Leopard Frog is thinner and more distinct than the dorsolateral fold of the Pickerel Frog. Lastly, unlike Southern Leopard Frogs, Pickerel Frogs have a yellowish wash on the groin area. Tadpoles of these two species also are very similar but Southern Leopard Frog tadpoles typically have a vertical white line running down the middle of the snout between the nostrils.

Distribution: The native range of the Southern Leopard Frog extends from southern New York to Florida, west to east central Texas, eastern Oklahoma, and southeastern Kansas, and north to Missouri, central Illinois, Indiana, and extreme southern Ohio. In Tennessee, the Southern Leopard Frog can be found nearly statewide, absent only in the higher elevations of the Blue Ridge Mountains in eastern Tennessee. The Southern Leopard Frog has also been introduced to the Little Bahama Bank in the Bahamas and in California.

Habitat: The Southern Leopard Frog can be found in nearly any area where water is present, be it permanent or ephemeral, although they tend to be less common in flowing water habitats. They are also known to wander some distance from water into both open and wooded areas. It is speculated that they might even become terrestrial in moist areas with adequate ground cover during the warmer months. Southern Leopard Frogs breed in both ephemeral and permanent bodies of water, including roadside ditches, swamps, farm ponds, and creek and river wetlands.

Natural History: Breeding generally occurs following rainfall from late winter through early spring but can be year round in southern parts of their range. Females contain up to 5,000 eggs, each in a double envelope, which they lay in clutches of 1,000–1,500 eggs. The globular egg mass is usually attached to vegetation floating near the water surface. Hundreds of egg masses might be very closely grouped together at a breeding site. Eggs hatch in 3–14 days and the tadpole stage lasts 2–7 months. Maturity probably is reached in 1–2 years, with females taking slightly longer than males. The Southern Leopard Frog is a fairly indiscriminate predator, consuming a host of arthropods, snails, and occasionally smaller frogs. Known predators of tadpoles and adults include snakes, birds and mammals. Arthropods and Eastern Newts eat eggs of Southern Leopard Frogs.

Call: The advertisement call of the male Southern Leopard Frog is quite variable but typically includes a mixture of low-pitched chuckles and croaks. The call is best described as sounding like two balloons being rubbed together. The call is usually given at night from shallow water near the shoreline or while floating on the surface. This call can resemble that of the Wood Frog (*L. sylvaticus*) at lower temperatures.

Conservation Status: Southern Leopard Frogs are abundant in Tennessee and populations appear stable throughout the state.

Brad M. Glorioso

Wood Frog adult, Blount County. (Photo by Matthew L. Niemiller)

Wood Frog

Lithobates sylvaticus

Description: The Wood Frog is a small- to medium-sized ranid measuring 50–67 mm TL. Females are generally larger than males. The ground color of dorsum is variable but typically is pale brown to tan to dark brown. Males are usually darker than females that can be tan to reddish pink to pale brown. Scattered darker flecks are sometimes present on the dorsum. Widely spaced darker bars are present on the hind limbs. Two distinct dorsolateral folds run from the eye down the body to the groin. A dark facial patch is present and runs through each eye to the base of the forelimb appearing much like a robber's mask. The tympanum lies within this mask. A white to yellowish line runs along the upper lip beneath the mask. The venter typically is white and unmarked, although each side of the chest might have a darker spot. There are four toes on the front feet and five on the no-

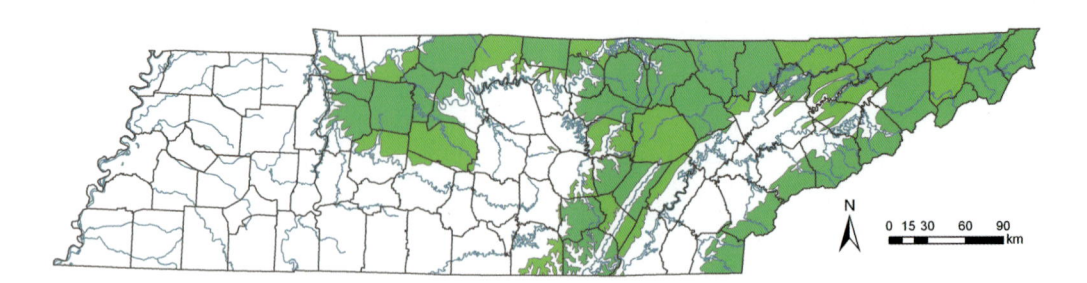

Left: Wood Frog red morph, Campbell County. (Photo by Matthew L. Niemiller) *Right:* Wood Frog tadpole, Blount County. (Photo by Matthew L. Niemiller)

ticeably webbed hind feet. Tadpoles have dorsal eyes and reach 60 mm TL before metamorphosis. Ground color is brown to greenish brown without any discernable markings. Bronze or golden flecks are occasionally present. Larger tadpoles often have a dark upper lip bordered by a white line. The tail fin is clear but occasionally will have small, darker markings. The tail is rounded dorsally and tapers to a sharp point. Froglets are 16–18 mm TL at metamorphosis. No subspecies are recognized.

Etymology: The specific epithet, *sylvaticus,* is Latin for "amid the trees," in reference to the common name.

Similar Species: No other frog in our state is brown with a black mask, though Wood Frogs can be confused with Green Frogs. Green Frogs lack a distinctive mask and usually are greenish in color. Wood Frog tadpoles are distinguished by a pale stripe on the lip, dark brown coloration, and very early appearance in the breeding ponds.

Distribution: The Wood Frog is the most widespread amphibian in North America, ranging from Alaska and northern Canada south along the Appalachian Mountains to Georgia and west diagonally from Kentucky to North Dakota and Montana. In Tennessee, Wood Frogs are found from the Cumberland Plateau east into the Blue Ridge Mountains, although this species appears to be absent from most of the Ridge and Valley. Additionally, populations are known from northern sections of the Interior Plateau in the state from just west of Nashville east and northward.

Habitat: Wood Frog breeding habitat consists of ephemeral aquatic habitats that do not have fish. Woodland pools, ponds, ditches, and tire ruts all serve as potential breeding sites, although survival of tadpoles assumes that water remains present long enough to complete metamorphosis. Outside of the breeding season, adults can be found in association with wooded upland moist habitats such as streams, and are frequently seen on roads on rainy nights. During the early spring in East Tennessee, adults can be seen by the dozens as they move to breeding ponds.

Natural History: Wood Frogs typically breed in Tennessee between January and March, when winter and spring precipitation has sufficiently accumulated in ephemeral wetland habitats. Because Wood Frogs are explosive breeders, females deposit many clutches into communal pools, with each clutch containing 300–4,000 eggs. There is some indication that communal oviposition confers a thermal advantage to some eggs in the clutches reducing the likelihood of freezing during a cold snap after breeding has begun. Eggs are bicolored like many ranids with the black embryo on top and the white yolk below. Egg masses can be tightly or loosely bound and are roughly 38–100 mm wide and are attached to vegetation. Eggs hatch in 2–4 weeks. Tadpoles feed on detritus and aquatic invertebrates, and might even feed on other amphibian eggs or cannibalize each other. Metamorphosis occurs after 65–130 days and the metamorphs move away from the pools to occupy the typical adult habitats. Adults and juveniles consume a wide variety of invertebrate prey, including beetles, flies, and spiders. Both conspecifics and larval ambystomatid salamanders prey upon larvae, and adult Wood Frogs likely are prey for a variety of woodland predators, including raccoons, foxes, owls, and snakes.

Call: The advertisement call of the Wood Frog sounds like medium-pitched, short "chuckles" repeated 2–3 times per interval and are frequently heard as a chorus. This call has been described as a quacking duck. Choruses typically occur at night, although males are known to call during the daytime when temperatures are warmer.

Conservation Status: Wood Frogs appear to be common in their range and no specific management plans exist. Threats to this species include significant road mortality during spring breeding migrations and the loss of ephemeral pond habitat. Short or reduced hydroperiods can cause breeding habitats to dry before metamorphosis occurs.

R. Graham Reynolds and
Matthew L. Niemiller

22
Family Scaphiopodidae (American Spadefoot Toads)

American Spadefoots are a unique group of amphibians with seven species occurring in North America from Mexico to Canada. The common name comes from the distinct spade-like projection on the hind feet, which facilitates burrowing backward into the substrate, where these frogs spend most of their lives outside of the breeding season. The family name is from the Greek *skaphis* "spade" and *pode* "foot." Spadefoots are squat with distinct blunt noses and vertical elliptical pupils. They inhabit areas with loose soil and can be extremely difficult to locate when they are not surface active. When heavy rainfall triggers breeding, they can be found in the hundreds. Fossil scaphiopodids are known from the Oligocene of North America. This family is composed of two genera—*Scaphiopus*, the Southern Spadefoots (three species), and *Spea*, the Western Spadefoots (four species)—with only a single species of the former occurring in Tennessee.

Eastern Spadefoot

Scaphiopus holbrookii

Description: The Eastern Spadefoot is a medium-sized frog measuring 44–57 mm TL as adults with a known maximum of 83 mm TL. Females attain larger sizes than males. Two distinctive yellowish or brownish lines run from each eye down the back, somewhat resembling reverse parentheses. An additional pale-colored line can be present on the sides of the body. The skin is relatively smooth, with many small tubercles scattered on the back and sides. The ground coloration is variable but is usually a shade of brown, olive, gray, or black. A distinct tympanum and round parotoid glands are present on the head, though cranial ridges and an interorbital boss are lacking. The venter is white to pale gray, with a pair of distinct pectoral glands. The Eastern Spadefoot has large protruding eyes with vertical catlike pupils. The common name is derived from the sickle-shaped black spade present on the inside of each hind foot used for digging. The hind limbs are extensively webbed. Four toes are present on the front limbs and five on the hind limbs. Tadpole dorsal coloration is brownish to bronze, with clear tail fins and no dark markings on the tail musculature. The eyes are very closely set on the dorsum, more so than any other native species of frog. The venter is practically transparent, making the internal organs and gills visible through the venter. The tail is short and rounded with a clear tail fin. Tadpoles can reach up to 50 mm TL but are usually smaller with newly metamorphosed individuals 8–15 mm TL. No subspecies are recognized.

Eastern Spadefoot adult, Williamson County. (Photo by Matthew L. Niemiller)

Etymology: The specific epithet, *holbrookii*, honors John E. Holbrook, a member of the National Academy of Sciences and often referred to as the "father of modern herpetology."

Similar Species: The Eastern Spadefoot is easily distinguished from all other frog species native to Tennessee by the presence of vertical pupils and the conspicuous sickle-shaped black spade on each hind foot. Perhaps only American Toads (*Anaxyrus americanus*) and Fowler's Toads (*A. fowleri*) could be confused with this species; however, these species have more conspicuous warts and horizontal pupils.

Distribution: The native range of the Eastern Spadefoot extends from Massachusetts down the East Coast to the Florida Keys and west to eastern Louisiana, eastern Arkansas, and southeast Missouri, with several disjunct populations in the northern part of its range. In Tennessee, the Eastern Spadefoot can be found nearly statewide but is absent at high elevations of the Blue Ridge Mountains in eastern Tennessee.

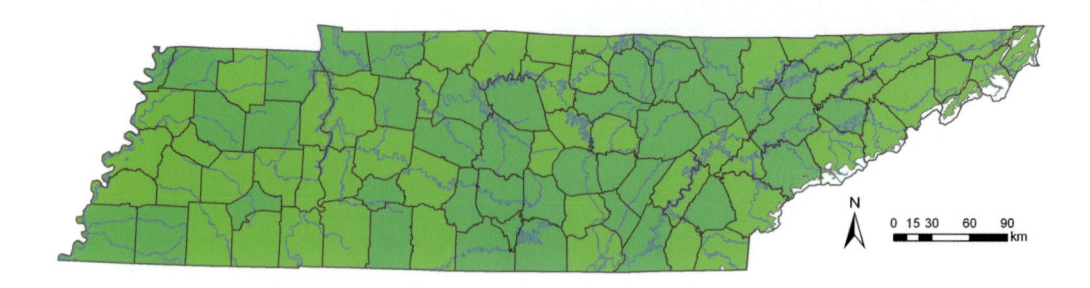

Top left: Eastern Spadefoot adult, Coffee County. (Photo by Brian T. Miller) *Top right:* Spade on hind foot. (Photo by Matthew L. Niemiller) *Bottom right:* Eastern Spadefoot tadpole, Union County. (Photo by Nathan Haislip)

Habitat: The Eastern Spadefoot is known to live in a wide variety of habitats, including upland and bottomland forest sites, meadows, and agricultural fields. The most important habitat variable is loose, well-drained loam or sandy soils to facilitate their secretive fossorial existence. They are most easily detected by listening for advertisement calls in appropriate habitat at night on a warm, rainy night as they emerge from their burrows en masse. Breeding occurs in ephemeral wetlands, such as flooded fields, roadside ditches, and borrow pits.

Natural History: Breeding is explosive and can occur in any month where the air temperature is above 7–10°C and is triggered by very heavy rains during warm weather. In Tennessee, the peak of breeding activity probably occurs from late spring through early autumn. Females are known to lay as many as 5,500 eggs in stringy masses attached to vegetation in shallow, temporary water. Eggs hatch in 1–15 days and the tadpole stage lasts 14–60 days. Tadpoles often congregate in massive schools of thousands of individuals, and some can become cannibalistic in such conditions. After metamorphosis, sexual maturity is typically reached in 2–3 years, with males often maturing quicker than females. Eastern Spadefoots have been documented to live at least 9 years in the wild, with a captive individual living 12 years. The Eastern Spadefoot is a predator of a host of arthropods. It affords itself some protection from predators by remaining underground most of the year and with a toxic skin secretion. Still, some frogs, birds, snakes, and mammals are known predators of adults, while carnivorous aquatic insects and salamanders are known predators of tadpoles, though this list is likely incomplete. Eastern Spadefoots dig their own burrows and some individuals can remain underground for weeks without feeding. Although most individuals only use a burrow for a short duration, some individuals are known to use the same burrow for more than four years.

Call: The advertisement call of the male Eastern Spadefoot, usually given afloat on the water surface, is an explosive, nasal *waaagh* given at intervals of typically 3–4 seconds but sometimes longer. It is sometimes described as the sound a person would make if they were experiencing severe gastrointestinal distress. The call can carry a long distance under the right atmospheric conditions, more than a mile away for large choruses.

Conservation Status: Eastern Spadefoot populations have severely retracted and some have even been extirpated in the Northeast, due chiefly to urbanization. In Tennessee, however, populations appear stable, though the secretive nature of this species precludes certainty.

Brad M. Glorioso

23
Erroneous Species and Species of Possible Occurrence

Several species of amphibians with distributions far removed from Tennessee have been erroneously reported, either because of misidentification or errors in cataloging of specimens. The following amphibian species are considered either erroneous, in that they have previously been reported to occur in the state but lack sufficient verification or originate from questionable records, or of possible occurrence, in that they might yet be found in our state. It is possible that some of these species occurred historically, but as of this writing these species are not thought to be established in Tennessee. Subsequent surveys might overturn these conclusions, and we along with others are currently engaged in investigating unverified reports of several of the following species. Verifiable sightings or photographs should be reported to wildlife authorities or university herpetologists, so that we might further our understanding of the state's faunal composition. Erroneous records of salamanders include Jefferson's Salamander (*Ambystoma jeffersonianum*), Blue-Spotted Salamander (*A. laterale*), Gulf Coast Waterdog (*Necturus beyeri*), and Dwarf Salamander (*Eurycea quadridigitata*). Likewise, several anuran species have been erroneously reported from Tennessee, including Southern Toads (*Anaxyrus terrestris*), Squirrel Treefrogs (*Hyla squirella*), and Northern Leopard Frogs (*Lithobates pipiens*). Two species of frogs might yet occur in Tennessee: Illinois Chorus Frogs (*Pseudacris streckeri illinoensis*) and Plains Leopard Frogs (*Lithobates blairi*).

Family Ambystomatidae: Jefferson's Salamander

Ambystoma jeffersonianum

As previously reviewed and discussed by Redmond and Scott in 1996, Rhoads first reported Jefferson's Salamander in Tennessee in 1895 from Roan Mountain in Carter County at high elevation. However, Rhoads likely was observing Northern Gray-Cheeked Salamanders (*Plethodon montanus*). Other erroneous reports of Jefferson's Salamander from Tennessee include records from Decatur County (Maldonado-Koerdell and Firschein in 1947) and Hardeman County (Gentry in 1955 and 1956; Gentry et al. in 1965). These records might be Smallmouth Salamanders (*A. texanum*) based on range. Jefferson's Salamanders most closely resemble Smallmouth Salamanders but have distinctly broader heads and longer legs and toes. Although these records are believed to be invalid, Jefferson's Salamander distribution nears the northern border of Tennessee in Kentucky and southwest Virginia. In fact, records exist north of Kingsport (East Tennessee) from Scott County, Virginia. This species potentially could be added to Tennessee's herpetofauna in the future.

Family Proteidae: Gulf Coast Waterdog

Necturus beyeri

Gulf Coast Waterdogs are medium-sized necturids that differ slightly in physical appearance from the Mudpuppy (*N. maculosus*). Genetic evidence suggests that they are a distinct species. Larvae tend to be spotted, while Mudpuppy larvae have distinct stripes. Adults seem to have many small dark spots, whereas Mudpuppy adults usually have large blotches on the dorsum. Gulf Coast Waterdogs are distributed along the southern Mississippi River drainage, from central Mississippi south to the Gulf of Mexico, with a disjunct population in East Texas and West Louisiana. The only report of this species from our state comes from East Tennessee in the Tennessee River drainage. This report is based on old range maps and likely is a misidentification of Mudpuppies or a result of the previously confusing taxonomy of the genus. Were Gulf Coast Waterdogs to occur in Tennessee, it seems likely that they would be found in West Tennessee in the Mississippi River drainage as opposed to the Tennessee River drainage.

Family Bufonidae: Southern Toad

Anaxyrus terrestris

Southern Toads were once considered to be conspecifics of the American Toad (*Anaxyrus americanus*) based on the similarity of their call and appearance. Subsequent genetic analysis has indicated that they are in fact distinct species. Southern Toads are actually more closely related to Fowler's Toad (*A. fowleri*) and

Jefferson's Salamander, Indiana. (Photo by Todd Pierson)

can be distinguished from both American and Fowler's Toads by the presence of two parallel cranial ridges that extend along the top of the head adjacent to the back of the eyes and end in a distinct knob. Fowler's and American Toads have a similar ridge, but the posterior terminus of the ridge does not generally end in a prominent knob, instead remaining the same height and taking a 90-degree lateral turn. Southern Toads range along the Coastal Plain in the southeastern United States, reaching northern Mississippi and Alabama just south of Tennessee. The only reported specimens from our state were collected in Davidson and Hamilton counties by Rhoads in 1895. Redmond and Scott (1996) discussed these reports, indicating that revision of nomenclature and further examination of specimens from Tennessee indicate that this species does not actually occur in our state. Likewise, 31 specimens identified as Southern Toads are accessioned at the Florida Museum of Natural History (FLMNH 106490–106520) from Blount, McMinn, Meigs, Monroe, Polk, Rhea, and Unicoi counties. These specimens likely are misidentified Fowler's or American Toads.

Gulf Coast Waterdog, Lee County, Georgia. (Photo by John Jensen)

Southern Toad adult, Seminole County, Florida. (Photo by Matthew L. Niemiller)

Family Hylidae: Squirrel Treefrog

Hyla squirella

Named for its squirrel-like call, the Squirrel Treefrog is an attractive, small arboreal treefrog that closely resembles the Green Treefrog (*Hyla cinerea*). Adults are smaller than the Green Treefrog, measuring 20–40 mm TL and having a distinct nasal *waaaak* call that is not as loud as that of Green Treefrogs. These two species are perhaps best distinguished by the pale lateral stripe: in Green Treefrogs it is bold with a distinct lower edge, whereas in Squirrel Treefrogs the lower edge is not as sharp and the pale color might trail or fade toward the abdomen. Squirrel Treefrogs are a Coastal Plain species ranging across the southeastern United States to eastern Texas. They are found well into northern Alabama and up the Mississippi River drainage to at least central Mississippi. This species was previously reported to occur all the way up the Mississippi River to the confluence of the Tennessee and Ohio rivers. Subsequent analysis of these specimens determined that they were in fact unusually patterned Western Chorus Frogs (*Pseudacris triseriata*) and that *H. squirella* does not occur in Tennessee, Illinois, or Kentucky. However, individuals are easily transported and might yet turn up in our state, though it is unclear whether they would be capable of establishing a reproductive colony.

Squirrel Treefrog adult, Vermillion Parish, Louisiana. (Photo by Matthew L. Niemiller)

Illinois Chorus Frog adult, Scott County, Missouri. (Photo by Brad M. Glorioso)

Family Hylidae: Illinois Chorus Frog

Pseudacris streckeri illinoensis

Illinois Chorus Frogs are similar in appearance to Upland Chorus Frogs (*P. feriarum*) but typically are stouter and larger with a more toad-like appearance. This species has been reported from northeast Arkansas and southeast Missouri and likely would be found around the Reelfoot Lake area of northwest Tennessee if it occurs in the state.

Family Ranidae: Plains Leopard Frog

Lithobates blairi

Plains Leopard Frogs might occur around the Reelfoot Lake area. Similar to Southern Leopard Frogs (*L. sphenocephalus*), Plains Leopard Frogs have a dark spot on the snout that is lacking in Northern Leopard Frogs and also have a yellow wash on the groin and ventral surface of the thigh. Plains Leopard Frogs have been reported from northeast Arkansas and southeast Missouri.

Family Ranidae: Northern Leopard Frog

Lithobates pipiens

Dodd in 2004 included Northern Leopard Frogs in the list of amphibians occurring within Great Smoky Mountains National Park. However, there remains uncertainty regarding the taxonomic identify of specimens collected from the western edge of the park in Tennessee. Both King (1939) and Dodd (2004) agree that specimens in the park collection most closely resemble Northern rather than Southern Leopard Frogs. Living specimens that would resolve the matter have remained elusive in the last several years. Most recent distribution maps indicate Southern Leopard Frogs should occur within the park's boundaries. If valid, this would represent a significant range extension of the Northern Leopard Frog. Northern Leopard Frogs have spots with pale borders and lack a distinct pale spot in the center of the tympanum. Additionally, Northern Leopard Frogs have a shorter, more rounded snout and have more dark spots on the sides of the body.

Plains Leopard Frog adult, Cape Girardeau County, Missouri. (Photo by Brad M. Glorioso)

Northern Leopard Frog adult, Newton County, Indiana. (Photo by Matthew L. Niemiller)

Other Erroneous Amphibians

A specimen identified as a Blue-Spotted Salamander (*Amybstoma laterale*) was collected from Davidson County (ANSP 1378). However, the main distribution of the species occurs throughout the Great Lakes, the Northeast, and southern Canada. This specimen might be a misidentified Streamside Salamander (*A. barbouri*), Mole Salamander (*A. talpoideum*), or Northern Slimy Salamander (*Plethodon glutinosus*). A museum record (MCZ A-115140) exists for the Dwarf Salamander (*Eurycea quadridigitata*) from the Cosby Campground area in Great Smoky Mountains National Park in Cocke County. Dwarf Salamanders are distributed primarily in the Coastal Plain of the southeastern United States, and this record likely represents a Blue Ridge Two-Lined Salamander (*Eurycea wilderae*) instead.

A Cuban Treefrog (*Osteopilus septentrionalis*) was found recently in Davidson County, apparently having hitched a ride on a rental car driven from Miami, Florida (see photo in chapter 2). This is the only record of this species in Tennessee, and the individual was removed from the wild.

Checklist of the Amphibians of Tennessee

Salamanders

Family Ambystomatidae
☐ Streamside Salamander (*Ambystoma barbouri*)
☐ Spotted Salamander (*Ambystoma maculatum*)
☐ Marbled Salamander (*Ambystoma opacum*)
☐ Mole Salamander (*Ambystoma talpoideum*)
☐ Small-Mouthed Salamander (*Ambystoma texanum*)
☐ Eastern Tiger Salamander (*Ambystoma tigrinum tigrinum*)

Family Amphiumidae
☐ Three-Toed Amphiuma (*Amphiuma tridactylum*)

Family Cryptobranchidae
☐ Eastern Hellbender (*Cryptobranchus alleganiensis alleganiensis*)

Family Plethodontidae
☐ Green Salamander (*Aneides aeneus*)
☐ Cumberland Dusky Salamander (*Desmognathus abditus*)
☐ Seepage Salamander (*Desmognathus aeneus*)
☐ Carolina Mountain Dusky Salamander (*Desmognathus carolinensis*)
☐ Spotted Dusky Salamander (*Desmognathus conanti*)
☐ Northern Dusky Salamander (*Desmognathus fuscus*)
☐ Imitator Salamander (*Desmognathus imitator*)
☐ Shovel-Nosed Salamander (*Desmognathus marmoratus*)
☐ Seal Salamander (*Desmognathus monticola*)
☐ Allegheny Mountain Dusky Salamander (*Desmognathus ochrophaeus*)
☐ Ocoee Salamander (*Desmognathus ocoee*)
☐ Blue Ridge Dusky Salamander (*Desmognathus orestes*)

- ☐ Northern Pygmy Salamander (*Desmognathus organi*)
- ☐ Black-Bellied Salamander (*Desmognathus quadramaculatus*)
- ☐ Santeetlah Dusky Salamander (*Desmognathus santeetlah*)
- ☐ Black Mountain Dusky Salamander (*Desmognathus welteri*)
- ☐ Pygmy Salamander (*Desmognathus wrighti*)
- ☐ Brownback Salamander (*Eurycea aquatica*)
- ☐ Southern Two-Lined Salamander (*Eurycea cirrigera*)
- ☐ Three-Lined Salamander (*Eurycea guttolineata*)
- ☐ Junaluska Salamander (*Eurycea junaluska*)
- ☐ Long-Tailed Salamander (*Eurycea longicauda longicauda*)
- ☐ Cave Salamander (*Eurycea lucifuga*)
- ☐ Blue Ridge Two-Lined Salamander (*Eurycea wilderae*)
- ☐ Berry Cave Salamander (*Gyrinophilus gulolineatus*)
- ☐ Big Mouth Cave Salamander (*Gyrinophilus palleucus necturoides*)
- ☐ Pale Salamander (*Gyrinophilus palleucus palleucus*)
- ☐ Blue Ridge Spring Salamander (*Gyrinophilus porphyriticus danielsi*)
- ☐ Northern Spring Salamander (*Gyrinophilus porphyriticus porphyriticus*)
- ☐ Four-Toed Salamander (*Hemidactylium scutatum*)
- ☐ Tellico Salamander (*Plethodon aureolus*)
- ☐ Eastern Red-Backed Salamander (*Plethodon cinereus*)
- ☐ White-Spotted Slimy Salamander (*Plethodon cylindraceus*)
- ☐ Northern Zigzag Salamander (*Plethodon dorsalis*)
- ☐ Northern Slimy Salamander (*Plethodon glutinosus*)
- ☐ Jordan's Red-Cheeked Salamander (*Plethodon jordani*)
- ☐ Cumberland Plateau Salamander (*Plethodon kentucki*)
- ☐ Mississippi Slimy Salamander (*Plethodon mississippi*)
- ☐ Northern Gray-Cheeked Salamander (*Plethodon montanus*)
- ☐ Southern Ravine Salamander (*Plethodon richmondi*)
- ☐ Southern Red-Backed Salamander (*Plethodon serratus*)
- ☐ Red-Legged Salamander (*Plethodon shermani*)
- ☐ Southern Appalachian Salamander (*Plethodon teyahalee*)
- ☐ Southern Zigzag Salamander (*Plethodon ventralis*)
- ☐ Wehrle's Salamander (*Plethodon wehrlei*)
- ☐ Weller's Salamander (*Plethodon welleri*)
- ☐ Yonahlossee Salamander (*Plethodon yonahlossee*)
- ☐ Midland Mud Salamander (*Pseudotriton montanus diastictus*)
- ☐ Blue Ridge Red Salamander (*Pseudotriton ruber nitidus*)

☐ Northern Red Salamander (*Pseudotriton ruber ruber*)
☐ Black-Chinned Red Salamander (*Pseudotriton ruber schencki*)
☐ Southern Red Salamander (*Pseudotriton ruber vioscai*)

Family Proteidae
☐ Mudpuppy (*Necturus maculosus*)

Family Salamandridae
☐ Central Newt (*Notophthalmus viridescens louisianensis*)
☐ Red-Spotted Newt (*Notophthalmus viridescens viridescens*)

Family Sirenidae
☐ Western Lesser Siren (*Siren intermedia nettingi*)

Frogs

Family Bufonidae
☐ Eastern American Toad (*Anaxyrus americanus americanus*)
☐ Dwarf American Toad (*Anaxyrus americanus charlesmithi*)
☐ Fowler's Toad (*Anaxyrus fowleri*)

Family Hylidae
☐ Northern Cricket Frog (*Acris crepitans*)
☐ Southern Cricket Frog (*Acris gryllus gryllus*)
☐ Bird-Voiced Treefrog (*Hyla avivoca*)
☐ Cope's Gray Treefrog (*Hyla chrysoscelis*)
☐ Green Treefrog (*Hyla cinerea*)
☐ Barking Treefrog (*Hyla gratiosa*)
☐ Gray Treefrog (*Hyla versicolor*)
☐ Mountain Chorus Frog (*Pseudacris brachyphona*)
☐ Spring Peeper (*Pseudacris crucifer*)
☐ Upland Chorus Frog (*Pseudacris feriarum*)
☐ Western Chorus Frog (*Pseudacris triseriata*)

Family Microhylidae
☐ Eastern Narrow-Mouthed Toad (*Gastrophryne carolinensis*)

Family Ranidae
☐ Crawfish Frog (*Lithobates areolatus circulosus*)
☐ Gopher Frog (*Lithobates captio*)
☐ American Bullfrog (*Lithobates catesbeianus*)
☐ Bronze Frog (*Lithobates clamitans clamitans*)
☐ Green Frog (*Lithobates clamitans melanotus*)
☐ Pickerel Frog (*Lithobates palustris*)
☐ Southern Leopard Frog (*Lithobates sphenocephalus utricularius*)
☐ Wood Frog (*Lithobates sylvaticus*)

Family Scaphiopodidae
☐ Eastern Spadefoot (*Scaphiopus holbrookii*)

Glossary

A-1, A-2 row: The first and second anterior labial tooth rows in the mouth of a tadpole.

A-2 gap: Medial gap in the second labial tooth row in the mouth of a tadpole.

Abiotic: Nonliving components of a habitat, community, or ecosystem.

Adpressed limbs: Limbs pressed parallel to the lateral sides of the body.

Advertisement call: Vocalization produced by male frogs and toads to attract females during the breeding season.

Aestivation: State of dormancy in some organisms similar to hibernation in response to hot, dry conditions.

Aggression call: Vocalization produced by male frogs and toads to discourage rival males from establishing calling territories nearby.

Albinism: Devoid of pigment.

Allele: A variant of a particular gene, located in a specific position on a specific chromosome.

Allopatric: Two populations or species occurring in geographic isolation from one another; nonoverlapping ranges.

Alluvial: Referring to material deposited by flowing water.

Ambient: Surrounding, as in ambient temperature.

Amplexus: A mating embrace of frogs and toads in which the male tightly clasps the female and fertilizes the eggs released by the female.

Anterior: At or situated near the head of an organism.

Anthropogenic: Produced or caused by humans.

Aphotic zone: Region of caves where no light penetrates from the surface. Contrast with the cave twilight zone, where some light penetrates from the surface or cave entrance.

Aposematism: Possessing colors that serve to warn potential predators of an organism's toxicity, foul taste, or other defensive mechanisms.

Arboreal: Living in trees.

Arthropod: A group of invertebrates that have an exoskeleton, segmented body, and jointed appendages. Includes the insects, crustaceans, arachnids, chilopods (centipedes), and diplopods (millipedes).

Autotomy: The loss or breakage of the tail either reflexively or after being captured.

Band: A pigmented area that spans the dorsum of the body from one side to another extending onto, or nearly to, the ventral surface.

Barred: A pattern of stripes on the trunk or appendages.

Batesian mimicry: Imitation of a noxious species by a harmless or palatable species; mimicry of warning colors or signals to avoid predation.

Benthic: The ecological region in the lowest level of a body of water; the bottom of a lake or stream.

Biomass: The total mass of all or a group of living organisms in a given habitat.

Blotch: A pigmented area that is usually large and round or squarish that differs from the background coloration.

Body length: See **SVL**.

Boletoid: A characteristic of the tongue of salamanders in which the tongue is attached by a central pedicel only, as opposed to attached by the pedicel and the anterior or posterior edges.

Boss: A swelling or elevated rounded area between the eyes of Eastern Spadefoots (*Scaphiopus holbrookii*).

Canthus rostralis: A bony ridge often outlined with pigment that extends from the eye to the tip of the snout in *Gyrinophilus* salamanders. Thought to be used for aiming predatory strikes.

Capillaries: Smallest vessels of the arterial circulatory system. Site of gas exchange in tissues.

Caudal: At or near the tail.

Cepahlic amplexus: An amplexus position used by newts in which the male clasps the female around or behind her head with his front limbs.

Channelization: Artificial deepening and straightening of a body of water, typically rivers and streams.

Chert: Fine-grained sedimentary rock that contains quartz microcrystals.

Cirri: Soft structures protruding from the nostrils in some salamanders that contain the nasolabial grooves, which facilitate the detection of chemicals on the ground. Cirri are especially pronounced in some male salamanders, presumably to assist in locating reproductively receptive females. Singular cirrus.

Cladoceran: A type of tiny, aquatic crustacean also known as a water flea.

Class: A higher-level taxonomic group below the level of phylum but above the level of order, as in the class Amphibia.

Cloaca: See **vent**.

Copepod: A type of tiny, aquatic crustacean that are dominant members of zooplankton.

Costal fold: A bulge in the thoracic region of a salamander.

Costal groove: Vertical groove lying between costal folds on the lateral sides of a salamander, the number of which frequently assists in identification of a species.

Congeneric: Belonging to the same genus.

Conspecific: Belonging to the same species.

Cornified: See **keratinized**.

Cranial: Referring to the head or skull.

Cranial crests: Raised, bony ridges on the head of true toads.

Crepuscular: Active during dawn and/or dusk.

Cryptic species: Two or more related species that are morphologically indistinguishable but are genetically divergent.

Cusp: A pointed or rounded edge of a tooth or toothlike structure.

Cutaneous: Of or relating to the skin or epithelium.

Deciduous: Vegetation that loses foliage with the onset of cold weather (usually the autumn) and regrows it during the spring.

Depressed: Pressed down or flattened.

Desiccation: Drying out; loss of retained moisture.

Detritus: Nonliving particulate organic matter.

Diploid: Possessing two sets of chromosomes in each body cell.

Disjunct population: A population of organisms that is geographically separated from other populations of the same species.

Diurnal: Active during the day.

DNA: Deoxyribonucleic acid; nucleic acid that contains genetic information of an organism.

Dorsal: Referring to the uppermost surface of a bilateral organism; the back.

Dorsolateral: Pertaining to the back and sides of a bilateral organism.

Dorsolateral fold/ridge: Folds of skin on the dorsum of anurans that demarks the dorsal and lateral surfaces of the body.

Dorsum: The uppermost surface of a bilateral organism; the back.

Ecoregion: An ecological region that is characterized by similar landscape, climate, soil, vegetation, hydrology, fauna, and other ecological attributes.

Eft: The terrestrial, adolescent stage of the Eastern Newt (*Notophthalmus viridescens*).

Emarginate: Notches or indentations, in reference to the margin of the oral disc of tadpoles.

Endemic: Restricted to a particular region; found nowhere else.

Ephemeral: Existing for only a short time period, as in an ephemeral wetland.

Estivate: To spend a period of time in an inactive state, often underground during hot or dry weather.

Eutrophication: The natural or anthropogenic process of sedimentation and nutrient deposition in aquatic habitats leading to changes in community structure.

Extirpation: Local extinction of a population of a species.

Facultative: Refers to an optional process or behavior; contrast with obligate.

Family: A higher-level taxonomic group below the level of order but above the level of genus; as in the family Plethodontidae.

Fauna: The species of animal in a particular region or time period.

Fecundity: Reproductive capacity of an organism relating to the number of potential offspring.

Fimbriae: Hairlike projections of the external gills of salamanders; also known as gill filaments.

First-order stream: See **stream order**.

Floodplain: Low-lying area adjacent to rivers and streams that is subject to periodic flooding during heavy rainfall.

Fossorial: Living or adapted for life underground, typically in the soil or in burrows.

Froglet: A recently metamorphosed frog, often still possessing a tail.

Genus: A lower-level taxonomic group below the level of family that usually consists of several closely related species, as in the genus *Plethodon*. Plural genera.

Gill filament: See **fimbriae**.

Gill slit: Opening located along the neck of some salamander species that connects the pharynx to the surface of the body.

Gravid: Carrying developing eggs or young.

Gular fold: A transverse fold of tissue on the lower throat of salamanders.

Herpetofauna: The amphibians and reptiles of a region or time period.

Herpetology: The scientific study of amphibians and reptiles.

Herringbone pattern: Pigmentation pattern of bent vertical lines or chevrons that resemble the appearance of a fish's skeleton.

Hybridization: Reproduction between two different organisms, typically species, that results in the formation of offspring.

Hydroperiod: The period of time in which a wetland contains water.

Intergradation: Reproduction between morphologically distinguishable populations or subspecies.

Interorbital: Between the orbits or eyes.

Interorbital boss: A raised area between the orbits or eyes.

Intestinal coil: Coil of intestines of tadpoles. Visibility of this structure is used as a diagnostic character for taxonomic identification.

Introduced species: A species that has been transported by humans, either indirectly or purposely, outside of its native range. See **invasive species**.

Introgression: Movement of alleles from one species to another through hybridization, or mating of two species. Also called introgressive hybridization.

Invasive species: An introduced species that has become established and has spread, often causing detriment to local biotic communities.

Iridophore: Pigment cell containing reflective pigment, which imparts color to an organism.

Iris: The pigmented part of the eye.

Karst: An area or region characterized by irregular limestone or other carbonate bedrock in which erosion has produced numerous caves, sinkholes, fissures, and subterranean streams.

Keeled tail: Having a tail that tapers to a thin ridge on top; causing the tail to appear triangular in cross section.

Keratinized: Having deposits of keratin in the outer layer of the epithelium, such as hair, nails, scales, and feathers. In salamanders, keratinized structures are usually visible as rigid, dark-colored pads on the toe tips.

Labial teeth: One of several rows of keratinized teeth found on the upper and lower labia of the mouth of tadpoles.

Labium: Lip; plural labia.

Larva: The immature stage of amphibians, usually possessing gills and tail fins. Plural larvae.

Lateral line: Sensory system found on the head and sides of the body in some salamander larvae and adults that detects vibration caused by movement of water.

Lentic: Referring to nonflowing water, such as a lake or pond.

Life history: The history of changes undergone by an organism over its lifetime from conception to death.

Lineage: A group of individuals, species, or taxa related by a common ancestor.

Linnaean taxonomy: A hierarchical classification system based on the work *Systems of Nature* by Carolus Linneaus in 1758. Organisms are given standard Latin names that reflect the most recent and accepted evolutionary relationships.

Longitudinal: Referring to length or lengthwise.

Lotic: Referring to flowing water, such as streams, creeks, and rivers.

Marginal: Referring to the margin or edge, as in marginal papillae.

Melanistic: Possessing dark pigmentation due to the presence of melanin in the epithelium. Melanistic individuals are either aberrant individuals that are darker than normal members of a species or those that become more darkly pigmented with age.

Melanophore: Pigment cell containing the dark pigment melanin.

Mental gland: Gland on the chin of male salamanders that secretes chemicals used in courtship. Visible as raised patches of tissue, the shape of which occasionally allows discrimination between males of closely related species.

Mesic: Characterized by being moderately moist, as in a mesic habitat.

Metamorphosis: The transformation, often marked and rapid, of a larva into an adult.

Middorsal: Referring to the midline of the dorsum or back.

Mimicry: The resemblance of one organism to another or to an object in its environment, presumably for camouflage or reduced risk of predation.

Morphology: The study of the form and structure of an organism, especially external structure and form. Relating to the external characteristics of an organism.

Mottled: An indistinct pattern of spots or flecks of various sizes.

Nares: External nostril openings. Singular naris.

Nasolabial groove: A small channel extending from the nares to the upper lip, and occasionally out to the cirri of male salamanders; characteristic of the salamander family Plethodontidae.

Natural history: The study of the biology of species including their origins, evolution, behavior, and relationships with other species

Neotenic: An organism that reaches sexual maturity while retaining larval or juvenile characteristics.

Neurotoxin: A chemical that causes damage to nerves or nerve tissue, frequently similar in structure to neurotransmitters, which allows passage into and disruption of the nervous system.

Nocturnal: Active at night.

Nomenclature: A system of names that organizes organisms based on their relationships to one another.

Noxious: Irritating, painful, or otherwise harmful.

Nymph: The immature stage of certain insect groups that is often aquatic.

Obligate: A behavior or process that is not optional. Also used to imply that an organism is only able to survive in a specific habitat or environment. Contrast with **facultative**.

Olfaction: The sense of smell.

Ontogenetic: Describing changes in the traits or behaviors of an organism as it ages.

Oral disc: Referring to the lips surrounding the mouthparts of some tadpoles.

Order: Higher-level taxonomic group below the level of class but above the level of family, as in the order Caudata.

Ostracod: A type of tiny, aquatic crustacean often referred to as seed shrimp.

Ova: Undeveloped eggs; singular ovum.

Oviposit: To lay eggs or egg masses.

P-1, P-2, P-3 row: The first, second, and third posterior labial tooth rows in the mouth of a tadpole.

Paedomorphosis: Reaching sexual maturity in the larval stage without undergoing metamorphosis, as in some species of salamanders.

Papillae: Small, fleshy projections, as in the papillae surrounding the mouthparts of tadpoles.

Papillose: Having the characteristic of small protuberances or fleshy bumps or projections. Some salamander species are characterized by having papillose cloacal lips.

Parotoid gland: A poison gland located behind each eye on the head of some toads and salamanders.

Pectoral: Referring to the chest.

Perennial: Lasting or active throughout the year or multiple years.

Phreatic zone: Areas within underground caverns, aquifers, or interstices that are either underwater or saturated with water. The phreatic zone may change seasonally, depending on hydroperiods and seasonal changes in moisture levels.

Physiographic province: A landscape region characterized by unique geological history and physical attributes.

Physiography: The study of the physical features of the surface of the earth.

Physiology: The study of the mechanical, physical, and biochemical functions of organisms.

Pleistocene: Geologic time period from 1.7–0.1 million years before the present.

Polymorphism: Multiple color or body forms in a species or population.

Population: A group of organisms of the same species living within a continuous area.

Premaxillary: Referring to the most anterior bones in the vertebrate upper jaw.

Protuberance: A bulging or knoblike feature.

Rachises: The central shafts of the external gills, which bear the branching fimbriae.

Rain call: The daytime call of male frogs of a few species of unknown purpose often in response to rainfall.

Regenerated: The repair and replacement of lost structures, such as the tail or toes in salamanders.

Release call: A distress call in male frogs and toads emitted by a male that is being amplexed by another male.

Reticulum: A network design or pattern (reticulation) of color that results in a netlike patterning of an organism.

Riparian: Pertaining to the edges of aquatic habitats, such as stream banks and floodplains.

Road cruising: The act of searching for animals by driving slowly along roads. A productive way of finding amphibians, particularly at night after heavy rains.

Rugose: Exhibiting folds or wrinkles.

Second-order stream: See **stream order**.

Seep/seepage: Moist habitat typically on a slope characterized by water trickling or seeping from the ground.

Sexual dimorphism: Morphological characters that differ between males and females of the same species.

Siltation: The natural or anthropogenic process of sediment deposition in aquatic habitats.

Spade: An elongate, keratinized protuberance on the hell of spadefoots and true toads.

Spatulate: Flattened in appearance; shaped like a spatula.

Species: The least inclusive taxonomic level below the level of genus and consisting of a group of individuals capable of interbreeding that are reproductively isolated from other such groups. This is known as the biological species concept, though it should be noted that species are not natural categories and hence many other species concepts exist.

Spermatophore: A gelatinous, stalk-like mass containing a sperm cap deposited on the substrate by male salamanders during courtship.

Silviculture: The practice of tree farming.

Sphagnum: A type of loose moss found in moist, acidic habitats; also known as peat moss.

Spiracle: The tubular vent that exits the gill chamber of a tadpole.

Stream order: A classification system for streams and rivers, ranging from first to twelfth in order of size. First-order streams are the smallest and form the first tributaries; hence they have no other water flowing into them. First- through third-order streams are considered headwaters and usually consist of faster flowing, more highly oxygenated water that contains less silt than higher-order streams.

Submarginal: Near or adjacent to a margin, in reference to submarginal papillae on the oral disc of tadpoles.

Subspecies: A taxonomic subdivision of a species typically consisting of a group of populations with unique characteristics and occupying a definable geographic region but capable of interbreeding with other such races. Subspecies are named using a trinomial with a third name following the species bionomial, such as in the Big Mouth Cave Salamander, *Gyrinophilus palleucus necturoides*.

Substrate: The soil or material on or in which an organism lives.

Subterminal: Referring to the location of the mouth. A subterminal mouth is located underneath the head or below the anterior end of the head, as opposed to a terminal mouth, which occurs at the very anterior end of the head. A subterminal mouth is usually associated with bottom feeding.

SVL: Snout-vent length, measured from the tip of the snout to the posterior opening of the cloaca, usually on the ventral surface of the organism. A common measurement used to assess body size in amphibians.

Sympatric: Populations or species occurring within the same regions with overlapping ranges.

Tail musculature: The central part of the tail excluding the tail fins that contains the muscles in tadpoles, or salamander larvae.

Talus: An aggregation of rocks, particularly at the base of steep slopes or cliffs.

Taxonomy: The science of naming and classifying organisms.

Terrestrial: Living on the land.

Tetraploid: Possessing four sets of chromosomes in each body cell.

Third-order stream: See **stream order**.

TL: Total length, measured from the tip of the snout to the tip of the tail.

Toadlet: A recently metamorphosed toad, often still possessing a tail.

Transverse: Crossing from one side to another.

Tubercle: A small, usually round nodule found on the skin of amphibians.

Tympanum: The outer layer of skin covering the ear opening in frogs, visible as an opaque, occasionally slightly translucent patch behind the eyes.

Unpalatable: The opposite of tasty; not good to eat; possessing a foul taste or offensive chemical(s).

Urbanization: Referring to the growth of cities into surrounding rural areas.

Vent: The opening of the reproductive, urinary, and digestive systems located on the underside of an amphibian; also known as the cloaca.

Venter: The underside of an organism; opposite of dorsum.

Ventral: Referring to the underside of an organism.

Vermiculation: A wormlike pattern.

Vestigial: Degenerate or atrophied, usually referring to limbs. Limbs that have evolved to be reduced in size or function.

Vocal sac: Flexible membrane of skin of a male frog's throat that amplifies its call.

Vomerine: Referring to the vomer bone in the anterior roof of the mouth, as in vomerine teeth.

Voucher: A specimen collected from a particular area and housed in a museum that provides evidence of that species' occurrence in that area. Some museums allow photograph vouchers instead of physical vouchers, reducing the need to collect wild animals.

Wart: A cornified, raised protuberance on the skin.

Xeric: Characterized by being dry, as in a xeric habitat.

Zooplankton: Small, frequently microscopic animals that inhabit aquatic environments; might be composed of larvae of larger organisms or adult small organisms.

Recommended Readings, Organizations, and Websites

Amphibian Conservation and Monitoring

Collins, J. P., and M. L. Crump. 2009. Extinction in our times: global amphibian declines. Oxford Univ. Press, New York.

Dodd, C. K., Jr. 2009. Amphibian ecology and conservation: a handbook of techniques. Oxford Univ. Press, New York.

Green, D. M. 1997. Amphibians in decline: Canadian studies of a global problem. Herpetological Conservation 1. Society for the Study of Amphibians and Reptiles.

Heyer, W. R., M. A. Donnelly, R. W. McDiarmid, L. C. Hayek, and M. S. Foster, editors. 1994. Measuring and monitoring biological diversity: standard methods for amphibians. Smithsonian Institution Press, Washington, DC.

Kraus, F. 2009. Alien amphibians and reptiles: a scientific compendium and analysis. Invading Nature: Springer Series in Invasion Ecology. Springer, New York.

Lannoo, M. J., editor. 2005. Amphibian declines: the conservation status of United States species. Univ. of California Press, Los Angeles.

Lannoo, M. J. 2008. Malformed frogs: The collapse of aquatic ecosystems. Univ. of California Press, Los Angeles.

Semlitsch, R. D., editor. 2003. Amphibian conservation. Smithsonian Institution Press, Washington, DC.

Southeastern Amphibians

Barbour, T. 1971. Amphibians and reptiles of Kentucky. Univ. Press of Kentucky, Lexington.

Bartlett, R. D., and P. P. Bartlett. 2006. Guide and reference to the amphibians of eastern and central North America (north of Mexico). Univ. Press of Florida, Gainesville.

Beane, J. C., A. L. Braswell, J. C. Mitchell, and W. M. Palmer. 2010. Amphibians and reptiles of the Carolinas and Virginia. 2nd ed. Univ. of North Carolina Press, Chapel Hill.

Conant, R., and J. T. Collins. 1998. A field guide to reptiles and amphibians of eastern and central North America. 4th ed. Houghton Mifflin, New York.

Dodd, C. K., Jr. 2004. The amphibians of Great Smoky Mountains National Park. Univ. of Tennessee Press, Knoxville.

Dorcas, M. E., and W. Gibbons. 2008. Frogs and toads of the Southeast. Univ. of Georgia Press, Athens.

Dorcas, M. E., S. J. Price, J. C. Beane, and S. S. Cross. 2007. The frogs and toads of North Carolina. North Carolina Resources Commission, Raleigh, NC.

Dundee, H. A., D. A. Rossman, and E. C. Beckham. 1996. The amphibians and reptiles of Louisiana. Louisiana State Univ. Press, Baton Rouge.

Huheey, J. E., and A. Stupka. 1967. Amphibians and reptiles of Great Smoky Mountains National Park. Univ. of Tennessee Press, Knoxville.

Jensen, J. B., C. D. Camp, W. Gibbons, and M. J. Elliot. 2008. Amphibians and reptiles of Georgia. Univ. of Georgia Press, Athens.

Johnson, T. R. 2000. Amphibians and reptiles of Missouri. Rev. ed. Missouri Department of Conservation, Jefferson City.

Martof, B. S., W. M. Palmer, J. R. Bailey, J. R. Harrison III, and J. Dermid. 1989. Amphibians and reptiles of the Carolinas and Virginia. Univ. of North Carolina Press, Chapel Hill.

Mitchell, J. C., and W. Gibbons. 2010. Salamanders of the Southeast. Univ. of Georgia Press, Athens.

Mitchell, J. C., and K. K. Reay. 1999. Atlas of amphibians and reptiles in Virginia. Virginia Department of Game and Inland Fisheries, Richmond.

Mount, R. H. 1975. The reptiles and amphibians of Alabama. Alabama Agricultural Experiment Station, Auburn Univ., Auburn.

Redmond, W. H., A. C. Echternacht, and A. F. Scott. 1990. Annotated checklist and bibliography of amphibians and reptiles of Tennessee (1835–1989). Center for Field Biology, Austin Peay State Univ., Clarksville, TN.

Redmond, W. H., and A. F. Scott. 1996. Atlas of amphibians in Tennessee. Center for Field Biology, Austin Peay State Univ., Clarksville, TN, and references therein.

Scott, A. F., and W. H. Redmond. 2002. Updated checklist of Tennessee's amphibians and reptiles with an annotated bibliography covering primarily years 1990 through 2001. Center for Field Biology, Austin Peay State Univ., Clarksville, TN.

Tilley, S. G., and J. E. Huheey. 2001. Reptiles and amphibians of the Smokies. Great Smoky Mountains Natural History Association, Gatlinburg, TN.

Trauth, S. E., H. W. Robinson, and M. V. Plummer. 2004. The amphibians and reptiles of Arkansas. Univ. of Arkansas Press, Fayetteville.

Amphibian Taxonomy

Collins, J. T., and T. W. Taggart. 2009. Standard common and current scientific names for North American amphibians, turtles, reptiles, and crocodilians. 6th ed. Publication of the Center for North American Herpetology, Lawrence, KS.

Crother, B. I., editor. 2008. Scientific and standard English names of amphibians and reptiles of North America, north of Mexico, pp. 1–84. Herpetological Circular 37. Society for the Study of Amphibians and Reptiles.

Frost, D. R. 2009. Amphibian species of the world: an online reference. Version 5.3 (12 February 2009). Electronic database accessible at http://research.amnh.org/herpetology/amphibia/. American Museum of Natural History, New York.

Powell, R., J. T. Collins, and E. D. Hooper. 1998. A key to amphibians and reptiles of the continental United States and Canada. Univ. Press of Kansas, Lawrence.

Amphibian Biology and Natural History

Beebe, T. J. C. 1996. Ecology and conservation of amphibians. Chapman and Hall, London.

Carroll, R. 2009. The rise of amphibians: 365 million years of evolution. Johns Hopkins Univ. Press, Baltimore.

Duellman, W. E. 1999. Patterns of distribution of amphibians: a global perspective. Johns Hopkins Univ. Press, Baltimore.

Duellman, W. E., and L. Trueb. 1994. Biology of amphibians. Johns Hopkins Univ. Press, Baltimore.

Elliott, L., C. Gerhardt, and C. Davidson. 2009. The frogs and toads of North America: a comprehensive guide to their identification, behavior, and calls. Mariner Books, New York.

Hillman, S. S., P. C. Withers, R. C. Drewes, and S. D. Hillyard. 2009. Ecological and environmental physiology of amphibians. Oxford Univ. Press, New York.

McDiarmid, R. W., and R. Altig, editors. 2000. Tadpoles: the biology of Anuran larvae. Univ. of Chicago Press, Chicago.

Mitchell, J. C., R. E. Jung Brown, and B. Bartholomew. 2008. Urban herpetology. Herpetological Conservation 3. Society for the Study of Amphibians and Reptiles.

Petranka, J. W. 1998. Salamanders of the United States and Canada. Smithsonian Institution Press, Washington, DC.

Pough, F. H., R. M. Andrews, J. E. Cadle, M. L. Crump, A. H. Savitsky, and K. D. Wells. 2004. Herpetology. 3rd ed. Pearson Education, Upper Saddle River, NJ.

Ryan, M. J., editor. 2001. Anuran communication. Smithsonian Institution Press, Washington, DC.

Stebbins, R. C., and N. W. Cohen. 1995. A natural history of Amphibians. Princeton Univ. Press, Princeton, NJ.

Vitt, L. J., and J. P. Caldwell. 2008. Herpetology: an introductory biology of amphibians and reptiles. 3rd ed. Academic Press, San Diego.

Wells, K. D. 2007. The ecology and behavior of amphibians. Univ. of Chicago Press, Chicago.

Videos

BBC Warner. 2007. Planet Earth: The Complete BBC Series.

BBC Warner. 2008. Life in Cold Blood.

BBC Warner. 2009. Life: The Complete BBC Series.

Audio CDs and Frog Calls

Bogert, C. 1998. Sounds of North American frogs. Smithsonian Folkways.

Dorcas, M. E., S. J. Price, J. C. Beane, and S. S. Cross. 2007. The frogs and toads of North Carolina. North Carolina Resources Commission, Raleigh. (Audio CD included.)

Elliott, L. 2004. The calls of frogs and toads. Stackpole Books,. Mechanicsburg, PA. (Audio CD included.)

Elliott, L., C. Gerhardt, and C. Davidson. 2009. The frogs and toads of North America: a comprehensive guide to their identification, behavior, and calls. Mariner Books, New York. (Audio CD included.)

Gibson, D. Frog song. Solitudes.

Jensen, J. B., C. D. Camp, W. Gibbons, and M. J. Elliot. 2008. Amphibians and reptiles of Georgia. Audio recordings available from: http://www.ugapress.org/AmphibsAndReptiles/.

Academic Journals

Catalogue of American Amphibians and Reptiles (Society for the Study of Amphibians and Reptiles)

Herpetologica (Herpetologist's League)

Herpetological Conservation and Biology (http://www.herpconbio.org)

Herpetological Monographs (Herpetologist's League)

Herpetological Review (Society for the Study of Amphibians and Reptiles)

Journal of Herpetology (Society for the Study of Amphibians and Reptiles)

Southeastern Naturalist

Regional and Professional Societies

American Society of Ichthyologists and Herpetologists (http://www.asih.org)

Georgia Herpetological Society

Herpetologist's League (http://herpetologistsleague.com)

Kentuckiana Herpetological Society

Kentucky Herpetological Society

Missouri Herpetological Association (http://www.moherp.org)

North Carolina Herpetological Society (http://www.ncherps.org)

Partners in Amphibian and Reptile Conservation (http://www.parcplace.org)

Society for the Study of Amphibians and Reptiles (http://www.ssarherps.org)

Southeast Partners in Amphibian and Reptile Conservation (http://www.separc.org)

Tennessee Herpetological Society (http://www.tnherpsociety.org)

Virginia Herpetological Society (http://fwie.fw.vt.edu/VHS/)

Other Relevant Websites

Amphibian Research and Monitoring Initiative (http://www.armi.usgs.gov)

Amphibian Specialist Group (http://www.amphibians.org)

AmphibiaWeb (http://www.amphibiaweb.org)

Center for North American Herpetology (http://www.cnah.org)

Facebook: The Amphibians of Tennessee Fan Page (http://www.facebook.com/#!/pages/The-Amphibians-of-Tennessee/285681405933?ref=mf)

HerpLit (http://www.herplit.com)

HerpNET (http://www.herpnet.org)

North American Amphibian Monitoring Program (http://www.pwrc.usgs.gov/naamp/)

Tennessee Amphibians and Reptiles (http://www.herpetology.us/tnherps)

Tennessee Atlas of Amphibians (http://www.apsu.edu/amatlas/)

Tennessee Wildlife Resources Agency (http://www.state.tn.us/twra/)

Selected References

AmphibiaWeb: Information on amphibian biology and conservation [Internet application]. 2009. AmphibiaWeb, Berkeley, CA. Available from: http://amphibiaweb.org/. (Accessed: 2008–2009.)

Anderson, J. A., and S. G. Tilley. 2003. Systematics of the *Desmognathus ochrophaeus* complex in the Cumberland Plateau of Tennessee. Herpetol. Monogr. 17:75–110.

Ashton, T. E. 1966. A revised annotated checklist of the order Caudata (Amphibia) of Davidson County, Tennessee. J. Tenn. Acad. Sci. 41:106–111.

Bailey, L. L., T. R. Simmons, and K. H. Pollock. 2004. Estimating site occupancy and species detection probability parameters for terrestrial salamanders. Ecol. Appl. 14:692–702.

Barbour, R. W. 1950. A new subspecies of the salamander *Desmognathus fuscus*. Copeia 1950:277–278.

Beltz, E. 2006. Scientific and common names of the reptiles and amphibians of North America—explained [Internet document]. Available from: http://ebeltz.net/herps/etymain.html. (Accessed: 2008–2009.)

Bishop, S. C. 1943. Handbook of salamanders: the salamanders of the United States, of Canada, and of lower California. Comstock, Ithaca, NY. 555 pp.

Bogart, J. P., and A. O. Wasserman. 1972. Diploid-polyploid cryptic species pairs: a possible clue to evolution by polyploidization in anuran amphibians. Cytogenetics 11:7–24.

Brandon, R. A. 1962. A systematic study of the salamander genus *Gyrinophilus*. Ph.D. diss., Univ. of Illinois, Urbana. 129 pp.

Brandon, R. A., J. Jacobs, A. Wynn, and D. M. Sever. 1986. A naturally metamorphosed Tennessee cave salamander (*Gyrinophilus palleucus*). J. Tenn. Acad. Sci. 61:1–2.

Brode, W. E. 1969. A systematic study of the genus *Necturus* Rafinesque. Ph.D. diss., Univ. of Southern Mississippi, Hattiesburg. 137 pp.

Bruce, R. C. 1968. Life history studies of the salamanders of the genus *Plethodon* (Caudata: Plethodontidae). Ph.D. diss., Duke Univ., Durham, NC. 222 pp.

Burton, E. C., M. J. Gray, A. C. Schmutzer, and D. L. Miller. 2009. Differential responses of post-metamorphic amphibians to cattle grazing in wetlands. J. Wildlife Manag. 73:269–277.

Bushnell, R. J., E. P. Bushnell, and M. V. Parker. 1939. A chromosome study of five members of the family Hylidae. J. Tenn. Acad. Sci. 14:209–215.

Caldwell, R. S., and S. E. Trauth. 1979. Use of the toe pad and tooth morphology in differentiating three species of *Desmognathus* (Amphibia, Urodela, Plethodontidae). J. Herpetology 13:491–497.

Carlin, J. L. 1997. Genetic and morphological differentiation between *Eurycea longicauda longicauda* and *E. guttolineata* (Caudata: Plethodontidae). Herpetologica 53:206–217.

Cash, M. N., and J. P. Bogart. 1978. Cytological differentiation of the diploid-tetraploid species pair of North American treefrogs (Amphibia: Anura: Hylidae). J. Herpetology 12:555–558.

Collins, J. T. 1991a. Amphibians and reptiles in the upper Mississippi River Valley: systematic and distributional problems. J. Tenn. Acad. Sci. 66:149–152.

Collins, J. T. 1991b. Viewpoint: a new taxonomic arrangement for some North American amphibians and reptiles. Herpetol. Rev. 22:42–43.

Conant, R., and J. T. Collins. 1998. A field guide to reptiles and amphibians of eastern and central North America. Houghton Mifflin, New York.

Corser, J. D. 2008. The Cumberland Plateau disjunct paradox and the biogeography and conservation of pond-breeding amphibians. Am. Mid. Nat. 159:498–503.

Crespi, E. J., L. J. Rissler, and R. A. Browne. 2003. Testing Pleistocene refugia theory: phylogeographical analysis of *Desmognathus wrighti,* a high-elevation salamander in the southern Appalachians. Mol. Ecol. 12:969–984.

Crespi, E. J., R. A. Browne, and L. J. Rissler. 2010. Taxonomic revision of *Desmognathus wrighti* (Caudata: Plethodontidae). Herpetologica 66:283–295.

Cupp, P. V., and D. T. Towles. 1983. A new variant of *Plethodon wehrlei* in Kentucky and West Virginia. Trans. Kentucky Acad. Sci. 44:157–158.

Davenport, J. M., and A. F. Scott. 2009. Amphibians and reptiles of Fort Donelson National Battlefield, Stewart County, Tennessee. J. Tenn. Acad. Sci. 84:83–89.

Dodd, C. K. 2003. Monitoring amphibians in the Great Smoky Mountains National Park. U.S. Geological Survey Circular 1258:1–117.

Dodd, C. K. 2004. The amphibians of Great Smoky Mountains National Park. Univ. of Tennessee Press, Knoxville.

Dodd, C. K., and R. M. Dorazio. 2004. Using counts to simultaneously estimate abundance and detection probabilities in a salamander community. Herpetologica 60:468–478.

Dunn, E. R. 1927a. *Hyla phaeocrypta* in Tennessee. Copeia 1927:19.

Dunn, E. R. 1927b. A new mountain race of *Desmognathus*. Copeia 1927:84–86.

Etnier, D. A., and W. C. Starnes. 1993. The fishes of Tennessee. Univ. of Tennessee Press, Knoxville.

Fitzpatrick, B. M., and H. B. Shaffer. 2007. Hybrid vigor between native and introduced salamanders raises new challenges for conservation. Proc. Nat. Acad. Sci., USA 104:15793–15798.

Fitzpatrick, B. M., K. Shook, and R. Izally . 2009. Frequency-dependant selection by wild birds promotes polymorphism in model salamanders. BMC Ecology 9:12.

Freak, M. J., and E. D. Lindquist. 2008. Geographic pattern analysis of pesticide exposure in salamander populations in the Great Smoky Mountains National Park. Herpetological Cons. Biol. 3:231–238.

Frost, D. R., T. Grant, J. Faivovich, R. H. Bain, A. Haas, C. F. B. Haddad, R. O. De Sá, A. Channing, M. Wilkinson, S. C. Donnellan, C. J. Raxworthy, J. A. Campbell, B. L. Blotto, P. Moler, R. C. Drewes, R. A. Nussbaum, J. D. Lynch, D. M. Green, and W. C. Wheeler. 2006. The amphibian tree of life. Bull. American Mus. Nat. Hist. 297:1–370.

Gentry, G. 1937. A preliminary survey of the Amphibia of Tennessee. M.S. thesis, George Peabody College for Teachers, Nashville, TN. 107 pp.

Gentry, G. 1955–1956. An annotated check list of the amphibians and reptiles of Tennessee. J. Tenn. Acad. Sci. 30:168–176; 31:242–251.

Gentry, G., R. M. Sinclair, W. Hon, and B. Ferguson. 1965. Amphibians and reptiles of Tennessee. Tenn. Game and Fish Comm., Nashville. 28 pp.

Griffith, G. E., J. M. Omernik, and S. H. Azevedo. 1998. Ecoregions of Tennessee. (Map poster). U.S. Geological Survey, Reston, VA.

Hairston, N. G. 1993. On the validity of the name *teyahalee* as applied to a member of the *Plethodon glutinosus* complex (Caudata: Plethodontidae): a new name. Brimleyana 18:65–69.

Heineke, T. E., and J. E. Heineke. 1984. New distribution record for the barking treefrog, *Hyla gratiosa* LeConte, in western Tennessee. J. Tenn. Acad. Sci. 59:57.

Highton, R. 1962. Revision of North American salamanders of the genus *Plethodon*. Bull. Florida State Mus. Biol. Sci. 6:235–367.

Highton, R. 1971. Distributional interactions among eastern North American salamanders of the genus *Plethodon*. In: P. C. Holt (ed). Distributional history of the biota of the southern Appalachians. Part III. Vertebrates. Vir. Polytechnic Inst. and State Univ. Res. Div. Monogr. 4:139–188.

Highton, R. 1983. A new species of woodland salamander of the *Plethodon glutinosus* group from the southern Appalachian Mountains. Brimleyana 9:1–20.

Highton, R. 1995. Speciation in eastern North American salamanders of the genus *Plethodon*. Annu. Rev. Ecol. Syst. 26:579–600.

Highton, R. 1997. Geographic protein variation and speciation in the *Plethodon dorsalis* complex. Herpetologica 53:345–356.

Highton, R., and S. A. Henry. 1970. Evolutionary interactions between species of North American salamanders of the genus *Plethodon*. Part 1. Genetic and ecological relationships of *Plethodon jordani* and *Plethodon glutinosus* in the southern Appalachian mountains. Evol. Biol. 4: 211-241.

Highton, R., and J. R. MacGregor. 1983. *Plethodon kentucki* Mittleman: a valid species of Cumberland Plateau woodland salamander. Herpetologica 39:189–200.

Highton, R., G. C. Maha, and R. L. Maxon. 1989. Biochemical evolution in the slimy salamanders of the *Plethodon glutinosus* complex in the eastern United States. Ill. Biol. Monogr. 57:1–153.

Highton, R., and R. B. Peabody. 2000. Geographic protein variation and speciation in salamanders of the *Plethodon jordani* and *Plethodon glutinosus* complexes in the southern Appalachian Mountains with the description of four new species. In: R. C. Bruce, R. G. Jaeger, and L. D. Houck, editors, pp. 31–93. The Biology of Plethodontid Salamanders. Kluwer Academic/Plenum Publishers, New York.

Highton, R., and T. P. Webster. 1976. Geographic protein variation and divergence in populations of the salamander *Plethodon cinereus*. Evolution 30:33–45.

Huheey, J. E. 1966. The desmognathine salamanders of the Great Smoky Mountains National Park. J. Ohio Herpetol. Soc. 5:63–72.

Huheey, J. E., and A. Stupka. 1967. Amphibians and reptiles of Great Smoky Mountains National Park. Univ. of Tennessee Press, Knoxville. 99 pp.

Hyde, E. J., and T. R. Simmons. 2001. Sampling plethodontid salamanders: sources of variability. J. Wildlife Manag. 65:624–632.

Jacobs, J. F. 1987. A preliminary investigation of geographic genetic variation and systematics of the two-lined salamander, *Eurycea bislineata* (Green). Herpetologica 43:423–446.

Johnson, R. M. 1958. A biogeographic study of the herpetofauna of eastern Tennessee. Ph.D. diss., Univ. of Florida, Gainesville. 221 pp.

Jones, R. L. 1982a. Distribution and ecology of the seepage salamander *Desmognathus aeneus* Brown and Bishop (Amphibia: Plethodontidae), in Tennessee. Brimleyana 7:95–100.

Jones, R. L. 1982b. Ecology and reproductive biology of two species of the *Desmognathus fuscus* complex (Amphibia: Plethodontidae) in the southern Appalachians. Ph.D. diss., Univ. of Tennessee, Knoxville. 124 pp.

Juterbock, J. E. 1975. The status of *Desmognathus welteri* Barbour (Caudata: Plethodontidae) and a comparison with two sympatric cogeners. M.S. thesis, Ohio State Univ., Columbus. 169 pp.

Juterbock, J. E. 1978. Sexual dimorphism and maturity characteristics of three species of *Desmognathus* (Amphibia, Urodela, Plethodontidae). J. Herpetology 12:217–230.

Juterbock, J. E. 1984. Evidence for the recognition of specific status for *Desmognathus welteri*. J. Herpetology 18:240–255.

King, W. 1936. A new salamander (*Desmognathus*) from the southern Appalachians. Herpetologica 1:58–60.

King, W. 1939. A survey of the herpetology of Great Smoky Mountains National Park (Tennessee). Amer. Midl. Nat. 21:531–582.

Kozak, K. H., A. Larson, R. M. Bonett, and L. J. Harmon. 2005. Phylogenetic analysis of ecomorphological divergence, community structure, and diversification rates in dusky salamanders (Plethodontidae: *Desmognathus*). Evolution 59:2000–2016.

Kozak, K. H., R. W. Mendyk, and J. J. Wiens. 2009. Can parallel diversification occur in sympatry? Repeated patterns of body-size evolution in coexisting clades of North American salamanders. Evolution 63:1769–1784.

Kozak, K. H., D. W. Weisrock, and A. Larson. 2006. Rapid lineage accumulation in a non-adaptive radiation: phylogenetic analysis of diversification rates in eastern North American woodland salamanders (Plethodontidae: *Plethodon*). Proc. R. Soc. B 273:539–546.

Kozak, K. H., and J. J. Wiens. 2006. Does niche conservatism promote speciation? A case study in North American salamanders. Evolution 60:2604–2621.

Kozak, K. H., R. A. Blaine, and A. Larson. 2006. Gene lineages and eastern North American palaeodrainage basins: phylogeography and speciation in salamanders of the *Eurycea bislineata* species complex. Mol. Ecol. 15:191–207.

Lannoo, M. J., editor. 2005. Amphibian declines: the conservation status of United States species. Univ. of California Press, Los Angeles, and references therein.

Lemmon, E. M., A. R. Lemmon, J. T. Collins, J. A. Lee-Yaw, and D. C. Cannatella. 2007. Phylogeny-based delimitation of species boundaries and contact zones in the trilling chorus frogs (*Pseudacris*). Mol. Phylogen. Evol. 44:1068–1082.

Maldonado-Koerdell, M., and I. L. Firschein. 1947. Notes on the ranges of some North American salamanders. Copeia 1947:140.

Martof, B. S., and F. L. Rose. 1963. Geographic variation in southern populations of *Desmognathus ochrophaeus.* Am. Midl. Nat. 69:376–425.

Mathews, R. C., and A. C. Echternacht. 1984. Herpetofauna of the spruce-fir ecosystem in the southern Appalachian Mountain regions, with emphasis on the Great Smoky Mountains National Park. In: P. S. White, editor, pp. 155–167. The southern Appalachian spruce-fir ecosystem. Natl. Park Service. Research/Resources Mgmt. Rep. SER-71.

McAllister, C. T., C. R. Bursey, M. L. Niemiller, and B. T. Miller. 2007. A noteworthy infection of *Clinostomum complanatum* (Digenea: Clinostomidae) in a cave salamander, *Eurycea lucifiga* (Caudata: Plethodontidae), from north central Tennessee. Texas J. Sci. 59:321–326.

Mead, L. S., S. G. Tilley, and L. A. Katz. 2001. Genetic structure of the Blue Ridge dusky salamander (*Desmognathus orestes*): inferences from allozymes, mitochondrial DNA, and behavior. Evolution 55:2287–2302.

Miller, B. T., and J. W. Lamb. 2004. A Tennessee conundrum: the gopher frog at Arnold Air Force Base. J. Tenn. Acad. Sci.79:8–12.

Miller, B. T., J. W. Lamb, and J. L. Miller. 2005. The herpetofauna of Arnold Air Force Base in the Barrens of Tennessee. Southeastern Nat. 4:51–62.

Miller, B. T., and J. L. Miller. 1998. Gill structure in embryonic and hatchling zig-zag salamanders, *Plethodon dorsalis.* Herpetol. Nat. Hist. 6:51–54.

Miller, B. T., and J. L. Miller. 2005. Prevalence of physical abnormalities in eastern hellbender (*Cryptobranchus alleganiensis alleganiensis*) populations of Middle Tennessee. Southeastern Nat. 4:513–520.

Miller, B. T., and M. L. Niemiller. 2008. Distribution and relative abundance of Tennessee cave salamanders (*Gyrinophilous palleucus* and *Gyrinophilous gulolineatus*) with an emphasis on Tennessee populations. Herpetol. Conserv. Bio. 3:1–20.

Miller, B. T., M. L. Niemiller, and R. G. Reynolds. 2008. Observations on egg-laying behavior and interactions among attending female red salamanders (*Pseudotriton ruber*) with comments on the use of caves by this species. Herpetol. Conserv. Bio. 3:203–210.

Miller, D. L., M. J. Gray, S. Rajeev., A. C. Schmutzer, E. C. Burton, A. Merrill, and C. A. Baldwin. 2009. Pathologic findings in larval and juvenile anurans inhabiting farm ponds in Tennessee, USA. J. Wildlife Diseases 45:314–324.

Mitchell, J. C., T. K. Pauley, D. I. Withers, P. V. Cupp Jr., A. L. Braswell, B. T. Miller, S. M. Roble, and C. S. Hobson. 1999. Conservation status of the southern Appalachian herpetofauna. Virginia J. Sci. 50:1–36.

Moriarty, J. J., and A. M. Bauer. 2000. State and provincial amphibian and reptile publications for the United States and Canada. Herpetological Circular 28. Society for the Study of Amphibians and Reptiles.

Mynatt, M., and B. T. Miller. 2002. Feeding habits of seepage-dwelling dusky salamanders (*Desmognathus fuscus*) of Short Mountain, Cannon County, Tennessee. J. Tenn. Acad. Sci. 77:88–90.

Nicholls, J. C. 1949. A new salamander of the genus *Desmognathus* from East Tennessee. J. Tenn. Acad. Sci. 24:127–134.

Niemiller, M. L. 2005. The herpetofauna of the upper Duck River watershed in Coffee County, Tennessee. J. Tenn. Acad. Sci. 80:6–12.

Niemiller M. L., B. M. Glorioso, C. Nicholas, J. Phillips, J. Rader, E. Reed, K. L. Sykes, J. Todd, G. R. Wyckoff, E. L. Young, and B. T. Miller. 2006. Status and distribution of the streamside salamander (*Ambystoma barbouri*) in Middle Tennessee. Amer. Midl. Nat. 156:393–399.

Niemiller, M. L., B. M. Glorioso, C. Nicholas, J. Phillips, J. Rader, E. Reed, K. L. Sykes, J. Todd, G. R. Wyckoff, E. L. Young, and B. T. Miller. 2009. Notes on the reproduction of the streamside salamander, *Ambystoma barbouri*, from Rutherford County, Tennessee. Southeastern Nat. 8:37–44.

Niemiller, M. L., B. M. Fitzpatrick, and B. T. Miller. 2008. Recent divergence with gene flow in Tennessee cave salamanders (Plethodontidae: *Gyrinophilus*) inferred from gene genealogies. Mol. Ecol. 17:2258–2275.

Niemiller, M. L., D. Fenolio, G. O. Graening, and B. T. Miller. 2009. Observations on oviposition and reproduction of the cave salamander, *Eurycea lucifuga* (Caudata: Plethodontidae), from Arkansas and Tennessee. Speleobiology Notes 1:17–19.

Niemiller, M. L., and B. T. Miller. 2005. Common salamanders of Tennessee caves. Tenn. Caver 2:12–18.

Niemiller, M. L., and B. T. Miller. 2007. Subterranean reproduction of the southern two-lined salamander (*Eurycea cirrigera*) from Short Mountain, Tennessee. Herpetol. Conserv. Bio. 2:106–112.

Niemiller, M. L., and B. T. Miller. 2009. A survey of the cave-associated amphibians of the eastern United States with an emphasis on salamanders. Proc. 15th Int. Cong. Speleol., Kerrville, Texas 15:249–256.

Niemiller, M. L., B. T. Miller, and B. M. Fitzpatrick. 2009. Systematics and evolutionary history of subterranean *Gyrinophilus* salamanders. Proc. 15th Int. Cong. Speleol., Kerrville, Texas 15:242–248.

Niemiller, M. L., R. G. Reynolds, B. M. Glorioso, J. Spiess, and B. T. Miller. 2011. Herpetofauna of the cedar glades and adjacent habitats of the inner central basin of middle Tennessee. Herpetol. Cons. Biol. 6: 135–149.

Norton, V. M., and M. J. Harvey. 1975. Herpetofauna of Hardeman County, Tennessee. J. Tenn. Acad. Sci. 50:131–136.

Parker, M. V. 1937. Some amphibians and reptiles from Reelfoot Lake. J. Tenn. Acad. Sci. 12:60–86.

Parker, M. V. 1939. The amphibians and reptiles of Reelfoot Lake and vicinity, with a key for the separation of species and subspecies. J. Tenn. Acad. Sci. 14:72–101.

Parker, M. V. 1948. A contribution to the herpetology of western Tennessee. J. Tenn. Acad. Sci. 23:20–30.

Petranka, J. W. 1982. Geographic variation in the mode of reproduction and larval characteristics of the small-mouthed salamander (*Ambystoma texanum*) in the east-central United States. Herpetologica 38:475–485.

Petranka, J. W. 1998. Salamanders of the United States and Canada. Smithsonian Institution Press, Washington, DC, and references therein.

Petranka, J. W., C. K. Smith, and A. F. Scott. 2004. Identifying the minimal demographic unit for monitoring pond-breeding amphibians. Ecol. Appl. 14:1065–1078.

Platz, J. E., and D. C. Forester. 1988. Geographic variation in mating call among the four subspecies of the chorus frog: *Pseudacris triseriata* (Wied). Copeia 1988:1062–1066.

Pritts, G. R. 1995. Identification and distribution of the gray treefrog complex (*Hyla chrysoscelis/Hyla versicolor*) in the Central Basin of Middle Tennessee. M.S. thesis, Middle Tennessee State Univ., Murfreesboro. 50 pp.

Pritts, G., and B. T. Miller. 2001. Identification of gray treefrog populations in Middle Tennessee: chromosome counts from squashed tadpole tail tips. J. Tenn. Acad. Sci. 76:65–67.

Redmond, W. H. 1980. Notes on the distribution and ecology of the Black Mountain dusky salamander *Desmognathus welteri* Barbour (Amphibia: Plethodontidae) in Tennessee. Brimleyana 4:123–131.

Redmond, W. H. 1985. A biogeographic study of amphibians in Tennessee. Ph.D. diss., Univ. of Tennessee, Knoxville. 290 pp.

Redmond, W. H. 1991. Biogeography of amphibians in Tennessee. J. Tenn. Acad. Sci. 66:153–160.

Redmond, W. H., A. C. Echternacht, and A. F. Scott. 1990. Annotated checklist and bibliography of amphibians and reptiles of Tennessee (1835–1989). Misc. Publ. Center for Field Biol., Austin Peay State Univ., Clarksville, TN. No. 4. 173 pp.

Redmond, W. H., and A. F. Scott. 1996. Atlas of amphibians in Tennessee. Center for Field Biology, Austin Peay State Univ., Clarksville, TN, and references therein.

Redmond, W. H., A. F. Scott, and D. Roberts. 1982. Comments on the distribution of *Ambystoma talpoideum* (Holbrook) in Tennessee. Herpetol. Rev. 13:83–85.

Reynolds, R. G., M. L. Niemiller, and S. Pasachnik. 2011. Distribution and range extension of the Pigmy Salamander (*Desmognathus wrighti*) in Tennessee. J. Tenn. Acad. Sci. 86: 53–55.

Rhoads, S. N. 1895. Contributions to the zoology of Tennessee. No. 1, reptiles and amphibians. Proc. Acad. Nat. Sci. Philadelphia 47:376–407.

Ritke, M. E., and M. L. Beck. 1991. An interspecific satellite pair association between *Hyla chrysoscelis* and *Hyla versicolor*. Herpetol. Rev. 22:49–51.

Rose, F. L., and F. M. Bush. 1963. A new species of *Eurycea* (Amphibia: Caudata) from the southeastern United States. Tulane Stud. in Zool. 10:121–128.

Rossman, D. A. 1958. The treefrog, *Hyla gratiosa* in Tennessee. Herpetologica 14:40.

Schmutzer, A. C., M. J. Gray, E. C. Burton, and D. L. Miller. 2008. Impacts of cattle on amphibian larvae and the aquatic environment. Freshwater Biol. 53:2613–2625.

Scott, A. F. 1991. The history and literature of Tennessee herpetology. J. Tenn. Acad. Sci. 66:145–148.

Scott, A. F., and D. F. Harker. 1968. First records of the barking treefrog, *Hyla gratiosa* LeConte, from Tennessee. Herpetologica 24:82–83.

Scott, A. F., B. T. Miller, M. Brown, and J. W. Petranka. 1997. Geographic distribution. *Ambystoma barbouri*. Herpetol. Rev. 28:155.

Scott, A. F., and W. H. Redmond. 2002. Updated checklist of Tennessee's amphibians and reptiles with an annotated bibliography covering primarily years 1990–2001. Center for Field Biology, Austin Peay State Univ., Clarksville, TN.

Scott, A. F., and D. H. Snyder. 1968. The amphibians and reptiles of Montgomery County, Tennessee. J. Tenn. Acad. Sci. 43:79–84.

Sever, D. M. 1983b. Observations on the distribution and reproduction of the salamander *Eurycea junaluska* in Tennessee. J. Tenn. Acad. Sci. 58:48–50.

Simmons, D. D. 1976. A naturally metamorphosed *Gyrinophilus palleucus* (Amphibia: Urodela: Plethodontidae). J. Herpetology 10:255–257.

Sinclair, R. M. 1965. Variation in the cave salamander, *Eurycea lucifuga* in Middle Tennessee. J. Ohio Herpetol. Soc. 5:27–28.

Snyder, D. H. 1972. Amphibians and reptiles of Land Between the Lakes. Tennessee Valley Authority, Golden Pond, KY. 90 pp.

Stevenson, H. M. 1959. Some altitude records of reptiles and amphibians. Herpetologica 15:118.

Taylor, M. K. 1938. The distribution of Amphibia in Knox County, Tennessee. M.S. thesis, Univ. of Tennessee, Knoxville. 52 pp.

Thurow, G. R. 1963. Taxonomic and ecological notes on the salamander, *Plethodon welleri*. Univ. Kansas Sci. Bull. 44:87–108.

Tilley, S. G. 1981. A new species of *Desmognathus* (Amphibia: Caudata: Plethodontidae) from the southern Appalachian Mountains. Occ. Papers, Mus. of Zool., Univ. of Mich. No. 695. 23 pp.

Tilley, S. G. 1988. Hybridization between two species of *Desmognathus* (Amphibia: Caudata: Plethodontidae) in the Great Smoky Mountains. Herpetol. Monogr. 2:27–39.

Tilley, S. G., and J. R. Harrison. 1969. Notes on the distribution of the pygmy salamander, *Desmognathus wrighti* King. Herpetologica 25:178–180.

Tilley, S. G., R. B. Merritt, B. Wu, and R. Highton. 1978. Genetic differentiation in salamanders of the *Desmognathus ochrophaeus* complex (Plethodontidae). Evolution 32:93–115.

Tilley, S. G., and M. J. Mahoney. 1996. Patterns of genetic differentiation in salamanders of the *Desmognathus ochrophaeus* complex (Amphibia: Plethodontidae). Herpetol. Monogr. 10:1–42.

Timpe, E. K., S. P. Graham, and R. M. Bonett. 2009. Phylogeography of the brownback salamander reveals patterns of local endemism in southern Appalachian springs. Mol. Phylogen. Evol. 52:368–376.

Titus, T. A., and A. Larson. 1996. Molecular phylogenetics of desmognathine salamanders (Caudata: Plethodontidae): a reevaluation of evolution in ecology, life history, and morphology. Syst. Biol. 45:451–472.

Todd-Thompson, M., D. L. Miller, P. E. Super, and M. J. Gray. 2009. Chytridiomycosis-associated mortality in *Rana palustris* collected in Great Smoky Mountains National Park, Tennessee, USA. Herpetological Review 40:321–323.

Van Norman, D. E., and A. F. Scott. 1987. The distribution and breeding habitat of the barking treefrog, *Hyla gratiosa* LeConte, in south-central Kentucky and north-central Tennessee. J. Tenn. Acad. Sci. 62:7–11.

Wallace, J. M. 1975. Biochemical genetics of *Eurycea bislineata* and *Eurycea aquatica* (Amphibia: Plethodontidae) in Davidson County, Tennessee. M.S. thesis, Austin Peay State Univ., Clarksville, TN. 40 pp.

Weisrock, D. W., K. H. Kozak, and A. Larson. 2005. Phylogeographic analysis of mitochondrial gene flow and introgression in the salamander, *Plethodon shermani*. Mol. Ecol. 14:1457–1472.

Weller, W. H. 1931. A preliminary list of the salamanders of the Great Smoky Mountains of North Carolina and Tennessee. Proc. Junior Soc. Nat. Sci. Cincinnati 2:21–32.

Withers, D. I. 2009. A guide to rare animals of Tennessee. Division of Natural Heritage, Tennessee Department of Environment and Conservation, Nashville.

Wright, A. H., and A. A. Wright. 1949. Handbook of frogs and toads of the United States and Canada. 3rd ed. Comstock, Ithaca, NY. 640 pp.

Yeatman, H. C., and H. B. Miller. 1985. A naturally metamorphosed *Gyrinophilus palleucus* from the type-locality. J. Herpetology 19:304–306.

Lake
Obion
Weakley
Henry
Stewart
Montgomery
Robertson
Sumner
Houston
Cheatham
Davidson
Wilson
Dyer
Gibson
Carroll
Benton
Humphreys
Dickson
Williamson
Rutherford
Lauderdale
Crockett
Haywood
Madison
Henderson
Decatur
Perry
Hickman
Maury
Tipton
Lewis
Marshall
Bedford
Chester
Shelby
Fayette
Hardeman
McNairy
Hardin
Wayne
Lawrence
Giles
Lincoln
Moore

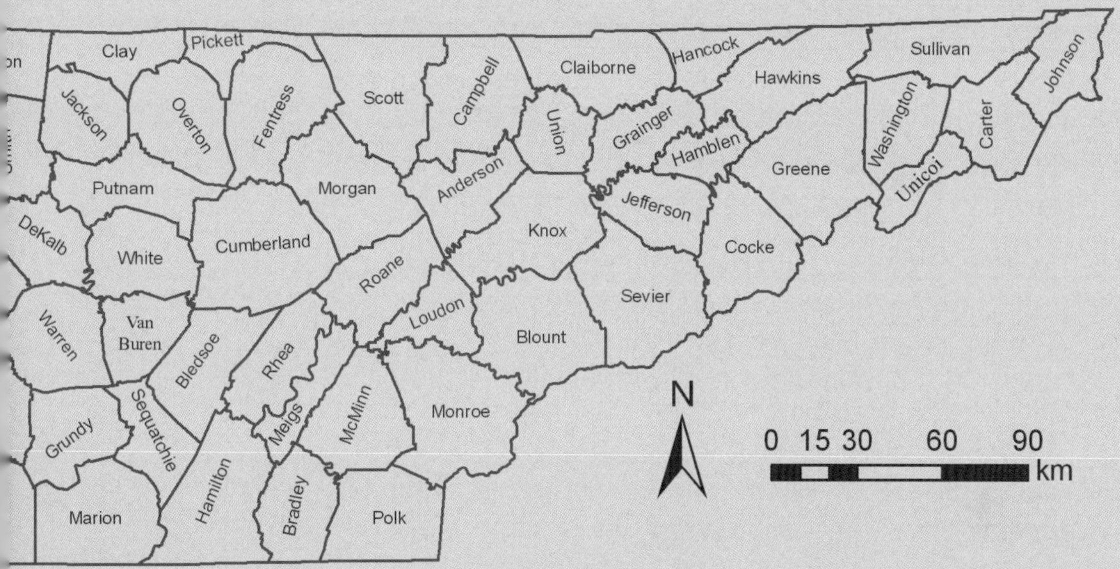

Clay
Pickett
Jackson
Overton
Fentress
Scott
Campbell
Claiborne
Hancock
Hawkins
Sullivan
Johnson
Union
Grainger
Hamblen
Washington
Carter
Unicoi
Greene
Putnam
Morgan
Anderson
Knox
Jefferson
Cocke
DeKalb
White
Cumberland
Roane
Sevier
Loudon
Blount
Warren
Van Buren
Bledsoe
Rhea
Meigs
McMinn
Monroe
Grundy
Sequatchie
Marion
Hamilton
Bradley
Polk
N
0 15 30 60 90
km

Index of Common and Scientific Names

Page numbers in **boldface** refer to species accounts and illustrations.

Acris blanchardi, 264–65
Acris crepitans, **246**, 247, 250, **264–65**, 267–68
Acris gryllus, 15–17, 40, **246**, 247, 250, 265, **266–68**
Adelges tsugae, 33
adelgid, hemlock wooly, 33
Agalychnis, 4
Agkistrodon contortrix, 196
Agkistrodon piscivorus, 93, 261, 279
Ambystoma barbouri, xiii, 20, 40, **58**, 59, 70, **73–76**, 84, 87, 194, 327
Ambystoma californiense, 31–32
Ambystoma jeffersonianum, **323–24**
Ambystoma laterale, 323, 327
Ambystoma maculatum, **37**, **57**, 59, 70, **77–79**, 89
Ambystoma opacum, 58, 70, 78, **80–82**
Ambystoma talpoideum, 3–4, 14–16, 18–19, 59, 69, 78, 81, **83–85**, 87, 327
Ambystoma texanum, 14–16, 18–19, 59, 70, 73, 84, **86–87**, 194, 260, 323
Ambystoma tigrinum, 58, 70, 78, 87, **88–90**, 238
Ambystoma tigrinum mavortium, 31–32
Ambystomatidae, 73
Amphiuma tridactylum, xiii, 14, 16, 44, 57, 67, **91–93**, 240
amphiuma, three-toed, xiii, 14, 16, 44, 57, 67, **91–93**, 240
Amphiumidae, 91
Anaxyrus americanus, **6**, 7–8, **9**, 18, 30, 41, 46, **245**, 246, 250, **253–56**, 258–60, 302, 320, 324

Anaxyrus fowleri, 7–8, 30, 41, **245**, 249, 254–55, **257–59**, 302, 320, 324
Anaxyrus terrestris, 323–324, **325**
Aneides aeneus, 22, 40, 62, 99, **102–4**, 216–17
Anguilla rostrata, 91
Apalone ferox, 302
Atelopus, 30

bass, largemouth, 31–32
bass, smallmouth, 238
Batrachochytrium dendrobatidis, 30–31, 41
black-bellied salamander, 26–27, 46–47, 52, **61**, 68, 100, 118, 121, 123, 126, 133, **139–42**, 198, 214
blue-spotted salamander, **323**, 327
bolitoglossine, 2
bronze frog, 248, 252, **307–9**
brownback salamander, 64, 71, **150–53**, 155–56, 170–71
Bufo periglenes, 30
Bufonidae, 253
bullfrog, American, 6, **20**, 22, **246**, 248, **249**, 251, 261, 298, **304–6**, 308, 311; invasive, 31; predator, 238, 259, 309, 312; game, 38, 297

caecilian, 1
cave salamander, 18, 20, 22, 24, 64, 70, 156, 158–59, 164–65, **166–69**, 171
cave salamander, berry, 40, 62, 72, **172–74**, 176, 180

cave salamander, big mouth, 62, 72, **175–78**
cave salamander, pale, 62, 72, **175–78**
cave salamander, Tennessee, xii, 4, 19, 40, 44, 173–74, **175–78**, 180
chorus frog, Illinois, 323, **326**
chorus frog, mountain, 22, 28, 247, 251 **280–82**, 284, 287–88, 290
chorus frog, upland, 46, 82, 247, 250, 251, 263, 281–82, 284, **286–88**, 290–91, 326
chorus frog, western, 17, 247, 250–51, 281, 284, 287–88, **289–91**, 325
common mudpuppy, 51, **54–55**, 57, 67, 96, 98, 182, **231–33**, 240, 324
copperhead, 196
cottonmouth, western, 93, 261, 279
crawfish frog, 15–16, 248, 252, **297–300**, 301
cricket frog, Blanchard's, 264–65
cricket frog, northern, **246**, 247, 250, **264–65**, 267–68
cricket frog, southern, 15–17, 40, **246**, 247, 250, 265, **266–68**
Cryptobranchus alleganiensis, xiv, 2–3, 18–20, 24, 27, 34, 40, 45, 51, **52–53**, 58, 67, **95–98**
Cryptobranchidae, 95
Cumberland plateau salamander, 23, 40, 66, 193, **199–201**

Desmognathus abditus, **9**, 22, 40, 60, 69, **105–7**, 129, 132, 190
Desmognathus aeneus, 28, 40, **59**, 61, 68, 106, **108–10**, 148–49
Desmognathus carolinensis, 40, 60, 69, **110–12**, 137
Desmognathus conanti, 16–18, 24–25, 38, 46, 62, 69, **113–15**, 116–118, 126, 132, 143, 146
Desmognathus fuscus, 38, 62, 69, 100, 113–114, **116–18**, 126, 143, 146
Desmognathus imitator, 27, 46, 60, 69, 114, **119–21**, 132, 196, 198–99
Desmognathus marmoratus, 27, 44, **61**, 68, **122–24**, 126, 140–41

Desmognathus monticola, 23, 27, 46, 62, 68, 114, 117, **125–27**, 130, 133, 146
Desmognathus ochrophaeus, 60, 69, 105–6, 110–11, 119–20, **128–30**, 131–32, 134–35
Desmognathus ocoee, 27, 46, 60, 69, 106, 111, 120, 126, **131–33**, 191
Desmognathus orestes, 26, 60, 69, 100, **134–36**, 137
Desmognathus organi, 26, 40, 61, **136–38**
Desmognathus quadramaculatus, 26–27, 46–47, 52, **61**, 68, 100, 118, 121, 123, 126, 133, **139–42**, 198, 214
Desmognathus santeetlah, 27, 40, 62, 69, 114, 117, 126, 132, **142–44**
Desmognathus welteri, 40, **59**, **61,** 62, 68, 126, 130, **145–47**
Desmognathus wrighti, xii, 2, 28, 40, 61, 109, **147–49**
Diadophis punctatus, 206, 217
dusky salamander, Allegheny mountain, 23, 60, 69, 105–6, 110–11, 119–20, **128–30**, 131–32, 134–35
dusky salamander, Black Mountain, 40, **59**, **61**, 62, 68, 126, 130, **145–47**
dusky salamander, Blue Ridge, 26, 60, 69, 100, **134–36**, 137
dusky salamander, Carolina mountain, 40, 60, 69, **110–12**, 137
dusky salamander, Cumberland, **9**, 22, 40, 60, 69, **105–7**, 129, 132, 190
dusky salamander, northern, 38, 62, 69, 100, 113–114, **116–18**, 126, 143, 146
dusky salamander, Santeetlah, 27, 40, 62, 69, 114, 117, 126, 132, **142–44**
dusky salamander, spotted, 16–18, 24–25, 38, 46, 62, 69, **113–15**, 116–18, 126, 132, 143, 146
dwarf salamander, 323, 327

eel, American, 91
Eleutherodactylus, 5

Eurycea aquatica, 64, 71, **150–53**, 155–56, 170–71
Eurycea bislineata, 155, 161, 170
Eurycea cirrigera, 19–20, 22, 24–25, 64, 71, 151–52, **154–57**, 159, 161, 165, 168, 170–71
Eurycea guttolineata, 64, 70, **157–60**, 164–65, 167–68
Eurycea junaluska, 27, 40, **46**, **57**, 63, 71, 151–52, 155–56, **160–62**, 170–71
Eurycea longicauda, 17–18, 22, 27, 64, 70, 103, 156, 158–59, **163–65**, 167–68, 171
Eurycea lucifuga, 18, 20, 22, 24, 64, 70, 103, 156, 158–59, 164–65, **166–69**, 171
Eurycea quadridigitata, 323, 327
Eurycea wilderae, 26–27, 46, 64, 71, 151, 155–56, 159, 161–62, 165, 168, **169–71**, 196, 327

Farancia abacura, 93
four-toed salamander, 40, 59, 67, **181–83**, 231

gartersnake, 87, 90, 118, 181, 206, 238, 279
Gastrophryne carolinensis, 246, 249, **293–96**
gopher frog, xiii, 19, 40, 248, 252, 297, **300–3**, 308
gray-cheeked salamander, northern, 26, 65, 100–101, 194, **202–4**, 323
green frog, 6, 22, 24, **35**, 46, **246**, 248, 252, 298, 305, **307–9**, 311–12, 317
green salamander, 22, 40, 62, 99, **102–4**, 216–17
Gyrinophilus gulolineatus, 40, 62, 72, **172–74**, 176, 180
Gyrinophilus palleucus, xiii, 4, 19, 40, 44, 62, 72, 173–74, **175–78**, 180
Gyrinophilus porphyriticus, **9**, 22–24, 27, 44, 46, **57**, 62–63, **71**, 72, 173, 176, **178–81**, 224, 228, 236, 238; predator, 112, 118, 121, 130, 133, 149, 198, 212, 214

hellbender, eastern, xiv, 2–3, 18–20, 24, 27, 34, 40, 45, 51, **52–53**, 58, 67, **95–98**
hellbender, Ozark, 96
Hemidactylium scutatum, 40, 59, 67, **181–83**, 231
hemlock, 22, 34
Hyla avivoca, 14–16, 18, 247, 250, **260–61**, **268–70**, 272, 276
Hyla chrysoscelis, 18, 20, 22, 46, 247, 251, 260, 263, 269, **271–74**, 276
Hyla cinerea, 14–15, 18, 248, 251, 263, 272, **274–77**, 278, 325
Hyla gratiosa, 17–19, 40, 248, 250, 276, **277–79**
Hyla squirella, 276, 323, **325**
Hyla versicolor, 247, 251, 260, 269, **271–74**, 276
Hylidae, 263

imitator salamander, 27, 28, 46, 60, 69, 114, **119–21**, 132, 196, 198–99
Iridoviridae, 31

Jefferson's salamander, **323**
Junaluska salamander, 27, 40, **46**, **57**, 63, 71, 151–52, 155–56, **160–62**, 170–71

kingsnake, black, 46

Lampropeltis getula nigra, 46
leopard frog, northern, 323, **326–27**
leopard frog, plains, 323, **326**
leopard frog, southern, **246**, 248, 252, 298, 301, 305, 308–9, 311, **313–15**, 326
Lithobates areolatus, 15–16, 248, 252, **297–300**, 301
Lithobates blairi, 323, **326**
Lithobates capito, xiii, 19, 40, 248, 252, 297, **300–303**, 308

Lithobates catesbeianus, 6, **20**, 22, **246**, 248, **249**, 251, 261, 298, **304–6**, 308, 311; invasive, 31; predator, 238, 259, 309, 312; game, 38, 297

Lithobates clamitans, 6, 22, 24, **35**, 46, **246**, 248, 252, 298, 305, **307–9**, 311–12, 317

Lithobates palustris, 22, 46, **246**, 248, 252, 298, 308, **310–12**, 314

Lithobates pipiens, 323, **326–27**

Lithobates sevosus, 303

Lithobates sphenocephalus, **246**, 248, 252, 298, 301, 305, 308–9, 311, **313–15**, 326

Lithobates sylvaticus, **5**, 9, 23, 27, 46, 79, 82, 248, 251, 281, 287, 308, 315, **316–18**

long-tailed salamander, 17–18, 22, 27, 64, 70, 103, 156, 158–59, **163–65**, 167–68, 171

marbled salamander, 2, **36**, 58, 70, 78, **80–82**

Microhylidae, 293

Micropterus salmoides, 31–32

mole salamander (species), 3–4, 14–16, 18–19, 59, 69, 78, 81, **83–85**, 87, 327

mole salamanders (family). *See* Ambystomatidae

mountain dusky salamander. *See* Dusky Salamander

mudpuppy. *See* Common Mudpuppy

mud salamander, 19, 22, 63, 71, 179, **223–25**, 228, 236

mudsnake, 93

narrow-mouthed toad, eastern, 246, 249, **293–96**

narrow-mouthed toads, 293

Nasturtium officinale, 152

Necturus beyeri, 323, **324**

Necturus maculosus, 51, **54–55**, 57, 67, 96, 98, 182, **231–233**, 240, 324

Nerodia fasciata, 302

newts, 235

newt, central. *See* Red-Spotted Newt

newt, eastern. *See* Red-Spotted Newt

newt, red-spotted, 3, 41, **58**, 69, 79, 90, **235–38**, 315

Notophthalmus viridescens, 3, 41, **58**, 69. 79, 90, **235–38**, 315

ocoee salamander, 27, 46, 60, 69, 106, 111, 120, 126, **131–33**, 191

Oncorhynchus mykiss, 31

Oophaga, 5

Oophila ambystomatis, 79

Osteopilus septentrionalis, **33**, 34, 327

peeper, spring, 6, 46, 247, 250–51, 281, **283–85**, 287, 290

pickerel frog, 22, 46, **246**, 248, 252, 298, 308, **310–12**, 314

pileated woodpecker, 270

Pipa, 5

Plethodon aureolus, 28, 40, 46, **65**, 66, **184–86**, 193–94, 211–13

Plethodon cinereus, 26, 65–66, 100, 111, 135, **186–88**, 203, 205, 207, 219

Plethodon cylindraceus, 26, 66, 100–101, **192–95**, 203

Plethodon dorsalis, 22, 24, 64, 66, 187, **189–91**

Plethodon glutinosus, xiii, 18–19, 22, 24, 66, 184–85, **192–95**, 198, 200, 203, 213–14, 216, 327

Plethodon jordani, 2, 28, 64, 100, 119–21, 194, **196**, **197–99**, 202, 203, 210–11, 214

Plethodon kentucki, 23, 40, 66, 193, **199–201**

Plethodon mississippi, 15–17, 66, **192–95**

Plethodon montanus, 26, 65, 100–1, 194, **202–4**, 323

Plethodon richmondi, 26, 65, 101, **204–6**, 219

Plethodon serratus, 27, 65–66, 109, 187, 190–91, 196, **207–9**

Plethodon shermani, 40, 64–65, 185, 194, **210–12**, 214
Plethodon teyahalee, 27, 46, 66, 185, 193–94, 211–12, **213–15**
Plethodon ventralis, 17, 20, 64, 66, 187, **189–91**, 208
Plethodon wehrlei, 23, 40, 65, 200, **215–17**
Plethodon welleri, 26, 40, 65, 101, 112, 203, **218–20**
Plethodon yonahlossee, 26, 40, 66, **100–101**, 203, **221–23**
Plethodontidae, 99
Proteidae, 231
Pseudacris brachyphona, 22, 28, 247, 251, **280–82**, 284, 287–88, 290
Pseudacris crucifer, 6, 46, 247, 250–51, 281, **283–85**, 287, 290
Pseudacris feriarum, 46, 82, 247, 250, 251, 263, 281–82, 284, **286–88**, 290–91, 326
Pseudacris streckeri illinoensis, 323, **326**
Pseudacris triseriata, 17, 247, 250–51, 281, 284, 287–88, **289–91**, 325
Pseudotriton montanus, 19, 22, 63, 71, 179, **223–25**, 228, 236
Pseudotriton ruber, **4**, 16, 18–19, 27, 46, 50, 63, **71**, 179, 196, 224, **226–29**, 236
pygmy salamander, xii, 2, 28, 40, 61, 109, **147–49**
pygmy salamander, northern, 26, 40, 61, **136–38**

Rana aurora, 31
Rana boylii, 31
Rana muscosa, 31
Ranavirus, 31, 41
Ranidae, 297
ravine salamander, southern, 26, 65, 101, **204–6**, 219
red salamander, black-chinned, 27, 46, 50, 63, **71**, 179, 224, **226–29**, 236

red salamander, Blue Ridge, 50, 63, **71**, 179, 224, **226–29**, 236
red salamander, northern, **4**, 18–19, 50, 63, **71**, 179, 224, **226–29**, 236
red salamander, southern, 16, 50, 63, **71**, 179, 224, **226–29**, 236
red-backed salamander, eastern, 26, 65–66, 111, 135, **186–88**, 190–91, 203, 205, 219
red-backed salamander, northern. *See* Eastern Red-Backed Salamander
red-backed salamander, southern, 27, 65–66, 109, 190–91, **207–9**
red-cheeked salamander, Jordan's, 2, 28, 64, 100, 119–21, 194, **196**, **197–99**, 202, 203, 210–11, 214
red-legged frog, 31
red-legged salamander, 40, 64–65, 185, 194, **210–12**, 214
Rhinella marina, 31
Rhinoderma, 5
ribbonsnake, 279
ring-necked snake, 206, 217

Salamandridae, 235
Scaphiopus holbrookii, 8, 22, 43, 245, 249, **319–22**
Scaphiopodidae, 319
seal salamander, 23, 27, 46, 62, 68, 114, 117, **125–27**, 130, 133, 146
seepage salamander, 28, 40, **59**, 61, 68, 106, **108–10**, 148–49
shovel-nosed salamander, 27, 44, **61**, 68, **122–24**, 126, 140–41
Siren intermedia, xiii, 3, 14, 15–16, 44, 57, 67, 91, 232, **239–41**
siren, lesser, xiii, 3, 14, 15–16, 44, 57, 67, 91, 232, **239–41**
Sirenidae, 239
slimy salamander, Mississippi, 15–17, 66, **192–95**

slimy salamander, northern, xiii, 18–19, 22, 24, 66, 184–85, **192–95**, 198, 200, 203, 213–14, 216, 327
slimy salamander, white-spotted, 26, 66, 100–1, **192–95**, 203
small-mouthed salamander, 14–16, 18–19, 59, 70, 73, 84, **86–87**, 194, 260, 323
softshell turtle, Florida, 302
southern Appalachian salamander, 27, 46, 66, 185, 193–94, 211–12, **213–15**
spadefoot, eastern, 8, 22, 43, 245, 249, **319–22**
spadefoot, western, 319
Spea, 319
spotted salamander, **37**, **57**, 59, 70, **77–79**, 89
spring salamander, Blue Ridge, 27, 46, **57**, 63, 72, 112, 121, 149, **178–81**, 198, 212, 214
spring salamander, Kentucky
spring salamander, northern, **9**, 22–24, 44, 62, **71**, 72, 118, 130, 133, 173–74, 176, **178–81**, 224, 228, 236, 238
streamside salamander, xiii, 20, 40, **58**, 59, 70, **73–76**, 84, 87, 194, 327

Tellico salamander, 28, 40, 46, **65**, 66, **184–86**, 193–94, 211–13
Thamnophis proximus, 279
Thamnophis sirtalis, 87, 90, 118, 181, 206, 238, 279
three-lined salamander, 64, 70, **157–60**, 164–65, 167–68
tiger salamander, barred, 31–32
tiger salamander, California, 31–32
tiger salamander, eastern, 58, 70, 78, 87, **88–90**, 238
toad, American- eastern, dwarf, **6**, 7–8, **9**, 18, 30, 41, 46, **245**, 246, 250, **253–56**, 258–60, 302, 320, 324
toad, cane, 31
toad, Fowler's, 7–8, 30, 41, **245**, 249, 254–55, **257–59**, 302, 320, 324

toad, southern, 323–324, **325**
treefrog, barking, 17–19, 40, 248, 250, 276, **277–79**
treefrog, bird-voiced, 14–16, 18, 247, 250, **260–61**, **268–70**, 272, 276
treefrog, Cope's gray, 18, 20, 22, 46, 247, 251, 260, 263, 269, **271–74**, 276
treefrog, Cuban, **33**, 34, 327
treefrog, gray, 247, 251, 260, 269, **271–74**, 276
treefrog, green, 14–15, 18, 248, 251, 263, 272, **274–77**, 278, 325
treefrog, squirrel, 276, 323, **325**
trout, rainbow, 31
Tsuga caroliniana, 33–34
turkey, 274
two-lined salamander, Blue Ridge, 26–27, 46, 64, 71, 151, 155–56, 159, 161–62, 165, 168, **169–71**, 196, 327
two-lined salamander, northern, 155, 161, 170
two-lined salamander, southern, 19–20, 22, 24–25, 64, 71, 151–52, **154–57**, 159, 161, 165, 168, 170–71

watercress, 152
waterdog, Gulf coast, 323, **324**
watersnake, 87, 118, 181, 233, 270, 279, 302
watersnake, banded, 302
Wehrle's salamander, 23, 40, 65, 200, **215–17**
Weller's salamander, 26, 40, 65, 101, 112, 203, **218–20**
wood frog, **5**, 9, 23, 27, 46, 79, 82, 248, 251, 281, 287, 308, 315, **316–18**

Xenopus, 30

yellow-legged frog, 31
Yonahlossee salamander, 26, 40, 66, **100–101**, 203, **221–23**

zigzag salamander, northern, 22, 24, 64, 66, 187, **189–91**
zigzag salamander, southern, 17, 20, 64, 66, 187, **189–91**, 208

The Amphibians of Tennessee was designed and typeset on a Macintosh computer system using InDesign software. The body copy is set in Kepler Light 10/15 and display type is set in Century Gothic and News Gothic. This book was typeset and designed by Chad M. Pelton, and manufactured by Everbest Printing Company Limited.